BUFFALO BILL'S WILD WEST
& CONGRESS OF ROUGH RIDERS OF THE WORLD.

COL. W.F. CODY PRES.

NATE SALSBURY VICE PRES. & MAN'G'R

RUSSIAN COSSACKS

COW-BOYS & INDIANS.

SOUTH AMERICAN GAUCHOS.

MEXICAN VAQUEROS

ARABS OF THE DESERT

CAVALRY OF ALL NATIONS

30

A. HOEN & CO. BALTIMORE, U.S.A.

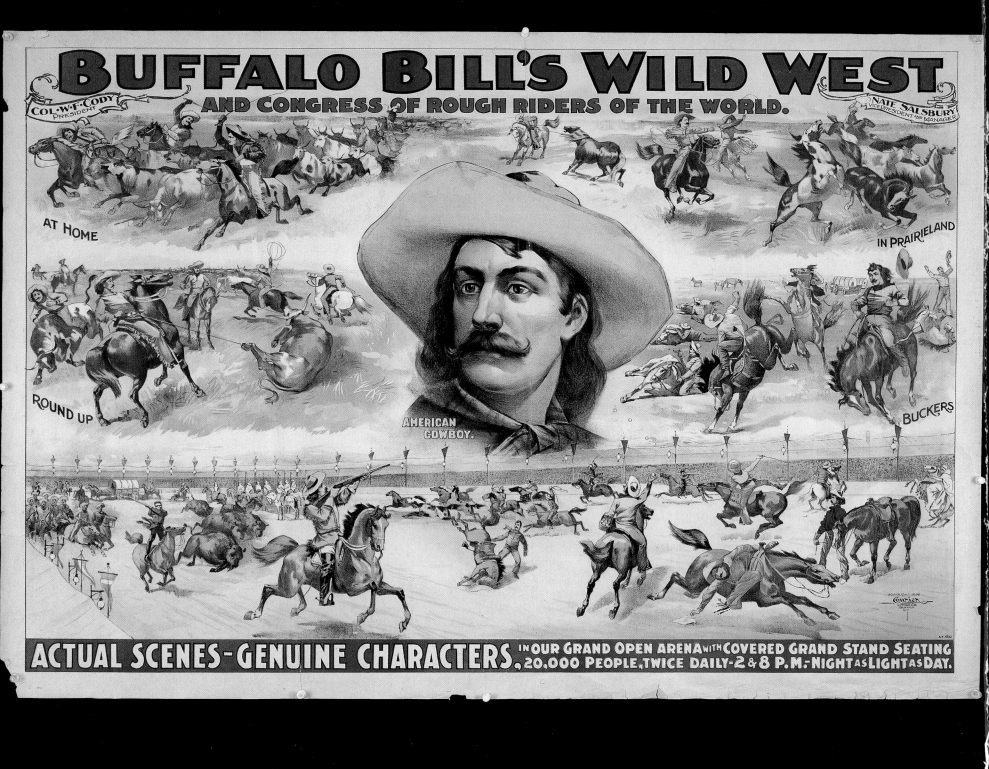

DAD: 7/8/00

WELL, THE DAY HAS FINALLY ARRIVED. THE LAST FEW MONTHS HAVE BEEN A LITTLE HECTIC, BUT THE ONLY CASUALTY HAS BEEN OUR FISHING TRIP. TO RECOGNIZE THAT, I HAD COPIES MADE OF SOME GREAT PHOTOS OF YOU, ME AND JIM. UNFORTUNATELY, THEY WERE NOT COPIED IN TIME FOR ME TO PUT THEM IN THIS BOOK FOR YOU. I WILL GET THEM TO YOU SHORTLY. I HAD THREE PHOTOS TO PICK FROM. THE FIRST WAS A PICTURE OF US THREE HOLDING AN IMPRESSIVE STRINGER OF WALLYE. A VERY NICE PICTURE, BUT THE OTHER TWO WERE OF YOU AND JIM TOGETHER AND ONE OF ME ALONE. WE APPARENTLY JUST GOT OFF THE WATER ON A RAINY DAY. THE THREE OF US ARE

Buffalo Bill's Wild West

IN NO OTHER PICTURE HAVING A GOOD TIME

SMILING AND LAUGHING LIKE I HAVE. WE OBVIOUSLY WERE IN SPITE OF THE WEATHER.

THOSE ARE THE PICTURES I'M SO GLAD TO HAVE THEM EVEN MORE GLAD THAT WE KNOW, I DON'T EVEN CARE IF WE

THAT I'LL PUT IN THIS BOOK. MEMORIES OF OUR TRIPS, BUT I'M HAVE MORE TO COME. AND YOU CATCH ANY FISH.

IT'S EASY TO SAY "THANK YOU FOR EVERYTHING" DAD, BUT THERE IS SO MUCH TO THANK YOU FOR I WOULD BE WRITING FOR A LONG TIME. I AM HAPPY WITH WHO I HAVE BECOME AND I HAVE YOU TO THANK FOR THAT. THEY SAY THAT IMITATION IS THE MOST SINCERE FORM OF FLATTERY. SO MANY PEOPLE HAVE TOLD ME HOW MUCH I REMIND THEM OF YOU. I COULDN'T BE MORE PROUD OF THAT.

LOVE-

Kay

CAPITAL STOCK $500,000

ISSUED FOR PROPERTY PURCHASE

N° 1

Buffalo Bill's Wild West

AN AMERICAN LEGEND

R. L. WILSON WITH GREG MARTIN

PHOTOGRAPHY BY PETER BEARD AND DOUGLAS SANDBERG

FEATURING THE MICHAEL DEL CASTELLO COLLECTION OF THE AMERICAN WEST

WITH PORTFOLIOS OF TREASURES FROM THE BUFFALO BILL HISTORICAL CENTER, CODY, WYOMING,

AND THE AUTRY MUSEUM OF WESTERN HERITAGE, LOS ANGELES, CALIFORNIA

Treasurer.

President.

RANDOM HOUSE NEW YORK

INCORPORATED UNDER THE LAWS OF THE STATE OF NEW JERSEY

Copyright © 1998 by R. L. Wilson and Greg Martin

Photographs copyright © 1998 by Peter Beard and Douglas Sandberg, excepting photographs from the Buffalo Bill Historical Center and the Autry Museum of Western Heritage.

Library of Congress Cataloging-in Publication Data

Wilson, R. L. (Robert Lawrence)
    Buffalo Bill's Wild West: an American legend / by R. L. Wilson with Greg Martin; photography by Peter Beard and Douglas Sandberg.
        p.   cm.
    "Featuring the Michael Del Castello Collection of the American West, with portfolios of treasures from the Buffalo Bill Historical Center, Cody, Wyoming, and the Autry Museum of Western Heritage, Los Angeles, California."
    Includes bibliographical references and index.
    ISBN 0-375-50106-1
    1. Buffalo Bill's Wild West Show—History.
    2. West (U.S.)—History—Pictorial works.
    3. Entertainers—West (U.S.)—Biography.
    I. Martin, Greg.   II. Beard, Peter H. (Peter Hill), 1938– .   III. Sandberg, Douglas.   IV. Michael Del Castello Collection of the American West.
    V. Buffalo Bill Museum (Cody, Wyo.)
    VI. Autry Museum of Western Heritage.
    VII. Title.
GV1821.B8W55   1998   978'.02'0922—dc21   98-12868
[B]

Random House website address:
www.randomhouse.com
Printed in the United States of America on acid-free paper

98765432
First Edition
Book design: Georgiana Goodwin

Note: Dimensions for posters are correct within approximately half an inch and listed by height and then width. Several have been measured within frames; therefore, dimensions given cover imprinted size—since some posters were trimmed for framing or other reasons, the imprinted size was considered the most practical one for reference.

Front endpaper: From Prairie to Palace, 1910, by the U.S. Lithograph Company, Russell Morgan print, number 12761, Cincinnati and New York. Various scenes from the life of Buffalo Bill. 26 × 39½ inches. Michael Del Castello Collection. *Buffalo Bill's Wild West and Congress of Rough Riders of the World,* by A. Hoen and Company, Baltimore. 29⅟₁₆ × 39¼ inches. Michael Del Castello Collection.

Frontispiece: An overview of the Wild West of Buffalo Bill, Annie Oakley, and their partners. Historic firearms from left: Colt Lightning rifle, gift to Dr. Longstreet from friends at Kickapoo Medicine Encampment; Colt Single Action Army "Nighthawk" given to Dr. David Powell by Buffalo Bill; Stevens single-shot target pistol given to Ben Thompson by Buffalo Bill; Remington Rolling Block pistol given to Captain Jack Crawford by Remington Arms Co.; Colt Model 1895 revolver of Johnny Baker; S&W American given to the Earl of Dunraven by Texas Jack Omohundro; and Annie Oakley Model 1873 Winchester, presented to her young English friend W. R. C. Clarke. Three target coins, shot by Cody, Oakley, and Baker. Cased masonry trowel given to Buffalo Bill by Ned Buntline. Tomahawk given to David Powell by friends. Buffalo-head letter opener, gift to Buffalo Bill. Orator H. M. Clifford's silver badge of the 1891 season, near the Nighthawk Colt. Note also dime novel, show programs, letterhead, glass target ball, memorial Cody book, shooting medals, sundry ephemera, and memorabilia. Firearms and majority of other items from Michael Del Castello Collection; balance from Greg Martin Collection.

Title page: Adapted from 1887 Buffalo Bill's Wild West company stock certificate. Buffalo Bill Historical Center, Buffalo Bill Museum.

Back endpaper: American Cowboy, 26¼ × 39½ inches, 1895, number 1610. *The American,* 26¼ × 39½ inches, 1896, number 1616. Both by Courier Lithograph Company, Buffalo, New York.

Back cover: Entertainment promotions of 1883 Buffalo Bill Cody and Doc Carver show program. Buffalo Bill Historical Center, Buffalo Bill Museum.

❧Contents❧

Illustration accompanying the headliners to the Wild West troupe, from the 1886 program. From a Manchester, England, press report, January 6, 1888: "Apart from the intrinsic merit of the performance given by Buffalo Bill's [Wild West] company, the interest attached to it, on account of the fact that those who take part in the representation have actually been participators in the stirring scenes depicted, lends an additional charm and value to the wonderful exhibition. The company is not composed of the ordinary actors, who in their time play many parts. The Indians are "real live" Indians, who have fought for their lives and rights; the cowboys have seen service on the "wide rolling prairie"; the scouts have suffered innumerable hardships and passed through thrilling adventures in the Wild West. The remarkable realism thus imparted to the unparalleled series of tableaux arranged for our enjoyment—and may we not add education—has never yet been approached by any other combination."

(*opposite*) Buffalo Bill shooting at glass-ball targets; Buffalo Bill's Wild West 1886 program.

❧ Introduction ❧

Growing up in an era of heroes, when there was still widespread respect for parental authority, we looked forward to the Saturday matinee Westerns as the highlight of each week. On our pedestal were film stars such as Gene Autry and Roy Rogers, who carried on a tradition begun decades before by authentic pioneers of the Western frontier. And it was those originals—Buffalo Bill, Annie Oakley, and the like—who reigned supreme in our imaginations.

They still do.

Fully aware of that adulation, we have tried to make this book an accurate reflection of reality: a chronicle of lives and foibles, hopes and disappointments. At the same time, the work considers material objects familiar, often vital, to our characters: their firearms, cabinet cards, posters, and much, much more—striking and beautiful as these often were. The men and women were greatly intriguing, colorful, brave, and bigger than life. Their artifacts, memorabilia, ephemera, and art speaks volumes of them and is justifiably lusted after today by collectors and museums alike.

Little did we know, as children growing up in a society imbued with the romance and ethos of the Old West, that some day our individual experiences would lead to producing a volume of this type on so uniquely American a subject. This book is about an America that once was and will never be again. But with hope, our illustrated chronicle of these Wild West figures will contribute to a new appreciation of their lives and times.

These were the people who first brought the great American West to eager audiences in America and Europe, to crowned heads and socialites, to millionaires and the public at large. Many times, these performers acted out their own frontier exploits, becoming the first superstars of show business. But unlike most of those who followed, these characters were the real thing: genuine, authentic, valiant icons, entirely worthy of admiration, respect, and affection. They were also patriotic Americans in their real-life roles. Whether on the winning side or the losing one, they were concerned about saving the West's resources (including the buffalo and all other wildlife). They believed in America's destiny. Billed as America's national entertainment, Buffalo Bill's shows were generally and genuinely thought of as educational experiences.

Over his career, Buffalo Bill performed before an audience estimated collectively to be in excess of fifty million, and he became arguably the most famous American in the world. To count but a few of his many achievements: creating the Western as an art and entertainment form; advocating adoption of "The Star-Spangled Banner" as America's national anthem; endorsing the vote for women; volunteering to raise a company of Rough Riders first for the Spanish-American War and then for World War I; promoting the Boy Scout movement; and reigning as the most popular and effective ex officio ambassador in American history. His death in 1917 produced an outpouring of emotion and international sorrow, the likes of which had not been seen since the passing of President Abraham Lincoln over fifty years before.

Annie Oakley's frailness in old age moved none other than Will Rogers to write: "She will be a lesson to you. . . . Annie Oakley's name, her lovable traits, her thoughtful consideration of others, will live as a mark for any woman to shoot at."

We hope that *Buffalo Bill's Wild West: An American Legend* will be worthy of the memory of its extraordinary subjects. To maintain authenticity, we made no attempt to correct the colorful spelling in the many quotations from original sources. Should there be any doubt as to meaning, information is provided in brackets.

Without further ado, therefore, and to paraphrase the Berliner Gramophone recording of Buffalo Bill himself, speaking over a century ago: "Ladies and gentlemen, permit us to introduce to you a Congress of Rough Riders of the World!"

R. L. Wilson and Greg Martin
November 1, 1997

The life and times of W. F. Cody through about 1876. Guns and knives among types he saw and used on the plains. Henry Deringer rifle at *center,* with a Deringer pistol beneath its butt. Colt and Remington revolvers. Winchester Model 1866 rifle. Engraved Model 1851 Navy Colt with silver-mounted belt and matching holster has a wagon-master history. Elaborate Sheffield Bowie knife with scabbard *above* Deringer rifle's wrist. Naval ball commemorated historic visit to the United States of Grand Duke Alexis. Moccasins picked up by trooper W. O. Taylor after Custer's battle at the Little Bighorn.

Chapter 1

❖

From Reality to Legend

1846-1876

Buffalo Bill, Buffalo Bill,
Never missed and never will,
Always aims and shoots to kill,
And the company pays his buffalo bill.
—Frontier jingle

Almost from the day of his birth in an Iowa log cabin, February 26, 1846, William F. Cody's life was an adventure. The frontier was still wild and woolly, the pacification of the Indians nearly a half century away. The boy who became Buffalo Bill would see it all. He would know more real-life Western figures—including his personal hero Kit Carson—than anyone before or since. In his latter years, he would be remembered as the last of the great scouts. And long before his life's end, Cody—more than any other Westerner—would have truly "seen the elephant."

In Buffalo Bill Cody's seventy-one action-packed years, America moved from being a frontier society to being the world's foremost industrial and financial powerhouse. Once-rural communities were transformed into urban centers, magnets attracting immigrants and country folk alike. Sophisticated machine tools replaced cottage industries. Stagecoaches and covered wagons gave way to trains, planes, and automobiles. And America's entertainment evolved as well, from traveling minstrel and medicine shows to the three-ring circus and the Wild West extravaganza and finally to motion pictures.

As the most famous American of his time, Cody was involved, directly or indirectly, in all of these things. From Iowa farm boy to America's most popular entertainment figure—its first superstar—Cody influenced the lives of his partners and employees (some of whom became his rivals) and helped create new national entertainments in which careers and money were made . . . and lost.

And, not least, Cody inspired, mainly in the twentieth century, whole new areas of collecting: firearms, Western wear, cowboy gear, Indian artifacts and weaponry, saddles, posters, photographs, documents, ephemera, Wild West–show memorabilia, and much, much more. Buffalo Bill and his national entertainment were the first to effectively capitalize on the merchandising of the Wild West, with dime novels, souvenir books and pictures, pennants, programs, and games—even cigars and tobacco. In time, his printed programs carried advertising from a myriad of manufacturers, patent medicines, and services. The art of slick promotion owes a great debt to Cody's master promoters and merchandisers.

In retrospect, the stars of the Wild West shows were the precursors of the modern stadium performers: the Beatles, Pink Floyd, Elton John, Aerosmith, Tina Turner, Garth Brooks, and Dolly Parton (not to mention the Three Tenors!). The similarities do not stop with gigantic audiences and mass merchandising: exotic costumes, fancy boots, long hair, and even a penchant for American Indian culture, exotic foods, and a bohemian, footloose lifestyle all hark back to Buffalo Bill's Wild West–show originals. On the other hand, a drug culture did not exist in Cody's day, and the Wild West performers had to deal only infrequently with the demon alcohol. Further, present-day superstars don't grow up dodging arrows, spears, tomahawks, and bullets on a harsh and unforgiving frontier.

A PRAIRIE SCHOONER.

YOUTHFUL ADVENTURES.

Harrisburg Arkansas Oct 4th 1893
W F Cody Buffalo Bill

Dear Old Friend
it has Bin A long time since I have heard from you Seeing in the Dailys that you Would be in Memphis to day I thought I Would like to hear from you Personly and I Would have come over but it seems that I am out of luck at this time I am county Judge of Bissett County Arkansas only three hours from Memphis and I have to hold Court to day and I see that you will be in Memphis only one day I would like very Much to shake your hand Billy and talk over the old grand how you rode at my heels on the little gray Mule while I was killing Buffalo oh theirs Wer happy days of course you recolect the time the Buffalo run through the train and stampeded the teams and you stoped the Stampede Well write as soon as you get this or send Answer by Telegraph to Harrisburg Ark as I will be holding court there to day your Freind and old Wagon Master
John R Willis

Buffalo Bill and the Tall Story

In any attempt to know the real Buffalo Bill, the embroidery of folklore ("stretching the blanket") must be dealt with from the outset. Storytelling was a long-standing Western tradition, and Buffalo Bill Cody came from a long line of tall-tale tellers; former scouts and frontiersmen such as Davy Crockett and Jim Bridger delighted in the imaginative "improvements" they made on their own experiences. Cody, on his way to becoming a premier show-business personality, had even more reason to weave the webs of imagination.

No less an authority than Don Russell has concluded that Cody's 1879 autobiography was not only written in nearly its entirety by Cody himself but was "as accurate as are most autobiographies written from memory, unchecked by notes or records."[1] The major drawback is that Cody occasionally relied on previously published material, not always written by him, in recounting some details. *The Life of Hon. William F. Cody* is a delightful read for any Cody devotee or enthusiast of the West—but beware of the embroidery therein.

As his phenomenal career took off, and he made the transition from scout, guide, and part-time showman to full-time star, Cody's stories sometimes assumed the proportions of Paul Bunyan, Mike Fink, and Pecos Bill tales. Throughout, Cody had plenty of help from gifted promoters such as Ned Buntline and Arizona John M. Burke.

HOLDING THE FORT.

BRINGING MEAT INTO CAMP.

MY ESCAPE FROM THE HORSE THIEVES.

THE KILLING OF TALL BULL.

A DUEL WITH CHIEF YELLOW HAND.

TONGUES AND TENDER LOINS.

BEHIND THE FOOTLIGHTS.

The story of Cody and the Pony Express is a case in point. Some historians have maintained that Cody never rode with the Pony Express. An eyewitness who claimed otherwise was philanthropist Edward E. Ayer:

About six or seven years ago I attended a reception and dinner given by all the diplomats of Paris to Buffalo Bill. I said it wasn't necessary to introduce me to Bill Cody; that I had crossed the plains in 1860, and that he was riding by our train about a month, and would give us news in a loud voice as he rushed by, so that we all became much attached to him. At the reception Bill wouldn't let me get out of his sight, and insisted that I should sit at his side, thereby disarranging the seating plan at the banquet.

In *Seventy Years on the Frontier*, Alexander Majors, a founder of the Pony Express, states, "Among the most noted and daring riders of the Pony Express was Hon. William F. Cody, better known as Buffalo Bill." Majors elaborates on Cody's heroic deeds as an Express rider. But Majors's book had been underwritten by Cody—who had other extenuating involvements with it—and the stories must thus be considered suspect. It is generally accepted, however, that late in the 1850s, Cody worked for some two months as an express messenger for the firm of Russell, Majors, and Waddell, before it established the Pony Express. His route covered a distance of three miles, from the company's office to Fort Leavenworth. Cody was at risk on this circuit, and it can be said that, at the least, he was an express rider, though possibly not with the Pony Express.

In any event, one of the most popular features of Buffalo Bill's Wild West for over thirty years was the Pony Express ride, which contributed significantly to the legend of one of the most glamorous episodes in the development of the West. Whether or not Cody actually rode with the Pony Express itself, he, more than any other person, immortalized that enterprise.

Unlike his predecessors, who occasionally told some tall tales while recounting their real-life adventures, Cody blurred the line between fact and fiction. He did not have a good memory for dates or for names and places, and he was a gifted storyteller. A popular figure with the media, he became a widely published author and the subject of other authors, as well as an international show-business celebrity. To quote the then-prominent journalist Amy Leslie, in the Chicago *Daily News* (June 26, 1893): "No such an engaging story-teller as Buffalo Bill figures in history or romance. He is quiet, rich in humor and mellow as a bottle of old port . . . and not a dozen men I know have his splendid magnetism, keen appreciation and happy originality. He sticks to the truth mainly and is more intensely beguiling than the veriest makers of fiction."

In order to appreciate Cody for the heroic figure he was, those of his adventures generally accepted as whole cloth—or nearly so—by experts are used to develop a picture of the man and his times. Some of these exploits are in Cody's own words and have been researched as thoroughly as possible to separate the tall tale from the real thing. In the process of reviewing highlights from his frontier career, Cody's prowess as a hunter, guide, Indian fighter, and scout become real.

CLOSE QUARTERS.

Twelve-Year-Old Wagon-Master

According to his own recollections and those of his sisters, Julia, Helen, and Eliza, the young Cody, known to his family as Will, made three long trips over the plains in the company of wagon master John R. Willis. Though only about twelve years old at the time, Cody carried a revolver provided by the teamster. On one of these sojourns, following an incident involving a knife and a confrontation with a young rival—prompting Cody to disappear for a while—he made a forty-day trip to Fort Kearny, Nebraska.

Some forty-nine years later, Willis, then a judge in Harrisburg, Arkansas, authenticated Cody's impressive credentials as a teamster and plainsman:

Dear Old Friend it has bin a long time since I have herd from you. Seeing in the Dailys that you would be in Memphis today I thought I would like to hear from you personly and I would have come over but it seems that I am out of luck at this time. I am county judge of Poinsett County, Arkansas, only three hours from Memphis and I have to hold court today and I see that you will be in Memphis only one day. I would like very much to shake your hand, Billy, and talk over the old grand hours you rode at my heels on the little gray mule while I was killing Buffalo. oh them were happy days. of course you recolect the time the Buffalo run through the train and stampeded the teams and you stoped the stampede. Well write as soon as you get this or send answer by Telegraph to Harrisburg, Ark., as I will be holding court there all day. Your Freind and old Wagon Master, John R. Willis.[2]

The youthful Cody's presence at Fort Bridger, Wyoming, was confirmed by First U.S. Cavalry Trooper Robert Morris Peck, in memoirs written for the *National Tribune* and published May 9, 1901:

[He] was then a boy of 11 or 12 years old, employed by Lou Simpson, a bull-train wagon boss, as an extra hand . . . or something of that kind.

He gave no visible signs then of future fame, and only impressed me as a rather fresh, "smart-ellick" sort of a kid. The bull-whackers had made quite a pet of him and one of them informed me that Billy was already developing wonderful skill at riding wild horses or mules, shooting and throwing a rope, etc. I had almost forgotten that I had ever seen the little dirty-faced bull-whacker when, just after the war, I heard the name of "Buffalo Bill" mentioned frequently in connection with frontier affairs. I thought at first it was another nick-name that had been conferred on "Wild Bill," whom I had known on the plains by several sobriquets, as "Injun Bill" and "Buckskin Bill," but on asking an old comrade who had been with me in Utah, "Who is this Buffalo Bill I hear so much about?" he answered "Why don't you remember Bill Cody, that smart little fellow that was with Lou Simpson's bull-train as an extra hand?" my recollection of him was revived.[3]

Cody at *left*, with his favorite buffalo-hunting rifle, Lucretia Borgia, and three unidentified men. Rifle was in .50-70 caliber, fired a 450-grain projectile, pushed by 70 grains of black powder; muzzle velocity was approximately 1,500 feet per second, more than adequate for dropping buffalo; serial number unknown. At ranges fired by Cody, sometimes with the muzzle virtually touching the beast's hide, the flash could well ignite the animal's fur. Ca. 1867–1870.

The Consummate Buffalo Hunter

Cody's reputation, his nickname, and his future were based on his bravery, courage, and skill as a scout and on his prowess as a hunter—more specifically, as a buffalo hunter. Several episodes in his autobiography deal with hunting these creatures and mention clients, specific hunts, and specially trained mounts. Early on, he speaks affectionately of his favorite horse: "I was mounted on my celebrated horse Brigham, the fleetest steed I ever owned. On several subsequent occasions he saved my life, and he was the horse that I rode when I killed sixty-nine buffaloes in one day."

Once, near Fort Hays, Kansas, in 1867, Cody was alerted that a herd of buffalo was coming over a hill. Not having sighted buffalo for a while, Cody gave chase:

I immediately told one of our men to hitch his horses to a wagon and follow me, as I was going out after the herd, and we would bring back some fresh meat for supper. I had no saddle, as mine had been left at the camp a mile distant, so taking the harness from Brigham, I mounted him bareback and started out after the game, being armed with my celebrated buffalo-killer, "Lucretia Borgia,"—a newly-improved breech-loading needle gun, which I had obtained from the government.[4]

This is Cody's first mention in his autobiography of his favorite buffalo-hunting gun. A single-shot trapdoor Springfield, this rifle became an icon of frontier firearms and survives today in well-used condition, lacking the triggerguard and buttstock.

Continuing the story, Cody describes how a group of five army officers came out of Fort Hays all "newly arrived . . . in that part of the country . . . a captain [George Wallace Graham], while the others were lieutenants [First Lieutenants Israel Ezekial, Myron J. Amick, William I. Reed, and Second Lieutenant John Milton Thompson]." The officers "scanned my cheap-looking outfit pretty closely, and as my horse was not very prepossessing in appearance, having on only a blind bridle, and otherwise looking like a work-horse they evidently considered me a green hand at hunting."[5]

"*Do you expect to catch those buffaloes on that Gothic steed?*" laughingly asked the captain.

"*I hope so, by pushing on the reins hard enough,*" *was my reply.*

"*You'll never catch them in the world, my fine fellow,*" *said the captain. "It requires a fast horse to overtake the animals on these prairies.*"

"*Does it?*" *asked I as if I didn't know it.*

"*Yes; but come along with us as we are going to kill them more for pleasure than anything else. All we want are the tongues and a piece of tender loin, and you may have all that is left,*" *said the generous man.*

"*I am much obliged to you, Captain, and will follow you,*" *I replied.*

There were eleven buffaloes in the herd and they were not more than a mile from us. The officers dashed ahead as if they had a sure thing on killing them all before I could come up with them; but I had noticed that the herd was making towards the creek for water, and as I knew buffalo nature, I was perfectly aware that it would be difficult to turn them from their direct course. Thereupon, I started towards the creek to head them off, while the officers came up in the rear and gave chase.

The buffaloes came rushing past me not a hundred yards distant, with the officers about three hundred yards in the rear. Now, thought I, is the time to "get my work in," as they said; and I pulled the blind-bridle from my horse, who knew as well as I did that we were out for buffaloes—as he was a trained hunter. The moment the bridle was off, he started at the top of his speed, running in ahead of the officers, and with a few jumps he brought me alongside of the rear buffalo. Raising old "Lucretia Borgia" to my shoulder, I fired, and killed the animal at the first shot. My horse then carried me alongside the next one, not ten feet away, and I dropped him at the next fire.

As soon as one buffalo would fall, Brigham would take me so close to the next, that I could almost touch it with my gun[.] In this manner I killed the eleven buffaloes with twelve shots; and, as the last animal dropped, my horse stopped. I jumped to the ground, knowing that he would not leave me—it must be remembered that I had been riding him without bridle, reins or saddle—and turning round as the party of astonished officers rode up, I said to them:

"*Now, gentlemen, allow me to present to you all the tongues and tender-loins you wish from these buffaloes.*"

Cody and the officers then introduced themselves, and one of them recognized Cody from Fort Harker. The men admired Brigham, and a general discussion developed on "the different subjects of horses, buffaloes, Indians and hunting." Cody noted that they

felt a little sore at not getting a single shot at the buffaloes, but the way I had killed them had, they said, amply repaid them for their disappointment. They had read of such feats in books, but this was the first time they had ever seen anything of the kind with their own eyes. It was the first time, also, that they had ever witnessed or heard of a white man running buffaloes on horseback without a saddle or a bridle.

Cody explained how well trained Brigham was in the art of buffalo hunting:

I told them that Brigham knew nearly as much about the business as I did, and if I had had twenty bridles they would have been of no use to me, as he understood everything, and all that he expected of me was to do the shooting. It is a fact, that Brigham would stop if a buffalo did not fall at the first fire, as to give me a second chance, but if I did not kill the buffalo then, he would go on, as if to say, "You are no good, and I will not fool away time by giving you more than two shots." Brigham was the best horse I ever owned or saw for buffalo chasing.[6]

Lucretia Borgia's recoil could become painful when a number of shots were fired. In the winter of 1868–1869, when scurvy broke out among the men of the Fifth Cavalry, Cody was assigned to kill a number of buffalo. In one day, he took forty-one, wearing out two of his mounts! Russell notes that the "recoil of his Springfield rifle left his right shoulder and breast so much swollen that he could not put on his coat without help. It took two days to gather up the scattered carcasses, and by that time Cody was ready to go again."[7]

Hunting Buffalo for the Railroad

One of the most often told tales of the American West involves Cody's contract to supply meat for the Kansas Pacific Railroad (then known as the Union Pacific, Eastern Division), which called for him to supply enough meat to feed 1,200 men. Although historians have noted discrepancies in some details, generally the events quoted in Cody's autobiography are correct:

Having heard of my experience and success as a buffalo hunter, Messrs. Goddard Brothers, who had the contract for boarding the employees of the road, met me in Hays City one day and made me a good offer to become their hunter, and I at once entered into a contract with them. They said that they would require about twelve buffaloes per day; that would be twenty-four hams, as we took only the hind-quarters and hump of each buffalo. As this was to be dangerous work, on account of the Indians, who were riding all over that section of the country, and as I would be obliged to go from five to ten miles from the road each day to hunt the buffaloes, accompanied by only one man with a light wagon for the transportation of the meat, I of course demanded a large salary. They could afford to remunerate me well, because the meat would not cost them anything. They agreed to give me five hundred dollars per month, provided I furnished them all the fresh meat required. . . .

Buffalo Bill and the Buffalo-Hunting Contest

I immediately began my career as a buffalo hunter for the Kansas Pacific Railroad, and it was not long before I acquired considerable notoriety. It was at this time that the very appropriate name of "Buffalo Bill" was conferred upon me by the road-hands. It has stuck to me ever since, and I have never been ashamed of it.[8]

Cody indicated that he was first called Buffalo Bill by Captain Graham's buffalo-hunting party. As to the terms of Cody's employment and the number of buffalo killed, Russell has determined that the length of time is more likely to have been eight months (October 1867 through May 1868) and that the approximate number of buffalo killed in that period was 2,928.

Shooting matches ranked among the most popular of all sports in nineteenth-century America. One of the most unusual—and renowned—was that between Cody and Billy "Medicine Bill" Comstock. Although some experts question whether the event ever took place, Russell sets the date sometime in 1868 and the place as two-and-a-half miles west of Monument, Kansas.[9] Cody described the contest in his autobiography:

Shortly after . . . I had my celebrated buffalo hunt with Billy Comstock, a noted scout, guide and interpreter, who was then chief of scouts at Fort Wallace, Kansas. Comstock had the reputation, for a long time, of being a most successful buffalo hunter, and the officers in particular, who had seen him kill buffaloes, were very desirous of backing him in a match against me. . . . We were to hunt one day of eight hours, beginning at eight o'clock in the morning, and closing at four o'clock in the afternoon. The wager was five hundred dollars a side, and the man who should kill the greater number of buffaloes from on horseback was to be declared the winner.

The hunt took place about twenty miles east of Sheridan, and as it had been pretty well advertised and noised abroad, a large crowd witnessed the interesting and exciting scene. An excursion party, mostly from St. Louis, consisting of about a hundred gentlemen and ladies, came out on a special train to view the sport, and among the number was my wife, with little baby Arta, who had come to remain with me for a while.

The buffaloes were quite plenty, and it was agreed that we should go into the same herd at the same time and "make a run," as we called it, each one killing as many as possible. A referee was to follow each of us on horseback when we entered the herd, and count the

Remarkable picture of Cody, believed taken at Fort McPherson, ca. 1871. Plains rifle at *top* with inlaid cheekpiece; rifle *below* a Frank Wesson; revolvers clockwise from *right*: Remington .44, possibly a Whitney, Colt Model 1851 Navy, and another Remington. Even at this early date, Cody had a flair for showmanship.

buffaloes killed by each man. The St. Louis excursionists, as well as the other spectators, rode out to the vicinity of the hunting grounds in wagons and on horseback, keeping well out of sight of the buffaloes, so as not to frighten them, until the time came for us to dash into the herd; when they were to come up as near as they pleased and witness the chase.

We were fortunate in the first run in getting good ground. Comstock was mounted on one of his favorite horses, while I rode old Brigham. I felt confident that I had the advantage of Comstock in two things—first, I had the best buffalo horse that ever made a track; and second, I was using what was known at that time as the needle-gun, a breech-loading Springfield rifle—calibre 50,—it was my favorite old "Lucretia," . . . while Comstock was armed with a Henry rifle, and although he could fire a few shots quicker than I could, yet I was pretty certain that it did not carry powder and lead enough to do execution equal to my calibre 50.

At last the time came to begin the match. Comstock and I dashed into a herd, followed by the referees. The buffaloes separated; Comstock took the left bunch and I the right. My great forte in killing buffaloes from horseback was to get them circling by riding my horse at the head of the herd, shooting the leaders, thus crowding their followers to the left, till they would finally circle round and round.

On this morning the buffaloes were very accommodating, and I soon had them running in a beautiful circle, when I dropped them thick and fast, until I had killed thirty-eight; which finished my run.

Comstock began shooting at the rear of the herd, which he was chasing, and they kept straight on. He succeeded, however, in killing twenty-three, but they were scattered over a distance of three miles, while mine lay close together. I had "nursed" my buffaloes, as a billiard-player does the balls when he makes a run.

After the result of the first run had been duly announced, our St. Louis excursion friends—who had approached to the place where we had stopped—set out a lot of champagne, which they had brought with them, and which proved a good drink on a Kansas prairie, and a buffalo hunter was a good man to get away with it.

While taking a short rest, we suddenly spied another herd of buffaloes coming toward us. It was only a small drove, and we at once prepared to give the animals a lively reception. They proved to be a herd of cows and calves—which, by the way, are quicker in their movements than the bulls. We charged in among them, and I concluded my run with a score of eighteen, while Comstock killed fourteen. The score now stood fifty-six to thirty-seven, in my favor.

Again the excursion party approached, and once more the champagne was tapped. After we had eaten a lunch which was spread for us, we resumed the hunt. Striking out for a distance of three miles, we came up close to another herd. As I was so far ahead of my competitor in the number killed, I thought I could afford to give an extra exhibition of my skill. I had told the ladies that I would, on the next run, ride my horse without saddle or bridle. This had raised the excitement to fever heat among the excursionists, and I remember one fair lady who endeavored to prevail upon me not to attempt it.

"That's nothing at all," said I; "I have done it many a time, and old Brigham knows as well as I what I am doing, and sometimes a great deal better."

So, leaving my saddle and bridle with the wagons, we rode to the windward of the buffaloes, as usual, and when within a few hundred yards of them we dashed into the herd. I soon had thirteen laid out on the ground, the last one of which I had driven down close to the wagons, where the ladies were. It frightened some of the tender creatures to see the buffalo coming at full speed directly toward them; but when he had got within fifty yards of one of the wagons, I shot him dead in his tracks. This made my sixty-ninth buffalo, and finished my third and last run, Comstock having killed forty-six.

As it was now late in the afternoon, Comstock and his backers gave up the idea that he could beat me, and there-upon the referees declared me the winner of the match, as well as the champion buffalo-hunter of the plains.[10]

In August of that year Billy Comstock was killed by Cheyenne Indians, who took his prized Colt revolver, reportedly with rare grips of mother-of-pearl.

Cody wrote that the railroad used to send mounted heads around to

all the principal cities and railroad centers in the country, having them placed in prominent positions at the leading hotels, depots, and other public buildings, as a sort of trade-mark, or advertisement, of the Kansas Pacific Railroad; and to-day they attract the attention of the traveler almost everywhere. Whenever I am traveling over the country and see one of these trade-marks, I feel pretty certain that I was the cause of the death of the old fellow whose body it once ornamented, and many a wild and exciting hunt is thus called to mind.[11]

Cody's Ride for General Sheridan

For much of the years 1868 to 1876, Cody served as an army scout, on the government payroll. In that capacity, while carrying dispatches for General Philip Sheridan, he performed one of his most heroic achievements on the plains. In 1868, Cody arrived at Fort Hays after riding sixty-five miles from Fort Larned to alert the general of an uprising of Kiowa and Comanche. Sheridan's *Personal Memoirs* continue the account of the scout's incredible ride.[12]

[The intelligence of impending Indian attacks] required that certain orders should be carried to Fort Dodge, ninety-five miles south of Hays. This too being a particularly dangerous route—several couriers having been killed on it—it was impossible to get one of the various 'Petes,' 'Jacks,' or 'Jims,' hanging around Hays City to take my communication. Cody learning of the strait I was in, manfully came to the rescue, and proposed to make the trip to Dodge, though he had just finished [a] long and perilous ride from Larned. I gratefully accepted his offer, and after four or five hours' rest he mounted a fresh horse and hastened on his journey, halting but once to rest on the way, and then only for an hour, the stop being made at Coon Creek, where

he got another mount from a troop of cavalry. At Dodge he took six hours' sleep, and then continued on to his own post—Fort Larned—with more despatches. After resting twelve hours at Larned, he was again in the saddle with tidings for me at Fort Hays, General Hazen sending him, this time, with word that the villages had fled to the south of the Arkansas. Thus, in all, Cody rode about 350 miles in less than sixty hours, and such an exhibition of endurance and courage was more than enough to convince me that his services would be extremely valuable in the campaign, so I retained him at Fort Hays till the battalion of the Fifth Cavalry arrived, and then made him chief of scouts for that regiment.[13]

Calculations by Russell indicate the actual distance to have totaled approximately 290 miles—still a formidable achievement.

Tall Bull and the Battle of Summit Springs

Scouts were more at risk than most army troops, as they went riding out ahead, carried dispatches, or were assigned to sneak close to Indians in camp or in the field.

While most of the Cheyenne had agreed to a peace treaty, a Cheyenne chief named Tall Bull remained a problem, leading a band of renegade Cheyenne, with some Arapaho and Sioux, who were known as Dog Soldiers. When Tall Bull's Dog Soldiers kidnapped two women, killing the husband of one and the baby of the other, General Eugene A. Carr and the Fifth Cavalry were determined to rescue the women and vanquish the Indians. In two skirmishes that led to a confrontation with Tall Bull, Cody played no direct role. However, a major battle, which proved to be a signal event in Cody's life, resulted in his being widely heralded for heroic conduct: that was Summit Springs, July 11, 1869, and it marked the end of Indian hostilities in Kansas and the neighboring territory.

In hot pursuit of the Indians who were holding the two women captive, General Carr moved his troops at a rapid pace, covering 150 miles in four days. On advice from Cody, they outmaneuvered the Indians. Carr later wrote: "Cody's idea was to get around, beyond, and between them and the river."[14] Cody was further credited by Captain George F. Price with intelligence that was instrumental in the victory:

... the arrival of the guide, William F. Cody, who reported large herds of ponies about six miles distant in a southwesterly direction, which was indubitable evidence that Tall Bull and his warriors were encamped and unconscious of approaching peril, as the pickets, who were watching their rear, had made no danger signals. ... [Cody] guided the Fifth Cavalry to a position whence the regiment was enabled to charge the enemy and win a brilliant victory.[15]

Still another endorsement of Cody's contributions to the battle came from Lieutenant Edward M. Hayes, quartermaster, who recalled that Cody had "discovered the village and led the troops to the position they were to occupy in the attack without the knowledge of the Indians. This was considered the greatest of the many great achievements of this wonderful scout."[16]

Cody himself describes the Fifth cavalry's charge against the Indian village:

The General at once ordered his men to tighten their saddles and otherwise prepare for action. Soon all was excitement among the officers and soldiers, every one being anxious to charge the village. I now changed my horse for old Buckskin Joe, who had been led for me thus far, and was comparatively fresh. Acting on my suggestion, the General made a circuit to the north, believing that if the Indians had their scouts out, they would naturally be watching in the direction whence they had come. When we had passed the Indians and were between them and the Platte river, we turned to the left and started toward the village.[17]

By this manoeuver we had avoided discovery by the Sioux scouts, and we were confident of giving them a complete surprise. Keeping the command wholly out of sight, until we were within a mile of the Indians, the General halted the advance guard until all closed up, and then issued an order, that, when he sounded the charge, the whole command was to rush into the village.

As we halted on the top of the hill overlooking the camp of the unsuspecting Indians, General Carr called out to his bugler: "Sound the charge!" The bugler for a moment became intensely excited, and actually forgot the notes. The General again sang out: "Sound the charge!" and yet the bugler was unable to obey the command. Quartermaster Hay[e]s—who had obtained permission to accompany the expedition—was riding near the General, and comprehending the dilemma of the man, rushed up to him, jerked the bugle from his hands and sounded the charge himself in clear and distinct notes. As the troops rushed forward, he threw the bugle away, then drawing his pistols, was among the first men that entered the village.

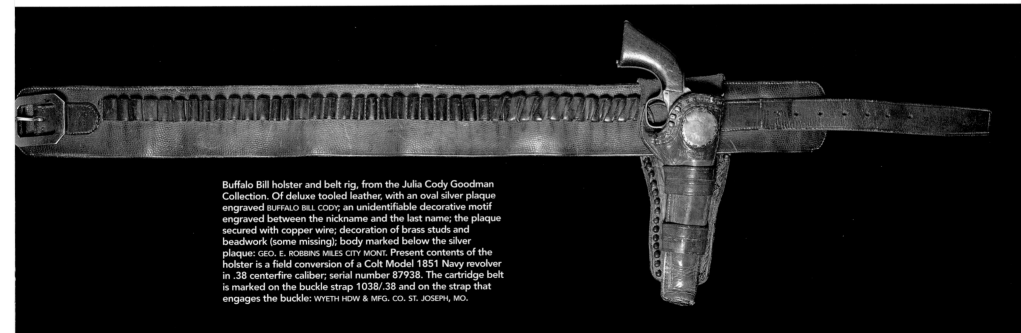

Buffalo Bill holster and belt rig, from the Julia Cody Goodman Collection. Of deluxe tooled leather, with an oval silver plaque engraved BUFFALO BILL CODY; an unidentifiable decorative motif engraved between the nickname and the last name; the plaque secured with copper wire; decoration of brass studs and beadwork (some missing); body marked below the silver plaque: GEO. E. ROBBINS MILES CITY MONT. Present contents of the holster is a field conversion of a Colt Model 1851 Navy revolver in .38 centerfire caliber; serial number 87938. The cartridge belt is marked on the buckle strap 1038/.38 and on the strap that engages the buckle: WYETH HDW & MFG. CO. ST. JOSEPH, MO.

off some stock near O'Fallon's Station. . . . Two companies, under command of Major Brown, had been ordered out, and next morning, just as we were about to start, Major Brown said to me:

"By the way, Cody, we are going to have quite an important character with us as a guest on this scout. It's old Ned Buntline, the novelist."

Just then I noticed a gentlemen, who was rather stoutly built, and who wore a blue military coat, on the left breast of which were pinned about twenty gold medals and badges of secret societies. He walked a little lame as he approached us, and I at once concluded that he was Ned Buntline.

"He has a good mark to shoot at on the left breast," said I to Major Brown, "but he looks like a soldier." As he came up, Major Brown said:

"Cody, allow me to introduce you to Colonel E.B.C. [sic] Judson, Otherwise known as Ned Buntline."

"Colonel Judson, I am glad to meet you," said I; "the Major tells me that you are to accompany us on the scout."

"Yes, my boy, so I am," said he; "I was to deliver a temperance lecture to-night; but no lectures for me when there is a prospect for a fight. The Major has kindly offered me a horse, but I don't know how I'll stand the ride, for I haven't done any riding lately; but when I was a young man I spent several years among the fur companies of the Northwest, and was a good rider and an excellent shot."

"The Major has given you a fine horse . . . and you'll soon find yourself at home in the saddle," said I. . . .

We reached O'Fallon's at eleven o'clock, and in a short time I succeeded in finding the Indian trail. . . . We followed their track to the North Platte, but as they had a start of two days, Major Brown abandoned the pursuit, and returned to Fort McPherson, while I went back to Fort Sedgwick, accompanied by Buntline.

During this short scout, Buntline had asked me a great many questions, and he was determined to go out on the next expedition with me, providing he could obtain permission from the commanding officer. I introduced him to the officers—excepting those he already knew—and invited him to become my guest while he remained at the post, and gave him my pony Powder Face to ride.[20]

Buntline resurfaced in Cody's life periodically, urging and cajoling the young scout and hunter into a consequential change in the direction of his life.

Cody as he appeared at about the date of the hunt with General Sheridan and party. The single-shot sporting rifle of best quality English make, half stocked, and likely of about .50 caliber. The pistol grip and forend checkered and capped in silver or in horn. A rifle of such distinction might well have been made for a British gentleman and brought along for hunting in the West.

While on a hunt with the Earl of Dunraven, Cody (in his autobiography) described the method of pursuing these elusive beasts on the plains:

"The elk hunt of those days was managed in about this way: six or seven of us would start at sunrise on our prairie horses and get as close as possible to the elk, which would be feeding in the open, two or three hundred, perhaps, in a bunch. These long-legged beasts were swifter than the buffalo, and they would let us get within a half mile of them before they would give a mighty snort and dash away after their leader. Then came the test of speed and endurance. They led the horses [on] a wild race, and it put our chargers to their mettle to overtake the game. Right in among them we would spur, and, dropping the reins, use the repeating rifle with both hands. The breech-loading [S]pringfield piece of fifty-caliber, the same as used in the regular army, was our favorite rifle at that time."

(opposite) Petite and handsome early example of Remington over-and-under .41 rimfire deringer, with presentation inscription WM FIELDER. / FROM / BUFFALO BILL, serial number 1848. A pair of percussion Henry Deringer pistols, inscribed W.F. CODY/1869 is in the collection of the Buffalo Bill Historical Center; set presented to early arms collector William Goodwin Renwick by his friend Louis A. Barker. Small-size Deringers measure 4½ inches overall.

General Sheridan's Party of Hunters

Equal in importance to Cody's future as his meeting with Buntline were several adventurous episodes that were instrumental in accelerating his national fame. One of these was a widely publicized hunt with General Sheridan and party. The experience was so important to the participants that a limited-edition book was published, one copy each for members of the party and one for Cody himself. Buffalo Bill's own description of the hunt appeared as Chapter XXIV in his autobiography. To some extent, the text was taken from the special-imprint book, written by General H. E. Davies, who was in the hunting party.

This was as distinguished a group of American sportsmen as ever was guided by Cody, not the least of whom was James Gordon Bennett, publisher of the New York *Herald*. Due to the significance of the expedition for Buffalo Bill's future, the event is covered in a lengthy quotation in Appendix A.

In this hunt, Cody proved his mettle to influential men, each of whom relished retelling their adventures with Buffalo Bill. He gained experience at mixing with such an elite company and soon made a trip to the East, where he was the guest of several such men, ensconced at the exclusive Union Club. That first eastern exposure moved him a step closer to the stage and to national stardom.

The Grand Duke Alexis's Grandiose Buffalo Hunt

No more regal hunts for buffalo were ever organized than the two expeditions put on by the U.S. government and the army for the entertainment of the Grand Duke Alexis of Russia, a son of the czar, and brother of the future czar. His highness's visit came only a few years after Russia had sold Alaska to the United States, a time when relations between the two countries were excellent. From a social standpoint, the grand duke's visit was unquestionably a major affair. At every stop on the several months'–long tour, young women especially attempted to meet this royal, the only Romanov up to that date to visit the republic.

One of the hunts was in the company of Lieutenant Colonel George Armstrong Custer, and the other was guided by Buffalo Bill. Cody gives the latter adventure an entire chapter in his autobiography, telling the story with considerable relish. Since the Fifth Cavalry had been reassigned to the Arizona territory, General Sheridan himself intervened to keep Cody, by then the best-known hunter and guide in America, on hand. The number of participants in the expedition, by Cody's own count, was some five hundred, including the regimental band of the Second Cavalry!

One of the newspapers reporting on the event—which was front-page news—referred amusingly to Cody's role as that of "Guide, Tutor, and [prophetically] Entertaining Agent." Cody wrote:

Hunting with a Grand Duke

About the first of January, 1872, General Forsyth and Dr. Asch, of Sheridan's staff came out to Fort McPherson to make preparations for a big buffalo hunt for the Grand Duke Alexis, of Russia; and as this was to be no ordinary affair, these officers had been sent by General Sheridan to have all the necessary arrangements perfected by the time the Grand Duke should arrive. They learned from me that there were plenty of buffaloes in the vicinity and especially on the Red Willow, sixty miles distant. They said they would like to go over on the Red Willow and pick out a suitable place for the camp; they also inquired the location of the Spotted Tail, Sioux Indians. Spotted Tail had permission from the Government to hunt the buffalo, with his people during the winter, in the Republican river country. It was my opinion that they were located somewhere on the Frenchman's Fork about one hundred and fifty miles from Fort McPherson.

General Sheridan's commissioners informed me, that he wished me to visit Spotted Tail's camp, and induce about one hundred of the leading warriors and chiefs, to come to the point where it should be decided to locate the Alexis hunting camp, and to be there by the

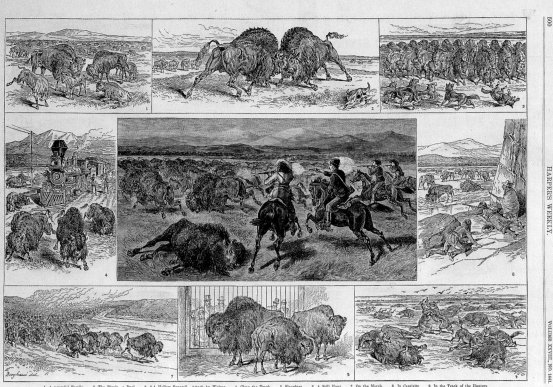

1. A peaceful Family.   2. The Rivals—a Duel.   3. "A Hollow Square"—Attack by Wolves.   4. Clear the Track.   5. Slaughter.   6. A Still Hunt.   7. On the March.   8. In Captivity.   9. In the Track of the Hunters.

BUFFALO HUNTING.—DRAWN BY BERGHAUS.—[SEE PAGE 499.]

(*opposite*) Studio photograph of the grand duke, with his deluxe presentation S&W Russian Model revolver and what is likely to have been a hunting sword. Lieutenant Colonel Custer holds his Springfield Officers Model Sporter rifle and a horsewhip. Both are ready for a grand buffalo hunt.

Harper's Weekly, on buffalo hunting. At *bottom center,* the nattily attired curious gawk at three captive buffalo, probably imprisoned in an eastern zoo. Press coverage for Alexis's travels in America was comprehensive.

time the Grand Duke should arrive, so that he could see a body of American Indians and observe the manner in which they killed buffaloes. The Indians would also be called upon to give a grand war dance in honor of the distinguished visitor. [Cody made arrangements with Chief Spotted Tail for his Indians to play a role in the grand hunt; done at some risk to Cody from Spotted Tail's young men: "Several of them were looking daggers at me. They appeared as if they wished to raise my hair then and there."] . . .

At last, on the morning of the 12th of January, 1872, the Grand Duke and party arrived at North Platte by special train; in charge of a Mr. Francis Thompson. Captain Hays and myself, with five or six ambulances, fifteen or twenty extra saddle-horses and a company of cavalry under Captain Egan, were at the depot in time to receive them. Presently General Sheridan and a large, fine-looking young man, whom we at once con-

cluded to be the Grand Duke came out of the cars and approached us. General Sheridan at once introduced me to the Grand Duke as Buffalo Bill, for he it was, and said that I was to take charge of him and show him how to kill buffalo.

In less than half an hour the whole party were dashing away towards the south, across the South Platte and towards the Medicine; upon reaching which point we halted for a change of horses and a lunch. Resuming our ride we reached Camp Alexis in the afternoon. General Sheridan was well pleased with the arrangements that had been made and was delighted to find that Spotted Tail and his Indians had arrived on time. They were objects of great curiosity to the Grand Duke, who spent considerable time in looking at them, and watching their exhibitions of horsemanship, sham fights, etc. That evening the Indians gave the grand war dance, which I had arranged for.

General Custer, who was one of the hunting party, carried on a mild flirtation with one of Spotted Tail's daughters, who had accompanied her father thither, and it was noticed also that the Grand Duke paid considerable attention to another handsome red-skin maiden. The night passed pleasantly, and all retired with great expectations of having a most enjoyable and successful buffalo hunt. The Duke Alexis asked me a great many questions as to how we shot buffaloes, and what kind of a gun or pistol we used, and if he was going to have a good horse. I told him that he was to have my celebrated Buckskin Joe, and when we went into a buffalo herd all he would have to do was to sit on the horse's back and fire away.

At nine o'clock next morning we were all in our saddles, and in a few minutes were galloping over the prairies in search of a buffalo herd. We had not gone far before we observed a herd some distance ahead of us crossing our way; after that we proceeded cautiously, so as to keep out of sight until we were ready to make a charge.

Of course the main thing was to give Alexis the first chance and the best shot at the buffaloes, and when all was in readiness we dashed over a little knoll that had hidden us from view, and in a few minutes we were among them. Alexis at first preferred to use his pistol instead of a gun. He fired six shots from this weapon at buffaloes only twenty feet away from him, but as he shot wildly, not one of the bullets took effect. Riding up to his side and seeing that his weapon was empty, I exchanged pistols with him. He again fired six shots, without dropping a buffalo.

Seeing that the animals were bound to make their escape without his killing one of them, unless he had a better weapon, I rode up to him, gave him my old reli-

17

able "Lucretia," and told him to urge his horse close to the buffalo, and I would then give him the word when to shoot. At the same time I gave old Buckskin Joe a blow with my whip, and with a few jumps the horse carried the Grand Duke to within about ten feet of a big buffalo bull.

"Now is your time," said I. He fired, and down went the buffalo. The Grand Duke stopped his horse, dropped his gun on the ground, and commenced waving his hat. When his suite came galloping up, he began talking to them in a tongue which I could not understand. Presently General Sheridan joined the group, and the ambulances were brought up. Very soon the corks began to fly from the champagne bottles, in honor of the Grand Duke Alexis, who had killed the first buffalo.

It was reported in a great many of the newspapers that I shot the first buffalo for Alexis, while in some it was stated that I held the buffalo while His Royal Highness killed it. But the way I have related the affair is the correct version.

It was thought that we had had about sport enough for one day, and accordingly I was directed by General Sheridan to guide the party back to camp, and we were soon on our way thither. Several of the party, however, concluded to have a little hunt on their own account, and presently we saw them galloping over the prairie in different directions in pursuit of buffaloes.

While we were crossing a deep ravine, on our way to camp, we ran into a small band of buffaloes that had been frightened by some of the hunters. As they rushed past us, not more than thirty yards distant, Alexis raised his pistol, fired and killed a buffalo cow. It was either an extraordinary good shot or a "scratch"—probably the latter, for it surprised the Grand Duke as well as everybody else. We gave him three cheers, and when the ambulance came up we took a pull at the champagne in honor of the Grand Duke's success. I was in hopes that he would kill five or six more buffaloes before we reached camp, especially if a basket of champagne was to be opened every time he dropped one.

General Sheridan directed me to take care of the hides and heads of the buffaloes which Alexis had killed, as the Duke wished to keep them as souvenirs of the hunt. I also cut out the choice meat from the cow and brought it into camp, and that night at supper Alexis had the pleasure of dining on broiled buffalo steak obtained from the animal which he had shot himself.

We remained at this camp two or three days, during which we hunted most of the time, the Grand Duke himself killing eight buffaloes.

One day Alexis desired to see how the Indians hunted buffaloes and killed them with bow and arrow; so Spotted Tail, selecting some of his best hunters, had them surround a herd, and bring the animals down, not only with arrows, but with lances. The Grand Duke was told to follow upon the heels of one celebrated Indian hunter, whose name was "Two Lance," and watch him bring down the game; for this chief had the reputation of being able to send an arrow through and through the body of a buffalo. Upon this occasion he did not belie his reputation, for he sent an arrow through a buffalo, which fell dead at the shot, and the arrow was given to Alexis as a souvenir of his hunt on the American plains.

When the Grand Duke was satisfied with the sport, orders were given for the return to the railroad. The conveyance provided for the Grand Duke and General Sheridan was a heavy double-seated open carriage, or rather an Irish dog-cart, and it was drawn by four spirited cavalry horses which were not much used to the harness. The driver was Bill Reed, an old overland stage driver and wagon master; on our way in, the Grand Duke frequently expressed his admiration of the skillful manner in which Reed handled the reins.

General Sheridan informed the Duke that I also had been a stage-driver in the Rocky Mountains, and thereupon His Royal Highness expressed a desire to see me drive. I was in advance at the time, and General Sheridan sang out to me:

"Cody, get in here and show the Duke how you can drive. Mr. Reed will exchange places with you and ride your horse." [Cody whipped up the team and produced a wild ride; the horses took off at their own speed] . . . The Duke and the General were kept rather busy in holding their positions on the seats, and when they saw that I was keeping the horses straight in the road, they seemed to enjoy the dash which we were making. I was unable to stop the team until they ran into the camp where we were to obtain a fresh relay, and there I succeeded in checking them. The Grand Duke said he didn't want any more of that kind of driving, as he preferred to go a little slower.

On arriving at the railroad, the Duke invited me into his car, and made me some valuable presents, at the same time giving me a cordial invitation to visit him, if ever I should come to his country.

General Sheridan took occasion to remind me of an invitation to visit New York which I had received from some of the gentlemen who accompanied the General on the hunt from Fort McPherson to Hays City, in September of the previous year. Said he:

"You will never have a better opportunity to accept that invitation than now. I have had a talk with General Ord concerning you, and he will give you a leave of absence whenever you are ready to start. Write a letter to General Stager, of Chicago, that you are now prepared to accept the invitation, and he will send you a pass.["]

Thanking the General for his kindness, I then bade him and the Grand Duke good-bye, and soon their train was out of sight.[21]

Inset shows Cody in frontier garb, ca. 1874. That year, Cody and his cast visited the Remington factory in Ilion, N.Y., and met with Elisha Green, Philo Remington's son-in-law. There he was presented with this .42 caliber Rolling Block rifle, engraved and plated, with select walnut stocks; serial number 3, from factory's special-order department. Remington New Model Army, serial number 73293, was presented by Buffalo Bill to his old friend Charles Trego (see R. L. Wilson, *The Peacemakers*, pp. 292–93, for details of its frontier use by Cody). Presenter's handwriting on card attests to its history and to the fact that "it never failed me." The Remington revolver in Cody's waistband is a deluxe model, with plated finish and likely with ivory grips—the gleaming appearance better suited for the stage than the plains.

The revolver that the grand duke used to shoot at buffalo would have been a large-caliber handgun, likely the one presented to him while visiting the Smith & Wesson factory. In .44 Russian, that revolver had been richly engraved and gold inlaid by the celebrated craftsman Gustave Young, and fitted with relief-carved mother-of-pearl grips. Among the embellishments were the Romanov coat of arms and patriotic symbols of the United States. Dropping a buffalo bull with a handgun demanded careful shot placement and firing at close range. Thus, his highness found Lucretia Borgia a better alternative to a .44-caliber topbreak revolver.

The gifts presented to Cody by the grand duke were gold cuff links and shirt studs—some later altered into other forms of jewelry. But it was the publicity that was the most lasting reward. And in the process of putting on a show for his highness, Cody had a dress rehearsal for what would become the Wild West Show. Buffalo hunting, by rifle from horseback, became a standard reenactment episode of show performances.

Cody Wins the Medal of Honor

The nation's highest award for valor, the Congressional Medal of Honor, was awarded to William F. Cody on May 22, 1872. In his capacity as a scout, Cody had distinguished himself, his life at risk, in an action against members of a band of Indians who had raided the McPherson Station, located some five miles from Fort McPherson, in April 1872. Third Cavalry Company B, commanded by Captain Charles Meinhold and First Lieutenant Joseph Lawson, was

dispatched to deal with the Indians. Cody was their scout and guide.

Two days later, the contingent arrived at the south fork of the Loup River, in Nebraska. The Indians had split up, so the soldiers struck camp. Cody and six men, under a Sergeant Foley, went out on a reconnaissance; under his guidance, an Indian encampment was located within a mile's distance. To quote the official report filed by Captain Meinhold: "Mr. Cody had guided Sergeant Foley's party with such skill that he approached the Indian camp within fifty yards before he was noticed. The Indians fired immediately upon Mr. Cody and Sergeant Foley. Mr. Cody killed one Indian; two others ran toward the main command and were killed."[22]

Cody tells the story of the charge and shoot-out:

We had gone but a short distance when we discovered Indians camped, not more than a mile away, with horses grazing near by. They were only a small party, and I determined to charge upon them with my six men, rather than return to the command, because I feared they would see us as we went back and then they would get away from us entirely. I asked the men if they were willing to attempt it, and they replied that they would follow me wherever I would lead them. That was the kind of spirit that pleased me, and we immediately moved forward on the enemy, getting as close to them as possible without being seen.

I finally gave the signal to charge, and we dashed into the little camp with a yell. Five Indians sprang out of a willow tepee, and greeted us with a volley, and we returned the fire. I was riding Buckskin Joe, who with a few jumps brought me up to the tepee, followed by my men. We nearly ran over the Indians who were endeavoring to reach their horses on the opposite side of the creek. Just as one was jumping the narrow stream a bullet from my old "Lucretia" overtook him. He never reached the other bank, but dropped dead in the water. Those of the Indians who were guarding the horses, seeing what was going on at the camp, came rushing to the rescue of their friends. I now counted thirteen braves, but as we had already disposed of two, we had only eleven to take care of. The odds were nearly two to one against us.

While the Indian reinforcements were approaching the camp I jumped the creek with Buckskin Joe to meet them, expecting our party would follow me; but as they could not induce their horses to make the leap, I was the only one who got over. I ordered the sergeant to dismount his men, and leaving one to hold the horses, to come over with the rest and help me drive the Indians off. Before they could do this, two mounted warriors closed in on me and were shooting at short range. I returned their fire and had the satisfaction of seeing one of them fall from my horse. . . .

By this time the soldiers had crossed the creek to assist me, and were blazing away at the other Indians. Urging Buckskin Joe forward, I was soon alongside of [one of the Indians and] shot him through the head.

The reports of our guns had been heard by Captain Meinhold, who at once started with his company up the creek to our aid, and when the remaining Indians, whom we were still fighting, saw these reinforcements coming they whirled their horses and fled; as their steeds were quite fresh they made their escape. . . . Securing the scalps of the dead Indians and other trophies we returned to the fort.[23]

Captain Mcinhold's report noted that three Indians had been killed; he also gave due credit to the bravery and resourcefulness of Cody:

Mr. Cody discovered a party of six mounted Indians and two led horses running at full speed at a distance of about two miles down the river. I at once sent Lieutenant Lawson with Mr. Cody and fifteen men in pursuit. He, in the beginning of the chase, gained a little upon them, so that they were compelled to abandon the two led horses, which were captured, but after running more than twelve miles at full speed, our jaded horses gave out and the Indians made good their escape. . . . Mr. William Cody's reputation for bravery and skill as a guide is so well established that I need not say anything else but that he acted in his usual manner.[24]

Ned Buntline in frontier costume; the Bowie knife appears to have an elaborately carved ivory handle and an elegant crossguard, with a silver or German silver mounted-leather scabbard. The revolver is likely a Moore teat-fire, one of the least practical handguns of the period, in a contoured leather holster.

Based on the captain's report, Cody was awarded the Medal of Honor. Many years later, in an act of Congress dated June 16, 1916, the medal was revoked, since "at the time of the act of gallantry he was neither an officer nor an enlisted man, being at that time a civilian." Despite that legislation, some forty-four years later, the fact remains: Cody had been awarded the nation's most exalted recognition for heroism. Today, Cody's medal is a featured display at the Buffalo Bill Historical Center, in a gallery of treasures.

Buntline's Impact on Cody and His Legend

While Cody's name and reputation were escalating rapidly in the West, Ned Buntline was having ideas for a Buffalo Bill dime-novel character and a stage career in the East. Some three years after their chance meeting at Fort McPherson, Cody accepted the invitation from the participants of General Sheridan's hunt of 1871 and traveled to New York City. Although Buffalo Bill asked to meet Buntline, then at the Brevoort Place Hotel, his hosts, dignitaries of the likes of James Gordon Bennett and August Belmont, expected him to socialize with them, and Buntline was well outside their social circle.

Cody was lodged at the Union Club and was the subject of much popular attention in New York. Buntline, opportunist that he was, saw a chance for some self-promotion. Conveniently, a play based on a Buntline story about Cody was scheduled for the Bowery Theater. To the annoyance of Bennett and his circle, Cody attended the opening night and was introduced to the throng:

Ned Buntline and Fred Maeder had dramatized one of the stories which the former had written about me for the New York Weekly. *The drama was called "Buffalo Bill, the King of Border Men." While I was in New York it was produced at the Bowery Theater; J. B. Studley, an excellent actor, appearing in the character of "Buffalo Bill," and Mrs. W. G. Jones, a fine actress, taking the part of my sister, a leading role. I was curious to see how I would look when represented by some one else, and of course I was present on the opening night, a private box having been reserved for me. The theater was packed, every seat being occupied as well as the standing-room. The drama was played smoothly, and created a great deal of enthusiasm.*

The audience, upon learning that the real "Buffalo Bill" was present, gave several cheers between the acts, and I was called on to come out on the stage and make a speech. Mr. Freleigh, the manager, insisted that I should comply with the request, and that I should be introduced to Mr. Studley. I finally consented, and the next moment I found myself standing behind the foot-lights and in front of an audience for the first time in my life. I looked up, then down, then on each side, and everywhere I saw a sea of human faces, and thousands of eyes all staring at me. I confess that I felt very much embarrassed—never more so in my life—and I knew not what to say. I made a desperate effort, and a few words escaped me, but what they were I could not for the life of me tell, nor could any one else in the house. My utterances were inaudible even to the leader of the orchestra, Mr. Dean, who was sitting only a few feet from me. Bowing to the audience, I beat a hasty retreat into one of the canons of the stage. I never felt more re-lieved in my life than when I got out of the view of that immense crowd.

That evening Mr. Freleigh offered to give me five hundred dollars a week to play the part of "Buffalo Bill" myself. I thought that he was certainly joking, especially as he had witnessed my awkward performance; but when he assured me that he was in earnest, I told him that it would be useless for me to attempt anything of the kind, for I never could talk to a crowd of people like that, even if it was to save my neck, and that he might as well try to make an actor out of a government mule. I thanked him for the generous offer, which I had to de-cline owing to a lack of confidence in myself; or as some people might express it, I didn't have the requisite cheek to undertake a thing of that sort. The play of "Buffalo Bill" had a very successful run of six or eight weeks, and was afterwards produced in all the principal cities of the country, everywhere being received with genuine enthusiasm.[25]

While in the East, Cody traveled with Buntline to Philadelphia, to see relatives in West Chester. Bunt-line took him to see a play at the Chestnut Street The-atre and arranged for an interview with the Philadelphia *Public Record*. Shortly after Cody and Buntline returned to New York, Cody headed back West, while Buntline launched into a dime novel: *Buffalo Bill's Best Shot; or, The Heart of Spotted Tail*. The article ran in serial form in *New York Weekly*, be-

Ned Buntline, Buffalo Bill, Texas Jack.

As evidenced by this picture, Buntline simply did not fit into the company of Buffalo Bill and Texas Jack. In time, both personalities distanced themselves from the irascible character.

ginning March 25. Still another Buffalo Bill piece by Buntline, *Buffalo Bill's Last Victory; or, Dove Eye, the Lodge Queen*, began its serial publication July 8.

Cody's autobiography notes that Buntline was badgering him to return to New York and to appear on the stage:

During the summer and fall of 1872, I received nu-merous letters from Ned Buntline, urging me to come East and go upon the stage to represent my own charac-ter. "There's money in it," he wrote, "and you will prove a big card, as your character is a novelty on the stage."

At times I almost determined to make the venture; but the recollection of that night when I stood on the stage of the Bowery Theatre and was unable to utter a word above a whisper, would cause me to stop and think and become irresolute. I feared that I would be a total failure, and wrote Buntline to that effect. But he insisted that I would soon get over all that embarrass-ment, and become accustomed to the stage, so that I would think no more of appearing before five thousand people than I would before half a dozen. He proposed to organize a good company, and wished me to meet him in Chicago, where the opening performance would be given.

I remained undecided as to what I ought to do. The officers of the fort as well as my family and friends to whom I had mentioned the matter, laughed at the idea of my ever becoming an actor. That I, an old scout who had never seen more than twenty or thirty theatrical performances in my life, should think of going upon the stage, was ridiculous in the extreme—so they all said.[26]

Finally, at the urging of John Burwell "Texas Jack" Omohundro, Cody agreed to Buntline's offer. The play was written in quick time by Buntline, adapting it from *Buffalo Bill's Last Victory* and using the title *The Scouts of the Prairie*. The December 17, 1872, Chicago *Evening Journal* published the title, with the heading "NED BUNTLINE—COL. E.Z.C. JUDSON" and smaller type noting, "The real heroes of the Plains, Buffalo Bill and Texas Jack in a great sensation drama entitled, *The Scouts of the Prairie*, written expressly for them by Ned Buntline. Morlacchi as Dove Eye. Matinees Wednes-day and Saturday—Every lady visiting the matinees will be presented with portraits of the boys." Cody's career as a scout had all the heroic proportions to which Buntline's piece should have aspired. Unfortu-nately, the story was fantasy fluff when it could have been stirring just by being true.

The *Evening Journal* treated the play generously, with a review that took into consideration the amateur status of nearly all of the lead players:

Nixon's Ampitheatre was last night the scene of a most extraordinary character and one in which the audience bore quite as prominent a feature as did the occupants of the stage. The occasion was the first appearance of Ned Buntline's play with the blood-curdling and hair-raising title of *The Scouts of the Prairie; or Red Deviltry As It Is,* being a descriptive affair of life on the plains and in the mountains of the West, and in which the noted characters 'Buffalo Bill' and 'Texas Jack' in their own original selves were presented, as well as 'Ned Buntline' the author of the play. Last night not less than 2,500 boys and young men crowded the ampitheatre to catch a glimpse of their heroes. Mlle. Morlacchi, the Italian danseuse, essayed the part of the Indian maiden Dove Eye with great success, . . . largely sustained the dramatic interest from first to last and was an interesting connecting link in the chain of events.

This initial performance of *The Scouts of the Prairie* was nothing less than the birth of the Western. Although Cody clearly was not a polished thespian, as a showman he was a natural. The awkward, amateurish stage debut was also nothing less than the beginning of one of the most extraordinary show-business careers in American history. Few know or care about the vehicle that began that success—a play unworthy of restaging—but the star that emerged became an American legend.

Following the Chicago engagement, the show traveled to St. Louis. There, Buntline was arrested for the riot of some twenty years before, having fled the city while out on bail. After again posting bail, the show was not interrupted. Performances followed in Cincinnati, Rochester, Buffalo, and Boston. Then, while in New York, a reviewer for Bennett's New York *Herald* panned Buntline, who was disliked by Bennett: "Ned Buntline is simply maundering imbecility. Ludicrous beyond the power of description is Ned Buntline's temperance address in the forest." Cody was also panned: "ridiculous as an actor," while

Buntline was clearly not a shooter. His grip on the double-barrel rifle or shotgun—particularly with the right hand—and the way the stock sets against his cheek were unconventional. A better view of the large and striking Bowie knife.

Omohundro was "not so ridiculous." The critic must have relished his summation: "Everything is so wonderfully bad it is almost good!" The *New York Times* was complimentary of Cody and noted that "his use of the revolver and rifle indicate extensive practice, and were vastly relished by the audience. . . . There is a certain flavor of realism and of nationality about the play well calculated to gratify a general audience."

Wild Bill.   Texas Jack.   Buffalo Bill.

Three authentic frontiersmen, photographed ca. 1873–1874, when they performed together.

As the show wound down, Buntline had big plans, even thinking of taking the show to England and of doing the performance in a tent on horseback! But

Buffalo Bill and Texas Jack, realizing they were now comfortable on the stage, had had enough of Buntline. After the final performance, June 16, 1873, in Port Jervis, New York, the stage association of Cody, Omohundro, and Buntline ended.

Buntline wrote his fourth and last dime novel about Cody, *Buffalo Bill's First Trail; or, Will Cody, the Pony Express Rider.* He also tried to develop another stage program, with other performers, but met with failure. Without Buffalo Bill, Buntline's later shows flopped.

When Buntline met Cody, he was not specifically seeking a frontier hero for his dime novels, but he did recognize Cody's potential. Buntline wrote four novels about Cody, appeared in stage productions with him, and helped to guide the novice into a theatrical career. Buntline's *The Scouts of the Prairie* gave Cody the vehicle that led to lasting fame and stardom. Buntline was a rascal, but his impact on Cody's career was positive and substantial.

As to his own career, Buntline summed that up in his inimitable and devilish way: "I might have paved for myself a far different career in letters but my early lot was cast among rough men on the border; they became my comrades, and when I made my name as a teller of stories about Indians, pirates, and scouts, it seemed too late to begin over again. And besides, I made more money than any Bohemian in New York or Boston."[27]

(*right*) Period photograph showing trophies taken by Cody from Yellow Hair. Some of these artifacts were detailed in a Rochester (New York) *Union and Advertiser* article on July 27, 1876; note reference to Yellow Hand due to interpreter's mistake at time of fight:

BUFFALO BILL'S TROPHIES
ARRIVAL OF YELLOW HAND'S SCALP AND ENTIRE OUTFIT

"This forenoon Moses Kerngood of the Pickwick cigar store, received from Buffalo Bill . . . a collection of novel trophies, including the scalp of the Cheyenne warrior, Yellow Hand, who was slain by the intrepid scout in an almost hand-to-hand conflict. Bill was in pretty close quarters in this conflict, but by dint of his superior skill and undaunted bravery laid his victim low. He now sends to his friend Kerngood the spoils of his victory, which inventory as follows: the scalp of the brave; bridle; blanket; whip; bowie knife; head dress; girdle; shield. To the latter is suspended several Indian scalps but no white scalps, showing that Yellow Hand had not killed any whites, but had confined his operations to hostile tribes of savages.

Yellow Hand's scalp consists of a piece of skin about three inches square to which adheres a switch of straight, jet black hair nearly two feet long. This [is] neatly braided to the tip and is more ornamental than useful. The scalp is not yet dry, but has been sprinkled with some chemical to preserve it. The head-dress referred to and its appendages constitute the chief ornament of the warrior.—It consists of a strip of limber buffalo skin five or six inches wide and as many feet long, set as close as they can stand with eagle feathers. There must have been several of the national birds stripped of their plumage to make up this piece of savage finery. On the tips of many of the feathers are locks of some kind of hair, some of it fine enough to be human; it is attached to the feather by a cement. Scarlet cloth sewed with green thread covers the flowing end of the ornament, and the whole would probably float out from the wearer's head horizontally if he was on horseback and moving rapidly. A number of small bells are attached to the cloth and jingle when it is stirred. Yellow Hand must have been a gay ranger and fond, as his tribe usually are, of bright colors.

"These trophies can be seen at Kerngood's store where they will no doubt attract much attention."

The Remington percussion revolver was not sent to Rochester, at least not in time for the newspaper article.

23

The Fight with Yellow Hair

The most famous and most controversial of Cody's clashes with the Indians took place on Hat Creek, near today's Montrose, Nebraska. Yellow Hair, whose Indian name was Hay-o-wei, was a son of Cut Nose, a chief of the Cheyenne. The fight was part of the Sioux War of 1876 and has been called "the first scalp for Custer."

By June 10, 1876, Cody was back in the employ of the army as a scout, following another successful theater season of what became known as his Combination, a theater troupe. For months, Colonel Anson Mills had been sending him letters, urging him to join the command of Brigadier General George Crook, one of the officers assigned to settle problems with the Sioux Indians. Finally agreeing to do so, Cody left Wilmington, Delaware, where he had played a benefit performance and, on reaching Chicago, determined that the best way to meet up with the Fifth Cavalry was by taking a train to Cheyenne. There he was met by Lieutenant Charles King, who took him to camp. A press report of the day stated:

At noon on the 9th [of June] W. F. Cody (Buffalo Bill) joined the command as scout and guide. There is very little change in his appearance . . . except that he looks a little worn, probably caused by his vocation in the East not agreeing with him. All the old boys in the regiment upon seeing General Carr and Cody together, exchanged confidences, and expressed themselves to the effect that with such a leader and scout they could get away with all the Sitting Bulls and Crazy Horses, in the Sioux tribe.[28]

While on a scout, on July 3 Cody was involved in a chase after Indians that stretched over thirty miles in the vicinity of the south branch of the Cheyenne River. The Indians had become aware of the presence of troops. By July 7, Cody had heard the tragic news of Custer's death, as reported in a memoir later published by King:

A party of junior officers were returning from a refreshing bath in a deep pool in the stream, when Buffalo Bill came hurriedly towards them from the general's tent. His handsome face wore a look of deep trouble,

and he brought us to a halt in stunned, awe-struck silence, with the announcement, "Custer and five companies of the Seventh wiped out of existence. It's no rumor—General Merritt's got the official dispatch."[29]

After some outmaneuvering and second-guessing of the Indians, on the morning of July 17 Cody had advised Chris Madsen, assigned to a butte for signaling purposes, that the Cheyenne would be moving their camp. Cody then rode beyond Madsen, who was to send signals by torch or flag, and delivered the same message in person to General Wesley Merritt. Merritt and Carr mobilized the men into position for fighting what appeared to be oncoming Indians.

Two couriers had been spotted some distance away, and a small band of Cheyenne began chasing after them. Cody saw this and suggested riding down to cut off the Indians. Merritt gave the order, and Cody was told to lead the charge. There were approximately eight men with him, two of them scouts and the remainder troopers. Seven Indians were seen in pursuit of the couriers.

The Indians came by where Cody and his men lay in wait, and the fight was on. Other Cheyenne were appearing on the ridge, and shots were being fired. Trooper Madsen was in perfect position to report what happened next:

Cody was riding a little in advance of his party and one of the Indians was preceding his group. I was standing on the butte where I had been stationed. It was some little distance from the place where they met but I had an unobstructed view of all that happened. Through the powerful telescope furnished by the Signal Department the men did not appear to be more than 50 feet from me. From the manner in which both parties acted it was certain that both were surprised. Cody and the leading Indian appeared to be the only ones who did not become excited. The instant they were face to face their guns fired. It seemed almost like one shot. There was no conversation, no preliminary agreement, as has been stated erroneously in some novels written by romantic scribes.

They met by accident and fired the moment they faced each other. Cody's bullet went through the Indian's leg and killed his pinto pony. The Indian's bullet went wild. Cody's horse stepped into a prairie dog hole and stumbled but was up in a moment. Cody jumped clear of his mount. Kneeling, he took deliberate aim and fired the second shot. An instant before Cody fired the second shot, the Indian fired at him but missed. Cody's bullet went through the Indian's head and ended the battle. Cody went over to the fallen Indian and neatly removed his scalp while the other soldiers gave chase to the Indian's companions. There is no doubt about it, Buffalo Bill scalped this Indian, who, it turned out, was a Cheyenne sub-chief called Yellow Hair.[30]

Cody's own account, in his autobiography, is somewhat embellished but states that he did indeed slay the chief and took his scalp and other trophies. Madsen, who later earned fame with Bill Tilghman and Heck Thomas as the "Three Guardsmen," distinguished lawmen in the Oklahoma territory, is considered a reliable witness.

In a letter to his wife, Cody wrote of the fight:

We have had a fight. I killed Yellow Hand [an interpreter had mistakenly come up with "Hand" instead of "Hair"] a Cheyenne Chief in a single-handed fight. You will no doubt hear of it through the papers. I am going as soon as I reach Fort Laramie the place we are heading for now send the war bonnet, shield, bridal, whip, arms and his scalp to Kerngood to put up in his window [Moses Kerngood was the owner of a clothing store in Rochester, New York]. I will write Kerngood to bring it up [to] the house so you can show it to the neighbors. . . . I have only one scalp I can call my own that fellow I fought single handed in sight of our command and the cheers that went up when he fell was deafening.[31]

Cody had prepared for the action by dressing in a costume from his theatrical appearances. This way he could wear it onstage in the future as the garb of the triumphant plainsman and Indian fighter. Of black velvet, with scarlet and lace decor and silver buttons, the outfit had been inspired by the attire of a Mexican vaquero.

Unfortunately, the Yellow Hair story became so embellished by dime-novel writers and by Cody's own exaggerations that the veracity of the identity of the chief's killer became a casualty itself. In fact, based on searches of official records, Cody was engaged in no less than sixteen fights with Indians from the date of his appointment as a scout with the Fifth Cavalry in 1868 until his slaying of Yellow Hair eight years later.

Shortly after killing the chief, Cody was named chief scout with the Bighorn and Yellowstone Expedition. As there were some twenty other scouts in the command, the honor was real. Before long, however, Cody despaired of any more battles. As he wrote in his autobiography:

> There being but little prospect of any more fighting, I determined to go East as soon as possible to organize a new "Dramatic Combination," and have a new drama written for me, based upon the Sioux war. This I knew would be a paying investment as the Sioux campaign had excited considerable interest. So I started down the river on the steamer Yellowstone en route to Fort Beauford. On the same morning Generals Terry and Crook pulled out for Powder river, to take up the old Indian trail which we had recently left.[32]

Cody had not gone far when he was recruited to do some dispatch carrying through hostile Indian territory. On one such ride, he watched as about twenty or thirty mounted Indians killed ten or fifteen buffalo. After delivering the dispatches, he resumed his trip east, heading to Rochester to rejoin his family.

Thereafter, he hit the stage again, this time with a new five-act play:

> . . . without head or tail, and it made no difference at which act we commenced the performance. Before we had finished the season several newspaper critics, I have been told, went crazy in trying to follow the plot. It af-

forded us, however, ample opportunity to give a noisy, rattling, gunpowder entertainment, and to present a succession of scenes in the late Indian war, all of which seemed to give general satisfaction.[33]

Cody: A National Hero

Granted, there are more than a few tall tales associated with Buffalo Bill Cody over the years, in a saga confused by hundreds of dime novels written by armchair adventurers. However, the fact is that Cody grew up in bleeding Kansas; was employed by Pony Express founders Russell, Majors, and Waddell; was a teamster, trapper, and hunter on the plains; handled the reins on a stagecoach; survived the Civil War, in which he fought in bona fide battles; served as a scout against the Indians with such distinction that he won the Congressional Medal of Honor; had some fourteen armed encounters with Indians; killed thousands of buffalo for the Union Pacific railroad; guided the Grand Duke Alexis on his command buffalo hunt; served as a guide for General Sheridan and his party on their own plains hunting trip; and guided several other dignitaries on distinguished hunts. Furthermore, his riding and shooting skills cannot be disputed. For these reasons, Cody could rightfully lay claim to a frontier heritage well worth celebrating in his Wild West entertainments—many of these achievements before he stepped onto the stage as a budding thespian.

William Mathewson: The Original Buffalo Bill

William F. Cody was not the only plainsman to claim the title of "Buffalo Bill." Another was William Mathewson. Born in Broome County, New York, on January 1, 1830, Mathewson's boyhood was spent hunting and trapping throughout the eastern region, venturing into Canada and as far west as Wisconsin. At nineteen years of age, he headed west. He was employed by the Northwestern Fur Company, with headquarters at Fort Benton, Montana. Traversing

William Mathewson, the original "Buffalo Bill."

Montana, the Dakotas, Nebraska, and Wyoming, he trapped furs, trading with friendly Indians and fighting with hostile bands.

After two years with the fur company, he joined Kit Carson's party and explored the region of the Rocky Mountains, crossing into Colorado and back down through the plains. In 1853, he settled near the center of Kansas, on the old Santa Fe Trail. There, he opened a trading post, which eventually became the site of Wichita.

It was in this region that his most remarkable feat occurred. In 1860 and 1861, drought and a fierce winter had left many pioneer families near starvation. Mathewson's exploits are related in O. H. Bentley's History of Wichita, Kansas, published in 1910:

> All [from the area] were grateful and ever retained memories of the man who saved them from starvation in that terrible winter of 1860 and 1861. Till February, William Mathewson remained on the buffalo range, some days killing and sending eastward as many as eighty carcasses of fat cows. Each day brought its quota of gaunt, penniless settlers, and each day, no matter

25

what the weather, Mathewson shouldered his rifle and with a few hours of tramping sent his guests rejoicing homeward with all the choicest buffalo roasts and steaks they could carry.

Thus did William Mathewson earn his title of "Buffalo Bill."

His most acclaimed deed, however, was the saving of 155 lives and 147 wagons of government supplies, from the hands of hostile Indians. In recognition of this heroic feat, accomplished by riding through the Indians as they circled a wagon train, Mathewson was presented a magnificent cased set of etched, inscribed, silver- and gold-plated and ivory-gripped Colt model 1861 Navy revolvers.

Post trader C. H. Durfee made the presentation, which so overwhelmed Mathewson that he wrote:

You could have knocked me down with a feather when they gave me those guns with my name carved on them. I have been in tight places in my time, passed through many a danger, but nothing ever took my nerve away so completely as the presentation of those guns. I was speechless, but finally stammered some sort of appreciation and rode away over the starlit prairie that night, the proudest man on the frontier.[34]

For many years, a feud existed between friends of Bill Cody and Bill Mathewson as to who rightfully held the title of "Buffalo Bill." Mathewson wrote a pointed letter to Cody, laying the matter on the line in no uncertain terms:

You have no right to call yourself 'Buffalo Bill' and you know you haven't. . . . You know I am the original Buffalo Bill and was known by that name ten years before you ever worked for the Kansas Railroad. When I was post trader I was called Buffalo Bill because I killed buffaloes to supply meat for them that didn't have any meat or couldn't get it and I never charged them a cent for it. When you and

your show come to Topeka I aim to tell you to your face that you are using a title that doesn't belong to you.[35]

Wild West press agent Frank Winch was dispatched by Cody to smooth things out with Mathewson before the show reached Kansas. Winch found that Mathewson was having financial problems and had just sold a coveted rifle to raise some money. Winch was able to retrieve the rifle and present it to Mathewson with Cody's compliments. When the Wild West reached Topeka, Cody and the old pioneer met, and Cody acknowledged that Mathewson was indeed the original Buffalo Bill, and they shook hands. Both men were too big to hold any ill feelings, especially some forty years after the events took place.

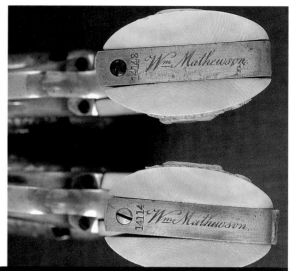

Colt Model 1861 Navy revolvers, presentation inscribed to William Mathewson, by C. H. Durfee, May 15, 1867. The exquisitely carved grips are the finest known ivory stocks on nineteenth-century Colt percussion revolvers. The casing and etched decoration, and possibly the grips, attributed to Tiffany & Co. Serial numbers 14143 and 14239 (buttstrap not matching number). See also R. L. Wilson, *The Peacemakers*, p. 232, and *Steel Canvas*, p. 273.

Life and times of Buffalo Bill from ca. 1878–1881. The Belmont Hotel register from November 22, 1877, when the Combination signed in. Captain Tom Custer's .44 Webley caliber Galand and Somerville revolver at *top* (a similar revolver belonged to his brother George, pictured at *left center*). Ben Thompson image under muzzle of Stevens pistol, which was presented to him by Buffalo Bill. Note period photos of Texas Jack, Wild Bill, Ned Buntline, and Cody. U.S. Centennial-period Colt Single Action at *upper left*; celebrated in same year Hickok and Custer were killed.

Chapter 2

⸻ ✕ ⸻

THE PRAIRIE TO THE NATIONAL STAGE
1876–1882

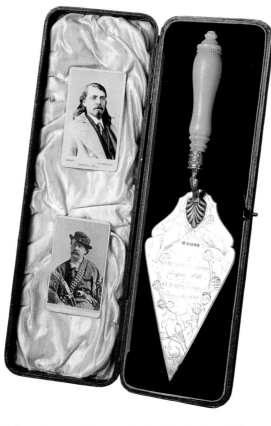

Buffalo Bill Cody's life, both on the plains and on-stage, was gaining a momentum that propelled him into national prominence with such power that he soon became an icon of the West. In part, this was due to the colorful characters who were his "pards" and to the numerous other personalities also gaining national press attention, thanks to the voracious public appetite for news from the West. Some of the cast of characters became celebrated stage performers, like Texas Jack Omohundro, James Butler "Wild Bill" Hickok, and Chief Sitting Bull. Others were friends or acquaintances of Cody, but their fame had nothing to do with show business: Kit Carson, George Armstrong Custer, Rain-in-the-Face, and generals such as Philip A. Sheridan and Nelson A. Miles. Even Yale University professor Othniel Charles Marsh became party to Cody's notoriety. Cody's autobiography notes that Marsh visited Fort McPherson in the summer of 1871 "with a large party of students to have a hunt and to look for fossils." The late 1870s

Elaborately engraved, presentation inscribed, and cased silver Mason's trowel, with turned ivory handle. Symbolic of influence by Buntline on Cody's burgeoning career in show business. Significance of the February 26, 1883, date is unknown.

and early 1880s were times that prepared Cody for his inevitable superstardom and for that extravaganza that became known the world over as Buffalo Bill's Wild West.

Texas Jack Omohundro: A "Pard" of Buffalo Bill

Army scout, hunter, guide, and pard of Cody, John Burwell "Texas Jack" Omohundro was one of the West's more colorful characters, perfectly suited for presentation on the stage before a public hungry for Wild West entertainment. A Southerner, Omohundro was born July 26, 1846, near Palmyra, Virginia. His Civil War record was distinguished, serving initially with former U.S. Secretary of War (later Major General) John B. Floyd, C.S.A., as a civilian mounted orderly. In February 1864, the youthful Omohundro joined Company G, Fifth Virginia Cavalry, which served under Major General Fitzhugh Lee and Lieu-

To Denver by the "Rock Island"; seated portrait of a well-armed Buffalo Bill, with pair of Model 1860 Colt revolvers and Winchester Model 1873. Ivory grips of the Colts carved in relief; butts forward in the style of Wild Bill Hickok. Note hammer cocked back on Winchester and Mexican-style saddle with deluxe trappings. Ca. late 1870s.

tenant General J. E. B. Stuart. In the Shenandoah Valley campaigns, Omohundro was both courier and scout.

After the war, Omohundro drifted west the long way—via Florida. Arriving in Texas, he managed to live through some armed scrapes with Indians and to ride on a cattle drive north. Among his pals were Wild Bill Hickok and the renowned scout, California Joe (Moses E. Milner), whom he met at Fort Hays. At Fort McPherson, Omohundro hired out as a scout. He became trail agent for the Pawnees in 1872 and accompanied them on a hunt for buffalo.

Most important, Cody and Texas Jack became fast friends.

Texas Jack's most enthusiastic hunting patron, the distinguished and adventurous English lord, the Earl of Dunraven, described Cody and Texas Jack as they appeared when greeting his lordship on arrival for a hunt in 1871:

Bill was dressed in a pair of corduroys tucked into high boots, and a blue flannel shirt. He wore a broad-brimmed felt hat, or sombrero, and had a little handkerchief folded like a shawl loosely fastened round his neck, to keep off the fierce rays of the afternoon sun. Jack's costume was similar, with the exception that he wore moccasins, and had his lower limbs encased in a pair of comfortably greasy deer-skin trousers, ornamented with a fringe along the seam. Round his waist was a belt supporting a revolver, two butcher [likely Bowie-type] knives, and in his hand he carried his trusty rifle, the 'Widow.'

Jack, tall and lithe, with light brown close-cropped hair, clear laughing honest blue eyes, and a soft and winning smile, might have sat as a model for a typical modern Anglo-Saxon—if ethnologists will excuse the term. Bill was dark, with quick searching eyes, aquiline nose, and delicately cut features, and he wore his hair falling in long ringlets over his shoulders, in true Western style.[1]

Dunraven was in for a memorable hunt, and became an addict thereafter, returning to the West several times. His many adventures were written up in fact and fiction, in books such as *Canadian Nights* and *Past Times and Pastimes.*

For Dunraven's next hunt, in 1872, he expected Cody to be his guide on a six weeks' excursion. However, in the midst of the festivities, Cody was called to guide a group of friends of General Philip Sheridan. Somewhat miffed, Dunraven had to settle for Texas Jack as a substitute. As Cody remarked: "The Earl seemed to be somewhat offended at this and I don't think he has ever forgiven me for 'going back on him.' "[2] To the delight of Dunraven, Texas Jack performed admirably; the next time, in 1874, his lordship arranged for his guide to be Texas Jack.

Meanwhile, Ned Buntline had been pestering the two scouts to come east and enter into the arena of the theater. When *Scouts of the Plains,* discussed earlier, went on tour, among the performers was the Italian-born Giuseppina Morlacchi, a talented dancer and actress. Morlacchi, a Milanese and an alumna of the legendary La Scala opera house, was born the same year as were Omohundro and Cody.

Richly engraved Smith & Wesson First Model American .44 caliber revolver; nickel plated, with 8-inch barrel and ivory grips; serial number 4868. The backstrap inscription commemorated the presentation: EARL DUNRAVEN FROM TEXAS JACK. Texas Jack, himself owner of a S&W .44, gave his friend the Earl of Dunraven one as well. Cooper painting of buffalo and wolves, 24 × 20½ inches.

Texas Jack Omohundro, Mlle. Morlacchi (clutching rifle), and pards. Revolvers are S&W Americans, as featured in pictures *opposite* and on *following page*, with A. D. M. Cooper paintings. Rare signed card at *left center*. *Center right* picture posed with full-stocked plains rifle and two revolvers; guns would have been part of the stage arsenal. Playbill from Opera House, Keokuk, Iowa, ca. 1877, when Texas Jack was performing on his own. Dime-novel cover art at *top left* is from later date than that published in *Beadle's* seen *below*. Mother-of-pearl chip at *lower right* also of later date.

31

Likely the favorite revolver of Texas Jack: Smith & Wesson First Model American, .44 caliber, 8-inch barrel; serial number 2008; walnut grips. On left side of the frame, the inscription: TEXAS JACK COTTON WOOD SPRING 1872. A. D. M. Cooper buffalo painting: 24 × 20 inches.

After performing extensively in Italy, London, and Portugal, she came to America under professional management in 1867. It was she who introduced the cancan to American audiences. By the time Morlacchi joined the original Cody-Omohundro troupe, she already had a professional reputation in America and Europe. In *Scouts of the Plains,* she played the role of Dove Eye.

After the show closed, Cody and Omohundro, with some intriguing sidearms, were on their way back to the West. They were saluted in the Omaha *Daily Bee:*

"The Scouts of the Prairie."

Return of Buffalo Bill and Texas Jack

Yesterday William Cody, otherwise known as Buffalo Bill, and J. B. Omohundro, or Texas Jack, arrived in the city from the east, accompanied by E. B. Overton, of Brevoort Place, New York; E. P. Green of Amsterdam, N.Y., and [J. A.] Scott, the hatter, of Chicago.

Buffalo Bill and Texas Jack, as is well known, have been treading the sensational stage for the last six months, and have in that short time made a comfortable fortune, which they intend to increase to mammoth proportions during the fall and winter season. . . . Everywhere they were greeted with immense audience, especially in Philadelphia, where Buffalo Bill and Texas Jack drew larger crowds than ever did [Edwin] Forrest in his palmiest days.

Buffalo Bill, Texas Jack and Ned Buntline each cleared $30,000 during the past eight months. Bill thinks this more remunerative than the honor of being a Nebraska Legislator, while Texas Jack is of the opinion that financially it eclipses buffalo hunting and scouting. Bill has invested some of his money in a place at Westchester, twenty miles from Philadelphia, where his family now reside. Both men are looking exceedingly well, and sport considerable jewelry, especially Jack, whose immaculate shirt bosom is orna-

men[t]ed with a $1,200 diamond pin, and diamond studs, and he wears a $1,000 chain [purchased from Tiffany & Co.] and a magnificent gold watch, while his little finger on his left hand is encircled by a valuable diamond ring. During Jack's trip in the East he was presented with a $650 breech-loading gun, by the Earl of Dunraven. He also has a splendid rifle, given to him by Remington, the great manufacturer. Buffalo Bill also had one given him by the same gentleman. Jack has the most beautiful six-shooter that was ever manufactured in this country. It is of the Smith & Wesson pattern, and is over a foot in length. Jack, by the way, is the best shot with a six-shooter now living. Mr. M. H. Brown, in whose employ Jack was for two years engaged in driving cattle from Texas to the plains, testified that he has seen him shoot with a six-shooter the heads off of four qua[i]ls out of five, while they were running in the grass. Jack will hunt the buffalo with the six-shooter in a match with any man for any sum from $1,000 to $5,000. He acknowledges that Buffalo Bill is the best shot and hunter in this country with the rifle, but he claims to rank next, and to be the best shot with the six-shooter.

The whole party left on this morning's train for Ft. McPherson, from which place, on the 20th, they intend to go on a grand buffalo hunt. The buffalo hunters are all well armed, and will be absent on the hunt for two weeks.

Next fall Buffalo Bill and Texas Jack will appear in an equestrian drama entitled "Alexis in America," the grand feature of which, we suppose, will be the Grand Duke's buffalo hunt when he was in Nebraska. It is quite possible that the Buffalo Bill and Texas Jack combination will play two nights in Omaha early in the fall.

As an added note, from the same paper:

"Texas Jack," before his departure for the West, presented the city editor of the BEE with a handsome and valuable rifle cane, manufactured by Remington. It will carry a ball thirty yards with great accuracy. It is loaded by unscrewing the handle and placing the cartridge in the tube; and it is cocked and fired by pulling back the handle, and touching a small spring. Besides being quite a novelty as a weapon it is a very fine walking-stick. It will ever be retained by the recipient as a token of the friendship and generosity of the famous scout and hunter.

Both men returned as stars, having tasted the big city, the adulation, the hero worship, and the money. After a summer of hunting and occasional revelry, they were on the road again that fall. The performances ran through the spring of 1874, with Wild Bill Hickok as a featured player. Texas Jack and Buffalo Bill remained in show business until 1876, working from late fall through early spring and then returning to hunting and guiding. Apparently, they worked well together.

In the fall of 1876, Omohundro set off on his own. He had married Morlacchi, and they had organized their own Combination. Arizona John M. Burke was a part of the new operation, as was a veteran of the Modoc War (1873), "the great chief and

From *left*, with a small arsenal, Elisha Green, Wild Bill Hickok, Buffalo Bill, Texas Jack Omohundro, and Eugene Overton, ca. 1874. Stage props of percussion Kentucky and plains rifles; Hickok also sporting a huge Bowie-type knife; Cody and Omohundro with two deluxe Remington Rolling Block rifles (gifts from the Remington Arms Company). Ivory-gripped 1860 Army Colt revolvers (in belt of Cody) and rare ivory-gripped squareback triggerguard 1851 Navy (in belt of Omohundro); a No. 3 American S&W tucked into the belt of Overton.

The star in *Texas Jack in the Black Hills*, with Mlle. Morlacchi, "The Premiere Danseuse of the World . . . in the Protean Comedietta" of *Thrice Married,* and Maud Oswald astride her Indian pony, Eagle Eye. The featured mount of Texas Jack was his Mexican mustang Modoc. Ca. 1878.

scout Donald McKay and his Warm Springs Indians." Burke performed in the program, *Texas Jack in the Black Hills,* which was reviewed in the St. Louis *Globe Democrat:* "In all of Texas Jack's retinue there is no one who can annihilate whole tribes of Indians with greater facility than 'Arizona' John. Armed with a revolver filled with blank cartridges, he kills six of the 'red demons' at a single fire."

Texas Jack engaged himself in writing and was a correspondent for *The Spirit of the Times,* a New York City newspaper. The Texas Jack Combination performed *Scouts of the Plains* as one of its productions in the 1877–1878 season. In 1880, in Denver, his troupe presented *The Trapper's Daughter,* and in Leadville, Colorado, *The Black Crook,* the latter featuring Morlacchi in what was termed the first musical comedy. In 1880, Texas Jack died in Leadville.

Wild Bill Hickok, ca. 1869, armed with pair of Colt 1851 Navies, butts forward. Compare with classic Buffalo Bill Combination image of Hickok (ca. 1873–1874) in buckskins, ivory-gripped Colt 1851 revolvers positioned same way, with large and menacing knife tucked into military belt (see R. L. Wilson, *The Peacemakers,* p. 147).

Wild Bill Hickok and Buffalo Bill

With Wild Bill Hickok's reputation as a shootist and marksman, it is not surprising that his association with Buffalo Bill often centers on firearms and shooting. The two knew each other from as early as 1859, when Hickok became a friendly visitor to the Cody household. Their adventures together were exaggerated in Cody's autobiography; nevertheless, these men were exposed to danger from Indians and from desperadoes. In one such instance, Hickok and Cody captured and brought to justice no less than eleven federal prisoners. Hickok was then living in Hays City as a saloon keeper and a deputy United States marshal. To quote from the Topeka *Leader* of April 2, 1868,

Band of Road Men Captured—

W. F. Cody Government detective, and Wm. Haycock [*sic*]—Wild Bill—deputy U.S. Marshal brought eleven prisoners and lodged them in our calaboose on Monday last. These prisoners belonged to a band of robbers having their headquarters on the Solomon and near Trinidad, and were headed by one Major Smith, once connected with the Kansas 7th. They are charged with stealing and secreting government property, and desertion from the army.

Seventeen men, belonging to this same band, were captured eleven miles from Trinidad, on the 13th of March, and sent to Denver, Colorado Territory, for trial.

Cody and Hickok also met from time to time while scouting for the army on the plains, though Cody continued for several years after Hickok ceased in 1869.

When Cody entered into his theatrical career, he became aware that Hickok was a public draw, with an already solid following in the East. Hickok had appeared in Niagara Falls as master of ceremonies in an entertainment billed as a "Grand Buffalo Hunt." A

(*opposite*) "General Custer's Death Struggle"—dramatization of one of the West's most heralded events, later elaborately commemorated in the Wild West entertainments of Buffalo Bill, with participants actually in battle. Several of the illustrated elements are from the collection of Private William O. Taylor, a participant and eyewitness to the event, as published in *With Custer on the Little Bighorn.* Taylor's photograph, with cavalry sword, at *lower left.* Two arrows removed by Taylor from trooper's body after battle; Custer's Sharps pepperbox at *left,* Tom Custer's Galand and Somerville revolver at *right.*

GENERAL CUSTER'S DEATH STRUGGLE.
The Battle of the Little Big Horn.

generous salary served as an enticement for Hickok to join Cody's Combination in New York City late in the summer of 1872. Cody found, however, that despite some experience before the public, Hickok was not quite ready for the stage: "[Hickok] had a fine stage appearance and was a handsome fellow, and possessed a good strong voice, yet when he went upon the stage before an audience, it was almost impossible for him to utter a word. He insisted that we were making a set of fools of ourselves, and that we were the laughing-stock of the people."[3]

The public was thrilled when they saw this well-known pistoleer and true man-killer, armed with a brace of Colt Navy revolvers, enter the stage, and open fire. A September 15, 1873, issue of the New York Clipper reported that Hickok "gave an exhibition of rapid pistol-shooting and fancy shots."

Hickok was accustomed to the rough frontier life and was disrespectful of many Easterners. Blanks that he fired in his matched Navy Colts were aimed at the legs of actors portraying Indians. These playful shots would cause the wounded to jump about the stage, sometimes in sorrowful pain. Cody's reaction to this was one of bemused concern, whereas Hickok thought it was good fun. Aggravating their association was the fact that Hickok did not enjoy the traveling life and never was comfortable on the stage.

Hickok left the Combination near the end of the 1873-1874 season, his theatrical career at an end. The split was in Rochester, New York, against the wishes of Buffalo Bill and Texas Jack. As parting gestures of friendship, the two presented Hickok with a pair of Smith & Wesson American model .44 revolvers and $500 from each of them. Later, Cody wrote that Hickok was one of several "Western" men who got "the big head" after seeing "their names in print a few times" and wanted "to start a company of their own."

Others continued to play Hickok in stage roles, and he remained the subject of a number of dime novels. On August 2, 1876, while peacefully enjoying a card game in Saloon No. 10, Deadwood, South Dakota, Hickok was shot from behind by a frontier lowlife. In later years, Cody visited the gravesite and lamented the loss of his friend in notices in early programs of the Wild West show.

Buffalo Bill's Gift to Ben Thompson

Another of the West's stalwart shootists and yet another "pard" of Buffalo Bill was English-born Ben Thompson, Austin city marshal and chief of police. The deluxe Stevens-Lord No. 36 Target model pistol presented by Cody to Thompson is one of the most historic firearms from the annals of the Old West. The pistol's documentation dates back to the marshal's receipt, directly from Buffalo Bill. The presentation was inspired by a target match between Cody and Thompson, as recorded in the Austin Statesman, December 10, 1879, and further described in the Statesman, June 15, 1881. Besides his law-enforcement duties, Thompson was also renowned as a professional gambler and gunfighter. He was known to his friend and fellow gunfighter Bat Masterson as "[unequaled] in his time . . . with a pistol in a life and death struggle."[4]

The deluxe, engraved, and presentation-inscribed Stevens-Lord No. 36 Target pistol, serial number 32, is inscribed on the backstrap BUFFALO BILL TO BEN THOMPSON. The engraving and inscription were by L. D. Nimschke. The pistol is in .32 short Colt centerfire caliber with pearl grips. The barrel is finished in nickel plating, the brass frame and triggerguard in gold plating; the brass buttplate was engraved and gold plated to match.

From the December 10 Statesman: "Buffalo Bill went out of town yesterday with Mr. Ben. Thompson and some other gentlemen, and he showed them a little crack shooting. With Mr. Thompson's rifle he struck six half dollars out of seven that were thrown up." From the June 15 issue:

Yesterday morning Marshal Thompson received a very handsome present from Buffalo Bill. It is a handsome and costly target pistol, manufactured by Stevens Co., Chicopee Falls, Massachusetts. The mountings are of gold, handle beautifully tinted pearl, while the glittering metal barrel is most artistically and beautifully carved. It has engraved on the handle [BUFFALO BILL TO BEN THOMPSON]. It is the only pistol of the kind in the city, and is a marvel of skilled workmanship.

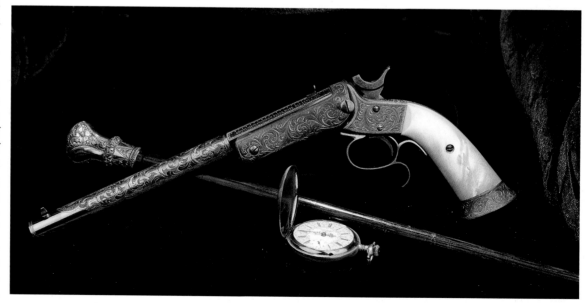

(above) Ben Thompson's presentation from Buffalo Bill: Stevens-Lord No. 36 Target pistol, serial number 32.

Stevens-Lord single-shot pistol made for Cody, and inscribed on backstrap;
.32 caliber; 10-inch barrel, serial 29; plated in silver and gold; a gift from Buffalo Bill
to John M. Phillips (1861–1953), prominent Pittsburgh industrialist, hunter, conservationist,
and friend of numerous celebrities of his day. Like the Ben Thompson gift,
engraving by L. D. Nimschke.

Thompson's pistol is nearly a match of Buffalo Bill's Stevens-Lord No. 36 Target pistol. The Cody pistol is serial number 29, virtually identically engraved, gold and nickel plated, and also fitted with pearl grips. The pistol is believed to have been a gift from the Stevens Company, the manufacturers.

The backstrap of number 29 is inscribed: W. F. CODY. Judging from the close proximity of serial numbers, the two pistols were made at the same time. Cody's Stevens pistol was eventually presented by him to John M. Phillips, a Pittsburgh industrialist.

If any one firearm capsules the color, romance, excitement, and life-and-death adventure of the great American West *and* the supreme significance of firearms on the frontier, it is the Cody-to-Thompson Stevens No. 36 Target pistol.

Bat Masterson was one of the West's most renowned characters—a buffalo hunter, lawman, gambler, and gunfighter. Further, as a journalist of no little ability, he was eminently qualified to pay tribute to Thompson in writing, which he did as part of an article on shootists in *Human Life* magazine in 1907:

I have been asked . . . to write something about the noted killers of men I am supposed to have personally known in the early days on the western frontier and who of their number I regarded as the most courageous and the most expert with the pistol. . . . I have known so many courageous men in that vast territory lying west and south-west of the Missouri River—men who would when called upon face death with utter indifference as to consequences, that it would be manifestly unjust for me even to attempt to draw a comparison.

Courage to step out and fight to the death with a pistol is but one of three qualities a man must possess in order to last very long in this hazardous business. A man may possess the greatest amount of courage possible and still be a pathetic failure as a "gun fighter," as men are often called in the West who have gained reputation as "man-killers." Courage is of little use to a man who essays to arbitrate a difference with the pistol if he is inexperienced in the use of the weapon he is going to use. Then again he may possess both courage and experience and still fail if he lacks deliberation.

Any man who does not possess courage, proficiency in the use of fire-arms, and deliberation had better make up his mind at the beginning to settle his personal differences in some other manner than by an appeal to the pistol. I have

known men in the West whose courage could not be questioned and whose expertness with the pistol was simply marvelous, who fell easy victims before men who added deliberation to the other two qualities. . . .

Ben Thompson was a remarkable man in many ways, and it is doubtful if in his time there was another man living who equalled him with the pistol in a life and death struggle. . . . He stood about five feet nine inches in height and weighed, in later years, in the neighborhood of 180 pounds. His face was pleasant to look upon and his head was round and well-shaped. He was what could be called a handsome man. He was always neat in his dress but never loud, and wore little if any jewelry at any time. . . . He had during his career more deadly encounters with the pistol than any man living and won out in every single instance. . . . [He] was absolutely without fear and his nerves were those of the finest steel. He shot at an adversary with the same precision and deliberation that he shot at a target. . . . Others missed at times, but Ben Thompson was as delicate and certain in action as a Swiss watch.

Evolution of the Wild West Show

With the growing popularity of the Buffalo Bill Combination, by the early 1880s the performances had the potential to become a bigger and more complex show. Even as early as the mid-1870s, Cody had announced his intention to organize an entertainment that could be taken to Europe. The Buffalo Bill Com-

bination did not qualify, despite the novelty of having real frontiersmen on the stage.

What soon debuted as Buffalo Bill's Wild West was not, however, the first of the genre. If they had any idea of the potential of Wild West entertainments, the pioneers of these events still lacked that all-important element: timing. The West had to be a more identifiable entity, with distinct characters and an array of action-packed vignettes, before it could be re-created onstage or in an arena.

Thus, the first of the genre, like P. T. Barnum and Grizzly Adams, was limited in its appeal and quickly fizzled into distant memories. Regarded as the first, Barnum introduced to New Yorkers the Western theme as outdoor entertainment in 1843. Buffalo had been part of the festivities surrounding the dedication of Boston's Bunker Hill Monument, and Barnum had the small herd of yearlings brought to Hoboken, New Jersey, for a "Grand Buffalo Hunt." The entertainment was free, but the wily promoter's profit came from supplying ferryboat rides to the site from New York City. A band concert and a hunter roping calves added to the amusements.

Another event, this one on tour, was Tyler's Indian Exhibition, also featuring simulated buffalo hunting. The time-honored story of Pochahontas and Captain John Smith, Indian dances, and a corn festival added to the attraction. The Tyler show dated from 1855, traveling first with Van Amburgh's menagerie and Don Stone's circus. The year following, it toured with the Mable Brothers' menagerie and Don Stone, all entertainments of the day with circus overtones.

It was P. T. Barnum who contracted with California's Grizzly Adams for another menagerie; the date was 1860. The animals had been trapped by Adams, who trained them, as described by Barnum in his *Struggles and Triumphs:*

A band of music preceded a procession of animal cages down Broadway and up the Bowery, Old Adams dressed in his hunting costume, heading the line with a platform wagon on which were placed three immense grizzly bears, two of which he held by chains, while he was mounted on the back of the largest grizzly, which stood in the centre and was not secured in any manner whatever. This was the bear known as "General Fremont," and so docile had he become that Adams said

he had used him as a pack-bear to carry his cooking and hunter apparatus through the mountains for six months, and had ridden him hundreds of miles.[5]

Considering the potentially explosive behavior of the grizzly bear, such an act in modern times, on New York's public streets, would be a nightmare scenario for the impresario, in dire need of liability insurance and of a live-entertainment license from the labyrinthine bureaucracy of the city of New York!

Among other acts or events that were precursors of the Wild West show was a July 4 commemoration in 1869 in Deer Trail, Colorado, in which one Emilne Gardenshire was honored with the title Champion Bronco Buster of the Plains. Another Fourth of July celebration, this one in Cheyenne, Wyoming, in 1872, featured the riding of an unruly steer. As noted earlier, a Grand Buffalo Hunt took place late in August 1872 at Niagara Falls, with Wild Bill Hickok a celebrated member of the cast.

The buffalo hunt for the Grand Duke Alexis was a hint of an institution to come. Cody's hunting forays

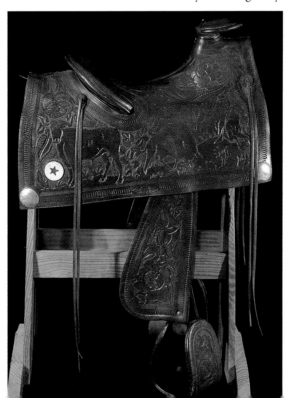

with General Sheridan, James Gordon Bennett, and their friends, as well as such stalwarts as the Earl of Dunraven, were also preludes to the main event. The Combination would soon be a thing of the past, and the big event loomed in the future. The stage was set for Buffalo Bill Cody to enter the arena with an extravaganza that was destined to become America's national entertainment.

(opposite, left) *Beadle's Weekly,* with feature article on "The League of Three or Buffalo Bill's Pledge," by Prentiss Ingraham. Though Texas Jack and Wild Bill were both deceased by the date of this publication, they remained popular dime-novel heroes. Cody's appreciation to Ingraham for his imaginative output of Buffalo Bill adventures was inspiration for a presentation Remington over-and-under deringer pistol, inscribed BUFFALO BILL TO COL. P.I.; serial number 5181 (see Wilson, *Peacemakers,* p. 291).

(opposite, right) Program of Buffalo Bill "Eleventh Annual Season of the Great Scout and Guide," "Buffalo Bill's Pledge." Rifle-shooting demonstration by Cody was a part of the performance, with twenty different positions assumed by him.

(above) Buffalo Bill Colt Single Action Army revolver, from the Julia Cody Goodman Collection: serial number 77284 (ca. 1882), 7½-inch barrel, .45 Colt caliber. Top of each side of oil-stained walnut grips with stamping; that on right side 03 over ICP. Backstrap and triggerguard strap with hand-filed or cut striations, perhaps to improve handhold. On lid of the revolver's contemporary Single Action Army case of mahogany.

(left) Hand-tooled saddle of Buffalo Bill. Carved buffalo and longhorn steer on skirt. On the cantle the tooled inscription: WM. F. CODY. Made by G. H. and J. S. Collins, Omaha, Nebraska, makers of several saddles for the Wild West and a few special ones for Buffalo Bill himself. CN brand stands for Cody-North. So-called Mother Hubbard skirt and oversize pommel. From the late 1870s, when Cody and Major Frank North set up a ranching operation on the south fork of the Dismal River, Nebraska, approximately sixty-five miles north of North Platte. In Hartford on tour in 1884, North was trampled by a horse and hospitalized for several months. He died from those injuries in March 1885.

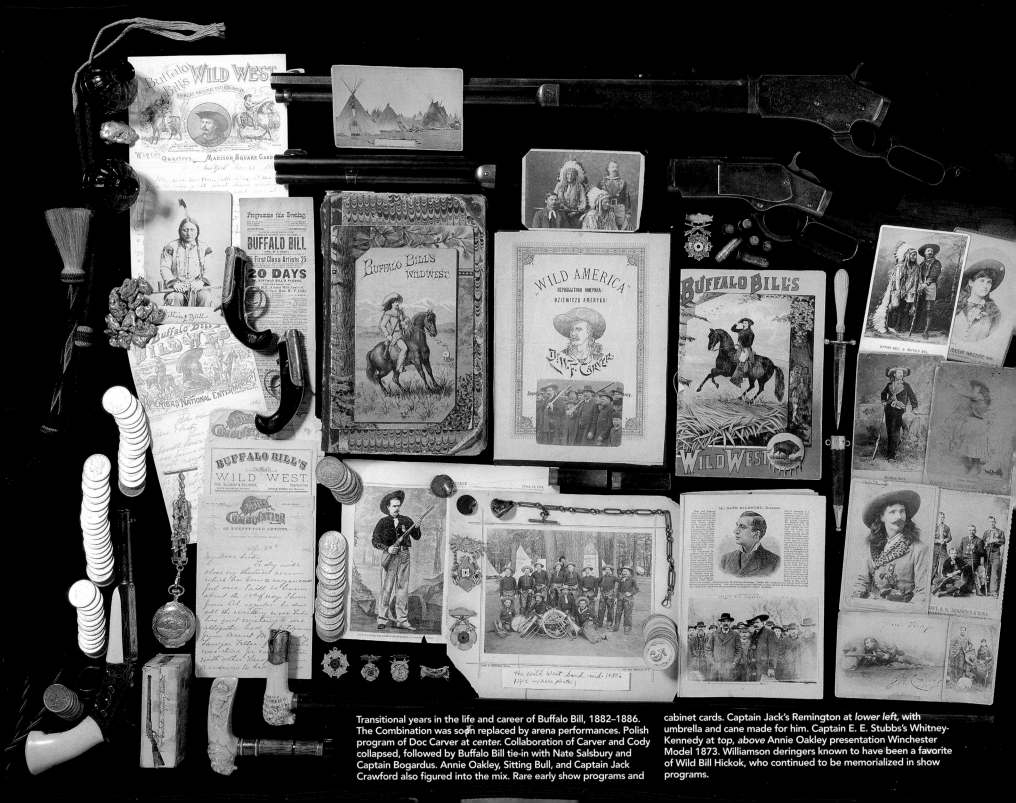

Transitional years in the life and career of Buffalo Bill, 1882–1886. The Combination was soon replaced by arena performances. Polish program of Doc Carver at *center*. Collaboration of Carver and Cody collapsed, followed by Buffalo Bill tie-in with Nate Salsbury and Captain Bogardus. Annie Oakley, Sitting Bull, and Captain Jack Crawford also figured into the mix. Rare early show programs and cabinet cards. Captain Jack's Remington at *lower left*, with umbrella and cane made for him. Captain E. E. Stubbs's Whitney-Kennedy at *top, above* Annie Oakley presentation Winchester Model 1873. Williamson deringers known to have been a favorite of Wild Bill Hickok, who continued to be memorialized in show programs.

Chapter 3

❦ ✦ ❦

From the Stage to the Arena
1882-1886

With a dozen seasons under his belt as a stage performer, Buffalo Bill Cody had reached the point where something bigger and more complicated, even approaching the grandiose, was in the offing. The Combination was restricted by being a theater production; developing an outdoor entertainment would be crucial to creating a substantial show-business success. The exhibition should present to the public a realistic reenactment of life on the frontier of the West.

What propelled Cody into his celebrated career as a Wild West arena showman began in an innocent way. At an impromptu gathering of local dignitaries, Cody expressed surprise that the city of North Platte had not planned a big event to celebrate the Fourth of July 1882. In response, he was asked to organize the party himself. The result came to be known as the Old Glory Blow Out, of which Cody was appointed chairman. A thousand cowboys competed for prizes in shooting, riding, roping, and bronco busting, and Cody put on a

demonstration (with blanks) of hunting buffalo from horseback. The outdoor show was a success and has been characterized as "the original, not only of the Wild West Show, but of the rodeo."[1]

Organizing the Blow Out was not as complex and difficult as it would be to put together a touring Wild West show, with hundreds of performers, horses, buffalo, and other animals, a stagecoach or two, and the rest of the logistical nightmare of staff and equipment—not to mention cash for expenditures.

In the meantime, another character had the potential of competing with Cody and had an impressive background as a marksman and showman. This was W. F. "Doc" Carver, known as the "Evil Spirit of the Plains," the "Champion Marksman of the World," and so on.

Doc Carver: Self-Styled Champion

Born May 7, 1840, in Winslow, Illinois, William Frank Carver was called "Little Doc" by his father, since the boy cared for wounded and maimed animals and wildfowl. A crack rifle shot at sixteen, Carver hunted in the wilds of Minnesota, among the Santee Sioux. At twenty, he made his way to the Great Plains and vast herds of buffalo. His skills as a rifleman earned him the nicknames "Spirit Gun" and "Evil Spirit of the Plains"—or so he claimed.

By his own account, Carver mingled with the illustrious personalities of the frontier: Wild Bill Hickok, Texas Jack Omohundro, George Armstrong Custer, and many others. Carver's adventures on the plains are open to conjecture, but his feats as a marksman are well documented.

Moving to Oakland, California, in 1875, he set his sights on becoming the champion rifle shot of the world. For two years, he practiced, quietly determined to make a name for himself in California and

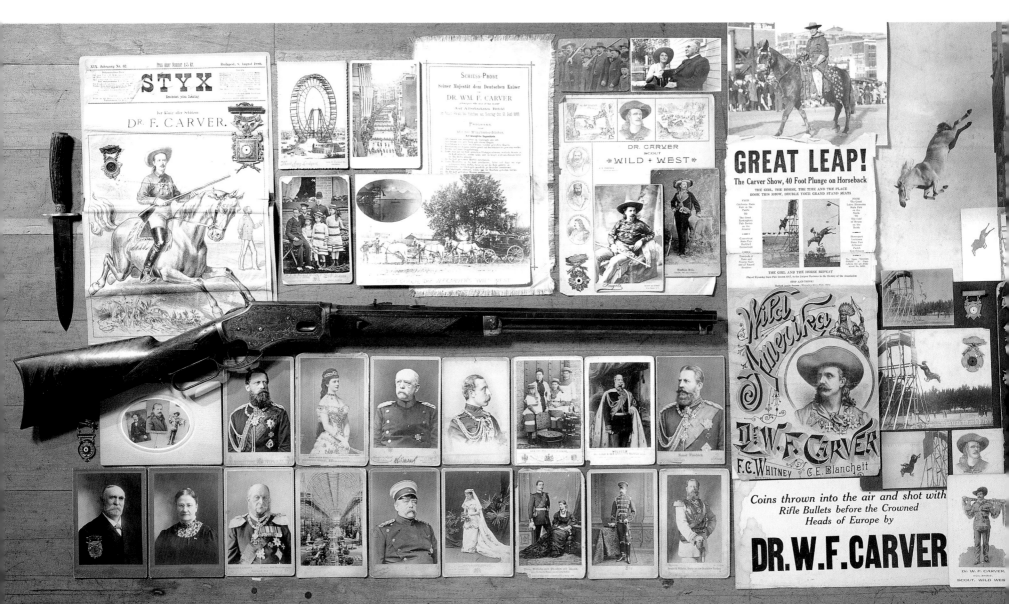

The flamboyant Doc Carver, whose reputation was based on brilliance with rifle. Collected cabinet cards of dignitaries for whom he claimed to have done shooting exhibitions during his grand European tour, before Cody undertook such a venture. Photographed in competition series with Captain Bogardus, *top center, above* rare letterhead. Program of Wild Amerika show before the German kaiser on June 13, 1880, printed on silk. Whitney-Kennedy .38-55 rifle belonged to a would-be challenger, E. E. Stubbs. Exhibition shooters often wore shooting medals on their chests in photos or lithographs. The famous Carver saddle, with coins shot by him, at *upper right;* friend and frontiersman Charles Nordin in seat. Diving horses from the end of Carver's show-business career.

then to take on the world. As a member of the Sportsmen's Club of California, he had ample opportunity to test himself in the company of competent and experienced shooters.

On December 13, 1877, feeling he was now ready to shoot against the best, his bold challenge was published in the pages of the San Francisco *Chronicle*:

To the Editor of the Chronicle—SIR:

I will shoot any man in the world at 500 glass balls, 25 yards rise, Bogardus trap, for $250 or $500 a side. I will bet from $250 to $500 a side that I can break 1000 glass balls quicker than Captain A. H. Bogardus or any other man living, and I will go to any part of the world to shoot. I will bet from $250 to $500 a side that I can break more glass balls and shoot from a horse's back, the horse to be on a run, the balls to be thrown into the air at 21 yards rise, than any man in the world can break and stand on the ground and shoot 30 yards rise from a Bogardus trap. I will shoot any man in the world 250 glass balls for from $250 to $500 a side, letting him shoot a shotgun, 30 yards rise, Bogardus trap, and I will shoot a parlor rifle and have the balls thrown into the air for me. I will bet $250 to $500 a side that I can make more fancy shots with a rifle than any man in the world. I will bet $250 to $500 that I can break 100 glass balls quicker with a Winchester rifle, using two or more guns, than any man can with a shotgun and shoot the same distance I do with the rifle. I will bet $250 against $350 that I can break two glass balls thrown into the air at the same time, and will shoot a Winchester rifle, loading the gun once while the balls are in the air, making a double shot. I will bet $1000 that I can go on the plains and kill more buffalo on one run shooting from a horse's back, than any man in the world, and if buffalo are not to be found, will run elk.

DR. W. F. CARVER.

Having gone public with his challenge to all, Carver attained one major step toward his goal on February 22, 1878: with a rifle, he broke 885 aerial glass balls out of 1,000. His opponent, champion wing shot John Ruth, gave up after fifty tries. Carver was awarded a massive gold medal that boasted a grizzly bear and contained a lengthy inscription. The Sportsmen's Club of California also recognized his feat with another gold medal—a miniature horse head, with the eyes made of diamonds, the nostrils of rubies, and in its mouth, a Winchester rifle!

Carver then left on a cross-country tour that drew national recognition. The striking characteristics of his act were that he preferred shooting a rifle against his opponents' shotguns and that he preferred flying targets. In matches in over thirty cities between San Francisco and the East Coast (including New York and Boston), he took on all comers. His skill was such that the press and public lauded him as "The Human Mitrailleuse" (after a famous repeating gun of the day), "The California Deadshot," "The Rifle King," "The Magical Marksman," and "The Modern Hawkeye." In New York, in an unprecedented tour de force of endurance, he broke 5,500 balls out of 6,212, launched in seven hours, thirty-eight minutes, and thirty seconds of nearly continuous shooting. (See Appendix D.)

With the support and encouragement of the Winchester factory, Carver was sure to include New Haven in his schedule of exhibitions. From that city's *Evening Union*, Wednesday, June 5, 1878:

The Wonderful Marksman

Dr. Carver, the "dead shot," practiced at Quinnipiac range today, in the presence of William Winchester, Colonel Smith, and a number of other gentlemen. He performed some fifteen or twenty phenomenal feats of marksmanship, the like of which has never been seen in these parts before. One feat was the throwing of eighteen silver dollars in the air some twenty-five feet, every one of which he struck with a bullet ere it could fall to the ground. If hit in the center, the ball went through; if on the edge of the coin, it shattered it. A passing "chipper" bird he brought down with ease. Another remarkable exhibition was—it was the best he showed—was to allow his assistant to throw a large piece of rock in the air. While it

was ascending he broke it with a bullet, and then, ere the largest fragment could reach the ground he shattered it with a bullet. Small stones, nickels and other articles thrown high in the air he hit with ease. His man took a number of stones, and one after the other, with hardly a second's intermission, threw them in the air, the Doctor hitting each in succession with a bullet, as long as his cartridges lasted. These and other exhibitions of his wonderful skill with the rifle were given, to the great astonishment and delight of his spectators.

Carver continued touring. He made a sweep through the South and mastered shotgun shooting. This proved important in his matches, since it was difficult to entice some shooters to compete against him unless he, too, was firing a shotgun.

Sepia-tone photographs of Doc Carver, who appears to have preferred his left three-quarter-view image. Carver's Winchester Model 1873 with checkered deluxe pistol-grip stocks; special finishes; appears to be engraved. Impressive shooting medals on chest in prints where he wears what appears to be a crushed velvet shirt.

Carver's Medals and Arsenal

Among numerous press pieces in which Carver was lauded, another major story appeared in the New Haven *Evening Union*—a convenient promotion sure to reach the desks of the crucial executives from the Winchester factory. Entitled "The King of the Rifle. Dr. Carver, the Great Marksman, in New Haven," the piece described in detail some of Carver's medals and firearms.

Next in order the Doctor favored his visitor with an exhibition of his trophies. His medals . . . have been increased by two additions. One he got at Pittsburgh. It is a large solid gold keystone-shaped affair, suspended by a finely wrought chain from a bar, which is attached to the vest. The inscription reads, "Presented to Dr. W. F. Carver by the Pittsburgh Exposition Society, October 12, 1878." Another present is a neat little gold rifle pin about two inches long, with a gold cartridge suspended from it. Another is a handsome velvet-lined, hard wood, brass-mounted gun case. It is inscribed "Presented to Dr. W. F. Carver by his friend G. V. De Graaf, Augusta Ca." In this case were the Doctor's twelve rifles and five shotguns. One of them is the favorite Winchester rifle which has been used . . . 100,000 times, has not cost ten cents for repairs, and works as easy now as the first day it was used, and is just as trustworthy. There were also two other gold plated rifles shown, with the stock plates adorned with engraved hunting scenes in which the Doctor has taken a prominent part. These rifles are used solely for coin and fancy shooting, and they have fine buckhorn sights and are very reliable.

This article is one of several from a collection of the Carver scrapbooks at the Buffalo Bill Historical Center. The front cover of the subject volume is identified: *"Dr. W. F. Carver, Champion Rifle Shot etc." San Francisco CA Feb. 22, 1878."*

Unable to engage renowned shot Captain Adam H. Bogardus in a match, Carver sailed for Europe and carried on a tour in a new and lucrative arena. He brought along two Parker shotguns for competitions and his rifles for exhibitions. Although Captain Bogardus had already shot in England, Carver went him one better by also touring on the Continent. Carver later claimed to have shot before the crowned heads of Belgium, Saxony, Dresden, and Vienna, besides a command performance at Sandringham before the Prince of Wales and a selected party of aristocrats and other dignitaries.

His European tour over, Carver returned to America in 1882. From his performing and match-shooting experiences, he reportedly had cleared $80,000, an enormous sum in those days. Immediately, he resumed his challenge to Captain Bogardus for a series of public matches.

The Single Season of Doc Carver and Buffalo Bill

While preparations were under way for another shooting tour, Carver met his old friend Buffalo Bill, and the two formed their historic alliance. According to Carver:

[Cody] came to my home in New Haven, Conn., down and out. I told him I was getting ready to bring out the Wild West Show, and he gave me his solemn promise not to drink another drop if I would take him outdoors with me, and I agreed to do so. The result was that I invested $27,000 in the enterprise and signed a note with him on the First National Bank of Omaha for $2,000, all of which I had to pay. In addition to this, he failed to live up to his promise and was dead drunk all summer. So we separated.[2]

WILD WEST—CODY & CARVER'S ROCKY MOUNTAIN AND PRAIRIE EXHIBITION.
BEACON PARK,

ONE WEEK COMMENCING MONDAY, JULY 2.

WILD WEST—CODY & CARVER'S ROCKY MOUNTAIN AND PRAIRIE EXHIBITION.
BEACON PARK,

ONE WEEK COMMENCING MONDAY, JULY 2.

(*opposite, top*) Indicative of the cooperation and support extended to Doc Carver by the Winchester factory is this Model 1873, serial number 30182, which appears in company ledgers as a rifle, 26-inch octagon barrel, set trigger, 1 of 1000, gold and engraved; received in the warehouse June 22 and shipped June 24, 1878. The mortise cover is inscribed H.G. PARKER FROM DR. W.F. CARVER. Hubbard G. Parker served as Nevada's first Indian agent from 1864 and later served as a fish-and-game commissioner.

(*opposite, bottom*) Headliners and promotion, last page of the 1883 Cody and Carver program; two broadside pages from the Carver and Cody program.

(*above, left and right*) Two of the greatest prizes from the history of Wild West show entertainments. For the one-season-only existence of the Cody-Carver entertainment, this spectacular pair of posters, each measuring 22 × 29 inches, was made by an unknown lithographer. It has been said that the heroes are awash in a collage of achievement.

Posters played a vital role in promoting Cody and the Wild West. Far more of the public was introduced to the West through the proliferation of posters than was able to view Buffalo Bill's Wild West performances. The period from 1880 to 1910 is regarded as the golden age of the American poster. Those of the Wild West were among the very best of the genre (thanks partly to Cody's own dedicated involvement) and as many as a half-million sheets or more might be printed in a single year.

Carver's tendency toward hyperbole has placed a great many of his statements in question, including his claim that it was he who created the Wild West show. No matter, the Cody and Carver's Rocky Mountain and Prairie Exhibition opened in May 1883.

Six months later, it closed in acrimony. Carver accused Cody of constant intoxication and with demoralizing the members of the cast. Carver himself, however, was known to imbibe, and on the opening day at Omaha's Fair Grounds on May 17, Carver's lackluster shooting was likely a result of too much celebrating the night before. In response to cheers from the audience, Cody fired away at the glass-ball targets. These shots were so true that firing at glass balls from horseback became a standard performance for Cody in the Wild West.

When the split between the two partners took place, Carver claimed he was due funds invested in the production. In the controversial book *Doc Carver: Spirit Gun of the West*, a receipt dated October 23, 1883, is pictured, showing that Carver paid "expenses of Wild West Show" worth $525. However, this could simply be his share of expenditures and not an obligation of Cody's assumed by Carver.

In the end, in true Old West fashion, the two divided their assets by the toss of a coin, and Carver formed a new show in partnership with Captain Jack Crawford. Known as the Carver and Crawford Wild West, the show lasted until 1885. In 1887 and 1888, Carver performed with Adam Forepaugh's New and Greatest All-Feature Show and Wild West Combination. From 1889 to 1893, Carver operated his Wild America, touring in America as well as in Europe (1889–1890) and in Australia (1890 and 1891). Surprisingly, among the sites visited in Europe were Poland and Russia; performances were given in Moscow and St. Petersburg. When leaving Europe, the troupe stopped for some sight-seeing. While in Nice, on the French Riviera during a flower festival, roses were thrown affectionately at the cowboys and Indians.

(*top*) Rare cover for first Wild West program, partnership of Carver and Cody.

(*bottom*) Magnificent pair of gauntlets, beaded and sewn, of Buffalo Bill, ca. 1880s.

Marksmanship and the New Entertainment

Besides Cody and Carver, another heralded showman was Adam H. Bogardus, a marksman of international distinction. Bogardus was a former market hunter who pioneered in the sport of trapshooting. Among other showmen—but not marksmen—associated with Cody in those early years were the Indian fighter Major Frank North, cowboy sheriff of the Platte "Con" Groner, and Buck Taylor, "King of the Cowboys."

Studying the earliest of show programs from 1883—heralding the partnership formed by Cody and Carver—no litany of performances was presented. Toward the back of that publication, however, was a double-page spread with intriguing headings that previewed what the audience could expect to see. Clearly, the spectacle of guns and shooting played major roles in the entertainment. All three of the top stars—Cody, Carver, and Bogardus—were known for their prowess with firearms. And prominent within the largest headlines were

Buffalo Bill in show costume, holding deluxe semi–pistol grip Winchester Model 1873 rifle, which appears to have been engraved. Beaded buckskin shirt complemented by scarf, silk or satin shirt, trademark large belt and buckle, elegant leather hip riding boots, and fancy spurs. Ca. 1880s.

Presentation Model 1873 rifle from Buffalo Bill to Robbie Campbell Adams. Built as a short rifle, this Ulrich-engraved factory-built custom Winchester was presented to the son of a partner in the Beadle and Adams dime-novel publishing company. Nickel- and gold-plated finish, checkered select walnut stocks (length specially abbreviated for a boy), 22-inch octagonal barrel. Elaborate inscription attests to presentation, made in 1883, a good year for dime-novel sales. Serial number 121153.

Grand Shooting Fete
On Foot and Horseback, Rifle and Shot-gun.
and
Revelations in Clay Pigeon Contests.
and
The Great Bogardus and his Shot-Gun.
and Buffalo Bill
in a Series of Feats of Agility, Grace and Skill.

Since Cody's skills as a marksman were highly touted elsewhere in the program, these feats seem largely directed at his uncanny ability to hit flying objects. His skill and experience as a hunter was reinforced by listing distinguished clients who had been privileged to have Cody as a guide:

As another evidence of the confidence placed in his frontiersmanship, it may suffice to mention the celebrities whose money and position most naturally sought the best protection the Western market could afford, and who chose to place their lives in his keeping: Sir George Gore, Earl Dunraven, James Gordon Bennett, Duke Alexis, Gen. Custer, Lawrence Jerome, Remington, Professor Ward of Rochester, Professor Marsh of Yale College, Major J. G. Hecksher, Dr. Kingsley (Canon Kingsley's brother), and others of equal rank and distinction. All books of the plains, his exploits with Carr, Miles, and Crook, published in the New York *Herald* and *Times* in the summer of 1876, when he killed Yellow Hand in front of the military command in an open-handed fight, are too recent to refer to.

In addition to all of the above, the smaller print promoted: "Ne Plus Ultra in Sharp-Shooting. The Phenomenally Eagle-Eyed Dr. W. F. Carver, Famed BOGARDUS, Old Reliable BUFFALO BILL." Most of what the program said about Carver and Bogardus flaunted their remarkable marksmanship.

In General Manager John M. Burke's "Salutatory" near the beginning of the program, he described the stars as "a part of the development of the great

West." These men were "keen of eye, sturdy in build, inured to hardship, experienced in the knowledge of Indian habits and language, familiar with the hunt, and trustworthy in the hour of extremest danger, they belong to a class that is rapidly disappearing from our country."

He went on to note that

in the Eastern States, or even east of the Mississippi, the methods of these people are comparatively unknown, and it is for the purpose of introducing them to the public that this little pamphlet has been prepared. Hon. William F. Cody ("Buffalo Bill"), in conjunction with Dr. W. F. Carver (known as the "Evil Spirit of the Plains"), the famous shot, has organized a large combination that, in its several aspects, will illustrate life as it is witnessed on the plains: the Indian encampment; the cowboys and vaqueros; the herds of buffalo and elk; the lassoing of animals; the manner of robbing mail coaches; feats of agility, horsemanship, marksmanship, archery, and the kindred scenes and events that are characteristic of the border. The most completely-appointed delegation of frontiersmen and Indians that ever visited the East will take part in the entertainment, together with a large number of animals; and the performance, while in no wise partaking of the nature of a "circus," will be at once new, startling, and instructive.

Particularly promoting the shooting were three pages in the Cody and Carver program as pictured on p. 44.

Route-Books

The pocket-size Wild West *Route-Book* series published exhaustive details of the company, its employees down to the stake drivers, a listing of sites where performances were planned, a history of the organization, and even listings of railroad companies used on tour in different municipalities. This tiny but exhaustive source is a useful tool for keeping track of the Wild West by year, though they were not introduced until the 1890s. For 1883, the listing (from the 1899 book), reads as follows (note the lack of any mention of W. F. "Doc" Carver):

The Buffalo Bill Wild West Show was organized as an outdoor show in 1883, and opened in Omaha, Neb., in May, and traveled through the States of Nebraska, Iowa, Illinois, Kentucky, Indiana, Pennsylvania, New York, Connecticut, Massachusetts and Rhode Island, giving the performance in Fair Grounds with the exception of Coney Island, where a temporary stand was erected, and they remained there five weeks. It was at this place that the first horse race was ever given by electric light.

The Rifle as an Aid to Civilization

From as early as the 1883 Cody and Carver Rocky Mountain and Prairie Exhibition show program, a statement was included about the role of the rifle in the conquering of the West. At first, these remarks were made without credit to a source, implying it was written by the show management or publicists. Later programs indicated the essay was from a publication entitled Buel's *Heroes of the Plains*.

This educational quotation was not only a means of explaining the frequent rifle fire that was a hallmark of the Wild West but was presented as part of the entertainment's educational concept. Cody himself, of course, pulled the trigger at various stages of the performances.

The Rifle as an Aid to Civilization

There is a trite saying that "the pen is mightier than the sword." It is an equally true one that the bullet is the pioneer of civilization, for it has gone hand in hand with the axe that cleared the forest, and with the family bible and school book. Deadly as has been its mission in one sense, it has been merciful in another; for without the rifle ball we of America would not be to-day in the possession of a free and united country, and mighty in our strength.

And so has it been in the history of all people, from the time when David slew Goliath, down through the long line of ages, until, in modern times, science has substituted for the stone from David's sling the terrible missiles that now decide the fate of nations. It is not, therefore, so harsh an expression as it seems to be at first sight, that it is indeed the bullet which has been the forerunner of growth and development.

It is in the far West of America, however, and along our frontier, that the rifle has found its greatest use and become a part of the person and the household of the venturesome settler, the guide, the scout, and the soldier; for nowhere else in

Christendom is it so much and so frequently a necessity for the preservation of life and the defence of home and property. It is here, too, among the hunters on the plains and in the Rocky Mountains, that one sees the perfection of that skill in marksmanship that has become the wonder of those who are not accustomed to the daily use of weapons. Yet if it were not possessed—if there were not the quick eye, the sure aim, coolness in the moment of extreme danger, whether threatened by man or beast—life in that section would be of little value, and a man's home anything but a safe abiding place.

There are exceptional cases of men like Buffalo Bill, Dr. Carver, and others, whose names are more or less familiar among the mighty hunters of the West, who excel in the use of rifle and pistol, and to which, time and time again, they and those around them have owed their lives. And they are the worthy successors of a long line of marksmen, whose names are also "familiar as household words." Who does not recall David Crockett and his death-dealing rifle in the Alamo? Daniel Boone, of Kentucky, and the heroic exploits that have been written concerning them in the early pages of our country's history?

It is to the end that the people of the East, or rather those who are not acquainted with the rough life of the border, and especially that portion of it in which the rifle plays so important a part, may personally witness some of the feats of Western men, that Messrs. Cody & Carver have determined to introduce in their "great realistic pictures of Western life" a series of shooting exhibitions, in which they will both have the assistance of the celebrated pigeon shot, Capt. Bogardus. The manner in which buffalo are hunted, the exciting chase at close quarters, the splendidly trained horses who participate in the chase, the hunt for elk, the stealthy devices of Indians in capturing the fleet-footed animals—all these will be illustrated in a manner that never have been witnessed east of the Mississippi River.

(*above, left*) Detail of right side of Robbie Campbell Adams's Winchester Model 1873 rifle; similar hunting scene engraved on Kickapoo Indian Encampment presentation Colt Lightning rifle; see Chapter 9.

(*left*) Buffalo Bill's Wild West "Programme," the early troupe of Cody, Salsbury, and Bogardus, with John W. Burke, General Manager. Printed in New York City by Torrey and Clarke. The other side of lithograph is a portrait of Buffalo Bill, with signature.

Nate Salsbury and the Origin of the Wild West Show

Although the first successful onetime Wild West show was the 1882 North Platte Blow Out, a memoir about the origin of Buffalo Bill's Wild West by Nate Salsbury is deserving of consideration. Salsbury was a Civil War veteran and experienced actor and showman. His very convincing claim to credit in the establishment and success of Buffalo Bill's Wild West was the subject of his own lengthy discourse. The narrative rings true, but it is equally true that without a star, a Buffalo Bill, there would have been no show at all.

Salsbury's memoir begins with his return following a year's theater engagement in Australia in 1876 with his troupe, the Salsbury Troubadours. He was deckside on the steamer *City of Sydney* with an agent of Cooper and Bailey's Circus, J. B. Gaylord:

Gaylord and I were talking over the experiences we both had in the Colonies, among others the pleasure we had mutually enjoyed at the Melbourne races that year. During the conversation I remarked that "while the riding of the Australian jockeys was to be admired from a professional standpoint I did not think they were any better riders than jockeys of any other nation." We had quite a heated argument over the question and Gaylord expressed himself as believing that Australians could give cards and spades to any riders in the world. This rubbed my patriotism a bit and I ventured the opinion that our cowboy and Mexican riders could beat the civilized, or uncivilized world in all that the term horsemanship implies.

We argued this question until the gong sounded for supper but the subject stuck in my mind even after I had gone to bed that night, and the train of thought thus engendered grew upon me until it naturally turned into professional channels and I began to construct a show in my mind that would embody the whole subject of horsemanship and before I went to sleep I had mapped out a show that would be constituted of elements that had never been employed in concert in the history of the show business. Of course I knew that various circus managers had tried to reproduce the riding of the plains made up of professional circus riders but I knew they had never had the real thing.

Some years passed but I had never lost sight of my plan to originate my show and put it on the road. Finally the think took the form of resolve and I began to look up the elements of the show. I decided that such an entertainment must have a well known figure head to attract attention and thus help to quickly solve the problem of advertising a new idea. After a careful consideration of the plan and scope of the show I resolved to get W. F. Cody as my central figure. To this end I waited [for] a favorable opportunity to confide the scheme to him and in 1882 while we were both playing an engagement in Brooklyn or perhaps he was in New York, I made an appointment with him to meet me at the restaurant that adjoined Haverly's Theatre where the Troubadours were playing that week. Cody kept the appointment. As he was about at the end of his profit string on the theatrical stage I dare say he was pleased at the chance to try something else, for he grew very enthusiastic over the plan as I unfolded it to him and was sure that the thing would be a great success. It was arranged at the lunch that I would go to Europe the following summer and look the ground over with a view to taking the show to a country where all its elements would be absolutely novel. I was quite well aware that the Dime Novel had found its way to England especially and wherever the Dime Novel had gone Cody had one along for Ned Buntline had so firmly written Cody into contemporary history of the Great Plains that he had made a hero on paper at first hand. While on this subject I want to note what I consider a most remarkable feat. The man who today is known in the uttermost parts of the earth as a showman would never have been a showman at all if Ned Buntline not made him notorious and he dripped from the point of Buntline's pen as a hero. Buntline was looking for somebody to make a hero of and first tried to boost Major Frank North into that position but the Major being a real hero would not listen to that sort of thing but said, "Buntline if you want a man to fill that bill he is over there under that wagon." Buntline went over to the wagon and woke up

the man he made famous as Buffalo Bill. Between story and the stage Cody became a very popular man with a certain class of the public and was notorious enough for my purpose.[3]

The following summer, Salsbury did go to Europe, checking out the potential for such an entertainment. He concluded that "it would take a lot of money to do the thing right." Both agreed the sum was then too much for either of them, and it would be wise to wait another year: "We had arrived at a perfect understanding that we were to share and share alike in the venture. So far so good."

But Cody must have agreed to drop the matter for another year with a strong mental reservation for I was astonished in the Spring of 1883 to get a telegram (which I now have in my possession) asking me if I wanted to go into the show for this country if DR. CARVER DID NOT OBJECT. Of course I was dumfounded and replied that I did not want to have anything to do with Doctor Carver who was a fakir in the show business and as Cody once expressed it "Went West on a piano stool."

Events proved that Cody did not wait for our plan to go to Europe to ripen but no sooner had my ideas than he began to negotiate with Carver who had a reputation as a marksman to go in with him and was kind enough, when they had laid all their plans, to let me in as a partner. Of course I turned them down and they went on the road and made a ghastly failure. Their failure was so pronounced that they separated at the end of the season, each blaming the other for the failure.

I was playing an engagement in Chicago while they were there and Cody came to see me and said that if I did not take hold of the show he was going to quit the whole thing. He said he was through with Carver and that he would not go through such another summer for a hundred thousand dollars. As I had seen their show and knew that they had not developed my ideas in putting it together at all I felt that there was still a lot of money in it if properly constructed. At the end of their term in Chicago they divided the assets of their firm

and I took hold of the show under a partnership contract between Cody and myself which was drawn by John P. Altgeld who at that time was my legal adviser, when I needed one.

What following the signing of that contract is the history of the Wild West Show and it is too long to recite here.

Salsbury then revealed his annoyance at claims of "John Burke and other hero-worshippers who have hung on to Cody's coat tails for their sustenance to make Cody the originator of the show for in doing so they can edge in their own feeble claims to being an integral part of the success of the show." These men had been part of that first failure with Carver. Salsbury did recognize Burke's skills in public relations and advertising, though begrudgingly: "I do not believe there is another man in the world in his position that would have had the gall to exploit himself at the expense of the show as much as John Burke!"

Burke and [Jule] Keen [for many years treasurer of the Wild West] and the rest of the Codyites who have followed the show from the day I took hold of it have never forgotten me for taking the reins of management out of their hands where they had been placed by Cody and Carver. They have always resented me because it unseated their hero in the business saddle of the show, which needed somebody that could ride it.

Mr. Keen is honest and able in his department but that lets him out. He is absolutely nothing else to make him of value to any show. I mention these two men because they have been prominent in the affairs of the show, the small fry don't count for much in this summing up.

I know that there will be a world of protest to these lines, but that the Wild West Show was an invention of my own entirely, is proven the letters in Cody's own hand which I have preserved as indeed I have preserved every scrap of writing he has ever signed and addressed to me. It is lovely to be thus fortified against protestations and abuse that would surely follow if proof did not exist of what I have stated.

Cody versus Carver: Bitter Rivals

The following newspaper article reveals that tension between Cody and Carver did not end with their split in 1883; the rivalry was sometimes dangerously intense. The *San Francisco Examiner* of August 28, 1890, reported:

Cowboys Painting Hamburg

—

The Staid Old German Town Is Almost in a State of Siege.

—

Buffalo Bill and Carver Have a Bitter Quarrel.

—

The Adherents of Each Leader Take Up the Fight—The Residents of the City Badly Scared—Hostilities Threatened—Germany May Have a Realistic Show Very Soon—Bad Blood Very Hot. [Special to the EXAMINER.]

HAMBURG, August 26.—The following cablegram is forwarded by the New York *World* correspondent:

There is intense excitement here over a fierce row which has occurred between Buffalo Bill and Dr. Carver. The people are afraid to come out of doors after dark and the place is in a state of siege. The members of each troupe have openly declared their intention of fighting for their respective masters, even if the quarrel ends in a general fight. There can be no doubt that it is only through the efforts of the civic authorities that bloodshed has up to the present time been avoided. Carver has been following Cody through the latter's tour of cities of the continent and his performances have been so much better patronized that Buffalo Bill's jealousy was aroused. Cody announced his intention of staying some time in Hamburg, and Carver then stole a march on his rival.

Cleverly Outwitted.

He arrived in Hamburg three days ahead and opened his Wild West show in fine style. When Cody got here he found that he was obliged to pitch his tent within a few feet of Carver's show.

Carver had made arrangements for the exclusive supply of electric lights, and this left Cody's place in the dark. Then the members of both companies took up the matter, and it was only through the strenuous efforts of the police that a fearful fight has been prevented.

Hamburg is filled with a howling mob of Indians and cowboys who are waiting the chance to scalp each other. The town is crowded with the posters of both parties. As soon as Cody's bills are pasted up then Carver's assistants come along and tear them down and put their own in the place.

Cowboys Take It Up.

The bad blood between Cody and Carver has also aroused such a jealous feeling among their Indian and cowboy followers that serious trouble is expected any moment. It is an open secret that while Carver made enormous business in Berlin and Vienna, Cody fell flat, and Carver's men are going around spreading the fact and saying Bill's ill-success is due to his inferior show.

On Sunday both Cody and Carver opened at the same time. Both shows are in the center of Hamburg. Carver gave two performances and had 30,000 visitors, while Cody only gave one, which was attended by 7,000 persons.

Carver's show-business career continued until his death in 1927. In later years, his productions featured a diving-horse act, in which a horse and an Indian girl named Two Feathers plunged forty feet into a pool! Sadly, Carver never achieved the fame or financial rewards attained by Cody, despite occasional successes, remaining hostile and resentful toward his former partner.

Captain Adam H. Bogardus and Sons

In an age when marksmanship was at an all-time peak of respectability and popularity, one of the most famed of all shooters was Captain Adam H. Bogardus. Inventor of the trap for launching glass balls and credited with the development of the glass-ball target, Bogardus was instrumental in creating the sport of trapshooting. The new glass-ball targets and the trap for launching them evolved into yet another innovation: clay pigeons, the origin of the target for today's skeet, trap, and sporting clays competitions. These artificial bird targets also reduced the pressure on live pigeons. Unfortunately, passenger-pigeon populations had already been widely decimated by market hunters. In the late 1870s and early 1880s, millions were shot.

In 1884, with his exhibition-shooting sons—Edward, Peter, and Henry—the captain was the main shooting act in Buffalo Bill's Wild West. Very little is known of the family other than from newspaper reports of the day and from the 1884 program of the Wild West.

In piecing together the story of this remarkable Bogardus clan, a letter addressed to the Chicago *Field* is indicative of the reputation held by the captain in the late 1870s. One of his most extraordinary feats is revealed in detail:

Captain A. H. Bogardus, posed proudly with the American flag, a lineup of exhibition guns, and his three eldest sons: from the *left*, Eugene, twenty-one, Edward, fifteen, and Peter, thirteen. Not shown, Henry, then about eleven. Ca. 1886. Resting atop the shooting rack is a nickel-plated Remington Model 1875 single-action revolver with holster and cartridge belt. From *left*, Winchester Model 1873 rifle, an unidentified single-shot rifle, a double-barreled hammerless shotgun, two more Model 1873 Winchesters (that on the *left* with specially shortened stock), and a Model 1876 Winchester. The military musket to the *right* is a flintlock. All the Winchesters were made with checkered pistol-grip stocks.

EDITOR CHICAGO FIELD:—Captain Adam H. Bogardus has proven his claim of being the champion wing shot of the world. At Gilmore's Garden, New York, on Jan. 3, he accomplished his undertaking of breaking 5,000 glass balls in 500 minutes, a test of skill and endurance unparalleled. The shooting commenced at forty minutes past two o'clock, P.M., and at thirty-one minutes past ten o'clock P.M., his task was successfully completed. The shooting was from two of his patent traps, at eight yards rise, and the excellent arrangements introduced added largely to the success of the match. Between the loading and firing there was scarcely any intermission, except when an exchange of barrels was deemed advisable, and then the space consumed rarely exceeded more than half a minute.

At the breaking of the 2,000th glass globe he rested for 47 minutes and 15 seconds for refreshments, and recommenced shooting at 5h. 46m. 15s. He rested again at the end of the 3,000 score, at 6h. 54m. 15., for 20 minutes and 15 seconds, and resumed at 7h. 14m. 13s., most of the time being taken up in adjusting the stock of his shotgun and in oiling the barrels, which were of Scott's manufacture, the weapon weighing ten pounds, the cartridges used being charged with 3½ drahms of powder and 1½ ounces of No. 8 shot.

At the second recess it was found necessary to rehabilitate the wooden partition which prevented discharges doing damage to the Fourth avenue side of the building by intercepting the shot. It was draped with white sheeting to throw the dark brown balls, as they were spun into the air from the trap, into bold relief. Immediately to the rear of the marksman a large calcium light was situated, which threw its brilliant rays in the direction of the sheeting, marking the course of the flying balls.

Captain Bogardus showed painful traces of his laborious task as the blackboard recorded the score by the thousand. His right arm was swollen and pained him very much. His assistants bathed and rubbed the injured member with arnica and brandy, and he again resumed his work with great spirit, while his indomitable will was traceable in every line of his strongly marked features. After he had broken 4,000 balls, he took another recess, and expressed himself as feeling very much fatigued.

He completed the breaking of his first 1,000 balls in 1h. 5m., his second 1,000 in 1h. 2m. 30s., when he rested for 47 minutes 15 seconds at 5h. 46m. 15s. He continued his labors with slightly slower results to the end, making six rests of short duration in the last 1,000 score. He was so exhausted toward the end that he was obliged to complete the last 500 points sitting on a chair. He finally completed his task at 10h. 40m. 35s., thereby having 19m. 35s. to spare. In the total score 163 misses were recorded against him. GOTHAM.

Clay Pigeons Popularized by Buffalo Bill's Wild West

With its educational entertainment for the public, the Wild West promoted an understanding of wildlife and environmental issues. In the 1884 program, a special section was devoted to "The Clay Pigeon," identifying it simply as a recently invented "device . . . that is well calculated to put to a severe test the best of marksmen."

Considering the dominant role of shooting and marksmanship in American life of the nineteenth century and the importance of shooting to the settlement of the West, it is no surprise that gun-related sports were influenced by Cody and his troupe of champions. Such is the case with the use of glass balls and the clay pigeon. A dissertation on the latter appeared as early as the Cody and Carver Rocky Mountain and Prairie Exhibition show program and appeared later in somewhat altered form. The following is from an 1884 edition:

In deference to the humanitarian sentiment, [our exhibition] matches are all shot at Ligowsky "clay pigeons," an ingenious mechanical contrivance that furnishes an exact imitation of the bird's flight, and produces all the exciting and pleasurable sensation induced by fine workmanship when live birds are used. Ladies and children can, therefore, witness and enjoy this unique exhibition with no violence to the feelings, while the expert and experienced sportsman can still appreciate the excellence of the shooting, the clay pigeons heightening rather than diminishing the sport.

The pigeons are made of red clay, in the shape of a saucer. They measure four inches in diameter, and are a trifle over an inch in depth. They are very thin and light. Each of them has a flat handle of iron at its side about an inch long. The traps from which they are thrown give every variety and eccentricity of direction to the pigeons projected from them. They are made of iron, and consist of an arm revolved by a spring around a short upright column. At the end of the arm is an apparatus that holds the handle of the pigeon. The trap is set by forcing back the arm and securing it by a drop-catch. When the line attached to the catch is pulled the arm is released, and the spring that works it hurls the pigeon into the air. A joint in the middle of the supporting column enables the trap to be so set that it will throw the pigeon to any desired altitude within the possibilities of the spring. As they are projected sidewise, with the concave side down, their form enables them to float through the air for a distance and with a rapidity that the balls do not attain to. They can be made to describe a long and low or a short and high flight, and as their course is affected by a breeze or sudden gust of wind, as well as by the manner in which the trap is set,

Anxious crowds at Union Square, New York City, as the Wild West lined up for a parade on September 4, 1884. At center, Buffalo Bill astride his horse, awaiting beginning of the preshow parade. At *left*, band members in wagon, the sides painted handsomely with scenes and BUFFALO BILL and WILD WEST emblazoned on the side.

a shooter can never anticipate what direction any given pigeon will take.

Opposite this description on the bottom of the facing page were these credit lines:

Captain Bogardus uses the Wm. & C. Scott of Birmingham, England, shot-gun.
W. F. Cody uses rifles and arms manufactured by the Winchester Firearms Co.
The lightning powder of the Laflin & Rand Powder Co. was used in Bogardus's champion matches.
The "Life of Buffalo Bill," Bogardus's "Field, Cover, and Trap Shooting," Bogardus's "Record, Score, and Instruction Book," are for sale on the grounds.

In the earlier Cody and Carver program, the close of the clay-pigeon piece lent the support of their partnership to a newly formed association, which had adopted the Ligowsky as a standard target. The notation appeared on the same page as a scene in

(*above*) Cigarette-card colored lithograph of Annie Oakley, Buffalo Bill, Doc Carver, and Captain A. H. Bogardus, each like a playing card and each portrait bust accompanied by depictions of firearms. Note target-launching device at *upper left*.

(*right*) In this Union Square, New York City, picture, ca. 1885, Cody's embroidered satin or silk shirt is accompanied by an extremely deluxe pair of holstered Colt revolvers, with grips of relief-carved ivory. The rifle is the Colt-Burgess lever-action, serial number 285, presented by the Colt factory, the embellishments including the date, July 26, 1883. The right side of the frame is decorated with scene of Cody shooting buffalo from horseback; see Chapter 5.

which two frontiersmen lassoed a buffalo, captured for the Wild West show. The statement read: "The Lagowsky [*sic*] Clay Pigeons have been adopted as a Standard Target by the National Gun Association, an incorporated organization composed of the best sportsmen in the country. Send stamp for details to the Secretary, Box 1292, Cincinnati, Ohio."

The fate of the association is unknown; however, this was not the National Rifle Association. The NRA has never maintained an address in Cincinnati and has retained its name since its initial incorporation in 1871.

Bogardus Featured in Buffalo Bill's Wild West

The rare 1884 program of the Wild West published a detailed biographical portrait of Bogardus and his stirring record. In the flowing prose of the inimitable

John Burke, Bogardus was celebrated for his mastery of shooting and the sometimes physical and mental energy required in endurance competitions:

This rugged specimen of the hardy American hunter and honored sportsman was born in Berne County, New York State, and commenced shooting when but fifteen years of age, his first armament consisting of the "old flint lock" musket, his career thus covering the era of advancement in gunnery from that ancient arm to his present superb piece of mechanism known as the "William and C. Scott & Sons' gun," of Birmingham, England. Removing in 1856 to the broad prairies of Illinois, he found himself in the then paradise of the hunter, and where his acquired skill could be used to commercial advantage. Game being plenty, he commenced hunting, trapping for the market, and with his tent and outfit making expeditions of three and four months' duration year after year, and passing through the inevitable adventures attendant on such a life, relishing its joys, overcoming its obstacles by his natural enthusiasm in his work, while at the same time he handsomely supported a wife and large family, while not neglecting the injunction regarding "the rainy day." During the Rebellion he served as a captain in the 145th Regiment, Ill. Vol, from whence he derives the title that he has so worthily worn in many a victorious struggle in friendly contests at home and abroad when representing in foreign lands his country's colors as its "champion" against "the best men of the Old World." . . .

He first won the title of "Champion of America" at Fleetwood Park, New York, 1871, afterwards shooting matches from the Atlantic to the Pacific, and going to England with the American Rifle Team, he added to our national honors by winning sixteen matches and the "World's Championship Medal," and, as he has never *been defeated* for these titles and holds undisputed possession of the coveted trophies that he has honorably retained—"according to the rules"—he can look calmly back on an unblemished professional record that fully justified him to issuing:—

CAPTAIN A. H. BOGARDUS'S VALEDICTORY.

The Bogardus valedictory of November 26, 1883, presents the most detailed review of his career yet to be brought to the attention of the authors. From his Elkhart, Illinois, home base, the captain expounded on his claim to the title "Champion Rifle Shot of the World" and to the titles of "Champion Shot of the World" *and* "Champion Wing Shot of the World"! This lengthy and interesting discourse is published in Appendix C.

Captain Bogardus's Sharpshooting Sons

The 1884 Wild West program continued its tribute to Captain Bogardus with a brief review of his sons. The boys seemed to have been imbued with the eyes, coordination, quickness, and concentration of their father:

The distinguished exponent of marksmanship, Captain A. H. Bogardus, has been singularly blessed in his domestic relations, and is the proud father of a large family—three daughters, all married, and four sons. The eldest, Eugene Bogardus, is nineteen years of age, and became so early imbued with a love for his father's profession that, when eleven years old, he was quite an expert in the field, having the practical experience that association with such an adept tutor could alone give. When the father went to England, in 1878, young Eugene accompanied him, and shot his first match with a gentleman at Woolwich Gardens, London. The contest [w]as at eleven birds, twenty-six yards rise, English rules, when he astonished the natives by tieing his opponent, each scoring 9 birds—English swift-flying bluerocks—out of 11. He gave exhibitions throughout England and at the Paris Exhibition—everywhere the "young American" creating genuine surprise, and receiving many tokens of appreciation. Returning home, he won the "Boys' Champion Medal," and having added rifle shooting to his accomplishments, entered for the championship of glass-ball shooting with rifle from the trap. The conditions were "to shoot with Winchester rifle at 100 glass balls sprung from a Bogardus trap," and he won the same with a score of 77, and retained it for the required two years over all-comers. All the known rifle feats seem to him easy of accomplishment—hitting two glass balls thrown in the air, half dollars, quarters, nickels, marbles, etc., with a bullet. The correspondent of the very reliable *American Field* thus notes an exhibition at Leadville last summer:—

"The rifle-shooting of Eugene is simply marvelous, and his feat of shooting double balls, both thrown into the air at the same time, will be found difficult to equal by any living person with a rifle. Who can equal that? The truth, is he captured the town, and Eugene can find five thousand dollars backing him here against any rifle-shot in the world, barring no man living," and from present indications it seems highly probable that in young Eugene Bogardus the auditor sees "the coming man," the future champion marksman of the world.

Edward is now thirteen years of age, and has been behind the gun for the last three years, is a good shot with the rifle and is very successful as a wing shot after quail, snipe, etc., in the field.

Peter commenced practice at eight years of age, is now eleven, and is fast becoming proficient with both rifle and shot-gun.

Henry is now nine years old and began his public career when seven, traveling with his father exhibiting I Cole's Circus, shooting with a 32-calibre rifle glass balls from the captain's fingers. He handles a shot-gun with skill, and is without doubt "a chip of the old block" and the most precocious marksman before the public.

The record of this remarkable family speaks for itself, and their personal popularity is founded on the possession of those social, moral and refined traits that go to make the American gentleman and enthusiastic sportsman.

Captain Bogardus versus Doc Carver

Bogardus and Carver were recognized as two of the greatest exhibition shooters in the world, the men to beat over all others. While Carver was on tour in England during the summer and fall of 1881, the burly marksman showed the British a thing or two about exhibition and competition shooting. Feeling he was conquering the world of shooting, he issued a challenge for a match with Bogardus, published in the *London Sportsman:* "I will shoot Captain Bogardus a match at 100 pigeons, 30 yards rise, [London] Gun Club rules, for any sum from $1,000 to $5,000 a side. I will allow him $250 for his expenses here, and deposit that amount with the editor of the *Sportsman* the day he sails from New York. The match to be shot in February." Carver received no response to this challenge, but the day came when the two had a string of twenty-five matches between them as they traveled around the United States. Their intense rivalry was the subject of innumerable articles in the press of the day and no little talk among shooters.

While in Louisville in February 1883, Carver and Bogardus met at the Louisville Hotel, where both were staying. According to an article in the Louisville *Commercial,* this was "the first time in four years the two champions spoke to each other." The next day, on February 22, at the Jockey Club, they fired a match, one hundred live pigeons, the stakes at $500 each plus money from the gate. Carver won 83 to 82. This time,

Bogardus challenged Carver; more matches followed.

Two matches were shot in Chicago, both won narrowly by Carver: one was live pigeons, 82 to 79, and the other clays, 72 to 63. Heading for St. Louis for yet another match, they were met with a challenge by the Ligowsky Clay Pigeon Company:

We herewith make to [Doc Carver] and Captain Bogardus the following proposition . . . to shoot 25 matches at the Ligowsky clay pigeons, 100 clay pigeons each, five traps, 18 yards rise, use of both barrels, English rules, same conditions as the recent match in Chicago.

Should [either] on any occasion, break 82 or more birds the winner, or if both should accomplish the feat, to receive $100 extra, and the winner of the match to receive $300 for each match. The first match to be shot at St. Louis during the present week; the second at Cincinnati March 10; and the balance to be shot in the principal cities in the United States before the 1st of May.

Armed with their best shooting guns, Carver's a W. W. Greener hammerless, and Bogardus's a W. C. Scott and Son's hammerless, both 12 gauge, the matches commenced. All told, these were held in the following cities: St. Louis (twice), Cincinnati, Kansas City, St. Joseph, Omaha, Leavenworth, Des Moines, Davenport, Council Bluffs, Burlington, Quincy, Peoria, Terre Haute, Indianapolis, Dayton, Columbus, Pittsburgh, Philadelphia, Jersey City, New Haven, Springfield, Worcester, Providence, and Boston. The match already held in Chicago was counted as the first in the series.

Carver won the series, with nineteen victories; there were three ties, and three wins for Bogardus. Both men shot with a vengeance; Bogardus, though in a losing effort, better than any previous best.

Captain E. E. Stubbs:
Champion Rifle Shot of the World

A far-from-modest letterhead proclaimed to any and all that "Captain Elmer E. Stubbs" was "The Hero of many a Thrilling Adventure, and the Monarch of all Wing-Shots!" Decorated with a picture of Stubbs with medals on his chest and vignettes of Western figures and Indians, the letterhead also claimed Stubbs to be "The Celebrated Rocky Mountain Scout, Indian Traiter [*sic*] Guide and Hunter." Further, Stubbs had spent "Twenty Years in the Wild West" and was heralded as the "Champion Combination Wing Shot of the World, whose Life is Crowned by Victory Won on Many a Hard Fought Battle Field." Gainesville, Arkansas, was given as Stubbs's address.

The "Doc" Carver scrapbook dated San Francisco, February 22, 1878, contains a lively challenge from Stubbs to Carver, which went unanswered. Evidently, Carver was more than a bit hot under the collar and considered Stubbs unworthy of a match. Here is the challenge from Stubbs, directed to the Chicago *Field* and likely published therein:

Sir,—I notice a very windy communication in your issue of the 5th inst., in which Dr. Carver, of San Francisco, makes the following challenge, open to the world:

1st. He says he will wager $500 and shoot against any man in the world, and asserts that he can break more glass-balls, 25 yards rise, than any man living. 2d. That he can break 1,000 glass-balls with a shot-gun quicker than any man living. 3d. That he can break more glass-balls, 21 yards rise, on-horseback, the horse to be on a swift run, than any man living can at thirty yards rise and standing on the ground. 4th. That he can break more glass-balls thrown in the air, with a Winchester rifle, than any man living can with a shot-gun. 5th. That he can break 100 glass-balls thrown in the air from Bogardus'

"The Hero of many a Thrilling Adventure, and the Monarch of all Wing-Shots!"

Captain Elmer E. Stubbs.

The Celebrated Rocky Mountain Scout, Indian Trailer, Guide and Hunter.

TWENTY YEARS IN THE WILD WEST.

Champion Combination Wing Shot of the World, whose Life is Crowned by Victory Won on Many a Hard Fought Battle Field.

Gainesville, Ark., _____ 188_

Rare letterhead, ca. 1880s, of the "Celebrated Rocky Mountain Scout," etc.

traps with a Winchester rifle quicker than any man living with a shot-gun.

All I have to say to Dr. Carver is to come on with his money, and I will bet him $1,000 that I can break 100 glass-balls quicker than he can with his Winchester rifle, or any other gun he may choose. 2d. I will bet him $500 even that I can beat him shooting glass-balls or pigeons from a buggy, the horse to be on a run. 3d. I will bet him $1,000 that I can kill more wild pigeons from ground traps, 21 yards rise, than he can, out of 100 each; usual rules. 4th. I will bet him $2,000 to $5,000 that Captain A. H. Bogardus can break 1,000 glass-

balls in less time than he can; and, further, I will bet him $500 that Captain A. H. Bogardus can beat him nine matches out of ten, on time or at the score, if he will shoot; and I will bet him $1,000 that Eugene Lecompt, of Leavenworth, Kansas, can beat him in the field, shooting prairie chickens or quails, any place where they may be plenty, in the season. And further, I will bet him $2,000 to $1,000 that I can do all he says he can do.

[I propose we] stake the money in the hands of the Editors of the Chicago Field, *within the next thirty or sixty days, if he thinks I am playing the game at bluff, after*

which we can arrange for the shooting. Let Dr. Carver reply through your columns.

CAPT E. E. STUBBS.
Champion Wing Shot of the West
West Elkton, Ohio, January 9, 1878

Carver wasted no time in his response, published on the pages of the *Pacific Life*:

In answer to Captain Stubbs' challenge, I accept every one of the matches he proposes, on condition that he puts up $5,000 in the hands of the Chicago Field, *or in those of the* Forest and Stream, *or any other sporting paper of repute, and I will cover it, and, moreover, will give him $1,000 to make the matches, one and all. As soon as this money is deposited I will at once leave for the East to complete necessary details.*

Yours, respectfully, DR. W. F. CARVER.
San Francisco, January 22, 1878.

For some reason, Stubbs failed to fire a match with Carver, but he did challenge another well-known shooter in a letter sent to the Chicago *Field*:

Leavenworth, Kan., Jan. 26, 1878—Editor Chicago Field:—*I notice a challenge in your issue of this date, signed W. B. Hauworth. I except* [sic] *his challenge only from ground traps, and hereby request Mr. Hauworth to put up a forfeit of one half the amount, $50, in the hands of the Editor of the* CHICAGO FIELD, *at least thirty days prior to June 11, 1878, and I will cover it. I hereby challenge Mr. Hauworth to shoot me a match in Leavenworth, Kan., the 15th of May next, 500 glass balls each, against time, $250 a side, or at his place. Will give or take expenses.*

CAPT. E. E. STUBBS,
Champion Wing Shot of the West.

Beneath this challenge in a Doc Carver scrapbook is a challenge from R. T. Martin to Captain Stubbs:

Baltimore, Md., Jan. 26, 1878.—
Editor Chicago Field: *Please state to Capt. E. E. Stubbs that if he will state when and where he won the championship of the West, and the terms and conditions under which it is to be contended for, I will be happy to arrange a match with him for it to be shot in thirty days from date, either in Chicago, Peoria, Council Bluffs, or Omaha. I will be home Feb. 1, and will be pleased to hear from him at 79 Clark street.*

R. T. MARTIN.

No records exist of matches between Stubbs and Hauworth or between Stubbs and Martin or between Stubbs and Carver. Evidently, when it came to Doc Carver, Stubbs could not come up with the money required—or perhaps he was aware of the inevitable probability of a loss.

Yet in a shooting demonstration on November 25, 1883, Stubbs is reported to have fired at one thousand glass-ball targets with Kennedy rifles, using Bogardus traps from a distance of fifteen yards, with average hits at about thirty yards. The score indicates he hit 993 out of 1,000—a highly respectable achievement—with one run of 700 without a miss. No wonder the Whitney Arms Company was interested in supplying this man with rifles. The achievement surpasses Carver's record scores against glass balls: in his match against John Ruth, Carver smashed only 885 out of 1,000, using, like Stubbs, a rifle.

Judging from a Winchester and several Kennedy rifles that belonged to Stubbs, the gun factories regarded him with no little respect. It appears that his guns came at a discount, though some might well have been actual presentations. A Model 1873 Winchester with a rare 30-inch barrel was inscribed on the left sideplate: CAPT. E. E. STUBBS CHAMPION RIFLE SHOT OF THE WORLD. Since the inscription was en-

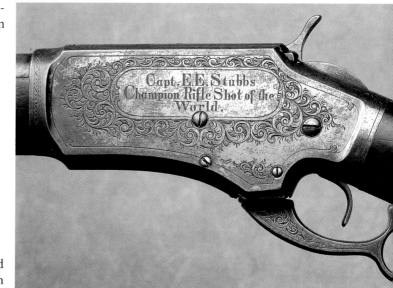

Inscription detail of the deluxe Whitney-Kennedy rifle, indicating ownership by Captain E. E. Stubbs, Champion Rifle Shot of the World; serial number 934.

graved at the Winchester factory, it seems likely that the company considered Stubbs to have been entitled to that recognition.

Two Whitney-Kennedy rifles were similarly inscribed. Serial number 934 is as pictured, and number 1586, a .44 caliber with double-set triggers and fancy wood, is elegantly engraved on the left side with scroll and border engraving and the inscription: CAPT. E. E. STUBBS CHAMPION RIFLE WING SHOT OF THE WORLD. The right side of the frame was engraved WHITNEY ARMS CO., which suggests that Stubbs was affiliated with the company in some way. Eli Whitney, Jr., wrote to Stubbs on May 18, 1883: "We see you have a Kennedy. How do you like the Kennedy. How is it for shooting glass balls? How does it compare with Winchester. Can you send us a recommendation of the Kennedy we can print?"

For a two-year period, correspondence was carried on between Stubbs and the factory. Shipping records show a Kennedy with checkered stocks in .44

caliber sent to Stubbs at his Gainesville address on July 12, 1883. In April 1885, Stubbs was shipped a "24[-inch] .38 Cal. Octagon Kennedy Rifle Fancy stock, checked butt and forearm, case hardened frame and trimming. Engraved 'Captain E. E. Stubbs' and 'Champion Rifle Shot of the World.' Easy trigger pull and quick spring." The rifle was sent by express to Gainesville. In May, Stubbs was shipped four thousand .44-caliber blank cartridges. And in July, he was sent another shipment of blanks.

But the Whitney records indicate that it was rumored Stubbs's "Wild West Show has gone to pieces. . . . Please let us hear from you." Stubbs continued to shoot Whitney rifles, as evidenced by the following order on July 22: two 24-inch barrel .44-40 rifles, each with set triggers, plus 1,400 primed shells, 1,000 bullets, and 1,000 blank cartridges, plus two sets of loading tools. On July 27, Whitney wrote to inquire what "length stock and drop of same for your boys [sic] gun. Give us his full name for engraving." In September, correspondence advises Captain Stubbs that the "guns [are] at engravers . . . [will] get them back next week."

In the 1884 Whitney Arms catalogue, Stubbs was quoted as endorsing Whitney rifles. The April 10, 1884, issue of *Forest and Stream* magazine wrote of shooting achievements by Stubbs using a Kennedy rifle. During a fire at the Whitney armory, records for 1884 were lost, but the correspondence with Stubbs picked up again in 1885, with the last of the communications in August.

The total number of Kennedy rifles that were shipped to Stubbs was no less than seven, of which six were in .44-40 caliber, and one in .38-40. At least three of these were engraved with Stubbs's name and his claims of being CHAMPION RIFLE SHOT OF THE WORLD, and CHAMPION RIFLE WING SHOT OF THE WORLD.

Early Days of the Wild West, 1884–1886

The 1899 *Route-Book* of the Wild West noted the 1884–1885 and 1886 seasons as follows:

1884–5.

Opened in May, in St. Louis, Mo., went through the Eastern States and Canada. October 31st took a boat down the Mississippi River, bound for New Orleans. The boat was wrecked at Rodney, Miss., and everything was lost except horses. Opened in New Orleans Christmas week [1884], and closed April 1, 1885, then worked north through the Central and Southern States, including Michigan and Wisconsin, and closed October 31st at St. Louis, Mo.

1886.

Opened in St. Louis in May, and then played through to New York, where they opened a season at Eristina, Staten Island, in June, and remained until September 30th, then opened a winter season at Madison Square Garden, Thanksgiving Eve, and closed Washington's Birthday, 1887. During their stay at the Garden they lost sixteen buffaloes, from lung trouble.

The Wild West Takes Off

Once the Wild West had Nate Salsbury in charge of business and showmanship matters, the future of the operation seemed assured. Salsbury's entrepreneurial brilliance would keep the Wild West on course for over a decade. The Wild West became the show to see and to be seen at. Among the hordes of the famous who saw the Wild West was Samuel L. Clemens (Mark Twain), a public figure who shared with Cody, at least for a while, the same publisher, Frank E. Bliss of Hartford.

Twain had a journalist's eye for the interesting and the unusual and was intrigued with mechanical contrivances, firearms among them. His novel *A Connecticut Yankee in King Arthur's Court* was inspired by his knowledge of Samuel Colt and of vice president and superintendent E. K. Root, and of the brilliantly run Colt factory. Twain is known also to have toured the Colt operation; furthermore, Edward

Early poster by the Forbes Company, Boston and New York, ca. 1885. Approximately ten years later, A. Hoen and Company, Baltimore, published the same image, with additions of text: "An American" (at bottom) and "Congress Rough Riders of the World" (at top). Dimensions of both posters approximately 40 × 28 inches. This is a rare example of Hoen later publishing a Forbes image but with altered text.

Tuckerman Potter, the architect of the author's palatial home in Nook Farm, Hartford, had his first commission in the city from Mrs. Samuel Colt—a museum gallery saluting the late colonel.

Twain's appreciation of the authentic Wild West prompted him to send an enthusiastic endorsement from Elmira, New York, on July 14, 1885:

I have now seen your Wild West show two days in succession, enjoyed it thoroughly. It brought back to me the breezy, wild life of the Rocky mountains, and stirred me like a war song. The show is genuine, cowboys, vaqueros, Indians, stage-coach, costumes, the same as I saw on the frontier years ago.

Your pony expressman was as interesting as he was twenty-three years ago. Your bucking horses were even

painfully real to me, as I rode one of those outrages once for nearly a quarter of a minute. On the other side of the water it is said the exhibitions in England are not distinctly American. If you take your Wild West over you can remove that reproach.

The entertainment that Twain enjoyed so immensely was detailed in the 1885 program, which was the first to spell out a formal sequence of performances. The program also listed a new star, destined to become the premier headliner, next to Cody himself, one Annie Oakley:

Programme.
Subject to Changes and Additions
1.—GRAND PROCESSIONAL REVIEW.
2.—ENTREE. Introduction of individual Celebrities, Groups, etc.
3.—RACE between Cow-boy, Mexican, and Indian on Ponies.
4.—PONY EXPRESS, ridden by Billy Johnson, Illustrating Mode of Conveying Mails on the Frontier.
5.—RIFLE SHOOTING by Johnnie Baker, the "Cow-boy Kid."
6.—DUEL between BUFFALO BILL and Chief Yellow Hand, and Indian Battle, "First Scalp for Custer."
7.—WING SHOOTING, by Miss Annie Oakley.
8.—THE COW-BOY'S FUN. Throwing the Lariat, Riding Bucking Ponies and Mules, by Buck Taylor, Bill Bullock, Tony Esquival, Jim Kidd, Dick Johnson, and Cow-boys.
9.—RIFLE SHOOTING, by Miss Lillian F. Smith, "The California Girl."
10.—RACE, ridden by Lady Riders.
11.—ATTACK UPON THE DEADWOOD STAGE COACH, by Indians. Repulsed by Cow-boys commanded by BUFFALO BILL.
12.—RACE between Sioux Boys on bareback Indian Ponies.
13.—RACE between Mexican Thoroughbreds.
14.—PHASES OF INDIAN LIFE. A nomadic tribe camps upon the prairie, the attack of the hostile tribe, followed by scalp, war, and other dances.
15.—MUSTANG JACK (Petz-ze-ka-we-cha-cha), the Wonderful Jumper.
16.—Hon. W. F. CODY, "BUFFALO BILL," America's Great Practical All-Around Shot.
17.—RIDING AND ROPING OF WILD TEXAS STEERS by Cow-boys and Mexicans.
18.—THE BUFFALO HUNT, BUFFALO BILL assisted by Sioux, Pawnee, Wichita, and Comanche Indians.
19.—THE ATTACK ON THE SETTLER'S CABIN by Marauding Indians; the Battle and Repulse by BUFFALO BILL Leading Cow-boys and Mexicans.
20.—SALUTE.

"A MAN WITH A HISTORY—RECORD—A NAME!"—*Gen. Wm. T. Sherman.*

THE SCOUT BUFFALO BILL

Lithograph of *The Scout Buffalo Bill*, by A. Hoen and Company. Established ca. 1835, the company is known to have printed more than fifty posters with Buffalo Bill's Wild West as their subject. The oldest lithographer in America, the company remained in business until ca. 1982, at which time an auction dispersed the remains of the historic firm. Among the lots: lithograph stones for printing, 32 × 25 inches.

LONG & HEPPNER. Photos.

The Buffalo Bill's Wild West band, some of them with Colt Single Action Army revolvers in holsters. Tepees in background; photographed on-site in New York City.

Cody with Sitting Bull at *lower right;* interpreter at *lower left.*

Sitting Bull and Buffalo Bill

The 1885 season had yet another star, one whose presence was surprising considering his role in the demise of Custer and the men under his command at the Little Bighorn. Yet just nine years after that, Sitting Bull was a star attraction in Buffalo Bill's Wild West. Others had tried for years to sign the chief to a personal-appearance contract, but Indian Agent Major James McLaughlin, who had jurisdiction over Sitting Bull at Standing Rock Reservation, resisted. The major felt that the chief would misinterpret what he saw in the big cities and return to the reservation more difficult to handle than ever.[4]

Among those who had tried to solicit the government to permit Sitting Bull to go on tour was Reverend Joseph A. Stephan, former agent at Standing Rock. Stephan thought the chief would be a suitable draw for a church fair in Jamestown, Dakota! Sitting Bull himself was agreeable to visiting cities of the East—as long as he had a suitable deal.

Finally, in hopes of impressing on Sitting Bull the importance of having his people adapt to farming and education, McLaughlin decided to give the concept a try. In March 1884, he took the chief on a ten-day trip to St. Paul. There, Sitting Bull met and became mesmerized by Annie Oakley while watching her performance at the Olympic Theater. Sitting Bull also visited a number of other sites, among them schools, stores, churches, and banks. He was visibly impressed. McLaughlin felt the trip had provided a picture of the power and grandeur of the white nation.

Following the St. Paul sojourn by a month, Cody made his initial approach to sign Sitting Bull for a tour with the Wild West. McLaughlin expressed to Cody that he could not accept "any such proposition at the present time when the late hostiles are so well disposed and are just beginning to take hold of an agricultural life." However, the agent felt that if permission was granted, he would "prefer to have them in your troupe to any other now organized that I have knowledge of."[5]

Soon, the decision-making was elevated up the chain of command, to the secretary of the interior,

Henry M. Teller. Approval was given—if Sitting Bull was in agreement—and McLaughlin then reluctantly sought the best venue for Sitting Bull's tour. Since the Wild West season was too far advanced to add Sitting Bull, arrangements were made for an eastern trip, under auspices of Alvaren Allen of St. Paul.

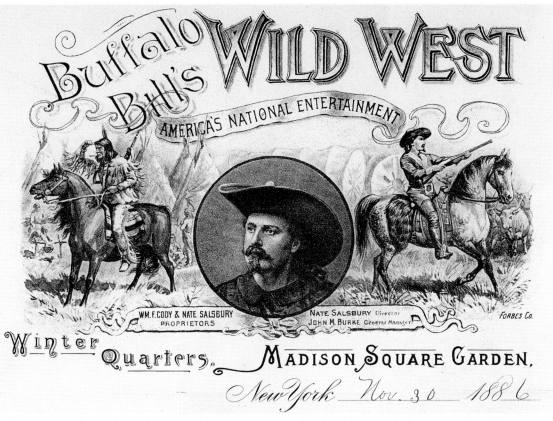

Letterhead of ca.1886; image of Cody shows him poised and ready to fire his Winchester from horseback. The saddle is of Mexican style.

The troupe, known as the Sitting Bull Combination, was made up of eight Indians and two interpreters. Their travels began September 2, 1884, and ended October 25; twenty-five cities were visited, from Minneapolis to New York. That tour proved unsuccessful; McLaughlin was confident, however, that Buffalo Bill and his Wild West would have been able to make it work.

Cody tried again the following April 29, with a wire to the secretary of the interior: "Sitting Bull has expressed a desire to travel with me and requests me to ask your permission for himself and seven of his tribe. I will treat him well and pay him a good salary." Acting at the request of the secretary, the commissioner of Indian affairs sent a refusal. Cody then asked General William Tecumseh Sherman and Colonel Eugene A. Carr to send letters in support as he tried anew. This time, the secretary agreed, sending a wire to Agent McLaughlin to allow Sitting Bull and some of his tribe to join the Wild West.

In two weeks, Burke was at Fort Yates, organizing the contract and collecting his new performers. The agreement called for a salary of $50 per week for Sitting Bull; a bonus of $125; two weeks' salary paid in advance; $25 a month each to five other Indians; "and to pay all expenses of the party from the show to Standing Rock at expiration of this contract." Added to the deal was the statement: "P.S. Sitting Bull is to have sole right to sell his own Photographs and Autographs."[6] This new entourage joined the Wild West at Buffalo, New York, in a matter of days.

Advertisements emblazoned Sitting Bull's name almost as prominently as that of Buffalo Bill. And the chief proved to be an attention-grabbing star. While on view in the United States, he was greeted with derision; in response, he was stoic and unimpassioned, his look one of contempt and disdain. (When the chief was in a foul mood, Annie Oakley was the most likely to be able to bring him out of it.) While touring in Pittsburgh, the chief was attacked by the brother of a trooper killed at Little Bighorn. Defending himself, the chief smashed the fellow in the face with a sledgehammer, pounding out several teeth! In Boston, an elaborate ceremony was held in which the chief adopted Nate Salsbury as a member of the Sioux tribe, accompanied by a well-orchestrated assembly of the press and members of the upper echelon of Cody's entourage; a barbecue was part of the festivities. Salsbury's Indian name was Little White Chief.

The Boston *Transcript* reporter detected a resemblance between Sitting Bull, dubbed "Sedentary Taurus," and the Honorable Daniel Webster. The advertisement in the Boston *Post* on July 25, 1885, referred to Sitting Bull as "The Renowned Sioux Chief."

Nearing Washington, D.C., arrangements were made for Sitting Bull to meet President Grover Cleveland. On the stationery of Buffalo Bill's Wild West, America's National Entertainment, a two-page letter was written by a cast member, signed by Sitting Bull, addressed "To my Great Father," and dated Washington, June 23, 1885. The original is now in the National Archives.

In U.S. appearances, Cody respectfully presented Sitting Bull as an honored statesman. Crowds, however, could not forget the havoc wreaked on Custer and the Seventh Cavalry. In Canada, the chief was welcomed as a heroic figure and cheered as if a monarch. His stock of souvenir cabinet cards sold so quickly that they had to be replenished. In Montreal, a famous photograph was taken, showing the chief and Cody together, both with a left hand on the barrel of Cody's Model 1873 Winchester. The chief's garments and headdress were nothing less than magnificent and regal.

SITTING BULL & BUFFALO BILL.

WM. NOTMAN & SON—MONTREAL.

Enemies in '76, Friends in '85. Photographed in Montreal, 1885, by W. Notman.

Sitting Bull was deeply concerned about conditions at the Standing Rock Reservation. Salsbury wrote on his behalf to the commissioner of Indian affairs. There were matters of trespassing by troops and cattlemen on reservation lands, the possible loss of timber, problems with the existence of only one trader at the agency, and the failure to speak the Sioux language by teachers sent to train the Indians as farmers. The letter was intended to inform the commissioner "what [Sitting Bull] considers will be for the benefit of his people, leaving it entirely to your sense of justice to give him a hearing."

The Wild West tour ended on October 11, in St. Louis. Following the last performance, in response to queries from the press, Sitting Bull informed them that "the wigwam is a better place for the red man. He is sick of the houses and the noises and multitude of men." As he departed for the reservation, the chief was presented with gifts by Cody: a sombrero and a trained circus horse.

As had been feared by McLaughlin, back on the reservation, Sitting Bull's attitude and outlook had changed for the worse. The agent was disappointed and dissatisfied:

He is inflated with the public attention he received and has not profited by what he has seen, but tells the most astounding falsehoods to the Indians. He tells every person who he sees that the "Great Father" in his interview with him told him that he was the only great Indian living, that he made him head chief of all the Sioux, that all Indians must do his bidding, that he was above his agent and could remove the agent or any employee whom he chose and that any Indian who disobeyed him or questioned his authority must be severely punished. Also that all Indian dances and customs that have been discontinued should be revived, "sun dance" included, and rations be issued in bulk.[7]

McLaughlin feared for the worse and even considered placing Sitting Bull under arrest.

When Cody and the Wild West requested Sitting Bull for the coming season, McLaughlin responded

Pawnee and Sioux chiefs, with Buffalo Bill on Staten Island, 1886. The Pawnee, all scouts, are, from the *left*, Brave Chief, Eagle Chief, Knife Chief, Young Chief, and, on the other side of Cody, American Horse, Rocky Bear, Flies Above, and Long Wolf. Most of these Indians sailed to Europe with the Wild West in 1887. The revolvers appear to be Colt Single Action Armies, in the holsters of four; Cody's elegant Model 1873 Winchester is a deluxe rifle, finished in blue and case hardening, with checkered select-walnut pistol-grip stocks. Extraordinary array of costumes, weapons, and accoutrements, including U.S. government peace medals.

by saying he felt the chief wanted to go but that it was unlikely the request would be approved by the Department of the Interior. The Wild West kept trying, but in April McLaughlin wrote a stern no. His letter referred to Sitting Bull as a "consumate liar" who was "too vain and obstinate to be benefitted by what he sees, and makes no good use of the money he thus earns." The agent added that the chief spent money

extravagantly among the Indians in trying to perpetuate baneful influences which the ignorant and nonprogressive element are too ready to listen to and follow. Of the money and property that he brought home last fall, he did not have a dollar, or anything else [except for the gray circus-trained horse] left, after being three weeks at home & it was all used in feasting the Indians and trying to impress upon the Indians his own great importance, and I had a great deal of trouble with him and through him with other Indians caused by his own bad behavior and arrogance. I, however, have him under control again and would dislike to run similar risks.[8]

Thus, the tours by Sitting Bull were over.

Buffalo Bill's friendship with the chief and concern over his future continued. In 1889, when the

ghost-dance revival took place, Sitting Bull was headed for serious trouble. Cody was called in by General Nelson A. Miles to intervene and bring about a peaceful resolution, to see the chief on the reservation, and to neutralize the impending crisis. If necessary, Cody could take the chief into custody and "deliver him to the nearest Commanding Officer of U.S. Troops."[9]

Accompanied by his friend Dr. Frank Powell (a.k.a. White Beaver), and by Pony Bob Haslam and G. W. Chadwick, Cody arrived in Mandan, Dakota, on November 27, 1890. A wire to Fort Yates alerted the post of their expected arrival there that evening.

Because Sitting Bull was uneasy and had "lost confidence in the whites," McLaughlin felt that Cody and his party should not be allowed to intervene. With some difficulty, the Cody contingent finally arrived at Fort Yates on the afternoon of the twenty-eighth. The post commander kept the group occupied, encouraging Cody to consume some whiskey, and no business was attended to that day or evening.

McLaughlin and the post commander wired Washington, attempting to get Miles's order reversed. Cody, accompanied by five newsmen and three others, continued to attempt to meet with Sitting Bull. Finally, Miles's order was reversed by the president himself, and Cody was so advised before he was able to locate the chief. Disappointed, the entourage left the post and caught a train back to Chicago. Suffering from a cold, Cody submitted an invoice to the government for transportation expenses and headed to his ranch in North Platte.

McLaughlin felt he had saved Cody from being killed and neutralized a potential uprising. Buffalo Bill, on the other hand, thought that he could have dealt with Sitting Bull, and in the long term might have saved the chief's life.

When the attempt to arrest Sitting Bull was made on December 14, 1890, Indians loyal to the chief opened fire on the Indian police. True to one of Sitting Bull's visions, one of his own people killed him: a policeman named Red Tomahawk shot the chief in the back of the head. In the fusillade that followed, six Indian policemen died, along with seven of the chief's men. One of the Indian police force leaped on Sitting Bull's circus horse and rode off for reinforcements, sped on his way by gunfire. This horse was subsequently sold to Buffalo Bill and was used by him in some of the Wild West's performances.

Could Cody have saved his friend and fellow frontier figure Sitting Bull? The great scout might well have done so; at the least, his concern for the chief's safety and well-being was genuine.

Lillian Smith: The California Girl

One of the early Wild West performers who ranks high in the annals of American exhibition shooters was Lillian Frances Smith, a headline performer with the Wild West during the 1886, 1887, and 1888 seasons. The show program of 1886 billed her as "The California Huntress; Champion Girl Rifle Shot," while Annie Oakley was "Champion Markswoman." However, since ballyhoo and hype were resorted to often in promoting circus, vaudeville, and Wild West performers, arriving at accurate information about some of them is challenging.

Private collectors Ruth and Jerry Murphey have assembled more information on Miss Smith than has been known since the days when she was one of America's best-known shootists. Her first recognition as a Wild West figure was in the 1886 season.

That year's show program published a lengthy biography, nearly two thirds of the page, with a portrait in which Smith sported an ostrich-feather hat, her plump face in a three-quarter view. The engraved image was accompanied by a picture of her soon-to-be husband, Jim Kid, Wyoming Cowboy, on horseback. The tribute was twice the length as that in the same program to Oakley and was positioned at the center, whereas Oakley's was in the back.

Miss Lillian T. [sic] Smith,
The California Girl, and Champion Rifle Shot.
Was born at Collville, Mono county, Cal., in the fall of 1871; is,

consequently, only past her 14th year. Born in a country where game was plenty, and good marksmanship as highly thought of as excellence in any particular accomplishment in the older localities of our variously constituted country, her childhood was passed amid an atmosphere well calculated to develop that precocious skill that has astonished the Pacific Coast and rendered her famous through the land. Horsemanship there being so nearly allied to the cradle—in fact, having been often carried in babyhood on the pommel of the saddle—it is little to be wondered at that she commenced horseback riding as soon as she could sit one, and whilst on foot still "a toddler," mounted she was an infantile expert. At six years of age she had a bow-gun and could kill birds readily, and at seven expressed herself as dissatisfied with "dolls," and wanted a "little rifle." When nine years old her father bought her a [Ballard] rifle, twenty-two calibre, weight seven pounds, (which she uses yet) with which, after a little practice and instruction, she, on her first foray, mounted on her little pony, bagged two cotton-tails, three jack-rabbits, and two quails. From this out her enthusiasm was such, that after her studies were over, she spent her leisure time with horse, dog, and gun, on the surrounding ranges hunting, and generally bringing home a plentiful supply of game. On her father accompanying her to a lagoon near the San Joaquin River in Merced county, when ducks were plentiful, he was greatly astonished by her killing forty red-heads and mallards, mostly on the wing. On another occasion when on a camping excursion in Santa Cruz county, hearing her dog bark in a [canyon], and thinking he had "treed a squirrel, sure," she mounted her mustang, and on her return amazed the campers and surprised her mother by depositing at her feet a very large wild-cat that she had shot on a limb of a high redwood tree, hitting it squarely in the heart. The admiring campers on their return proclaimed through publication her remarkable feats, and at a party given in her honor christened her the champion "California Huntress." Her fame spread throughout the "Golden State," and her father was induced to present her to the public of San Francisco, where in July, 1881, she gave seven successful receptions at Woodward gardens—her marvelous accuracy and extreme youth creating the greatest sensation, winning for her a host of admirers and many compliments from those who, before seeing, had been incredulous. After a short practice at shooting glass-balls thrown from the hand she made a score of 323 successive shots without a miss, and out of 500 breaking 495.

Miss Lillian, owing to the opportunities in that section, has made her reputation in practical shooting, such as a Turkey-shoot at Hollister, San Benito county, in the holidays of 1883, where at 150 yards she killed so many turkeys she was set back to 200 yards, but her dexterity at that distance

being equally destructive the managers arranged with her "to drop out and give the boys a chance at the turkeys too." Being invited to a mud-hut shoot, at 50 to 175 yards, according to the accessibility of the marshy ground, she, in one-half hour, bagged fifty, receiving a valuable prize. July 4, 1883, at Hollister, distance 30 feet at a swinging bell target, with a one-inch center, she scored 200 bells, with a Ballard rifle, in fifteen minutes, and on July 23d, at Dunn's ranch near San Filipe, she killed six dozen doves in two hours with *a rifle*. October 25, 1883, at a meeting of the Colusa Gun Club she was induced to try her skill at live pigeons thrown from three plunge traps, with a 10-pound shot-gun, 10 gauge, 2 drams powder, 1/2 ounce shot, and scored ten out of twelve, resulting in the club having the manufacturers at Meriden, Conn., present her as a testimonial, a 12 gauge Parker shot gun. This remarkable little lady has shot successfully, in tournaments with various gun clubs on the Coast, matches with such noted shots as Geo. I. Kingsley, Crittenden Robinson, John Kerrigan, taking two valuable prizes and the special prize given by Philo Jacoby, President of the Schuetzen Rifle Club, San Francisco, March 15, 1885. She will appear daily with the Wild West.

During the Wild West's first European tour, Smith did not fare well with the British at Wimbledon shooting grounds, as she offended by both missing outright and inadvertently hitting the rump of a running-deer target. She blamed the rifle she was using, promising to return with her own the next day. Not only did Smith fail to return, but she failed to pay a fine for hitting the running target in the haunch—each hit a penalty shot.

At least in her early entertainment years, Smith lacked the charismatic personality needed in a live-performance showperson, particularly in comparison to the charming and sprightly Oakley. That Smith's reputation in California did not match that of the raving press reports is clearly evident in the undated article that follows, from the Sacramento *Record Union:*

Many Sacramentans, especially those interested in shooting, will remember Miss Lillian Smith, the young girl that was such an expert rifle shot that she issued a challenge to anyone in the country, male or female, to contest with her. She resided in this city for quite a while, her parents maintaining a shooting gallery, where Miss Smith astonished all-comers by her remarkable ability. The Woodland *Mail* says of her:

"She was married some time ago to one of Buffalo Bill's scouts named Jim Kid, and the London *Topical Times* publishes an interview with the young lady, in which she tells how it was done. The story is simple and uninteresting enough, but what will interest Woodland people will be the highly polished language accredited to her—language that would do credit to the originator of English. In Woodland she usually said: "Swab off the target pap, and let me bang de eye," or else, "Swing de apple dere, young fellers, an' let me bust his skin." How great are the changes.

Annie Oakley had a trim figure but amazing strength and endurance. Double-barrel shotgun with outside hammers. Ca. 1885–1886.

Despite her remarkable shooting skills, Smith seems to have been unable to survive what was likely the wrath of Annie Oakley, who was intent on eliminating this rival from the roster of the Wild West. Jealous of the California Girl's youth (she was eleven years younger), Oakley altered her birth date by six years, from 1860 to 1866, to bring their ages closer.

After leaving the Wild West, Smith continued as an exhibition shooter. For several years, she was with Colonel Fred Cummins in an act shared with her partner, Frank. One of her most celebrated appearances was at the Pan American Exhibition in Buffalo, New York, in 1901, with Cummins's U.S. Indian Congress. In 1902 and 1903, she traveled in vaudeville, coast to coast, in the Orpheum theaters in performances billed as "Wenona and Frank." In 1910, they operated as California Frank's All Star Wild West Show. She is also known to have appeared with the 101 Ranch and as a member of the 101 Ranch and Buffalo Bill's Wild West in 1916.

In later years, Smith married E. W. Lenders, the well-known Western artist. The rare photograph on page 66 shows her as Princess Wenona with her rifle-toting partner, Frank. The interior of the lid of her elaborately cased set of Smith & Wessons is embossed in gold leaf with the tantalizing presentation: "PRESENTED TO WENONA BY SMITH & WESSON."

"Wenona" retired from the show ring to her home in Oklahoma around 1920. (She had become a resident of that state in 1907.) Smith's grave site is in Ponca City, where she was laid to rest February 5, 1930. Among her effects, as reported in a local newspaper, were four .44-40-caliber Winchester carbines, two gold-plated .22-caliber Winchester rifles, a gold-plated S&W .38 revolver, a gold-plated S&W .22 revolver—and a bulletproof vest!

Smith in frontier fringed costume, clutching a Low Wall single-shot Winchester rifle; to her *right* a Winchester Model 1873 in blued finish and a hammer-model double-barrel shotgun with pistol-grip stocks and an inlaid pistol-grip cap. Perhaps this is the 12-gauge Parker presented to her by the Colusa Gun Club. The two handguns tucked into her cartridge belt appear to be spur trigger tip-up Smith & Wessons, finished in nickel plating; shooting medal on her bodice. To her *left*, on the floor, a stack of glass ball targets await vaporizing.

Lillian Smith Smith & Wesson Single Shot First Model .22, serial number 19931, and .38 Hand Ejector, Military and Police Model, serial number 6244, were made specially for her, 1901. Rare medals; the largest is from the Willow Gun Club, Chicago, 1902; inscription on the reverse side of the *center* medal is shown on the *opposite* page. *Upper right*, shooting glass balls from around head of partner, California Frank. Card with club hit by .22, a souvenir to audience. Displayed against colorful buckskin show costume with ermine trim and accessories. Note banner sewn on dress in ca. 1887 photo, *upper left*. Trophy belt mounted in silver; diamond-inlaid gold buckle inscribed: PRESENTED TO "WENONA" CHAMPION RIFLE SHOT OF THE WORLD BY DIRECTORS OF INDIAN CONGRESS PAN AMERICAN EXPOSITION AUGUST 17, 1901.

Selected rifles of Lillian Smith (a.k.a. Princess Wenona), with show costume and memorabilia. Pair of Winchester Model 1890s custom-made for Smith in 1901; they bear the consecutive serial numbers 120374 (top) and 120375. On Model 1890 with deluxe stock, the opposite side is carved PRINCESS WENONA and frame is engraved CHAMPION RIFLE SHOT/OF THE WORLD/PRINCESS WENONA.; serial number 60912. Stevens rifle serial number 30668; the opposite side of the stock is carved WORLD CHAMPION RIFLE SHOT.

Large target with her signature. Postcard of ca. 1904 shows Wenona shooting a rifle from horseback. Three inscribed medals awarded to her (from left): 1903–1905; February 7, 1902 (reverse side visible); and 1906. Poster, 1914, by Strobridge; right half features Edith Tantlinger, another exhibition shooter.

Lillian Smith and California Frank in fancy show costumes, each holding Winchester gallery guns, the Model 1890 custom-built rifles noted previously. The cased set has three S&Ws, including a First Model Single Shot .22 rimfire pistol and a single-action topbreak revolver, likely the New Model No. 3, the latter with plated finish; the swing-out cylinder revolver is her Military and Police. In front of the cased set, a blued double-action S&W, at *left*, and a Model 1877 Colt Lightning double-action revolver, plated and with mother-of-pearl or ivory grips. Note shooting medals pinned on her bodice. Ca. 1901.

Some of the Famous Generals of the U.S. Army Under Whom Buffalo Bill Has Served. Custer figures most prominently, at *top center*, of all the officers. 29 × 19½ inches.

SOME OF THE FAMOUS GENERALS OF THE U.S. ARMY UNDER WHOM BUFFALO BILL HAS SERVED

From the Wild West 1886 program; note particularly items 8 and 12:

A FEW REASONS WHY YOU SHOULD VISIT "BUFFALO BILL'S WILD WEST"

1st—Over ONE MILLION people have set you the example.

2d—Because it is a LIVING PICTURE OF LIFE ON THE FRONTIER.

3d—It is an opportunity afforded YOUR FAMILY but once in a lifetime.

4th—You will see INDIANS, COWBOYS, and MEXICANS, as they live.

5th—You will see BUFFALO, ELK, WILD HORSES, and a multitude of curiosities.

6th—You will see an INDIAN VILLAGE, transplanted from the Plains.

7th—You will see the most WONDERFUL RIDERS the world can produce.

8th—You will see the GREATEST MARKSMEN in America.

9th—You will see INDIAN WARFARE depicted in true colors.

10th—You will see the attack on the DEADWOOD STAGE COACH.

11th—You will see the method of capturing WILD HORSES AND CATTLE.

12th—You will see a BUFFALO HUNT in all its realistic details.

13th—You will see YOUR NEIGHBORS there in full force.

14th—You will see BUFFALO BILL (Hon. W. F. Cody).

15th—You will see an Exhibition that has been witnessed and endorsed by—

PRESIDENT ARTHUR AND CABINET;

GEN. SHERIDAN AND STAFF;

GENERALS SHERMAN, CROOK, MILES, CARR, &C.;

RISTORI, PATTI, NEVADA, BOOTH, IRVING, BARRETT;

BENNETT, WATTERSON, CHILDS, VANDERBILT,

BELMONT, DREXEL.

and tens of thousands of well-informed people in EVERY WALK OF LIFE.

Hon. W. F. Cody, Buffalo Bill, lithograph by A. Hoen and Company. Note gold buffalo-head stickpin on cravat. 27 × 21 inches. Ca. 1886.

Buffalo Bill and the Winchester Factory

One of the perks of Cody's widespread fame was that Winchester catered to him. Although no records indicate that Cody was paid by Winchester in his exhibition shooting, the factory supported him through advertisements in programs and endorsements. The earliest known instance of Winchester quoting Cody in a factory catalogue was in 1875. The letter was from Fort McPherson; Cody waxed enthusiastic about the Model 1873:

> *I have been using and have thoroughly tested your latest improved rifle. Allow me to say that I have tried and used nearly every kind of a gun made in the United States, and for general hunting, or Indian fighting, I pronounce your improved Winchester the boss.*
>
> *An Indian will give more for one of your guns than any other gun he can get.*
>
> *While in the Black Hills this last summer I crippled a bear, and Mr. Bear made for me, and I am certain had I not been armed with one of your repeating rifles I would now be in the happy hunting grounds. The bear was not thirty feet from me when he charged, but before he could reach me I [put] more lead [in him] than he could comfortably digest.*
>
> *Believe me, that you have the* most complete *rifle now made.*

When performing in New Haven, it was not unusual for Cody and other cast members to visit the Winchester factory. It was said by the family of master engraver Conrad F. Ulrich that he was an admirer of Cody and sported a goatee after that of his hero. According to family tradition, Ulrich presented an engraved Winchester to Buffalo Bill. Still another story tells of him or his engraving brother John visiting Oliver F. Winchester's New Haven home with key members of the Wild West show troupe. One of the Indian chiefs is said to have guzzled down an alcoholic beverage and promptly pitched the empty container into the host's fireplace! Cody Combination cast member Wild Bill Hickok was subject of an oil painting by Ulrich in 1909; the picture shows Hickok shooting a revolver from horseback at aerial targets thrown aloft by Calamity Jane.

Of further interest is the apparent impact of early show programs on the Ulrich brothers and the scenes they engraved on Winchester firearms. Depicted here is a Buffalo Bill hunting scene from the 1884 program (printed by Forbes and Company, Boston and New York), which appeared in certain other programs as well. A similar rifle scene is represented by a pull, attributed to John Ulrich, from a Model 1894, serial number unknown.[10] A similar engraving scene appears on the left sideplate of Cody's own Model 1873 rifle, number 494993.

Cody was not the only exhibition shooter to be patronized by the Winchester Company: presentation rifles are known to have belonged to Captain E. E. Stubbs, Arizona Joe Bruce, and Captain Jack Crawford, though Doc Carver's inscribed rifle from the factory has yet to come to the attention of the authors.

National fascination with firearms and Cody's loyalty to Winchester were two factors in his ever-growing fame and fortune. Winchester's status as one of America's most powerful and successful manufacturers was given a boost by Cody—as he was by them. Both were on their way to becoming American legends. Soon, Buffalo Bill and his troupe would be every bit as famous in Great Britain and Europe as they were in the United States. Winchester was well on its way to superstar status as well.

Arizona Joe, the Shooting Star, recipient of this handsome Winchester Model 1873 as a present from the factory. It is of .38-40 caliber; serial number 447861. A New York stage performer, Joseph Alexander Bruce, subject of dime novel titled *Arizona Joe, The Boy Pard of Texas Jack. . . . [the] History of the Strange Life of Captain Joe Bruce, a Young Scout, Indian Fighter, Miner, and Ranger, and the Protégé of J. B. Omohundro, the Famous Texas Jack.* See also Chapter 9. At about the same time, Arizona Joe received another Model 1873 from the factory, serial number 510607, pictured in R. L. Wilson, *Winchester: An American Legend.*

The triumph of the Wild West in Europe and America. Westley Richards 12-gauge shotgun at *left,* custom-made for Buffalo Bill and well used by him. The Colt Single Action Army at *center* yet another example of his generous nature, a gift to friend Dr. George Powell (a.k.a. Night Hawk). Rare Wild West ledger at *left center,* entry open to New York. Show program at *top right* from English performance. Stylish letterheads at *top center* indicate Wild West practice of not infrequently printing new designs; most of letters in the book were written by Cody himself. Paris 1889 scrapbook kept by Cody, full of invitations, calling cards, menus, etc.; small invitation with French and American flags honoring July 4.

Chapter 4

✦❋✦

THE WILD WEST TRIUMPHS IN EUROPE AND AMERICA 1887–1892

When Cody and his troupe took Europe by storm, they did so at a time when relations between the United States and Great Britain were strained. There were still festering wounds from the Revolutionary War and the War of 1812 and from Britain's sympathy to the Confederacy during the Civil War. It took the master showman and celebrated Wild West figure William F. "Buffalo Bill" Cody to thaw the ice and to harmoniously bring together the two nations.

The Wild West so dominated public consciousness that the London *Globe* published a ditty that shows how completely and masterfully the great showman and his troupe had swept in with their unique entertainments and superbly orchestrated technique of distributing posters and billboarding:

> *I may walk it, or 'bus' it, or hansom it: still*
> *I am faced by the features of Buffalo Bill*
> *Every hoarding is plastered, from East-end to West,*
> *With his hat, coat, and countenance,*
> *lovelocks and vest.*

Of the myriad Buffalo Bill stories, one that richly reveals his wit, charm, quickness, and easy way with all classes took place in Earl's Court before a small but distinguished aristocratic audience, among them no less than four European kings and Edward, Prince of Wales, who went on a regal ride in the Deadwood stagecoach. The inimitable Cody held the record for being the subject of news pieces in the English press from 1887 through 1904, and no story outdid this "Royal Flush" incident. Reports of Wild West triumphs also made great press in the United States. The following piece was cabled to the New York *World* on June 21, 1887:

Buffalo Bill's Big Visitors
—
Four Kings and a Crowd of Notables at the Wild West Show.
—
They Ride on the Deadwood Coach and on
the Switchback Railroad—On Visiting the
American Bar They Try Every Variety of
American Drink from a Cocktail Up—
Buffalo Bill's Witty Reply to the Prince.
Copyright, 1887, by The Press Publishing Company
(New York World).

[SPECIAL CABLE DESPATCH TO THE WORLD.]

LONDON, June 20.—The royalties who now throng London, and who have assembled here in greater numbers than ever before in any one place in Europe, apparently take more interest in the Wild West Show than in the Jubilee performance. The Queen of Belgium said to one of the English gentlemen who called on her this morning that she did not come to London at all on account of the Jubilee, but that she came here because she was dying to see the Wild West performance. There was a private exhibition given this morning by Buffalo Bill and his men for the benefit of the visiting royalties. The general public was not admitted. There were not over twenty guests outside of the people who had been invited by the Prince of Wales. Judging by the interest displayed by the royal guests at the Wild West Show this morning, it is very evident that Col. Cody could go through Europe and command the same attention for his performance that he has obtained in London. There were never so many crowned heads before at any private or public entertainment given in Europe. The Prince of Wales brought with him four reigning sovereigns and the Crown Princes of the most prominent countries in Europe.

71

Wild West troupe in London, 1887, souvenir picture taken by Elliott and Fry, 55 and 56 Baker Street, London. Cody seated *front* and *center*; Lillian Smith and Annie Oakley stand in first row but they are separated by five people. Several performers have holstered firearms, one Indian brandishes his Winchester Model 1873. Some band members carry instruments.

ELLIOTT & FRY.   (COPYRIGHT.)   55 & 56, BAKER STREET, LONDON, W.

SOUVENIR OF BUFFALO BILL'S WILD WEST.

The royals present were four kings—of Denmark, Greece, Saxony, and Belgium. Other regal personages were Crown Prince Rudolph of Austria, the Hereditary Prince and Princess of Saxe-Meiningen, the Crown Prince and Crown Princess of Germany, as well as the Crown Prince of Sweden and Norway. Still more aristocrats present were the Prince and Princess of Wales, Prince Albert Victor and Prince George of Wales, and Princesses Victoria and Maud of Wales. Also on hand were Princess Victoria of Prussia, the Duke of Sparta, Prince George of Greece, and Prince Louis of Baden. The *World* story continued:

These were attended by a numerous suit of lords and gentlemen and ladies-in-waiting. The entire Wild West performance was gone through with from beginning to end, and the royal visitors became so excited and interested that they had to go into the arena in order to observe the shooting and manoeuvres at close range. All of the royal visitors wore black frock coats and high silk hats with the exception of the Prince

Signed "The VanderWeyne Light" and stamped with the London address, 182 Regent Street West. A seldom-seen cabinet card, available for the public to purchase and for Cody and staff to give away.

of Wales. He wore a light spring suit with a light drab overcoat buttoned tightly to his chin. In the button-hole of his coat there was a rose. He was the only one among the visitors who wore a high white hat. The Prince of Wales acted as the Master of Ceremonies. He gave the directions when the performance should begin, and could not remain in his seat in the box. In his capacity as exhibitor he walked uneasily up and down, and every time that there was anything that especially pleased him, he would go out into the arena with all the royal visitors. The shooting principally seemed to interest the King of Denmark and the Crown Prince of Austria. When Miss

In buckskins and elegant leather with riding quirt; signed "To my Secretary/W. F. Cody/Buffalo Bill/England 1888." Winchester Model 1873 rifle leaning against knee. Elliott and Fry, photographers, London.

Oakley had finished her shooting both the Danish King and the Austrian Crown Prince insisted upon examining her gun and sighted it, as if they were anxious to try their skill. The riding and shooting were greatly admired. The entire royal party seemed bent upon a lark.

The program was well under way when the Princess of Wales arrived, attended to the arena by Major John Burke and accompanied by her daughters and Prince Albert Victor. The princess appeared to consider the Wild West "as the place for a lark." As the Deadwood coach came into play, her highness climbed on board, onto the backseat, unassisted. Then others joined in:

She coaxed her father, the King of Denmark, to climb on to the crazy coach by her side. Then the grave and severe King of Saxony was invited to risk his life on the same wagon. This ancient King stroked his side whiskers with great calmness, as if to show that he had as much courage as the Princess of Wales. After him came the Crown Prince of Sweden and Norway, a very tall, melancholy-looking young man, with black eyeglasses, a crisp black mustache and short black whiskers. He wore a tightly buttoned gray frock suit. He languidly puffed his cigarette smoke into the face of the Princess of Wales, and indeed all of the royal party followed the example of the Prince of Wales and puffed cigars or cigarettes all through the performance. The Crown Prince of Austria clambered on to the centre seat and Prince George of Wales mounted the coach by the side of old John Nelson. Orator Richmond raised his hand and away the coach dashed. The Indians charged down upon the coach, and in a moment the royalties were encircled in a volume of smoke and fire. The cowboys came to the rescue after the usual fashion. There was a mad dash around the ring. Only one item in the programme was omitted. No death occurred during the short ride. All arrived safe and well in front of the royal box.

Buffalo Bill and the leading members of the show were subsequently presented to the various royalties. Mr. Cody, every one conceded, looked much more at ease among the Kings than any of the royal party. After he had cracked his bull whip the Prince of Wales sent out for it. He showed his relatives that the whip weighed thirty pounds, and that what looked so simple and easy required extraordinary strength and skill to handle. . . .

Towards the close, just before the Prince of Wales went away he asked Col. Cody if he had ever played before four kings before. Cody replied with a courtly bow to the group: "I have, Your Royal Highness, but I never held such a royal flush as this against four kings." The Prince had asked his question in all seriousness, but he was delighted with Col.

Cody's ready answer and laughed very loudly. He then turned around and explained all the complicated bearings of this answer of Col. Cody to the royalties, who—poor, benighted beings—do not understand the American game of poker.[1]

MISS LILLIAN SMITH.
The Celebrated Californian Rifle Shot.

BUFFALO BILL'S WILD WEST.

Lillian Smith, *The Celebrated California Rifle Shot*, with BUFFALO BILL'S WILD WEST. Copyright © Woodburytype, ca. 1887, London. Outfit appears to be of corduroy, with satin front.

The Wild West *Route-Book* for 1899 reviewed the years from 1887 through 1892 as follows:[2]

1887.

April 1st, sailed on the steamer "State of Nebraska" for London, England, where they remained a season of six months, and then went to Manchester, England, for six months, and closed April 30, 1888; then gave one performance at Hull, England, in the afternoon, and sailed the same night for New York City on the steamer "Persian Monarch."

1888.

Opened the season at Erastina, Staten Island, on Decoration Day [May], and remained six weeks; then went to Philadelphia, Baltimore and Washington, and closed at the State Fair in Richmond, Va., October 22d.

1889–1890.

Sailed April 12th on the Steamer, "Persian Monarch" for Havre, France, where a season of six months was played at Paris. They then toured through France, Spain, Italy, Germany and Austria, and closed in the City of Strasburg, Alsace-Lorraine, October 29, 1890. Some of the Troupe returned to the United States, while others remained there.

1891–1892.

Opened in Stuttgart, April 15th, and played through Germany, Belgium and England; closed at Croyden, England, October 31st. Opened again at Glasgow, Scotland, November 15th, and remained until April 15, 1892. May 9th opened again in London, and closed October 27, 1892, and sailed on the Steamer "Mohawk," October 29th, for New York City.

Buck Taylor: "King of the Cow-Boys"

One of the most popular cast members while on tour in England, Buck Taylor's billing presented him as "King of the Cow-Boys." He was America's first cowboy hero. A native of Texas, at about the age of seventeen Taylor first rode on a cattle drive from his home state to Wyoming. After returning to Texas, he repeated the feat, this time with his brother, Baxter. Together, they took up a homestead on Long Creek, some sixty miles from Lander, Wyoming.

A meeting with Buffalo Bill led to Taylor joining the Wild West. At six foot four—or, as he liked to say, five feet, sixteen inches—he weighed over three hundred pounds. Eventually, he became so large that he allegedly had to resign from the show since it was hard to find mustangs big enough to carry his increasing bulk. Despite his substantial weight and size,

BUCK TAYLOR,
"King of the Cow-boys."

BUFFALO BILL'S WILD WEST.

Buck Taylor, "King of the Cow-Boys." Diamond stickpin on cravat; heavy gold watch chain and fob. The varnished walnut butt of a Single Action Army revolver appears at *bottom*. Woodburytype, ca. 1887, London. See R. L. Wilson, *The Peacemakers*, for photo showing Taylor in jaguar chaps, with holster for 7½-inch Colt Single Action Army revolver, the cross-straps emblazoned with individual letters spelling out his name: BUCK TAYLOR.

Taylor was a trick rider, roper, and genuine cowpoke. He honed his masterful skills while he worked as a cowboy on Cody's ranch in Nebraska.

For nearly ten years, Taylor rode as one of the featured performers of the Wild West. The 1884 and 1885 programs give him a star billing, with this laudatory commentary:

Wm. Levi Taylor, known to his associates as "Buck," was born in Fredericksburgh, Gillespie County, Texas, and is now about thirty years of age. Frontiersmen come from all grades of society and classes of people, who develop peculiarities of their early surroundings and circumstances; therefore it is seldom the Eastern public meet face to face one so thoroughly "to the manor born" or who is so completely a typical Westerner by ancestry, birth and heritage of association as this noted herdsman, whose eminence is based on the sterling qualities that rank him as a "King of the Cowboys." His family lived in Taos, in the Lone Star State, when tributary to Mexico; fought for its independence with Crockett and Col. Travis at the Alamo, where a grandfather and uncle fell—under Sam Houston at San Jacinto, and after success had crowned a new empire with liberty, but two male members of the family were left, "Buck's" father and a younger brother. Joining the Texas Cavalry at the outbreak of the late war his father was killed in one of the first skirmishes, and in two years after, his mother dying, left him when about eight years old dependent upon his ranchman uncle and good luck to wrestle for existence. Texas—always famous for its immense herds of cattle roaming at will over the vast and fertile plains, was then, as now, the supply camp of the trade—gave unusual facilities; in fact, required the cultivation of sturdy qualities to follow daily a life so replete with privations, hardship and danger that it is a marvel to the luxuriously raised how a man can voluntarily assume it, much less come to actually like it to infatuation. Still this solitary life, with its excitements and adventures, has its charms for its votaries, who, often knowing of none other, never weary of its continuous duties, trials and exposures. Taylor from his childhood then knew no other ambition than to try and excel in his [occupation], and inheriting a strong physique, he early became hardy and proficient in horsemanship, lassoing, and general "cow-sense." Becoming able, he soon became famous as a "boss of the outfit" on the ranges and on the trail, conducting vast herds over the "Chisholm" to the Northern markets, leading in the stampede, excelling on the round-up, and gaining such distinction as a rider and tamer of the mustang and broncho that his surname has become obsolete among his confreres and he is known from Idaho to the Rio Grande by the cognomen of "Buck." A little worthily won in a profession of great risk and danger, and which his ap-

pearances in daily public exhibitions gives a very good idea of, but when seen in the corrall [sic] among herds of the obstinate equines, challenges the admiration of the spectator and the envy of his kind. His remarkable dexterity won the attention of Major North and Buffalo Bill and they secured his services for several seasons on their ranch on the Dismal River where his feats of strength, easily throwing a steer by the horns or tail, lassoing and tying single-handed, his mastery [of] wild horses, caused his engagement with the review of prairieland, "The Wild West." Standing six feet [four] inches, with a powerful, well-proportioned frame, possessed of a strength that is marvelous, he is a fine representative of his class. Amiable as a child, "Buck's" genial qualities combined with his well-known abilities, make him a favorite not only with his fellows, but on his first visit East last summer easily had the same position accorded him by an admiring public.

As a horseman of exceptional skill and daring, Taylor's performance at the 1887 London engagement was rated with comments such as "his exertions were rewarded with unlimited applause." A faded May 10 London newspaper story, from clippings Taylor sent home to his family, gave due credit to this dazzling rider:

Buck Taylor, 'King of the Cowboys,' is one of the most expert horsemen in the troupe. . . . A considerable amount of amusement was caused by the unwillingness of some of the ponies— for they are little more—to be mounted. Some of them nearly lay down; others circled around to the limit of their bridle, bucking and kicking furiously. Eventually they were mounted, but before the rider was fairly settled in his saddle, his steed had got his head down, and went across the spacious arena bucking in the most approved form.

Tricks from his repertoire included picking up coins or handkerchiefs from the ground while riding at full speed, for which he was sometimes termed a "pickup" rider.

A handful of dime novels were written about Taylor, with the first aptly titled *Buck Taylor, King of the Cowboys,* by Prentiss Ingraham, for Beadle's Half-Dime Library, in 1887. Other dime novels in which he was the headliner were entitled *The Wild Star Riders; Buck Taylor, The Saddle King; The Lasso King's League; The Cowboy Clan; Buck Taylor, The Comanche Captive;* and *Buck Taylor's Boys; or, The Red Riders of the Rio Grande.*

Apart from his career with the Wild West, Taylor played a major role in Denver's cowboy tournament and Wild West event of 1890. In 1894, he tried his own hand with a show, known as Buck Taylor's Wild West—thereby bringing disfavor from his friend Buffalo Bill. Although a newspaper story stated that he was one of the volunteers for Theodore Roosevelt's Rough Riders and was wounded in action at San Juan Hill, records do not indicate that to be the case.

In later years, he lived in or near Philadelphia, for a period with Cody's old frontier and ranching friend Charles Trego and his wife, and later in East Brandywine. A book that he had planned on his life and adventures never materialized, and he was plagued by ill health in later years. Death came to him at age sixty-seven, from bronchial asthma.

Taylor's impressive physique, appearance, performance, and behavior were instrumental in changing the image of the cowboy from a ne'er-do-well and rascal to a noble knight of the plains. Successor "Kings of the Cow-Boys," Roy Rogers among them, carried on traditions of respectability established by the original.

Buck Taylor on horseback.

Buck Taylor and His Guns

Though not an exhibition shooter, Taylor used a Colt Single Action as part of his props and was aware of the symbolic nature of this necessary Wild West piece of equipment. One of these pistols, though yet to be located—and a prize for any devotee of fine guns—was a custom-made .44-40 Frontier Six Shooter, ordered from the Colt factory in August of 1884. The order came from William Read and Sons, Boston, on Taylor's behalf:

Boston Aug. 19 '84

Colt's Pat Fire Arms Mnfg. Co.
Hartford, Ct.
Gents
We want for
"Buck Taylor", of Buffalo Bill's troupe now exhibiting here, one of your Frontier 44 caliber Revolvers, to take the Winchester 44 Cartridge, central fire to be <u>nickel</u> plated & <u>engraved</u> & with <u>Pearl</u> handle the strap on grip of handle to be left plain, not engraved, so that the name, <u>Buck Taylor</u>, can be engraved on it, and if you can have this name put on please do it, otherwise we will have it put on here. please send it at once, and at as <u>low</u> a <u>price</u> as <u>possible</u> as the purchaser says he will make it a good card for you and wants cheap price, and we are

Yours truly over
Wm. Read & Sons

P.S. Since writing the above we have wired you as party wanted to know how soon could have it, and if you send by tomorrow P.M., or Thursday, it will be in time. WR & S.

An annotation beneath the above, written by the factory, shows that the order was met, and the revolver, a 7½-inch nickel Frontier, .44-40, engraved, with pearl grips, inscribed, was shipped: "17½ nic Frontier S.A. Pistol nic Eng'd Pearl with "Buck Taylor" Engraved on strap." Unlike most Wild West guns, this six-shooter of the King of the Cow-Boys had the most striking of identifying features: the owner's name prominently engraved for all to see.

The Squaw Man

Another of the colorful characters from the real West was John Y. Nelson, billed as the Squaw Man. Like Taylor, Nelson found himself a popular figure with the British and Continental public. From the days of his youth, Nelson's life was one of countless exploits: at various times he was a mountain man, pioneer, trapper, guide, army scout, saloon keeper, peace officer, stagecoach driver, buffalo hunter, Indian trader, showman, and even author. His book *Fifty Years on the Trail* captured his inimitable personal style and related in frontier jargon many of his adventures—the extent of his exaggeration and hyperbole rivaling that of several of his contemporaries. His life's story, however, could be termed a panorama of Western history from 1840 to 1890.

As early as the mid-1840s, Nelson was a fur trapper and mountain man, somewhat beyond the tail end of the heyday of those vocations. His knowledge of the West and skills in the mountains and on the plains led to him guiding Brigham Young and his Mormons on their trek from the Mississippi Valley to the Salt Lake region. Nelson also hunted buffalo professionally for the Chicago market and became well known to the Indians as a trader; among his wares was whiskey.

The Squaw Man claimed to have known of gold in the Black Hills as early as 1850 and later guided prospectors who were illegally seeking the precious metal on Indian lands. Though Nelson served on several occasions as an army scout against certain tribes

JOHN NELSON,
Scout, Interpreter and Guide.
BUFFALO BILL'S WILD WEST.

John Y. Nelson, *Scout, Interpreter and Guide*, taken in London, with *BUFFALO BILL'S WILD WEST*. Woodburytype, ca. 1887. Nelson has a Winchester Model 1873 rifle and is wearing his unique holster and belt rig, butts forward, with pair of deluxe engraved, ivory-handled, and inscribed Colt Single Action Army revolvers.

of Sioux and Cheyenne, he was also well known as one who lived with the Indians.

Nelson was reputed to have had a total of nine Indian wives (three of them simultaneously) and fathered several half-breed children. At various times he ran saloons and casinos in the West and also had an appointment as a small-town peace officer. He drove the Deadwood stagecoach and achieved fame for this as a star performer in the Wild West. For approximately ten years, Nelson traveled throughout America, Great Britain, and Europe as a member of the troupe.

Nelson was an old friend of Buffalo Bill and received prominent billing wherever they appeared. The biography that follows appeared in the 1883 program of Cody and Carver's Rocky Mountain and Prairie Exhibition, continuing into at least the Wild West programs of 1886:

John Nelson—"Cha-Sha-Sha-na-po-ge-o",
And His Indian Family.

Will be one of the objects of interest in the camp of "The Wild West." To the majority of dwellers in the realms of civilization it is hard to realize that hundreds of our own race and blood, very often intelligent and even accomplished men, gladly exchange all the comforts and advantages of our mode of life for the privations and danger, relieved by the freedom and fascinations of the nomads of the Plains. Such, however, is the fact, and many by their marrying into the tribe are adopted as members, achieve tribal honors and possess great influence for good or evil, generally becoming interpreters, through whom all government communications pass. Among the most

honored and reliable of these in his section is John Nelson, who, by general honesty of character and energy, has gained fame and respect among whites and Indians. Being a thorough Plainsman, years ago his standing as a train guide was most enviable, being sought for by all. He guided Brigham Young and the Mormons across the then "Great Desert" to their present location in Utah. He married Chief Lone Wolf's daughter of the Ogallala tribe, has six children whom he supports in comfort by hunting, being especially expert as a trapper of beaver and otter. Nelson is a representative of the best class of "Squaw Men."

Cody and Nelson were considered "pards," and Cody is quoted as having said that Nelson was "a good fellow though as a liar he has few equals and no superior." In the show troupe, Nelson's role as stagecoach driver was shared with those of interpreter, sometime cowboy in frontier sequences, and occasionally as a thrower of glass balls during Cody's shooting act. Fittingly, his final days were on an Indian reservation.

John Y. Nelson's Single Action Army revolvers and matching holsters, an expression of his pride in being with the Wild West and of friendship and professional association with his old pard Buffalo Bill. Accurately rendered portraits of Nelson and Cody on the recoil shields; bold backstrap inscriptions. The holster plaques are of German silver, inscribed as illustrated. Serial numbers 98489 and 99615, .44-40 caliber, 7½-inch barrels, full nickel plating with two-piece ivory grips. Shipped from Colt's to Hartley and Graham, New York City, September 5 and 22, 1883. The engraving likely done in New York, possibly during the Wild West's long stint at Erastina. Number 99615 engraved with the portrait bust of Nelson, while 98489 has the portrait of his patron Buffalo Bill. The Cody pistol has animal figures engraved within cartouches on the cylinder. A unique set acquired in England in the 1960s by dealer and collector Herb Glass; some five years previously, the set left the hands of an elderly woman who was a granddaughter or great-granddaughter of Nelson himself.

The Famous Deadwood Coach/Buffalo Bill's Wild West. John Y. Nelson seated at *top back*. A treat for guests would be a ride in the coach, usually pulled by team of six mules. London, ca. 1887. Stagecoach now in collection, Buffalo Bill Historical Center.

THE FAMOUS DEADWOOD COACH.
BUFFALO BILL'S WILD WEST.

Mustachioed Mexican performer Joe Esquivel, for many years the Wild West's chief of cowboys. Antonio Esquivel was listed in programs as champion vaquero of Mexico.

A race that spread the gospel of the quarter horse in England was reported in the Hull *Daily Mail* on May 4, 1888:

AMERICAN BRONCHO HORSES V. ENGLISH THOROUGHBREDS. TEN MILES RACE FOR £500 A-SIDE.

"The second match between the English thoroughbred horses and bronchos supplied from the Wild West stud was decided yesterday before another large attendance of spectators. The conditions were slightly different from those of Tuesday, as yesterday the jockeys had to change their mounts without any assistance. The jockeys were J. Latham and A. Esquivel (the American), who had to change horses each half-mile, and although the Englishman's mounts showed much the greater pace[,] the alacrity with which the American mounted and dismounted fully counter-balanced any advantage that the Englishman gained in this respect. Immediately on starting the Englishman got off with a short lead, and passed the post slightly ahead at the end of the first lap, and also effected a further advantage in his change, but owing to a collision [at] the completion of the next lap, through an American horse getting on the track, he lost his lead, and the American quickly went to the head of affairs. Latham then gradually lessened the gap, but the American by his splendid dismounting rapidly gained and increased his lead to a couple of furlongs. The American then lost a considerable amount of ground, but Latham never succeeded in making anything like a diminution of his opponent's long lead, the American winning, amidst tumultuous applause, by 400 yards. Time, 22 minutes."

78

The Wild West at the Vatican

A first-person memoir of one of the most unforgettable experiences in the life and times of the Wild West is Nate Salsbury's description of their visit to the Vatican, in 1890.[3]

At the Vatican. . . .

While in Rome, the Wild West was invited to visit the Vatican, and the day set apart for it was the Anniversary of the Pope's Coronation.

About ninety percent of the company was in its best bib and tucker when I arrived at the ground that morning, and I had the heads of the departments get out their full strength, so that when we started for the Vatican we had every man and woman in the outfit in line, except the Camp Guards and one Indian who did not feel very well, so his comrades left him covered by a blanket and apparently asleep.

For a week before this day, John Burke, who is a devout Catholic, had worked on the Indians to impress them with the solemnity of the occasion we were about to assist in celebrating. He impressed them with the idea that they were going to see the Representative of God on Earth, and to those of them who had been under Catholic instruction at the Reservation, the coming event was of great interest.

Arriving at the Vatican we were escorted to the Courtyard that opens from the Sistine Chapel, and were finally bidden to enter the Chapel itself. Once inside, we found all the Diplomatic Corps assembled while the places reserved for the ladies were crowded with the hundreds of Catholics who were in Rome at that time for this very celebration. It was one of the most impressive human ceremonies that I have ever witnessed, as the Pope, borne on his Sedia, came down between the Wild West lines on his way to the Papal Throne, whereon he seated himself. We had massed the Wild West Company in open order along the corridor, in full war paint, and all the striking costumes that could be mustered for show and realism. It was a curious sight to watch the expressions on the faces of the people from the frontier of America, as they gazed in awestruck wonder at the magnificence displayed on all sides, and marked the exhibition of respect shown His Holiness, as borne aloft, he waved his blessing to the worshipping throng. As he passed the spot where Cody and myself were standing he looked intently at Cody, who towered a head and shoulders above everyone else, and who looked a picture in his dress coat and long hair. The combination seems incongruous, but he is the only man that I have ever known who could wear it [without] exciting laughter. As Cody bowed his head reverently His Holiness spread his hands in token of his blessing, and the good Catholics around us looked with envy at Cody during the rest of the ceremonies.

The pope then positioned himself on the throne, while the Sistine Choir sang in celebration of the High Mass. Salsbury was struck by the beauty and majesty of the music and said that attempting to describe its impact was comparable to "trying to initiate Niagara with a hand pump and a roadside ditch." Continuing his memoir:

At the conclusion of the ceremonies, His Holiness was again seated in his Sedia, and passed out of the Chapel through the ranks of the Wild West, followed by all the Cardinals and attendants of the Papal Court. I had passed a nervous half hour, for fear some of the Indians, not appreciating the sanctity of the Vatican, would utter an approving war whoop before the ceremonies were ended, in token of their approval of the whole affair. But fortunately Burke had schooled them in the conduct they must bear to the proceedings, but of this I knew nothing when I went into the Chapel. It would have seemed most irreverent if my fear had been realized, but as a matter of fact, would not have been so, because the war whoop is the natural expression of Indian approval or defiance, and would have been uttered in as much reverence as the lowest prostration made by any of the faithful present.

Taking my cue from the Master of Ceremonies, I motioned the Wild West to withdraw from the Chapel to the Courtyard, where they were regaled by a sight of the Vatican Guards drawn up for inspection. Indians rarely express their amusement at anything by laughter, but when they caught sight of the variegated colors that make up the uniforms of the Swiss guards their faces took on a broad grin, which deepened into guttural shouts of laughter when told that the men who wore uniforms were soldiers in the pay of His Holiness. They could not imagine anything clad in such outre costume to be a soldier.

The Indians had difficulty comprehending the numbers of the entourage who could be accommodated in the Vatican. They wanted to explore the premises on their own but were not allowed to do so—their reaction to this was that "they did not think much of God's Representative if his house was too good for anybody to go into." In their view, Indian tepees rated better in hospitality than "the etiquette of the Papal Court."

On returning to camp we were shocked to find that the solitary Indian who was left in camp had died of heart disease in our absence, if he had not died before we started, for none of his tent mates remembered to have spoken to him for some time before we left camp. The death of this man had a peculiar effect on the Indians' minds, for they immediately called a council among themselves, and sending for Burke demanded to know why the Representative of God had not protected their comrade while they were away from him, and if he had so much power on earth why he had not exerted himself to shield their comrade from death in their absence. As Burke could not make an explanation that satisfied them, his former efforts to impress the Indians with Papal power went to waste, for the catastrophe was followed by the usual mourning, and the expressed opinion that God should send another man to represent him if he expected the Indians to believe anything the missionaries might tell them in the future. Burke labored to destroy the unfortunate result of his labors, but they stuck to the primary facts, and would not be convinced that all he had told them beforehand was a bit of a humbug to say the least.

Cody's Cowboys Triumph over Roman Horses

In one of the most astounding achievements of American riders in history, Cody's cowboys took on the fiery and presumably unridable Italian wild horses, supplied by the Prince of Sermoneta. The story was told in various copies of the Wild West program and is quoted here from an 1897 edition:

Roman Wild Horses
Tamed by Cow-Boys, Ridden in Five Minutes.
How "Buffalo Bill's" Cow-Boys
Tamed the Roman Wild Horses
(Per the Commercial Cable to the "Herald") Rome, 4TH MARCH, 1890

All Rome was to-day astir over an attempt of "BUFFALO BILL'S" cow-boys with wild horses, which were provided for the occasion by the Prince of Sermoneta.

Several days past the Roman authorities have been busy with the erection of specially cut barriers for the purpose of keeping back the wild horses from the crowds.

The animals are from the celebrated stud of the Prince of Sermoneta, and the Prince himself declared that no cowboy in the world could ride these horses. The cow-boys laughed over this surmise, and then offered, at least, to undertake to mount one of them, if they might choose it.

Every man, woman and child expected that two or three people would be killed by this attempt.

The anxiety and enthusiasm was great. Over 2,000 carriages were ranged round the field, and more than 20,000 people lined the spacious barriers. Lord Dufferin and many other diplomatists were on the Terrace, and amongst Romans were presently seen the consort of the Prime Minister Crispi, the Prince of Torlonia, Madame Depretis, Princess Colonna, Gravina Antonelli, the Baroness Reugis, Princes Brancaccia, Grave Giannotti, and critics from amongst the highest aristocracy. In five minutes the horses were tamed.

Two of the wild horses were driven without saddle or bridle in the Arena. "BUFFALO BILL" gave out that they would be tamed. The brutes made springs into the air, darted hither and thither in all directions, and bent themselves into all sorts of shapes, but all in vain.

In five minutes the cow-boys had caught the wild horses with the lasso, saddled, subdued and bestrode them. Then the cow-boys rode them round the Arena, whilst the dense crowds of people applauded with delight.

Fancy Colt Single Action Army revolver, silver-plated, serial number 35521, inscribed on butt of silver grips: DE SUS AMIGOS/LOS CHARROS/MEXICO 1881 (bottom of left panel) and PARA EL MAJOR CHARRRO/DON VICENTE OROPEZA (bottom of right). Oropeza was the Wild West's chief of vaqueros for many years and, as a champion with the lariat, taught Will Rogers how to rope. Promotional scrapbook also featured in Chapter 7.

W. F. CODY,
(BUFFALO BILL.)

Done with patriotic flare and signed WOVEN IN PURE SILK BY THOMAS STEVENS, COVENTRY, portrait busts of Buffalo Bill, Nate Salsbury, and distinguished Indians from the Wild West. These scarce woven-silk souvenirs were done in various formats and styles, 5½ × 3¾ inches.

Command Performance before Queen Victoria

The popularity of Buffalo Bill's Wild West with the British royal family is clearly reflected in a first-person memoir by the inimitable Nate Salsbury.[5] The occasion was a command performance before Queen Victoria at Windsor Castle, June 26, 1892. The extensive interpretation of the performance for her majesty allowed Salsbury more direct contact with the queen than any other member of the show troupe in all of their royal appearances. Her majesty had indicated she would be "highly honored" if the Wild West management would allow the Cossack riders to perform; she was intrigued as well by Buffalo Bill's Winchester:

Wild West at Windsor

This polite request was construed, as it always is in England, to be a mild sort of command. . . . As the Cossacks only consumed about twelve minutes in their performance, I concluded that, no matter how startling it would be, it would hardly compensate for all the trouble of getting them down to Windsor, so I determined to take the whole outfit, and do something worthy of the occasion. To this end I engaged a train of cars, and loaded enough of our outfit to give a representative performance, leaving enough members of the company in London to satisfy the public, which was easily done, when it was explained to the afternoon audience that Colonel Cody had gone to Windsor by Royal command.

I preceded the company by one train, and repairing to the Castle, found Colonel McNeill, the Equerry for the day, awaiting my coming. He told me that I had carte blanche to use any part of the ground on the east side of the castle, and at once the servants of the castle began to environ the lawn with sheep fold fences. These fences are movable, and readily adjusted themselves to the purpose, which was to create a complete oval, inside of which we were to work. At the lower end of the lawn, a large tent was erected, in which was spread a splendid luncheon for the company when they should arrive. On the battlements of the castle wall was placed the canvas pavilion for the Queen and her immediate household. A carpet was spread over the rough stones, and a number of comfortable chairs were placed upon it. In due course the train bearing Cody and the rest arrived, and they were escorted to the castle ground, and after the company had lunched and otherwise refreshed themselves, I sent word to the Equerry-in-Waiting that we awaited Her Majesty's pleasure. The Queen (Victoria) indicated her desire to have the performance begin at once and so her pony carriage was driven around to the state apartments, and from there to the pavilion on the wall. The walls of the castle at that point are not less than fifteen feet wide. Her Majesty alighted from the carriage with difficulty, and was assisted by her Scotch Gillies to her chair in the pavilion.

Major Burke let his hair down, and we knew the afternoon was bound to be a success, for whenever the

Major let his hair down the world stood in awe. Her Majesty requested that someone connected with the Wild West should be with her to explain to her anything that she might not understand, and I nobly threw my-

RED SHIRT,
The Fighting Chief of the Sioux Nation.
BUFFALO BILL'S WILD WEST.

WA-KA-CHA-SHA (RED ROSE),
The Girl-pet of the Sioux.
BUFFALO BILL'S WILD WEST.

Red Shirt: The Fighting Chief of the Sioux Nation, ready for Wild West performance.

Wa-Ka-Cha-Sha (Red Rose), The Girl Pet of the Sioux. Both subjects photographed in England, ca. 1887. A number of descendants of Red Rose are still living at this writing, including her children.

PRINCE OF WALES.

B-2

Portraits of the Prince of Wales and Princess Alexandra, ardent fans of the Wild West.

self into the breach, and was escorted with much ceremony to the pavilion. Don't suppose for an instant that I look back on that experience with any but feelings of respect and admiration, for the methodical conduct of the whole affair. While there was much ceremony, there was also much courtesy shown to us. As I entered the pavilion, I removed my hat, as any gentleman would do in the presence of ladies in an enclosed place. After I was introduced to the Queen, I gave the signal to begin the performance, and took my place beside the Queen's place as Scout, Guide and Interpreter for the occasion. Noticing that I was standing, and uncovered, Her Majesty said, "Mr. Salsbury, please put on your hat, as I feel a strong draft here, and please take a chair."

"Your Majesty," said I, "I am very comfortable."

"But I would be more comfortable if you would take a chair."

All this is very commonplace I know, and I would not record it here except that it struck me at the time as being very thoughtful on the part of a woman who is not obliged to consider anything while in the pursuit of pleasure. Being an American, I followed the etiquette of such an occasion by addressing the Queen as Madame, after the first acknowledgment of her imperial title. An Englishman would have been required to address the Queen constantly as Majesty.

Our performance lasted the better part of an hour and a quarter, and during that time the Queen evinced the utmost interest in all she saw, and plied me with questions innumerable regarding the people in the show. And withal, she displayed a nice discrimination in her inquiries, which were all of a sensible, information seeking sort. As for instance:—while Cody was shooting glass balls, she turned to me and said, "Mr. Salsbury, what arm is Colonel Cody using?"

"He is using the Winchester rifle, Madame," I responded, "An American firearm."

"Ah," said she, "a very effective weapon, and in very effective hands."

Buffalo Bill standing by Wild West stagecoach; taken by Goldies, which enjoyed "the Patronage of Royalty and the Marquis and Marchioness of Bute," 66 Queen Street, Cardiff. John Y. Nelson armed to ride in protection. Note run-down condition of coach.

Distinguished Visitors to Buffalo Bill's Wild West, London, 1887.

Labels within illustration:
H.R.H. Princess of Wales
H.M. the Queen
H.R.H. Princess Beatrice. Battenberg
Countess of Dudley
Grand Duchess Serge of Russia
H.R.H. Princess of Saxe-Meiningen
H.R.N. Princess Mary Adelaide
Duchess of Leinster
Princess Louise
Queen of the Belgians

At a point in the performance when the Cossacks were doing their horseback work, Prince Henry of Battenberg, who was standing in the rear of the pavilion, said to the Queen in German, "Mamma, do you think they are really Cossack!" Before the Queen had time to reply to him, I said, "I beg to assure you, sir, that everything and everybody you see in the entertainment are exactly what we represent it or them to be."

Her Majesty turned to the Prince and said, "Prince, I think we had better speak English for the rest of the afternoon." Princess Beatrice, who was sitting beside the queen, was much amused at her husband's discomfiture, and smilingly said to him, "Mon chere, vous avez recu' votre premiere lecon Americaine." I immediately replied, "Oh Madam, j'espere non." At this there was a general laugh, which I wish Burke could have heard, for he could have used the incident in his own way in his description of the affair.

When the show was over, the Queen requested that Cody be presented to her, and after thanking me for assisting her to enjoy the Wild West, she arose, and was escorted to her carriage by her ever present body guard of Gillies. I sent for Cody, who came in his buckskins, and he was presented to the Queen, just before she started on her afternoon drive around the grounds of the castle. Her Majesty was very gracious to Cody, and complimented him very highly for the delightful afternoon she had enjoyed, and wished him good luck for the future.

Cody and I were then invited to the Equerry's apartments, where we were urged to partake of a lunch. We compromised by another act of self-sacrifice on my part, for as Cody did not drink anything that summer, I did duty for both of us in a glass of wine. The whole thing was delightfully informal, and wound up by our each being presented with a memento of the occasion in the Queen's name. Cody received a beautiful watch charm, and I was complimented with a scarf pin, set in diamonds, and bearing the Royal Monogram.

Distinguished Visitors . . . London 1887, lithograph with Buffalo Bill at *center* and portrait busts of ten distinguished aristocratic ladies, among them Queen Victoria, the Princess of Wales, Princess Mary Adelaide, the queen of the Belgians, the Countess of Dudley, the Duchess of Leinster, the Princess of Saxe-Meiningen, and Grand Duchess Serge of Russia. A. Hoen and Company, Baltimore, 33 × 23 inches.

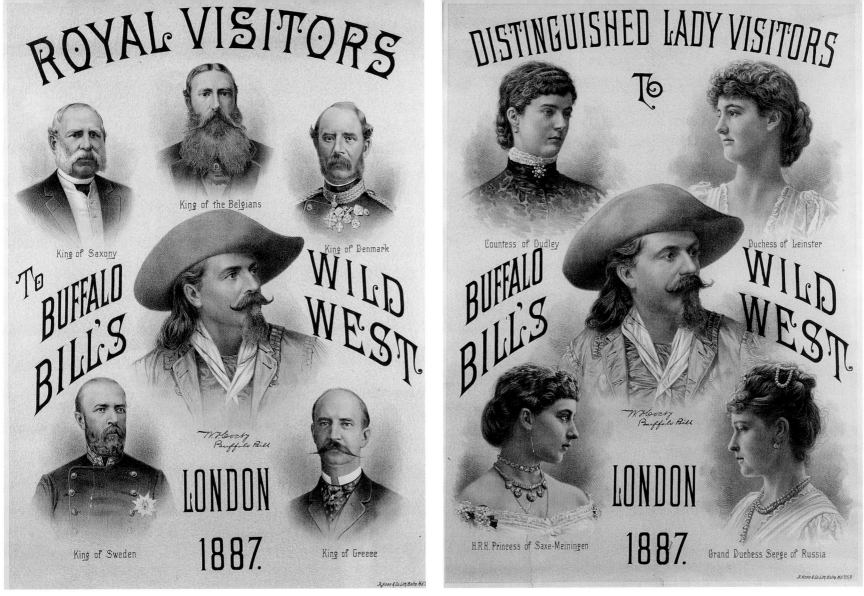

Our experience that afternoon proved to me that the higher you ascend the social scale in England, the more delightful do you find the surroundings. During the entire afternoon there was an utter absence of what a Montana lady would call "Lugs."

Of course there was ceremony, but it was of the purely perfunctory kind that goes with all court proceedings in Europ, or for that matter in all monarchies.

The Wild West had taken the United Kingdom and continental Europe by storm. The troupe's fame in those countries had not gone unnoticed in the American press. Salsbury and Burke recognized that America was now more eager than ever to enjoy the edifying entertainments of Buffalo Bill's Wild West. The time was ripe for yet another triumph—this time in the Midwest.

(*left*) *Royal Visitors . . . London 1887*, lithograph by A. Hoen and Company. The five royal gentlemen accompanied by a regal Buffalo Bill in the *center*. 26½ × 19½ inches.

(*right*) *Distinguished Lady Visitors . . . London 1887*, lithograph by A. Hoen and Company. The lovely royal ladies with host Buffalo Bill at *center*. 26½ × 19½ inches.

King of Sweden

King of the Belgians

King of Greeee

H.R.H. Prince of Wales.

Gen'l Lord Wolseley.

W.F.Cody
Buffalo Bill

18

W. E. Gladstone.

King of Saxony

King of Denmark

John Bright, M.P.

Distinguished Visitors to Buffalo Bill's Wild West, London, 1887.

WM. SWEENEY.
Buffalo Bill's Wild West.

(*left*) *Distinguished Visitors . . . London 1887.* This lithograph corralled six distinguished aristocrats, two politicians, and a general. Also by A. Hoen and Company. 33 × 23 inches.

(*top*) William Sweeney, a cornetist and longtime leader of the Wild West band, ca. 1887.

(*above*) Westley Richards 12-gauge double-barrel shotgun, custom-built for Buffalo Bill; pictured in the frontispiece to this chapter; serial number 6625; 30-inch side-by-side barrels. *Top* rib detail of Westley Richards shotgun, includes legend MADE FOR THE HON. W. F. CODY BUFFALO BILL NEBRASKA. At the same time, a similar gun, serial number 6624, was given as a present from Buffalo Bill to Johnny Baker.

Back cover from the 1895 Buffalo Bill's Wild West Historical Sketches and Programme, F. Less and Ridge Printing Company, Fifth Avenue, New York City. Shows "World's Wondrous Voyages from Prairie to Palace Camping on Two Continents." Poster by A. Hoen and Company of same image, 1894, 29 × 41½ inches.

Unique album kept by Colonel Cody and identified on an inside front page as "Col The Hon W. F. Cody's Souvenir & Invitation Book. Paris. May. 1889." The voluminous contents, all sixty-eight pages, are overflowing with business and personal calling cards, letters, invitations, telegrams, and menus, many from royalty and notables of the day. Among devoted visitors to the Wild West was artist Paul Gauguin. 12⅜ × 9¾ × 1⅝ inches; clothbound with leather spine and corners.

A similar volume, kept by Cody in London in 1887, is in the Buffalo Bill Historical Center collection. Both volumes reflect the seemingly unending avalanche of admiring communiqués directed at Cody on these European visits.

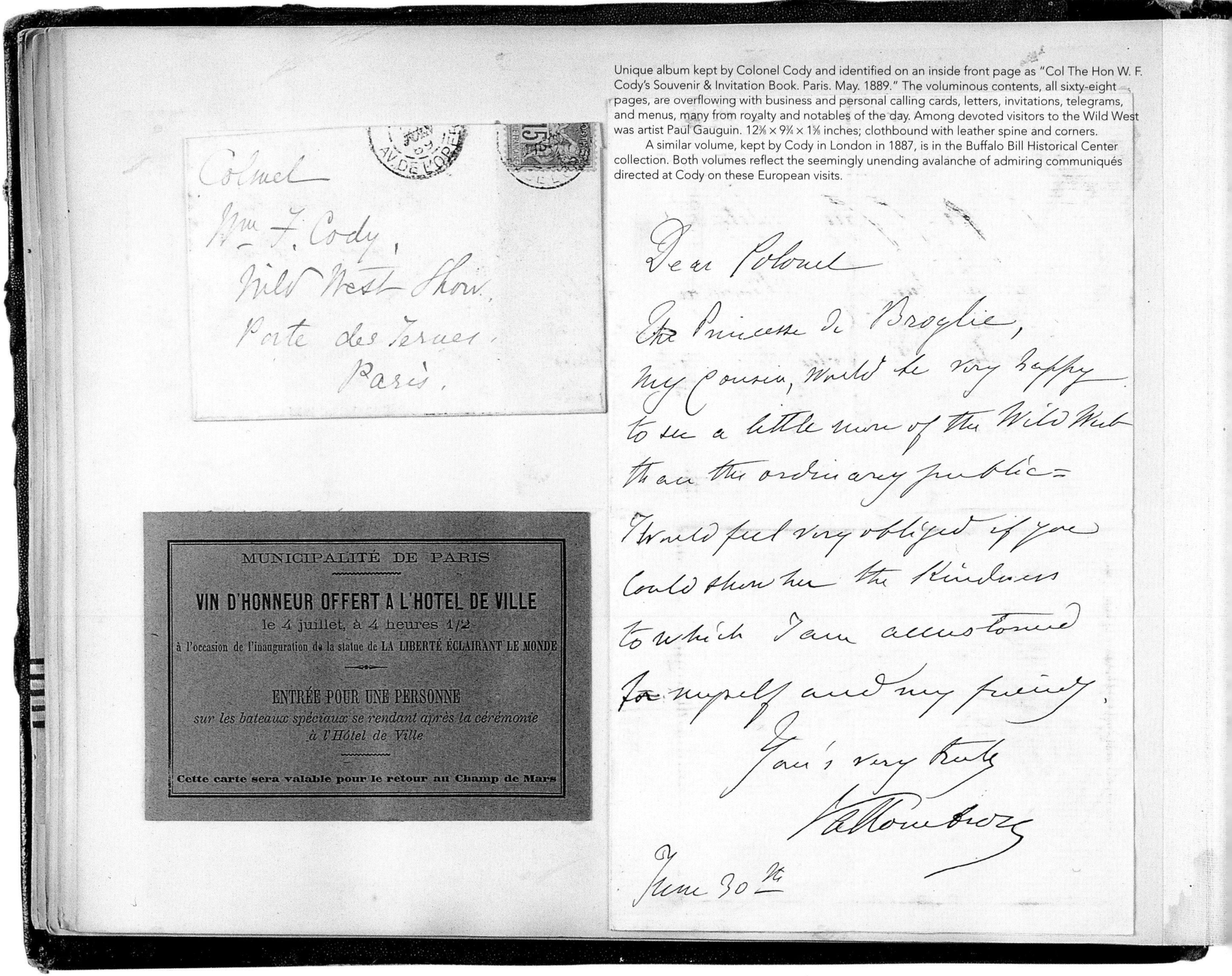

Colonel
Wm F. Cody,
Wild West Show,
Porte des Ternes,
Paris.
MUNICIPALITÉ DE PARIS
VIN D'HONNEUR OFFERT A L'HOTEL DE VILLE
le 4 juillet, à 4 heures 1/2
à l'occasion de l'inauguration de la statue de LA LIBERTÉ ÉCLAIRANT LE MONDE
ENTRÉE POUR UNE PERSONNE
sur les bateaux spéciaux se rendant après la cérémonie
à l'Hôtel de Ville
Cette carte sera valable pour le retour au Champ de Mars
Dear Colonel
The Princesse de Broglie,
my cousin, would be very happy
to see a little more of the Wild West
than the ordinary public —
I would feel very obliged if you
could show her the kindness
to which I am accustomed
for myself and my friends,
Yours very truly
June 30th

République Française

LIBERTÉ * ÉGALITÉ * FRATERNITÉ

La Municipalité de Paris

prie M. *Le Colonel W. F. Cody*

de vouloir bien assister à l'inauguration de la
Statue de la « Liberté éclairant le Monde » offerte
à la Ville de Paris par les Résidents Américains
qui aura lieu le 4 Juillet 1889, à 2 heures ½
midi, sur le môle de Grenelle.

Place reservée

Cette Carte est rigoureusement personnelle et n'est valable que pour une seule personne

Chief Justice Bermudez

Supreme Court of Louisiana

Fourth of July 1889

Buffalo Bill's Wild West Camp

PARIS

COMPLIMENTS OF CODY AND SALISBURY
TO THE BOYS IN CAMP PARIS
FOURTH OF JULY 1889

Municipalité de Paris

FÊTE FRANCO-AMÉRICAINE DU 4 JUILLET 1889

A deux heures inauguration de la statue
de la Liberté éclairant le monde sur le môle
de Grenelle.

A quatre heures et demie un vin
d'honneur sera offert aux invités dans les
salons de l'Hôtel de Ville.

Lithograph from celebrated Rosa Bonheur portrait, dated 1889. At *bottom right*, statement within scroll motif: LE DERNIER DES GRANDS/ECLAIREURS/PORTRAIT À CHEVAL DU/COLEL W. F. CODY (BUFFALO BILL)/D'APRÈS LE CÉLÈBRE TABLEAU DE/ROSA BONHEUR. A number of these were done in German and French, etc. 52 × 36½ inches. A particularly renowned artist of her day, Bonheur was a devoted admirer of Cody.

The Codys enjoying jolly England. Sitting in the boot of this English coach, quite in contrast to a Wild West stagecoach, Buffalo Bill himself, next to daughter Arta, who signed and dated the photograph. Nate Salsbury might be seated behind Arta. Her father has a cigar in his left hand. Cody enjoyed coaching so much that he purchased a coach of this style, as recorded in the 1887 ledgers.

Pair of nickel-plated and ivory-gripped Colt Single Action Army revolvers, presented to the Buffalo Bill Historical Center by W. F. Schneider, a longtime associate of Buffalo Bill. The pistols with matching leather holsters had been presented to Schneider by Cody himself. Serial numbers 54057 and 54070, .44-40 caliber, 7½-inch barrels.

Orator Henry Marsh Clifford

Proudly wearing an identification badge custom-made for the Earl's Court season in 1892, Henry Marsh Clifford was a distinguished thespian, well known in Great Britain for Shakespearean roles and a number of other plays. His interest in the theater began in boyhood. Quoting from a tribute published in *The Era* on April 25, 1903:

Originally intended for a commercial career, Mr. . . . . Clifford started as entering clerk in a wholesale hosiery warehouse in Wood-street, City [London], and for several months passed a humdrum existence. . . . But his youthful aspirations did not that way tend. At last the opportunity he had longed for came. An amateur performance of Hamlet at Myddleton Hall, Islington, was about to take place in aid of the Shakespearian Tercentenary Fund [1864]. Mr. Clifford was offered the part of Horatio, which suited him admirably. That performance settled the question as to his calling in life. . . . [He also played in] A Midsummer Night's Dream . . . Henry IV (second part), followed by Romeo and Juliet . . . [and as] William the Conquerer, in a production of Harold, also the King, in Hamlet, returning to Manchester for a revival of The Sultan of Mocha, Madame Angot, Grand Duchess, and The Bridge of Sighs, playing Louchard . . . Richard III, and Macbeth . . . [numerous plays and locations of performances listed, over a period of several years]. In 1890 he went to Tyne Theatre, Newcastle, under Augustus Harris, for the everlasting Giant. In 1891 a change came o'er the spirit of his dreams. He joined Colonel W. F. Cody (Buffalo Bill) as orator for his Wild West Show, and with him he remained for two years, terminating at Earl's-court. Then he returned to Drury-lane, under Sir Augustus Harris, to play the Ogre—another name for giant. The summer season Mr. Clifford spent at Blackpool Winter Gardens with Wm. Holland, and that was the last of his Giant performances. Then followed a tour of Two Orphans as the Count, also a tour of Ben-my-Chree as the Bishop, and a pantomime engagement at Cardiff. The autumn of 1898 found him at the Vaudeville, as the Sergeant, in Her Royal Highness. Engagements in The War Correspondent, &c, followed; and last year he toured with On Her Majesty's Service for Walter Melville.

The hand-engraved armorial-styled badge is of silver and measures three-and-a-half inches high. The cabinet-card photograph is of approximately the period of Clifford's stint with the Wild West.

Likely an identification badge worn for the Earl's Court season, 1892. The hand-engraved armorial-style badge is of silver and measures 3½ inches high. Cabinet-card photograph is of approximately the period of Clifford's stint with the Buffalo Bill's Wild West troupe.

Prime Minister Gladstone and wife and others, with the Wild West band, London, ca. 1887.

Buffalo Bill (fifth from *right*) and about a dozen men having a picnic on Staten Island, New York.

The Powell Brothers

Three of Buffalo Bill's most trusted and loyal friends were the Powell brothers, all doctors, and each with colorful nicknames. Most of the written record on the Powell brothers deals with "White Beaver," Dr. David Franklin Powell, who was known as a sometime drinking pard of Cody. While a contract surgeon at Fort McPherson and at the North Platte barracks, Powell officiated in the placement of degrees on Cody as a Mason. Dr. Powell was a dabbler in show business and had some skill as an exhibition marksman. Cody and White Beaver were also involved in various business deals, "White Beaver's Cough Cream"—a pseudo-Indian remedy—among them.

The 1886 Wild West program pictured Powell and presented the customary complimentary biographical study:

The life of White Beaver (Dr. D. Frank Powell) bears all the colors and shades of an idyllic romance; his character stands out upon the canvas of human eccentricities in striking originality, and finds never its counterpart, save in stories of knight-errantry. . . . A born plainsman, with the rough, rugged marks of wild and checkered incident, and yet a mind that feeds on fancy, builds images of refinement, and looks out through the windows of his soul upon visions of purity and fields elysian. A reckless adventurer on the boundless prairies, and yet in elegant society as amiable as a school-girl in the ball-room; evidencing the polish of an aristocrat, and a cultured mind that shines with vigorous lustre where learning displays itself. A friend to be valued most in direct extremity, and an enemy with implacable, insatiable, and revengeful animosities. In short, he is a singular combination of opposites, and yet the good in him so predominates over his passions that no one has more valuable friendships and associations than these strange complexities attract to him. . . .

A description of White Beaver is not difficult to give, because of his striking features; those who see him once are so impressed with his bearing that his image is never forgotten. He is almost six feet in height, of large frame, and giant muscular development; a full, round face, set off by a Grecian nose, a handsome mouth, and black eyes of penetrating brilliancy. His hair is long, and hangs over his shoulders in raven ringlets. In action he is marvellously quick, always decisive, and his endurance almost equals that of a steam engine. His appearance is that of a resolute, high-toned gentleman, conscious of his power, and yet his deference, I may say amiability, attracts every one to him. He is, in short, one of the handsomest as well as most powerful men among the many great heroes of the plains.

The "Night Hawk" Single Action Army Colt revolver, serial number 127109. A sister of the Powell brothers, Meta Bigelow Powell, had mistakenly thought this revolver was once property of Lieutenant Colonel George Armstrong Custer. It was actually property of Night Hawk and is now considered to have been a present to Dr. George Powell from Buffalo Bill. The revolver is a Frontier Six Shooter, and the engraved and carved mother-of-pearl grips have their left panel inscribed NIGHT HAWK with the date 1876. Colt factory ledgers indicate the engraved, nickel-plated, carved Mexican pearl-gripped .44-40 caliber, 7½-inch revolver was a shipment of one, sent to the Western Arms and Cartridge Company, Salt Lake City, Utah, August 23, 1888. Cased in a rare presentation-quality velvet-lined hardwood box, with rare satin ribbon embossed M. HARTLEY COMPANY/NEW YORK. In the photo, Cody with the three Powell brothers: George standing at *left*, William, standing *right*, and David, seated *right*. See also frontispiece to this chapter.

In addition to his other qualifications peculiarly fitting him for a life on the plains, he is an expert pistol and rifle shot; in fact, there are perhaps not a half-dozen persons in the United States who are his superiors; his precision is not so great now as it once was, for the reason that during the past three or four years he has had but very little practice, but even now he would be regarded an expert among the most skillful. For dead-center shooting at stationery [sic] objects he never had a superior; his eyesight is more acute than an eagle's, which enables him to distinguish and hit the head of a pin ten paces distant, and this shot he can perform now nine times out of ten. Any of his office employees will hold a copper cent between their fingers and let him shoot it out at ten paces, so great is their confidence in his skill; he also shoots through finger-rings held in the same manner. One very pretty fancy shot he does is splitting a bullet on a knife-blade, so exactly equally dividing it that the two parts will strike in a given mark; he also suspends objects by a hair, and at ten paces cuts the hair, which of course he cannot see, but shoots by judgment. Several persons have told me that they have seen him shoot a fish-line in two while it was being dragged swiftly through the water.

White Beaver and Buffalo Bill have been bosom friends and fellow-plainsmen since boyhood. History records no love between two men greater than that of these two foster brothers.[6]

Not as much is known of Dr. George Powell, "Night Hawk," but he did have a large firearms collection, and among these pieces were several given to him by Buffalo Bill. In a three-page article about White Beaver in *A History of La Crosse, Wisconsin, 1841–1900*, the author devoted a paragraph to the younger Powell brothers:

Dr. Frank Powell's two younger brothers lived in Lanesboro, Minnesota—George, a veterinarian, and William, a drug clerk. He sent both to a "medical college" for one year. They then opened offices in La Crosse, George as a general practitioner and William as a specialist in "Women's diseases." Both claimed to have had service in the Indian country and to have been given Indian names, the former "Night Hawk" and the latter "Blue Eyed Bill" [he was also known as "Broncho Bill"]. In those times there were many persons with a strange mental illusion, i.e., that there was some connection between the traditions of the Indians and good medical treatment. The Powells took full advantage of this idea.[7]

The "Night Hawk" Colt Single Action revolver is the most notable of the firearms that figure in the association between Cody and the Powell brothers. Another piece of interest is a Sharps Model 1874 Sporting Rifle (serial number C53101). The rifle bears similar inscriptions to the "Night Hawk" Colt, with a presentation from Night Hawk to White Beaver, and in turn to Prentiss Ingraham.[8] It is reasonable to deduce from the Night Hawk, the Sharps Model 1874, and other guns and documentary sources that gifts of firearms between Buffalo Bill and his friends were a part of their friendship. These were objects with great moment and meaning in their lives as frontiersmen and apostles of the frontier.

Finely engraved Single Action Colt, serial number 129108, made ca. 1889, its backstrap inscribed WILLIAM F. CODY. Blued and case-hardened finish; hard rubber grips, 4¾-inch barrel with etched marking of FRONTIER SIX-SHOOTER, .44-40 caliber. Displayed at the Buffalo Bill Historical Center. (Courtesy of Howell Howard)

REVOLVERS
OFFERTS
PAR LE PRINCE DE GALLES
ROI D'ANGLETERRE
AU
CAPITAINE LÉON MARTIN
Premier Tireur du Monde

Presentation pair of exquisitely decorated and gold-plated Smith & Wesson New Model No. 3 single-action revolvers. Presentation placard notes that this was a gift from the Prince of Wales to Captain Martin, premier pistol shooter of the world. Serial numbers 27378 and 27379, .38 caliber, 7½-inch barrels, leather-covered case of wood, lined in plush velvet.

GENERAL NELSON A. MILES AND "BUFFALO BILL"

VIEWING HOSTILE INDIAN CAMP, NEAR PINE RIDGE, S. D., January 16th, 1891.

A.Hoen & Co. Baltimore.Md.

14

(left) General Nelson A. Miles and "Buffalo Bill" viewing hostile Indian camp, near Pine Ridge, S.D., January 16th, 1891; imaginative lithograph by A. Hoen and Company, 28½ × 19 inches.

(above) Studio portrait of Buffalo Bill, accompanied by Julia Cody Goodman, with typed legend: "Wm. F. Cody and mother-sister Julia Goodman." Cody regarded Julia as both sister and surrogate mother.

(opposite) Indians and U.S. officials before Indian encampment at Pine Ridge, January 16, 1891, including W. F. Cody, John M. Burke, and Kicking Bear. Photograph by Grabill, number 3630. On occasion of Cody's unsuccessful effort at intervening on behalf of the military in an attempt to save Sitting Bull.

Facade of the Buffalo Bill Historical Center, Cody, Wyoming. The center houses the Buffalo Bill Museum, the Whitney Gallery of Western Art, the Plains Indian Museum, the Cody Firearms Museum, and the McCracken Research Library

Aerial view of the Autry Museum of Western Heritage, located in Griffith Park, near the Los Angeles Zoo. Grassed area to *right* portion of site is where celebrated annual fund-raising galas are held.

Chapter 5

✧✧

PORTFOLIO OF TREASURES:
BUFFALO BILL HISTORICAL CENTER AND THE AUTRY MUSEUM
OF WESTERN HERITAGE

As a tribute to their unique roles in honoring the history and traditions of the West through
public education and entertainment, selected showpieces from the Buffalo Bill Historical Center and
the Autry Museum of Western Heritage are featured in this pictorial section.
As frequent visitors to both institutions, the authors are pleased to have this opportunity to recognize
these two landmark sites for their appreciation and understanding of the life and times
of William F. Cody, his Wild West troupe, and his "pards."

Lucretia Borgia, Buffalo Bill's rifle for dispatching buffalo. Despite its present state, this arm stands supreme as one of the icons of the American West. 34½-inch barrel, .50 caliber.

Carriage or sleigh robe, ca. 1872. Given by Czar Alexander II to Buffalo Bill and by Buffalo Bill to General Nelson A. Miles. Sable, mink, snow leopard and other furs; 93 × 85 inches.

William F. Cody's Congressional Medal of Honor, 1872. Width of star; 2 inches. Back of the star engraved in commemoration of the award.

The Peerless Lady Wing-Shot; poster by A. Hoen and Company, Baltimore, ca. 1893, 28½ × 19 inches. The standing image was based on a photograph. Ample supply of medals pinned on bodice; note star device, frequently seen pinned to her Western-style hat; the rifle is a Marlin, in .32 caliber.

35

Selection of jewelry, gifts to Cody from royalty, *clockwise from left*: gold and diamond stickpin from King Edward VII; gold, diamond, and enamel ring from Luitpold Ludwig, Prince Regent of Bavaria; diamond and gold broach from Queen Victoria (inscription on back includes date, June 15, 1892); and diamond-encrusted gold pocket watch from King Victor Emmanuel III of Italy.

The Scout Buffalo Bill Hon. W. F. Cody, lithograph by the Forbes Company, ca. 1883, 39¼ × 26⅝ inches.

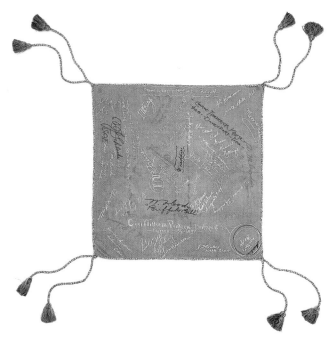

(*left*) Glass pitcher and sugar bowl of the Wild West.

(*bottom left*) Show trunk of Annie Oakley, made of wood, leather, brass, and fabric. 13¾ × 48 × 21 inches. Gift of Mr. and Mrs. William Self.

Pillow cover, embroidered by Annie Oakley, linen and thread, ca. 1887–1897, 20½ × 19½ inches.

Winchester Model 1892 rifle of Annie Oakley's, serial number 41023, .32-20 caliber; signed by J. Ulrich and with owner stamp OAKLEY in arc on left and right side of stock wrist. Gift of Spencer T. Olin.

Custom-made saddle of Buffalo Bill's by Collins and Morrison, Omaha. Silver mounted and extensively hand tooled, ca. 1893, sixteen-inch seat. Headlined "Buffalo Bill's Gorgeous Riding Equipment," a similar saddle was written up and pictured in a detailed article in the *Jeweler's Circular and Horological Review*, May 24, 1893: "A very handsome piece of work has just come from Omaha to Chicago, which deserves mention in THE CIRCULAR. Hon. W. F. Cody, . . . being a citizen of Nebraska, remembers his friends there, and among them the firm of Collins & Morrison, a large saddlery and harness manufacturing firm of Omaha. This Spring he gave them an order for the handsomest saddle they could make, and they sent to him in time for the opening of his show a saddle and bridle which they claim is the finest in America. What makes it interesting to readers of THE CIRCULAR are the silver mountings, which were manufactured in the jewelry establishment of Albert Edholm, by L. J. Kass, silversmith. Mr. Kass learned his trade in the cities of Christiania, Stockholm and Copenhagen, and although he has been long in America and is in advancing years his hand has not lost its cunning. Some years ago he manufactured a steam locomotive, tender and passenger coach, of solid silver, which was ordered as a gift to A. E. Touzalin, who had just been made general manager of the C., B. & Q. R.R. Mr. Kass was at this time in the employ of Max Meyer & Bro. Co.

"The saddle is made of russet saddle skirting, California tanned, on the sweat leather of which are

pictures of Buffalo Bill stamped from a photograph he had taken in Europe, in a standing position, with rifle, sombrero and full hunting or scout's costume. The saddle is mounted with solid silver, of which sixty-five ounces were used. In the seat inlaid in the leather is the name Hon. W. F. Cody, in silver letters one and one-half inches long; the horn is mounted with a silver crescent on which is engraved "World's Fair, Chicago, 1893;" the stirrup plates are elaborately engraved and chased; on each side of the saddle is a buffalo in repousse work; the rim of the seat is of silver, and buttons innumerable stud the handsome leather, two of them especially large and handsome having buffalo heads in repousse. The bridle is finished with loops so that not a buckle is required to hold the bits; two solid silver rosettes are on the sides and a silver plate is on the brow-band engraved with the owner's name. A quirt, the Mexican or cowboy name for whip, also accompanies the saddle, and is made like the bridle, of plaited rawhide mounted with silver.

"Buffalo Bill's friends know his fondness for handsome equipments, and can imagine him in his elegant scout's costume, mounted on his steed caparisoned with these gorgeous equipments, leading his Congress of Rough Riders of the World through daring feats for the edification of World's Fair visitors."

Multicolored gold pocket watch used by Buffalo Bill, gift from King Edward VII, ca. 1890, 2¼ inch diameter.

Wood and silver-plate cane, from Buffalo Bill to Jack Stilwell, 32-inch length. Gift of the Harris Family.

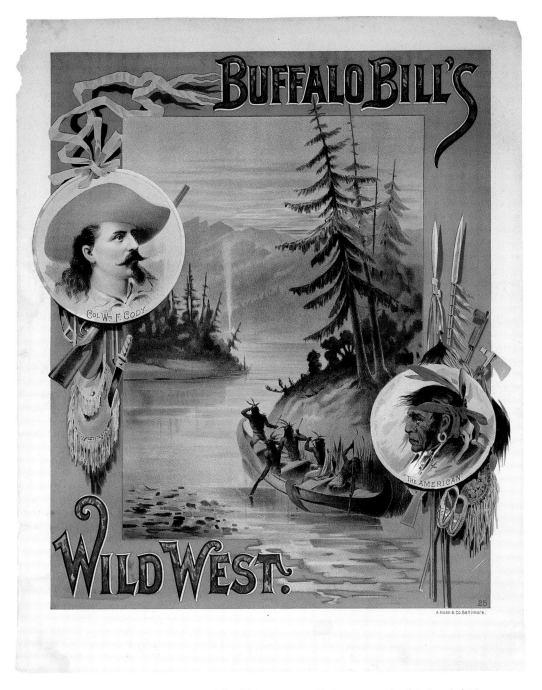

One of the most exquisite of all Wild West posters, with vignette portraits of Cody and of "The American" (an Indian warrior); primary scene of Indians in canoe, gazing across lake at white men. By A. Hoen and Company, ca. 1890, 28½ × 22 inches.

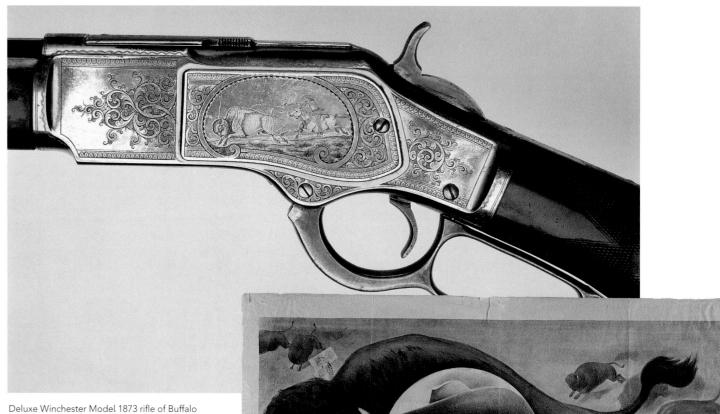

Deluxe Winchester Model 1873 rifle of Buffalo Bill, serial number 494993, .44-40 caliber. J. ULRICH signature on lower left tang; Winchester factory engraver, from a distinguished family of engravers and stockmakers. Sideplate scene depicts the owner and was likely inspired by Wild West program illustration. Gold-plated frame, forend cap, and buttplate; checkered and varnished select walnut stocks.

I am coming—poster made for appearances in France, early twentieth century. Buffalo Bill was so famous that his name or the name of his entertainment was unnecessary to draw crowds. By Weiners, Paris, 29½ × 39½ inches. Two other leading European lithographers for Wild West posters were Stafford and Chaix.

Sterling-silver spoon by Giles, Brother, and Company, depicting Cody lassoing a buffalo; Indian artifacts, lasso, and buffalo-head handle motif. Six inches overall length.

Humorous Italian poster promoting *La Rana*, a political satire magazine; lithograph by Stab. Tip. Lit. A. Noe, Bologna, ca. 1902, 38½ × 26 inches.

Poster of 1912, measuring 25½ × 17⅜ inches. By U.S. Lithograph Company.

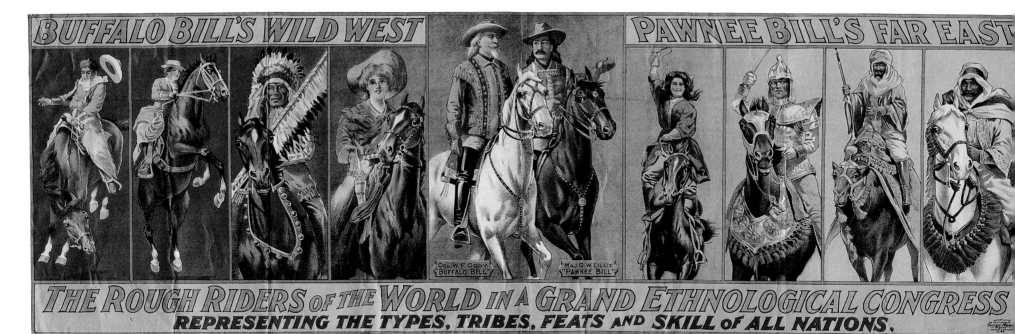

The Wild West and the Far East; poster copyright 1910 by U.S. Lithograph Company, Russell-Morgan Print, Cincinnati and New York; 13¼ × 39½ inches.

Mirror advertisement for Chancellor cigars. 15½ × 21¼ inches, ca. 1920. Maker unknown.

Sterling-silver loving cup, from grateful citizens of North Platte, Nebraska, 1911. Height: 14 inches. Maker unknown.

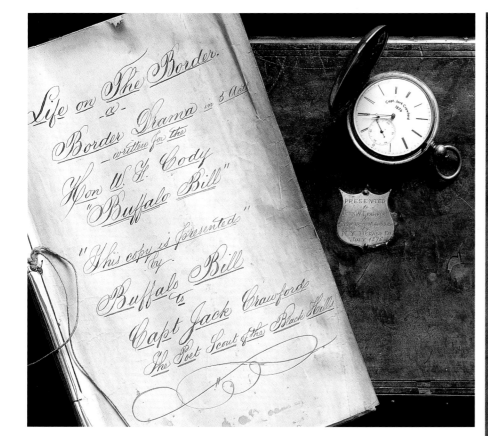

Presentation watch from Texas Jack Omohundro to Captain Jack Crawford; lap desk in background a gift to Captain Jack from the New York *Herald*. Script in longhand, "Life on the Border," written by Captain Jack, for Buffalo Bill.

From a pair of Wild Bill Hickok's Colt Model 1851 Navy revolvers, with holster, dead-man's hand, and ivory poker chips. Revolver number 138813; backstrap inscribed: J.B. HICKOCK [*sic*] 1869.

The Tiffany & Co. etched, silver-plated Smith & Wesson No. 2 cased set presented to George Armstrong Custer, with a pair of his binoculars. The Seventh Cavalry epaulettes worn by Irish mercenary and fellow casualty at the Little Bighorn, Captain Myles Keogh.

Ned Buntline's Model 1874 Sharps Sporting rifle, with factory case, and examples of his dime novels. Serial number 160009; invoiced (at a special discount) to E. Z. C. Judson, Stamford, New York, May 4, 1877, the document noting "assuming that you will become so greatly impressed with its merits, that you will be unable to resist the temptation to tell the *dear public* in some of your 'yarns' as to what you think of Sharps' OLD RELIABLE"; .45 2⅞-inch caliber, 30-inch barrel.

On a background of Doc Carver's Indian quilled-buckskin trousers are his Stetson, one of his ornate show boots, and a beaded gauntlet.

J. and S. Collins saddle of Buffalo Bill's; his portrait tooled onto fender; name on seat; and gold embroidery on back of cantle. Silver conchos from 1881 silver dollars, ca. 1882–1883, and likely one of the first rigs used in the Wild West performances. In 1890, Collins offered clients an identical design, the "Wild West."

Remington over-and-under deringer, an inscribed gift from Cody to the prolific Prentiss Ingraham; serial number 5181; .41 rimfire caliber.

Colt-Burgess lever-action rifle from factory to Cody; background of a Cody beaded jacket. Shotgun custom-made by Thomas of Chicago. Rifle serial number 285; .44-40 caliber.

(*opposite*) Presentation cased set, a gift from Frank Butler to Annie Oakley. The Smith & Wesson No. 3 Target Model revolver, serial number 27941, engraved by one of the Young family, gold plated, and with pearl grips. The First Model Single Shot S&W, number 19091; inscribed on the frame with Oakley's name, with checkered pearl grips, and engraving by one of the Youngs. The Stevens-Gould No. 37 Model, serial 10591, engraved, gold plated, and with pearl grips. All three pistols cased together in a velvet-lined leather set, designed so Oakley could carry the outfit to the center showring, set the case up on an accessory table, and then open the lid—sunlight glistening off the gold-plated finish. Embossed on lid in blind tooling: ANNIE OAKLEY. Deluxe engraved L. C. Smith Monogram Grade (by Hunter Arms Company) double-barrel shotgun, gold inlaid with Oakley's signature on the triggerguard and engraved with banknote-quality portraits on each lockplate. According to extensive documentation from Hunter Arms, decoration was by Tiffany & Co. Hunter's pride in the project was such that the gun, a gift from the company, was displayed for all the employees to admire on completion. Serial number 44937.

Captain Jack Crawford's Colt Model 1878 Frontier revolver and Lightning medium frame .38-40 slide-action rifle, serial numbers 8127 and 29649, respectively. Featured by Crawford in his lecture appearances.

Harry Brennan was one of the key cowboy stars with the Wild West and appears in group photo of cowboys in Europe. Spurs presented to Brennan by maker, G. S. Garcia. Brennan is considered the father of competitive bronco-riding rules for rodeo and was a world champion in 1906. Colt Single Action and matching rig worn by George Gardiner, another cowboy in Buffalo Bill's Wild West; serial number 224513, in .38-40 caliber.

113

Beginning in the early 1880s, the Dodge City Cowboy Band was a prominent feature at social events in that city and was notable for performances at stock-growers' conventions and similar get-togethers. Jack Sinclair served as leader for many years, even after the band officially relocated to Pueblo, Colorado. His extraordinary spurs, baton, and revolver were embellished by a jeweler in Pueblo in the early 1890s. The shirt collar is by S. C. Gallup, a prominent saddler in Pueblo.

Pawnee Bill Model 1892 Winchester, a gift to country singer Jimmie Rodgers. Compare shipping box to cases in the photograph of the Winchester ammo wagon in Chapter 9. Serial number 378806; a .44 smoothbore.

Odille "Dell" Jones left home at age fourteen to join the 101 Wild West show and became well known as a trick rider and roper; at age fifteen, she married Buck Jones. Together, they moved to Hollywood, working as stunt riders. Dell's trunk was used for her personal wardrobe in the 101, and she pasted pictures of friends inside. The cane is a special remembrance of the 101, made from compressed paper of unissued 101 show posters! The clothing, boots, and hat were also hers.

Poster promoting show of Sam Cody, a Texan who became an aviation pioneer in England, underwriting his ventures with a Wild West show. He played off his name, was a Buffalo Bill look-alike, and had some special-order Colt firearms in his arsenal. He was killed in a plane crash in 1913.

Solid-gold steer head with diamond and ruby inlays, a tie bar used by Joe Miller, one of the founders of the 101 Ranch. Later, he gave this to movie star and 101 alumnus Buck Jones.

115

Another 101 Ranch alumnus was Tom Mix. Bohlin spurs, gold and diamond pocket watch, gold and platinum cigarette case, and Cuno Helfricht–engraved Colt Single Action Army revolver all owned by Mix. The Colt revolver, serial number 331793, was one gun in a shipment to Ludwig William Ilfeld, with whom Mix was involved in filmmaking at the time, on November 24, 1915. Factory records also indicate: .32-20 caliber, 7½-inch barrel, silver plated, style 2 engraving, and inscription TOM MIX on barrel, ox head–carved pearl grips (both panels). Some engraved embellishment added at a later date, including the exotic grips of silver with gold signature and TM brand within diamond motif, TOM MIX inscription on buttstrap, and TEXAS RANGER on backstrap.

Charles Gebhardt became a lead performer with the 101 Wild West show; he changed his name to Buck Jones and gained fame as one of the greatest movie cowboys of all time. Colt .45 Single Action revolver, Bohlin engraved, with hint of Jones's Bohlin gun belt. The revolver was a gift for Christmas 1924 from his wife Dell; for the other side of the revolver, see R. L. Wilson, *The Peacemakers*, p. 314 and back endpaper.

Deluxe John Bianchi rig worn by Paul Newman in Robert Altman's *Buffalo Bill and the Indians*.

(*below*) If any of the Hollywood showmen followed in the footsteps of Buffalo Bill, it was cowboy, soldier, actor, and Indian authority Tim McCoy. Well known for his extremely tall Stetson hat, McCoy favored Indian imagery on his boots and shirts and used Bohlin spurs, saddle, and other accoutrements. The beaded gloves were given by him to Iron Eyes Cody, another performer with the show. Items courtesy of McCoy's son, Ronald.

(*opposite*) Joel McCrea gave one of the best interpretations of Buffalo Bill in the movie *Buffalo Bill*. Poster accompanied by pair of fine calf boots worn by McCrea in the film. Among other film stars who portrayed Cody were Charlton Heston and Melvyn Douglas.

Gene Autry followed in the footsteps of showmen like Buffalo Bill when putting together a traveling rodeo in 1939. The Gene Autry Rodeo appeared in Madison Square Garden, Boston Garden, and elsewhere. The consummate showman, Autry brought together great riders and performers; he himself sang and rode for the fans. Here, a show poster, saddle, and pair of chaps accompany his gun belt, Single Action Army, and Martin guitar.

From *left*, a customized William Cashmore 12-gauge shotgun, serial number 9270, 28½-inch barrels; Winchester Model 1873, with presentation stock plaque, a gift to W. R. C. Clarke, son of country gentleman Richard Edward Clarke of Shrewsbury, England. At *right*, the exquisite Stevens .25-20 falling-block rifle, a gift from the factory in the 1890s. Beaded brass-buckled belt of Oakley's own design and make, measures 2¾ x 33½ inches; she undoubtedly also designed and sewed the elaborate stage-shooting cloth for her husband, Frank Butler. *Rifle Queen* rare British souvenir tribute of 1887; adjacent to letterhead with ca. 1885 letter from Butler to gunmaker Freund. *Upper left*, extremely rare signed photo of Miss Oakley with side-by-side shotgun and in lady's print dress and bonnet; not standard attire for exhibition marksperson. Note shooting glove on left hand.

Chapter 6

Annie Oakley

Superstar, Athlete, and Modern Lady

Aim at a high mark and you'll hit it. No, not the first time, nor the second time and maybe not the third. But keep on aiming and keep on shooting for only practice will make you perfect. Finally, you'll hit the bull's eye of success.

Annie Oakley.

These words were hallmarks in the life of one of America's most remarkable figures. Of heroic stature for her time and for all time, Annie Oakley embodied those attributes proudly claimed for Victorian women yet was also imbued with the trailblazing qualities of the "modern woman." Further, as one whose living was derived from her brilliance with guns, she was in the unique position of being a woman who consistently and decisively beat men at the game they thought was theirs. All this from a tiny package five feet tall and weighing 110 pounds.

Born Phoebe Ann Moses on August 13, 1860, in Woodland, Darke County, Ohio, the girl who became Annie Oakley had what she later termed "an inherent love for fire-arms and hunting." By the time she was twelve, Oakley was supporting her impoverished family—Quakers who had migrated from Pennsylvania—by shooting game as a market hunter.

In her autobiography, "The Story of My Life," Oakley wrote fondly of her youth:

We children went to school and picked brush and helped Daddy build . . . fences around our little Ohio farm.

We always butchered a young beef when cold weather set in, and its hide was tanned for our shoes. Eight pairs, and the measurements were taken and the shoes made, from Daddy down. The tops were [stitched] with heavy white floss for the younger children. . . .

The corn was gathered, cribbed and the fodder all shocked. The hogs were butchered, the fine hams shoulders and bacon, together with the sausage were all smoked with hickory chips. A quarter of fine beef was smoked and hung for winter.

Pickled green beans, sweet pickles, preserves, dried apples, peaches and pears were ready for the winter. Cabbage, beets, turnips, parsnips, fine radishes, and a supply of good apples were all tucked away in dry straw beds and covered with turf so they would not freeze.

Two cows gave us milk, cream and butter. There were chickens and plenty of new laid eggs.

Black walnuts, hickory nuts, butternuts and hazel nuts had been garnered and a fat rick of wood stacked against the woodyard fence.

Suddenly and traumatically, the idyllic farm life changed. Her father went off "one morning to lay in coffee, sugar and rice and to take the corn and wheat to the mill, 14 miles away, to be ground. A blizzard came on and Daddy did not come home." Finally, her father returned at midnight, his hands frozen, his speech gone. The wagon remained outside in the snow, not to be dug out for another two days. "The doctor came to see daddy all winter but in [February 1866] he died." Like an early Hollywood melodrama, the family lost the farm and moved to another, on a cash lease for two years.

Oakley's natural affinity for the out-of-doors led her to learn trapping and shooting: "Somehow we managed to struggle along for several years. I remember how I struggled to master the 40 inch cap and ball Kentucky rifle, which I finally did, much to my pride, though my mother and sisters thought my prowess with the gun was just a little tomboyish. I was eight years old at the time."

Becoming a Champion Shooter

When Oakley was about ten, the family split up and she, then living at the county home, was hired as a live-in helper on the farm of a couple whom she later identified only as the "He-Wolf" and the "She-Wolf." She recalled the nightmare of abuse in her new position in her autobiography:

The "He-Wolf" explained that he wanted a small girl as company for his wife. The girl would have no work, he said, except to watch the three week old baby boy. He looked at [my sisters], then asked . . . about me.

When . . . told . . . how I loved to trap and shoot, he said, "Why she should go right home with me. We have quail, squirrel, partridges, pheasant and rabbits. She could go after them when she liked."

[Within two weeks my mother consented] and I went away with him.

All went well for a month. Then the work began to stack up. . . . Mother wrote for me to come home. But they wouldn't let me go. I was held prisoner. They wrote all the letters to my mother telling her that I was happy and was going to school. . . .

One night I nodded over the big basket of stockings I had to darn. Suddenly the "She-Wolf" struck me across the ears, pinched my arms and threw me out of doors into the deep snow and locked the door. I had no shoes on and in a few minutes my feet grew numb.

I was slowly freezing to death.

Oakley begged to be sent back to her mother but to no avail. After three miserable years, she ran away. Family and friends prevented attempts by the "He-Wolf" to reclaim her. Although the nightmare had ended, the influence of those scars on her personality and her career must have been enormous.

Shooting came naturally to Oakley, and the woods of Darke County proved a paradise. In an interview in 1914, she recalled those days:

When I first commenced shooting in the field of Ohio, my gun was a single-barrel muzzle-loader and, as well as I can remember, was 16-bore. I used black powder, cut my own wads out of cardboard boxes, and thought I had the best gun on earth. Anyway, I managed to kill a great many ruffed grouse, quail and rabbits, all of which were quite plentiful in those days. . . .

My game [was] exchanged for ammunition, groceries and necessities. A few years ago, I gave an exhibition at Greenville, and met the old gentleman who had bought all of my game [Charles Katzenberger]. He showed me some old account books showing the amount of game he had purchased [for hotels and restaurants in the vicinity of Cincinnati and Dayton]. I won't say how much, as I might be classed as a game-hog, but any man who has ever tried to make a living and raise a family on 27 acres of poor land will readily understand that it was a hard proposition, and that every penny derived from the sale of game shipped helped.

As a teenage shooting sensation, in an age where marksmanship, at least for most men, was a crucial part of one's identity, her reputation spread rapidly.

In 1881, a widely known traveling professional exhibition shooter, Irish-born Frank Butler, came to Cincinnati. Jack Frost, whose Cincinnati hotel was a buyer of Annie's game, arranged a match in the nearby North Star–Woodland area. Butler—whose skill was such that he felt only Adam Bogardus and Doc Carver could beat him—had no idea he was about to be defeated fair and square by a petite twenty-one-year-old girl! Later, he spoke of what became a pivotal moment in both their lives:

I got there late and found the whole town, in fact, most of the county out ready to bet me or any of my friends to a standstill on their 'unknown.' I did not bet a cent. You may bet, however, that I almost dropped dead when a little slim girl in short dresses stepped out

to the mark with me. . . . I never shot better in my life, but never did a person make more impossible shots than that little girl. . . . I was a beaten man the moment she appeared for I was taken off guard. . . . Never were the birds so hard for two shooters as they flew from us, but never did a person make more impossible shots than did that little girl. She killed 23 and I killed 21. It was her first big match—my first defeat.

In Oakley's version of the match, Butler lost on the final shot. The event remained a matter of excited conversation around Cincinnati for months thereafter. Already cool under pressure, Annie Moses was on her way to becoming history's most famous markswoman. In Butler not only did she find a manager, coach, press agent, shooting assistant, and all-around aide-de-camp, but she also found a husband.

They courted during the year after that match, by mail, while Butler continued his travels. He was then in partnership with an exhibition shooter named Baughman and later with a John Graham. The future of the Frank Butler–Annie Moses romance was somewhat complicated by the fact that he was ten years her senior and a divorcé with two children. Despite Victorian convention, the two were devoted to each other. Butler, a sometime poet, sent a Christmas missive, entitled "Little Raindrops":

There's a charming little girl
She's many miles from here
She's a loving little fairy
You'd fall in love to see her
Her presence would remind you
Of an angel in the skies,
And you bet I love this little girl
With the rain drops in her eyes.

On June 20, 1882, Phoebe Ann Moses became Mrs. Frank E. Butler.

Joining Buffalo Bill's Wild West

According to "The Story of My Life," Mrs. Butler did not become part of the show until Graham became ill. When it was clear that Oakley had extraordinary show-business potential, Butler set about not only to train her as the consummate exhibition shooter but to perfect her skills as a horsewoman, to master the art of training dogs, develop a stagecraft savvy, and improve her ability to read and write. At the same time, she adopted the stage name of Annie Oakley, the exact origin of which remains a mystery.

With practice and experience their program—first billed as Butler and Oakley—became Annie Oakley, the Peerless Wing Shot. In the first few years, the couple played variety theaters and skating rinks, traveled on a budget, and lived in moderately priced hotels. "I owe whatever I have to [my husband's] careful management. Of course, we were poor when we started, and I remember him saying to me, 'Well, Annie, we have enough this week to buy you a pretty hat.' "

In 1885, the act got its big break: signing with Buffalo Bill's Wild West. The timing was perfect. An approach the previous year, at New Orleans, had been unsuccessful; Cody then had too many shooting acts. In March 1885, Captain Bogardus and his sons quit the show, which left an opening. The Butlers approached Cody again, and this time were hired.[1] She became a headliner, one of the best paid of all the performers next to Cody himself, while Butler played a supporting role. Cody and the Butlers became good friends; Oakley was known to Buffalo Bill as "Missie," while she addressed him as "Colonel." Recalling their first introduction to the troupe, she wrote: "The cowboys, Mexicans and Indians . . . were all lined up on

Early carte de visite of Oakley with Butler and their poodle, George. Rifles by Stevens, with plated breeches, ca. 1883. Note her costume, customarily of skirts at knee length, with fancy fringes; she used starched collars and attractive cuffs and had a tiny waist and ample bodice. A silver star was customarily on her Western-style hat, and she performed with her dark hair down on her shoulders, then considered risqué. A reporter wrote of the multitalented star: "She told me . . . she cut and fitted every pair [of pearl-buttoned leggings] she wore as it was impossible to have them made to suit her." Here was a superstar who was a "crack shot in petticoats" and could design, cut, and sew her own outfits.

According to Butler himself, Oakley became the act as a result of his having trouble hitting a target. After missing several times, a spectator said, "Let the girl shoot." Oakley, though she had never practiced that shot, picked up a gun and hit the target on the

second try. Butler recalled, "The crowd went into an uproar, and when I attempted to resume my act I was howled down, and Annie Oakley continued. . . . From that day to this, I have not competed with her in public shooting. . . . She outclassed me."

George, who had been a part of Butler's act, then of Butler and Oakley's, and then of Oakley's herself, caught pneumonia while the show was playing Cleveland, Ohio. His death was the only bad news for the Butlers in the 1885 show season. On burial, George was wrapped in a satin and velvet table cover, used in the act before they joined the Wild West.

No cabinet cards shot in half came to the attention of the authors, though this difficult practice was a staple in her act for many years. Theater tickets came to be called "Annie Oakleys" because of the holes punched in them by ticket takers.

Oakley's amazing shooting skills and quickness meant that some thought she was cheating: "It is all so very easy and simple, and looks it, that the hardest thing in the world is to make people believe that there is no cheating. . . . Occasionally, I have indeed missed on purpose, because it looks so easy if you never miss and the spectators might think there was a trick in it. Once while performing in France, a gentleman threw his watch up, thinking she would miss it: He has never been able to tell the time by that watch since. [It was doubtful] whether he ever picked up a hundredth part of the pieces."

Remington-Beals rifle, engraved and in .32 rimfire caliber. One of the Oakley gun collection that eventually ended up in the hands of a relative. Total production of this model numbered not more than eight hundred, ca. 1866–1868. The only factory-engraved example known, this piece is also one of the earliest of Oakley's firearms. Displayed in the National Firearms Museum, Fairfax, Virginia, and accompanied by a gold-plated Hibbard .410 shotgun, given by Oakley to friend Mary Estell Beavers on a visit to Oklahoma.

Autographed cabinet photo of Sitting Bull with peace pipe. His friendship with Annie Oakley led to her historic nickname. The meeting between the two celebrities took place in St. Paul, Minnesota, on the night of March 19, 1884. The chief was in attendance in box B at the Olympic Theater, where Oakley was performing with the Arlington and Fields Combination. When she came onstage, and snuffed out a candle with a rifle shot, the chief came to life. She recalled: "He was about as much taken by my shooting stunts as anyone ever has been. . . . He raved about me, and would not be comforted. His messengers kept coming down to my hotel to enquire if I would come and see him. I had other things to do, and could not spare the time." When Sitting Bull sent sixty-five dollars to Oakley's room, that got her attention: "This amused me," she said, and she arranged to see him in the morning, returning the money, accompanied by a signed photograph of herself. The next day, she wrote that the chief "was so pleased with me, he insisted upon adopting me, and I was then and there christened 'Watanya Cecila,' or 'Little Sure Shot.' "

one side, Mr. Cody and Mr. Salsbury were on the other side, and my husband and I were called upon to pass down the line, meeting all of them. There I was facing the real Wild West, the first white woman to travel with what society might have considered an impossible outfit."[2]

Annie Oakley Press Biography

In an age of dime novels and rapidly evolving press gimmickry, not everything one read about public figures was accurate—much as is the case today. Probably the most widely published tribute, portions of which were on her letterhead for several years as well as in show programs, summed up her life through about 1887.[3] Clearly, she was destined to carve out a unique and celebrated career. The press agents promoting Buffalo Bill's Wild West were developing the arts of public relations and advertising to new and ever more grandiose heights, and in Annie Oakley they had a subject fully deserving of their talents:

At the age of fourteen she had paid off a mortgage on her father's homestead with money earned from the sale of game and skins, shot and trapped by herself alone. Then came a local reputation, and with improved firearms she attracted wider notice. For the past five years she has been shooting before the public with great success; though, like the modest little girl she is, she never laid claim to being a champion, yet in 1883–4 Richard K. Fox [proprietor, *The Police Gazette*] of New York had so much confidence in her ability that he offered to back her against any other so-called champion. Sitting Bull, the great Indian chief, after seeing her shoot in St. Paul, Minn., adopted her in the Sioux tribe, giving her the name of "Watanya Cicilia," or Little Sure Shot.

The first two years before the public she devoted to rifle and pistol shooting, and there is very little in that line she has not accomplished. At Tiffin, Ohio, she once shot a ten-cent piece held between the thumb and forefinger of an attendant, at a distance of 30 feet. In April, 1884, she attempted to beat the best record made at balls thrown in the air, using a 22 cal. rifle. The best record was 979, made by Dr. [John] Ruth. Miss Oakley used a Stevens 22 cal. rifle, and broke 943. Her first attempt at clay pigeon and trap shooting was made about three years ago, in Cincinnati, shooting with such fine shots as Bandle, McMurchy, and other noted shots.

In February, 1885, she attempted the feat of shooting at 5,000 balls in one day, loading the guns herself. In this feat she

Mid-1880s cabinet photograph of Oakley in shooting costume, with sash of Mexican style; customary medals on chest. Holding a Stevens tip-up rifle, with a tip-up long-barrel pistol at *lower left;* a double-barrel shotgun and Spencer pump shotgun at *lower right.* Oakley had blue eyes, "white and perfect teeth," and a "low sweet voice full of melody." She was also ambidextrous and could fire handguns from either hand or from both hands at the same time. Her skills as a shot were such that she nonchalantly said, "I feel now and then as if I could not miss." The Springfield (Massachusetts) *Republican* stated: "She handles a shotgun with an easy familiarity that causes the men to marvel and the women to assume airs of contented superiority."

used three 16-gauge hammer guns. The balls were thrown straight away from three traps fifteen yards rise. Out of the 5,000 shot at, she broke 4,772. On the second thousand she only missed 16, making the best 1,000 ball record—984. This feat was accomplished near Cincinnati, Ohio, in less than nine hours.

Besides the thousands of exhibitions she has given, she has shot in thirty-one matches and tournaments, winning twenty-five prizes. Her collection of medals and fire-arms, all of which have been won or presented to her, is considered the finest in America.

She has hunted in many of the game sections of America and Canada, and says, with a pardonable pride, that she has shot quail in Virginia, ducks in Illinois, prairie chickens in Kansas, and deer in Northern Michigan. Her style and position at the trap is considered perfection by such critics as Budd, Stice, Erb, Bogardus, Cody, Carver, and the English champions, Graham and Price. Shooting clay pigeons, she has a record of 96 out of 100. At live pigeons, her best record is 23 out of 25, made in a match for 100 dollars.

Besides her wonderful marksmanship, Miss Oakley is an accomplished housewife, as the neat and cheery appearance of her tent on Arapeah Avenue, within the encampment, and those visitors who are fortunate to be invited within cannot but admire the quiet and lady-like manner in which she acts the part of hostess. The Prince of Wales was particularly pleased with [Oakley], and complimented her most highly as did also the Queen.

Annie Oakley: Superstar

Because her act was made up of masterful shooting skills, combined with humor, drama, pantomime, and even pouting, Oakley's show captured the attention of the audience. She left them—after her customary ten minutes—wanting more. Within her act were moments spent standing in concentration, considering the difficult shot she was about to attempt. These were followed by little kicks, revealing her pleasure at making the attempt successfully. The New York *Sun* reported that "when she doesn't hit a ball she pouts. . . . She evidently thinks a good deal of her pout, because she turns to the audience to show it off." Columnist, writer, and friend Amy Leslie referred to Oakley as "an actress of no mean pretensions" in which comedy was "half the performance."

Studio photograph of Oakley with hammerless shotgun and fresh rabbit, harkening to her days in Darke County, Ohio. Note stylish shooting clothes with high collar and rakish hat.

Press agent Dexter Fellows stated: "There never was a question that she deserved her position as star performer. . . . She was a consummate actress, with a personality that made itself felt as soon as she entered the arena. Even before her name was on the lips of every man, woman, and child in America and Europe, the sight of this frail girl among the rough plainsmen seldom failed to inspire enthusiastic plaudits."

Elegant shooting costume and needlepoint by Oakley. Medals on shooting cloth, with presentation trophy against which is leaning an engraved, gold-plated, and pearl-gripped Stevens tip-up pistol.

Performing in New York City, 1886

The Wild West's summer 1886 season at Erastina marked Annie Oakley's ascent to stardom. The New York *Herald* said that New Yorkers were so keen to see the Wild West that they "trod on each other's corns with glee." Unfortunately for Oakley, the fifteen-year-old markswoman Lillian Smith had also been hired to perform. It was as a result of their intense rivalry that Oakley's birth date was changed to 1866, thereby eliminating six years of the age gap between them—though even in her early forties Oakley retained a look of youth.

In another match, at the Newton, New Jersey, fair, against English shooter William Graham (October 7, 1886), Oakley put up $100. The day before the shoot, in practicing with Butler, she cut her left hand between the first and second fingers so deeply that five stitches and a sling were required. During the next day's shoot, so determined was she to go through with the event despite the handicap, she broke the stitches and blood flowed. At that, Butler intervened to stop the match, saying her gate receipts could be given to the spectators. Oakley later recalled: "I retired, amid cheers."

Dedicated to hunting and fishing, Oakley went out of her way to promote these sports, as evident from this 1893 article of hers:

I am of the opinion that many people who have seen my shooting exhibitions, are under the impression that I neither favor [nor] indulge in any other pursuit with the shotgun and rifle. Such is not the case, however, for I am an enthusiast in the matter of game shooting and angling, and only engage in exhibition shooting for the money there is in the practice. Truly I long for the day when my work with the rifle and gun will be over with, and when I can take to the field and stream as often as true inclination may lead me there.

Nothing can be more noble and natural than to hunt and fish, and every body should love the gentle chase and the study of gameland, for the health and pleasure in these pursuits, if nothing else.

I have had quite my share of sports afield having hunted and fished in eleven countries, and bagged all species of game from the snipe to the grizzly bear.

For field shooting I use a light hammerless, 20-gauge double gun of the best make. Nobody should trust their lives behind a cheap gun—one costing less than one hundred dollars. I use the nitro powders, and have never considered them dangerous. They are all right if the shells are correctly loaded.

As for dogs, I favor Gordon setters. In the matter of field dress, I can not advocate any one costume, for I have been in the habit of clothing myself to suit each climate, always taking good care to keep my feet dry and warm.

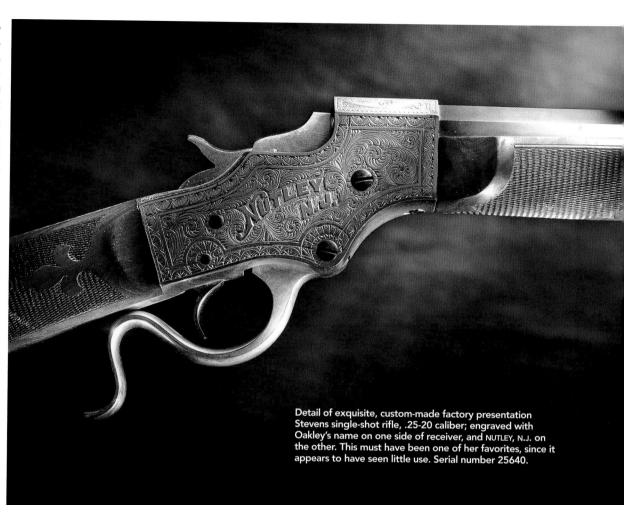

Detail of exquisite, custom-made factory presentation Stevens single-shot rifle, .25-20 caliber; engraved with Oakley's name on one side of receiver, and NUTLEY, N.J. on the other. This must have been one of her favorites, since it appears to have seen little use. Serial number 25640.

Fishing has always been a favorite sport with me, and if I have not handled the rod as expertly as the gun I have certainly used it with as much true gentle sporting exhilaration at all times.

For troutfishing I use a feather-weight rod—one of four ounces—and with this I have creeled many fine two-pound specimens. For bass and pickerel I use an eight-ounce split bamboo rod, rigged with a single click rubber reel and a silk enameled line. I prefer live bait for bass and pickerel, but often fly-fish for bass in waters

where they seem to prefer the fly in preference to any other lure.

Still, with all my experience, I have much to learn in shooting and fishing, and I learn something every day.
ANNIE OAKLEY.[6]

With Buffalo Bill's Wild West in Europe, 1889–1891

Thirty-two million people attended the Paris Exposition Universalle of 1889, one of the features of which was the recently completed Eiffel Tower. At first, the crowds of Paris did not understand the Wild West show. To quote Oakley: "[The French audience] sat like icebergs at first. . . . There was no friendly welcome, just a 'you must show me' air. . . . I wanted honest applause or none at all." Luckily, her performance was so dramatic and impressive that Nate Salsbury said Oakley had saved the show: "The icebergs were ready to fight for me during my six months stay in Paris." She was the toast of Paris, as she had been the toast of London.

After the close of the Paris engagement, the Butlers toured Europe with the Wild West, spreading Oakley's fame and popularity ever farther. While in Munich, she saved Prince Luitpold of Bavaria from being trampled by Dynamite, the show's most dangerous bronco, shoving him to the ground in the nick

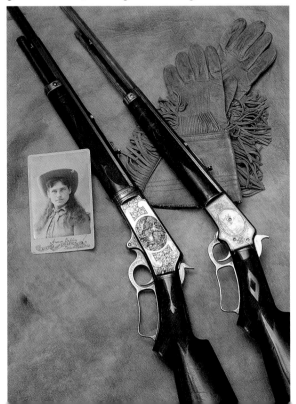

of time. She observed wittily, "I suppose I am the only person alive that ever knocked a ruling sovereign down and got away with it. . . . Well sir! He was a good sportsman. He got up and enjoyed the rest of the show five times as much for his realization that he was seeing the real thing and not a parlor fake." The appreciative prince send a diamond bracelet to Oakley and a cigarette case for Dynamite's handler, Jim Mitchell.

Oakley made the same impression on the sportsmen of the Continent as she had in the United Kingdom. Medals, loving cups, stuffed birds, and more were presented to her. When meeting the Emperor Francis Joseph I at his Schonbrunn palace in Vienna, she observed:

He arose with a smile and greeted me with a handclasp, but his face looked tired and troubled. I decided that being just plain little Annie Oakley, with ten minutes' work once or twice a day was good enough for me, for I had at least my freedom.

I spent part of a day on the emperor's game preserve, where we had planked fish and other dainties in our honor. The preserve was seven miles out, and we arrived [back in the show arena] one hour late, the only time in all my professional career that I was ever late, barring one time when three minutes were lost because someone stopped to greet me as I was entering the arena.

Annie Oakley was a favorite of the Marlin Firearms Company, as proven by these two presentation rifles from the company collection, displayed at the Buffalo Bill Historical Center. At *left*, Model 1893, serial 419119, gold and platinum inlaid, .38-55 caliber, a gift from the factory in 1917, then offered by Miss Oakley as a fund-raiser for war bonds.

Shooting and Fishing magazine ran a piece, commenting on the Butlers and two new Marlin rifles, ca. 1894: "Met on Broadway last Thursday Frank Butler, the efficient business manager of Miss Annie Oakley. He was arranging for a trip to England, where he goes immediately upon the close of the Buffalo Bill show season. Butler had just received two rifles from the Marlin company for Miss Annie's use, and each was a beauty—lock, stock, and barrel."

Some of the Marlin rifles she is known to have owned are: a Model 1891 .22 lever action; a Model 1889 presented to her by John M. Marlin (engraved and inscribed ANNIE OAKLEY, serial number 98560, .32-20 caliber); and the deluxe Model 1897 rifle, serial number 342637, pictured at *right*. Illustrated rifles presently on loan to the Cody Firearms Museum by the Marlin Firearms Company.

On holiday in England, while the Wild West was in winter quarters at Benfield, Alsace-Lorraine, the Butlers were shocked to learn of press reports of her supposed death from lung congestion in Buenos Aires! Frank Butler cabled to Buffalo Bill: "Annie just finished a full Christmas platter. No truth in report."

Enjoying her several obituaries, Oakley wrote to one of the journals, "I am, indeed, very grateful for your many kind words in my obituary." Butler told a friend that he had "answered more than a half thousand letters and telegrams. . . . How the report of her death gained circulation I do not know."

On the Wild West's second tour of Europe, beginning in April 1891, her most famous feat of marksmanship took place: shooting the ash off a cigarette held either in the hand or in the mouth of the future Kaiser Wilhelm—done at Wilhelm's own request! Oakley made the difficult shot with her usual aplomb, though in later years it was said that she missed a unique opportunity to eliminate the possibility of World War I.

Annie Oakley: Autograph Collector

Oakley's autograph book was the subject of press reports from time to time and was one of her most treasured possessions. The most detailed description of it found by the authors was in an article from the *American Field* by William Bruce Leffingwell, published between 1893 and 1895. The present whereabouts of the book remain a mystery:

The autograph album of Annie Oakley is a rarity. A noted collector offered her $500 for it, which she refused. He wanted her to name a price, which she declined to do as it was not for sale at any price. Among the noted names it contains are, Hilda de Clifford, considered one of the handsomest women of the nobility of Europe; Ralph Payne-Gallwey, the celebrated English writer; Henri Journu, the best revolver shot and one of the best pigeon shots in Europe; Capt. C. E. Speedy, who in the Soudan war disguised himself, stole into the enemy's camp at night and secretly regained the British flag which had been captured, and returned it to his regiment on the following morning. The Queen presented him with a jeweled watch as a partial recognition of his bravery. The album also contains the signatures of the whole of the Chinese and Japanese Embassy of London; Lord Wantage, the head of the Wimbledon Camp where international shooting is done; the King of Senegal, who wanted to buy Annie Oakley from Col. Cody, and offered 20,000 francs for her (he wanted her to kill off the wild beasts of his country and was very indignant that he could not buy her); Ira Paine, the greatest pistol shot that ever lived—his last signature, as he died a few days after signing his autograph; the Prince of Annam, a black prince; Thos. A. Edison, whose signature attracts more attention than any king or prince; the King of Boudon; Crispi, the Italian statesman who was invited to attend a banquet at the Queen's castle. Crispi's wife was not invited and he indorsed on the invitation that if his wife was not invited within a certain number of hours he would turn Italy into a republic. This was sent to the Queen. Crispi's wife went with him. Also the autographs of Prince Regent of Bavaria, the reigning prince; the Duchess of Cumberland, sister of the Prince of Wales; Lady Paget; the Duchess of Holstein, mother of the Empress of Germany; the King of Wirtemberg and his Queen; Mary Adelaide, the Duchess of Teck; the Duke of Teck; Victoria Mary of Teck, whose husband is the second heir to the throne of England; Lord Windsor; Lord Ruthven; Philipe, Duke of Orleans; Rain-in-the-face, the Indian chief who killed Gen. Custer, and who emphasized the importance of his autograph by saying that it was the first time he ever gave it without charging a dollar. Scores of prominent Americans have signed their autographs also, which makes it one of the most valuable albums in the world.

Also quoted in the press were tributes paid to Oakley in the autograph book:

"To the loveliest and truest little woman, both in heart and aim in all the world."
W. F. "Buffalo Bill" Cody

"You can do everything that can be done in the shooting line and then some."
Mark Twain

"When you feel like changing your nationality and profession there is a commission awaiting you in the French Army."
President Carnot of France

A description of a private exhibition by Oakley appeared in the *Shooting Times and Kennel News* of London on December 27, 1890.

Miss Oakley

At the Royal Oak Hotel Shoot, on Wednesday, the company, which included some of the best shots in the south of England, were unexpectedly gratified by having the opportunity of witnessing some of the wonderful shooting feats of Miss Annie Oakley. This lady, the "Little Sure Shot" of Buffalo Bill's troupe (which is now at Strasburg), is on a vacation visit for a few weeks to Mr. and Mrs. Graham, of the Royal Oak, they being old American friends, Mr. Graham having shot four or five matches with her during his sojourn in the States. Gentlemen will have the opportunity of seeing her performances at the next few meetings, and of taking part against her at her own game at the traps. The feats she performed on the ground seem scarcely credible. Thus, if Mr. Butler or Mr. Graham held out in their hands a visiting card edgeways to her, at a distance of from ten to twenty paces, she invariably hit the edge of the card with bullet from a pistol. With a Holland .320 bore double rifle she hit successively with bullets two marbles thrown in the air; and with a 10-shot repeating rifle she split at the first shot, a piece of brick as it was thrown up, and then knocked to pieces with a second shot, one of the fragments as it descended. Half-pence and coins the size of a sixpence were also struck with bullets in the same way. Thirteen competitors came out for the handicap. . . . Over a dozen sweepstakes were subsequently shot off, and a pleasant dinner party afterwards sat down at the Royal Oak.

From New York City to Nutley

A pleasant village, convenient to New York City, Nutley, New Jersey, was selected by the Butlers as the site of their first home, custom-built to their own design. The town was known as an artists' colony, but of all

the residents the Butlers were the most distinguished. Construction began in 1892, and the couple moved in prior to Christmas 1893. Due to their heavy travel schedule, it was said that the house was built without closets because they were so accustomed to living from trunks. Though that was not the case, the legend grew out of her remarking that the house was built "without thought to closets."

Indicative of the Butlers' appreciation of their public, Oakley wrote on Christmas Eve to *Field and Stream* magazine: "I beg of all friends and sportsmen not to pass by without stopping. They will find the latch string on the outside. No matter if they shoot a $30 or a $300 gun their welcome will be just the same." For a "sportsmen's room" in the house she asked readers for contributions of mounted heads, skins, and birds—each to be identified with the name of the donor. A number of donations were received, among them a solid-silver table service, presented to

Posed in shooting garb, with Winchester Model 1892 half-octagonal-barrel rifle; special front sights, shotgun-style composition buttplate, and checkered select-walnut stocks, serial number 41023 (see Chapter 5). Other images taken at the same time show only two medals on her bodice; note frilly collar, no gloves, a ring on fourth finger of her right hand. Other pictures reveal muscular hands like those of a modern bodybuilder. Ca. 1894.

Shotgun *at top*, a 20-gauge Parker, presented by Oakley to fellow exhibition shooter Curtis Liston (Young Buffalo Wild West show) on December 25, 1918. Serial number 181313, 27-inch barrels, with special safety device mounted on left side of receiver. Note length of stock for both guns, the other the exquisite Stevens presentation rifle, indicative of manufacture to Miss Oakley's measurements. Target at *center* shot by her in 1922. In photo at *upper left* she holds a deluxe L. C. Smith shotgun, which had her portrait on each lockplate and her signature in gold on triggerguard. At *right*, rare flier published at the time of a shooting demonstration at Greenville, July 25, 1900; this is one of the most sought-after of all Annie Oakley ephemera.

Most prized of all Annie Oakley posters, by the Enquirer Job Printing Company, Cincinnati, Ohio, ca. 1901. Note vignette of shooting from a bicycle. In an undated note in *American Rifleman* magazine, a drawing of Oakley riding and shooting was accompanied by the following:

FANCY RIFLE SHOOTING AWHEEL

"Annie Oakley, the world-famous rifle and pistol shot . . . also shoots at difficult moving targets and flying glass balls while riding her wheel.

"She has been an enthusiastic wheelwoman since 1889, and claims to have been the first woman to ride a wheel in London. She began shooting from a wheel in 1892, and rides with both hands off when performing this feat."

Little Annie Oakley . . . lives at hotels, but has her own private tent at the Cody show most beautifully decorated and comfortable as a parlor. It is carpeted with a cheery red brussels, has lounges, couches, rockers and satin pillows galore. The prairie canvas is ornamented with favorite pictures, stacks of guns, powder flasks, buffalo horns and a thousand relics and souvenirs of her triumphs everywhere. She has casks of delicious wine sent to her from England and though the charming little gunner does not care for the vintage luxuries herself, she is cordial enough to insist upon everybody who calls tasting the harmless and rich English wine.

About the guns, the Buffalo *Courier* wrote on August 25, 1895:

Out in the little dressing tent which Miss Oakley occupied at the Driving Park last week were her guns, about 25 in number, and her ammunition. She does not stay in the tent nights, but her ammunition-boy guards the guns constantly, as they are very valuable.

"I have a great many guns which have been given me by various gun factories—enough to line this tent on all four sides if they were stacked as closely as I could stack them. I usually take some of them on the road with me to show people, but most of them are at my home in New Jersey.

"You see, the guns I use are all made to order, and those which are given me are just for ornament. Some of them are very handsome, however, the handles being of various kinds of wood. I also have a handsome pearl-handled revolver."

Treasured silver cup, inscribed: TO MISS ANNIE OAKLEY FROM HER OLD HOME FRIENDS GREENVILLE, OHIO JULY 25, 1900. Prominently pictured *top center* on the poster, *left*.

Oakley and Butler in Retirement

Retired from exhibition shooting and distracted by her libel suits, Oakley's shooting diminished substantially while Butler's career as a marksman resumed. A professional with the Union Metallic Cartridge Company (UMC), Butler was a major figure in the promotion of the rapidly growing sport of trapshooting. The number of trapshooters in 1906 was estimated at one hundred thousand, and in that year alone he was present at no less than two hundred matches. In the next few years, the expansion of the sport was substantial, promoted adeptly by such firms as UMC, Remington, Winchester, and Parker.

Following the resolution of most of her libel suits, Oakley sometimes joined her husband on his travels. Exhibitions she fired in were covered enthusiastically in the press, and by 1907 her schedule rivaled the amount of shooting she had done in her career with the Wild West.

One of her demonstrations was at the March 1911 Sportsman's Show at Madison Square Garden in New York, where she was received with customary enthusiasm. Soon thereafter, the Butlers spent the season under contract with the Young Buffalo Wild West.

Along with Oakley, the "most noted quartette of sharpshooters ever on a single program" were Captain Adam Bogardus, Curtis Liston, and Captain O. G. Stevens. A reporter for *Billboard* gushed that "Annie Oakley looks as though she had discovered the secret that Ponce De Leon sought so long in vain. . . . She is as bright and alert, as when I saw her a slip of a girl with long braids 25 years ago when I was a kid."

The Butlers continued with the Young Buffalo Wild West troupe for the 1912 and 1913 seasons, and her shooting, according to the Rochester *Herald*, was "the feature of the entire exhibition." When the show appeared in Greenville, Ohio, the *Courier* honored their native daughter with a glowing tribute: "She has made a proud record by her wits, her activity, her genius, her naturalness, her brightness of mind, her courteous nature and her bravery." She gave complimentary tickets for use by wards of the Darke County Children's Home, along with free ice cream and refreshments.

Tired from all the traveling, at the close of the Young Buffalo season of 1913, Oakley rode in her last preshow parade and shot in her last Wild West exhibition. The show was in Marion, Illinois, on October 4, 1913. Soon, the Butlers moved into a new residence on Maryland's eastern shore, at Hambrooks Bay, near Cambridge, described by Butler as a "sportsman's paradise."

Ever restless, the Butlers soon had a new acquisition, an English setter named Dave and trained by Oakley. One of Dave's many tricks was allowing her to iron his ears; another was sitting in place while she shot an apple off his head. During this tranquil period, she wrote her monograph, *Powders I Have Used,* a publication of the Du Pont Company.

Taking aim to shoot an apple off the head of the remarkable Dave. Pinehurst, ca. 1920. Rifle appears to be a Remington Model 12 .22. After the apple had been shot from his head, Dave, according to an article in *Outlook,* "threw what was left of the apple into the air, caught it in his mouth and danced about in an ecstasy to exhibit the puncture." Oranges were also shot from his head and chalk from his teeth. An Annie Oakley Remington Model 12 .22-caliber rifle, serial number 600125, is in the Buffalo Bill Historical Center collection.

(*opposite*) From the Nutley Museum, unique photograph showing Annie Oakley firing her Colt Single Action Army Flat-top Target revolver. Her husband holds the target, while Oakley sights using a mirror!

The Butlers had also discovered Florida and began traveling there during the shooting days with the UMC team. They enjoyed four balmy Florida winters beginning in 1911, staying at the Lakeview Hotel in Leesburg. Among the game shot by the couple in the off-season were wild turkey, quail, deer, opossum, and dove. The fishing was also to their liking.

Once on a hunt, Oakley killed a threatening rattlesnake:

I happened to look at the ground less than a pace distant and saw the rattler. It was coiled and ready to strike. Another step forward and I would have received the strike. I never did such quick thinking in my life as was crowded into that second. I sprang backward and at the same instant raised my gun and fired quickly. . . . [Having shot off the head] I took it back to the hotel with me and had it skinned, and the skin tacked to a board.

The snake measured out at an impressive seven feet, four inches!

Occasional exhibition shooting and hunting kept her eye sharp, but the life of a retiree was not for Oakley: "You can't cage a gypsy," she said. "We had our own boat, dogs and oyster bed, and settled down to 'live happy ever after.' But I couldn't do it. . . . I went all to pieces under the care of a home. As Mr. Butler puts it, I am a complete failure as a housekeeper." Butler said that her "shooting record is much better than her housekeeping mark. . . . Riding, shooting and dancing came natural to her but she's a rotten housekeeper. Her record in this department is seven cooks in five days."

A tour the couple made of the United States in the summer of 1915 reflected their restless ways: with a rented car, the planned itinerary ran from Cambridge, Maryland, all the way to San Francisco. Among those whom the Butlers saw on the extended journey was an aging and sickly Buffalo Bill Cody, looking "feeble [and seeming] to be living his last days."

The Carolina Hotel, Pinehurst, North Carolina

A golfing and vacationing paradise, the Carolina Hotel drew the Butlers as visitors from as early as January 1909 for a trapshooting tournament in which Oakley competed. During the 1915 season, the Butlers stayed at the Carolina, the first of several long-term visits. Among the celebrity guests at the society spa were fellow shooters John Philip Sousa and Theodore Roosevelt and such luminaries as Warren G. Harding, Alexander Graham Bell, John D. Rockefeller, and Will Rogers.

The Carolina's lady guests were destined to be introduced by Oakley to the sport of shooting, while others had the opportunity to refine already existing skills. Oakley's coaching was restricted to women only. The lessons began by accident when the shooting star had overheard a wealthy New Yorker comment to another in the hotel's ballroom, "My, how I wish I were a man so that I could shoot." Oakley responded with an introduction and the remark, "Your sex does not prevent you from learning to shoot."

Soon, Oakley was teaching the art of shooting at the trap and rifle range. Butler began coaching male shooters as well. Their way at the Carolina was paid, and they enjoyed the company, the sportsmanship, and the shooting. Her coaching also extended to other resorts, particularly the Wentworth in Portsmouth, New Hampshire. The Butlers made a practice of wintering at the Carolina and summering at the Wentworth. The general consensus was that Oakley's skills as a shooter had not diminished, even though she was in her fifties.

World War I and the Butlers

With the start of the Great War in Europe, Oakley reflected on her shooting feat with Prince Wilhelm: "If I shot the kaiser, I might have saved the lives of several millions of soldiers. I didn't know then that he would swing the iron fist and shake the universe. Perhaps it was well for both of us that humans lack foresight."

Oakley offered to raise a regiment of women, intended for home defense. In a telegram to Secretary of War Newton D. Baker she declared: "I can guarantee a regiment of women for home protection every one of whom can and will shoot if necessary." This was clearly an idea ahead of its time.[11] She had also volunteered her services during the Spanish-American War. Her views on granting the vote for women, however, were less egalitarian and did not place her among the suffragettes: if "only the good women voted," she said, she would be supportive of the cause.

Not having the opportunity to raise her regiment, Oakley supported the war effort by visiting military camps and firing two exhibitions daily before thousands upon thousands of soldiers—the expenses assumed by her and Butler. Performing her feats before Camp Crane in Allentown, Pennsylvania, she "drew cheer after cheer from the soldier boys as she performed one feat after another."[12]

The *New American Shooter* in October 1918 quoted her as saying:

Honestly, words fail me when I attempt to describe my reception at the camps where I gave exhibitions. I'm the happiest woman in the world because I had the opportunity to 'do my bit' in a way which was best suited to me.... It has been my good fortune when with Col. W. F. Cody to shoot before thousands of enthusiastic people ... and there have been some proud and happy moments in my life when I rode into the big tent and heard the cheers of the thousands. But those days can't compare with the experiences I so recently have had when I was entertaining the boys who will fight for us 'over there.'

(*clockwise from upper left*) Several snapshots in an album kept by Oakley and Frank Butler. Eager pointer reaches out for a freshly hunted quail.

A string of birds taken by Oakley, with the enthusiastic pointer.

The pointer appears tired out, but not the shooter, with her game bag.

On point, but "nothing there."

The reward.

nothing there.

Dave, known as "The Red Cross Dog," helped by sitting on a stool, to which was attached a sign: "I am doing my bit are you? Let Me Find Your Money for the Red Cross." Money was placed in a handkerchief, then brought to him to take the scent. The handkerchief was hidden somewhere within a hundred yards of his post. Dave would proceed to find it, and the money was then donated to the Red Cross. Not once did Dave fail to find the funds. His keen nose and intelligence raised thousands and thousands of dollars.

Due to the costs, all borne by the Butlers, in time the exhibitions ceased. And then the war ended—suitably celebrated by the Butlers with an exhibition by Oakley and Dave in Pinehurst.

The Invincible and Generous Miss Oakley

When the New York *Tribune* published in the "Conning Tower" column a report stating that Annie Oakley was no more a "short-skirted, dashing girl of the plains, but a little old lady with spectacles and knitting," Oakley responded with a strongly worded rebuke:

> *My Dear Mr. Conning Tower Man:*
> *What did I hear you say? 'She is a little white haired lady who wears spectacles and knits?' I am guilty as to the first two charges owing to two trains trying to pass on the same track, but did not succeed. . . . Not guilty as to knitting. I graduated from the knitting school at the age of eight years. . . . So your correspondent, Mr. White, could not see at close range when he mistook the embroidering for knitting. Why did I give up the Arena? Because I made hay in the hay day of my youth, and felt that I had earned a change.*

Her sympathy toward sufferers from tuberculosis led her to give shooting exhibitions as fundraisers. Among those who fatally contracted the disease were her sisters Elizabeth and Lydia. Calling on hospitals and presenting candy and flowers were other ways in which she showed her concern. Unfortunately, it was the same generosity that led her to have twenty-seven shooting medals broken up, melted, and sold to raise funds for a tuberculosis sanitarium near Pinehurst. To date, only one Annie Oakley medal, from a Marseilles live-pigeon shoot, is known to have survived this misguided act of charity.

Determined to finally retire to Hambrooks Bay, Oakley's final act before leaving Pinehurst was shooting one hundred clay pigeons straight at the Carolina's shooting range on April 16, 1922. On return to Maryland, she had been invited by her old friend and shooting enthusiast, entertainer, and celebrity Fred Stone, to a major Long Island charity event he had organized for that summer. The affair was the Motor Hippodrome and Wild West show for the Occupational Therapy Society, held July 1 at the Mineola Fairgrounds. Though a number of celebrities and society dignitaries were involved in the benefit, Oakley was its star. According to the New York *Tribune*:

Annie Oakley has come back. Out of the memories of hot summer afternoons under a canvas tent, out of dreams in which cowboys and Indians eternally clatter around a smiling young woman with long yellow braids and an unerring rifle, she came yesterday to take part in Fred Stone's benefit circus. . . .

She carried over her shoulder the gun which Buffalo Bill himself gave her many years ago, and at her side tramped her husband, at whom she had been shooting for forty years, but never hurt. The gun and the husband remain unchanged, but the Annie Oakley of childish impressions has gone. In her place stands a white-haired, sweet-voiced little woman in a black dress with an old-fashioned lace choker.

Oakley herself had said that though she might have looked old, she was in fine shape, and "but a day or two of practice will show you that Annie Oakley can come back." She was greeted and feted with a "storm of applause." Remarkably, film footage has survived that shows her performance of that day. There was also talk of Oakley coming out of retirement and appearing in films—all this at the age of sixty-two!

Her last paid performance was in October 1922 at the Brockton Fair in Massachusetts. For $700 she put on five performances of five minutes each. To reporter Miles E. Connolly, though he missed seeing her perform, "she was worth finding." Commenting on the massive fair crowd, estimated at one hundred thousand people, Oakley said: "All this has its glamour. All this has its lure, especially after 38 years of it, but still, home is best." Connolly regarded her as a "sensitive little woman with the air of one who has looked out on a wood-and-meadow world all her life through a parlor window."[13]

The Automobile Accident

Thoughts of a comeback for Oakley were dashed forever when the Butlers were in a limousine accident on the Dixie Highway, north of Daytona Beach, Florida. Out of control, the car jumped over an embankment and turned over. Oakley was pinned beneath the car with a broken hip and right ankle. For the next six weeks, Butler and Dave stayed at a room across the street from Oakley's bed in Bohannon Hospital.

Butler wrote an article entitled "The Life of Dave, As Told by Himself," in which that sad November was imagined as if presented by Dave:

She looked very feeble and could only put out one hand to stroke my head. By putting my feet on a chair I managed to get close enough to lick her ear. . . . I didn't like the nurses there, as they seemed rough and hurt my mistress when they moved her. . . . She was always so gentle and careful in combing and brushing me that I enjoyed having it done. I often wondered if any other dog had a mistress as good and gentle as mine.

Early in 1923, Oakley, still recuperating, was moved to the Lakeview Hotel in Leesburg. She was on crutches, with a brace on her right leg. In appreciation of kindly wishes from friends and fans, she sent a public letter to the *American Field:* "Since my accident, I have received nearly 2,000 letters and telegrams, also loads of flowers from many kind and thoughtful friends. Only someone like myself, who has suffered and laid for weeks in a hospital, knows what such messages of sympathy mean and I certainly

Dave at work, awaiting the precise shooting of his mistress.

In retirement at Pinehurst; the Butlers with Dave.

do appreciate all that my friends have done for me." Despite doctors' assurances that she would recover completely, Oakley never walked again without a leg brace.

The next tragedy in the Butlers' lives occurred when Dave, who had been as close as a child, was killed by a car. Sadly, the Butlers were nearing the end of their own lives.

A Final Shooting Exhibition

While the Philadelphia Phillies baseball team was in spring training in Leesburg, the Butlers arrived at the field to do some shooting and see if she had lost her touch. The team halted their practice, took seats in the bleachers, and saw a demonstration of grit and marksmanship none of them would ever forget.

Not having shot since October 8, Oakley was concerned: "Still I think my eye is good and maybe I'll be able to shoot fairly straight." Complete with her braced right leg and having laid aside her crutches, Oakley opened fire. The display was termed "little short of miraculous." While still recuperating, she adopted her "Aim at a high mark" motto and had it copyrighted.

When she had finally recovered from the car wreck—though still wearing the leg brace—the Butlers paid a call back home in Ohio. For the winter of 1923–1924, the couple stayed at the home of Oakley's niece Bonnie Ann and her husband, Rush Blakeley, near the family homestead in North Star, Darke County.

"A Little Lady Made of Steel Wires"

For the summer, the Butlers returned to North Carolina, staying at Mayview Manor in Blowing Rock, a resort similar to Pinehurst's Carolina Hotel. The couple relaxed and enjoyed the surroundings and each other. Late in the fall, they returned to Ohio, this time

to Dayton, to reside near her half sister Emily. Also nearby was the headquarters of the Amateur Trapshooting Association in Vandalia. When visiting the 1925 championships that August, news spread rapidly that the Butlers were on the shooting grounds. They were surrounded by admirers, among them another distinguished shooting couple, Fred and Ethyl Etchen—champions of another generation.

Claiming that "sitting still is harder than any kind of work," Oakley danced a jig, a picture of which was published in the Newark *Star Eagle* on October 6, 1925. Oakley attempted to work on an autobiography, even corresponding with a New York City–based writer, but the work was never finished, existing only as a handwritten manuscript. The Amateur Trapshooting Association discussed buying the Moses home from North Star in order to move it to Vandalia and set it up with pictures and memorabilia from her life. The plan never materialized, and eventually the house was auctioned off and then leveled.

Oakley traveled to Newark to set up her last will and testament, signing the document on October 7, 1925. Her guns had been given away over the years, and those remaining were shipped by Butler to a dentist friend in Newark, Dr. Edwin Betts. Since most of these were not engraved with her name, several have long since lost their identification as hers, unless verified by factory shipping records. Arnott Millett purchased the remains of the collection from the Betts family: two shotguns and two revolvers—a Smith & Wesson .38 with pearl grips and a Colt New Line .38.

Frank Butler left his collection to a brother, William J., from Joliet, Illinois. These, too, are unknown to this day and could only be identified if engraved with his name, listed in factory records, or accompanied by strong pedigrees of ownership.

To a reporter from the Newark *Star Eagle*, Oakley remarked: "After traveling through fourteen countries and appearing before all the royalty and nobility I have only one wish today. That is that when my eyes are closed in death that they will bury me back in that quiet little farm land where I was born."

She purchased a plot at the Brock Cemetery near Ansonia, Ohio, and this was the site of the Butlers' final resting place. The blood disease anemia was worsening her condition. Fred Stone's wife, Allene, trying to wish Oakley well, wrote to her in February 1926 from Detroit: "We are all so sorry you have not been well. I know the 'stuff' you are made of 'Missie.' You will be well and strong again because you are just a little lady made of steel wires."

Will Rogers's Column: A Salute to Annie Oakley

The Butlers were both in weakened conditions when Will Rogers visited them in Dayton. His syndicated column of April 30, 1926, on Oakley is believed to have reached as many as 35 million readers. It told of an aging and weakened legend. The article appeared under the heading: "Worst Story I Have Heard Today." The response from well-wishers was estimated at one thousand letters.

This is not the worst story. It is a good story about a little woman that all the older generation remember. She was the reigning sensation of America and Europe during all the heyday of Buffalo Bill's Wild West show. She was their star. Her picture was on more billboards than a modern Gloria Swanson. It was Annie Oakley, the greatest woman rifle shot the world has ever produced. Nobody took her place. There was only one. I went out to see her the other day as I was playing in Dayton, Ohio. She lives there with her husband, Frank Butler, and her sister. Her hair is snow white. She is bedridden from an auto accident a few years ago. What a wonderful [C]hristian character she is. I have talked with Buffalo Bill cowboys who were with the show for years and they worshipped her. She for years taught the fashionable people at Pinehurst, N.C., to shoot. America is worshipping at the feet of Raquel Miller, the Spanish lady. Europe talked the same of Annie Oakley in her day, and she reigned for many a year. I want you to write her all you who remember her and those that can go see her. Her address is 706 Lexington Avenue, Dayton, Ohio. She will be a lesson to you. She is a greater character than she was a rifle shot. Circuses have produced the cleanest living class of people in America today, and Annie Oakley's name, her lovable traits, her thoughtful consideration of others will live as a mark for any woman to shoot for.

In the summer following, Oakley moved to Darke County. The end was near. She made arrangements for an undertaker, specifically female. That choice, Louise Stocker of Greenville, later recalled: "She wanted a woman to handle her body and I was the only female licensed embalmer and funeral director in those parts, maybe in the whole state. . . . She said she had no strength left and was ready to die. . . . Then she said softly and simply that she wanted me to embalm her. Miss Oakley had even selected the dress to wear for her funeral."

The news of her death on November 3, 1926, went far and wide on the Associated Press wire service. When her weakened husband learned she was no more, he "never ate a bite. . . . He said he could not swallow."

To keep her funeral private, the exact date and time of the service remained a family secret. The body was cremated, and the ashes sealed in an urn. Frank Butler died on November 21; his body was returned to Darke County to be buried beside his wife in the simple plot at Brock Cemetery. Her headstone said simply, ANNIE OAKLEY / AT REST / 1926. His was marked FRANK BUTLER / AT REST / 1926. They had been married fifty years.

The Remarkable Annie Oakley

Although she had every opportunity to enjoy polite society, both in America and Europe, Annie Oakley never lost her love of shooting and of the great outdoors: "Any woman who does not thoroughly enjoy tramping across the country on a clear frosty morning with a good gun and a pair of dogs does not know how to enjoy life. . . . God intended women to be outside as well as men, and they do not know what they are missing when they stay cooped up in the house enjoying themselves with a novel."

Of all the heroic figures associated with the American West, few could claim the purity and majesty of Annie Oakley and the nobility of her husband and partner, Frank Butler. Idolized by millions,

Aiming a self-loading rifle; note pose with both eyes open, her regular shooting style.

Oakley particularly represented stability and responsibility, strength and determination, hard work and natural skill, modesty and beauty. She was also a woman with whom many from modern times can associate: her background was a poor, in fact impoverished, family, she suffered from child abuse, and she had to call on her own inner strength to deal with childhood traumas. Later in life, she was confronted with severe physical setbacks. In an increasingly troubled and complex world and in a society that to many seemed in moral decline, she forever remained a lady.

153

Through letterheads, programs, cabinet cards, guns, souvenir pamphlets, Fourth of July and farewell dinner souvenirs, and a myriad of other artifacts, the Wild West saga continues, from ca. 1893 through 1908. "America's Entertainment" had achieved an international flavor. Sword presented to White Beaver, the Colt Model 1878 double-action revolver to Captain Jack Crawford, and the Savage self-loading pistol to Buffalo Bill.

Chapter 7

꧁❈꧂

THE CONGRESS OF ROUGH RIDERS OF THE WORLD
1893–1908

While the Wild West was in Europe from the spring of 1891 through late October 1892, Nate Salsbury instigated one of the most important innovations and improvements in the entertainments. Concerned that Indians would not always be permitted to perform in Europe, he sought a substitute that would capitalize on the public's fascination with horses. Harkening back to his original concept of a presentation that embodied "the whole subject of horsemanship," he came up with the "Congress of Rough Riders of the World."

Using a name that had no public recognition for any specific equestrian group, the choice was prescient—several years later Theodore Roosevelt found himself riding into the White House on the celebrity of his Rough Riders in the Spanish-American War. Salsbury's innovation proved to be a sensation.

W. F. Cody "Buffalo Bill," lithograph, with quotations from London press confirming Cody's status as America's foremost ambassador of goodwill. Originally a poster by Stafford for Cody's Earl's Court performances of 1892, the British flag had originally been the flag of Nebraska; endorsements at bottom also added. By A. Hoen and Company, 36 × 28 inches, ca. 1893.

Nate Salsbury's deluxe cased and ivory-gripped Colt New Army and Navy double-action revolver, number 15936; detailed in the factory ledgers as .38 caliber, 6-inch barrel, blued finish, rubber grips (shipping clerk in error—ivory grips on gun when shipped), gold inlaid and engraved monogram NS; shipped to Joseph Mayer, May 20, 1895, one gun in shipment (case of suede-covered wood, lined in velvet and satin, not pictured).

"A FACTOR OF INTERNATIONAL AMITY."—*Cartoon.*

"Buffalo Bill has done his part in bringing America and England together."—*London Times, Nov. 1, 1887.*

COL. W. F. CODY
"BUFFALO BILL"

This was the grand show that embarked in the spring of 1893 on its greatest run in history: at the Chicago World's Fair. The entertainment presented for these vast crowds was substantially that which was written about by artist and sometime correspondent Frederic Remington. His fast-paced review of the new Wild West show was published in *Harper's Weekly* in 1892. Cody and Salsbury were so enamored of the artist's observations that the piece was quoted in some of the show programs. John M. Burke's introduction to these remarks recognized Remington as the "most noted depicter of Western scenes of the present day" and that his "study of the subject renders him a most competent judge. In returning from an expedition in Russia, passing through London, he

From the back cover of an 1894 program; New Yorkers were especially dedicated fans of Cody and his entertainments. Rays of the sun cleverly emanate from the colonel himself.

visited Buffalo Bill's Wild West, and it is with pride that the projectors point to his endorsement, standing side by side in artistic merit as he does with the grand artiste, Rosa Bonheur." To quote from the 1902 program:

The Tower, the Parliament, and Westminster Abbey are older institutions in London than Buffalo Bill's show, but when the New Zealander sits on London Bridge and looks over his ancient manuscripts of Murray's Guide-Book, he is going to turn first to the Wild West. At present everyone knows where it is, from the gentleman in Piccadilly to the dirtiest coster in the remotest slum of Whitechapel. The cabman may have to scratch his head to recall places where the traveller desires to go, but when the "Wild West" is asked for he gathers his reins and uncoils his whip without ceremony. One should no longer ride the deserts of Texas or the rugged uplands of Wyoming to see the Indians and pioneers, but should go to London. It is also quite unnecessary to brave the fleas and the police of the Czar to see the Cossack, or to tempt the waves which roll between New York and the far-off Argentine to study the Gauchos. They are all in London. The Cossacks and Gauchos are the latest addition, and they nearly complete the array of wild riders. There you can sit on a bench and institute comparisons. The Cossacks will charge you with drawn sabres in a most genuine way, will hover over you like buzzards on a battlefield—they soar and whirl about in graceful curves, giving an uncanny impression, which has doubtless been felt by many a poor Russian soldier from the wheat fields of Central Europe as he lay with a bullet in him on some distant field. They march slowly around over imaginary steppes, singing in a most dolorous way—looking as they did in Joseph Brandt's paintings. They dance over swords in a light-footed and crazy way, and do feats on their running horses which bring the hand-clapping. They stand on their heads, vault on and off, chase each other in a game called "chasing the handkerchief," and they reach down at top speed and mark the ground with a stick. Their long coat-tails flap out behind like an animated rag-bag, while their legs and arms are visible by turns. Their grip on the horse is maintained by a clever use of the stirrups, which are twisted and crossed at will. They are armed like "pincushions," and ride on a big leather bag, which makes their seat abnormally high.

The Gauchos are dressed in a sort of Spanish costume, with tremendous pantaloons of cotton, and boots made of colt's skin, which in their construction are very like Apache moccasins. They carry a knife at their back which would make a hole which a doctor couldn't sew up with less than five stitches, if indeed he was troubled at all. They ride a saddle which one of the American cowboys designated as a "—— feather bed," and they talk Spanish which would floor a Castilian at once. They ride bucking horses by pairs, and amuse the audience by falling off at intervals.

The great interest which attaches to the whole show is that it enables the audience to take sides on the question of which people ride the best and have the best saddles. The whole thing is put in such tangible shape as to be a regular challenge to debate to lookers-on. I, for one, formed my opinion, and have sacrificed two or three friends on the altar of my convictions. There is also a man in a pink coat who rides a hunting seat in competition with a yellow savage on a clear horse, and if our Englishman is not wedded to his ideals, he must receive a very bad shock in beholding he is a cow-boy.

Next year the whole outfit is coming over the World's Fair with the rest of Europe, and they are going to bring specimens of all the continental cavalry. The Sioux will talk German, the cow-boys already have an English accent, and the "Gauchos" will be dressed in good English form.

The Wild West show is an evolution of a great idea. It is a great educator, and, with its aggregate of wonders from the out-of-the-way places, it will represent a poetical and harmless protest against the Derby hat and the starched linen—those horrible badges of the slavery of our modern social system, when men are physical lay figures, and mental and moral cog-wheels and wastes of uniformity—where the great crime is to be individual, and the unpardonable sin is to be out of the fashion.

Cody, the scout, on horseback, against an elaborately painted backdrop, on the lookout for Indians.

The cowboys assembled, on a roundup.

Two companies of artillery.

A unit of German cavalry.

A unit of British lancers, with flag bearer.

A unit of U.S. cavalry, with flag bearer.

Indians with tepees.

Cody and a group of cowboys.

Rescuing the Deadwood stagecoach from a holdup by the Indians.

Mexican vaqueros.

A unit of Rough Riders.

Indian attack on a log cabin.

158

The pocket-sized *Route-Books* proved a handy tool for broadcasting the itinerary of the organization, as reference for employees and their families, and, in some years, for listing performers and support crews, office staff, publicity, musicians, and so forth. Surviving copies are often in worn condition, usually from pocket wear by a Wild West member. In order to provide a picture of the intense performance schedule of the Wild West, the transition years—when the entertainments went from a somewhat sedentary routine in major cities in frequent stops at several sites—are listed. The 1900 *Route-Book* reviewed the years 1893–1900:

1893.

This was the World's Fair season. There was a Grand Stand erected at 62d and 63d streets and Grace Avenue, Chicago, with a seating capacity of 20,000 people. It was opened April 26th, and closed October 31st, making 186 days of continuous performance; not one show was missed, and it closed the most successful season known in show history.

1894.

Opened in Ambrose Park, Brooklyn, N.Y., May 12th, and closed October 6th. One show was missed September 14th, on account of heavy rain; no Sunday shows were given, making a run of 126 days.

The 1895 season extended from April 22 in Philadelphia through November 2 in Georgia. The grueling schedule was as follows, reproduced from pages 59–62 of the 1900 *Route-Book*:

ROUTE-BOOK
Buffalo Bill's Wild West
1900.

CONTAINING ALSO THE OFFICIAL
ROUTES, SEASONS OF
1895, 1896, 1897, 1898, 1899.

COMPILED BY
GEORGE H. GOOCH.

HUDSON-KIMBERLY PUBLISHING CO.,
KANSAS CITY, MO.

OFFICIAL ROUTE—Season of 1895.

APRIL.

DATE.	PLACE.	State.	RAILROAD.	Mls.
22 Mon	Philadelphia..	Pa.		147
23 Tue	"	"	"	
24 Wed	"	"	"	
25 Thu	"	"	"	
26 Fri	"	"	"	
27 Sat	"	"	"	
	SUNDAY.			
29 Mon	Philadelphia..	Pa.		
30 Tue	"	"		

MAY.

DATE.	PLACE.	State.	RAILROAD.	Mls.
1 Wed	Philadelphia..	Pa.		
2 Thu	"	"	"	
3 Fri	"	"	"	
4 Sat	"	"	"	
	SUNDAY.			
6 Mon	Pottsville	Pa.	Phila. & Read...	93
7 Tue	Reading	"	"	35
8 Wed	Easton	"	P. & R. and L. V.	53
9 Thu	Allentown. ...	"	Lehigh Valley..	17
10 Fri	Wilkes-Barre..	"	" "	82
11 Sat	Scranton ...	"	Del. & Hud. Co	19
	SUNDAY.			
13 Mon	Carbondale ...	Pa.	Del. & Hud. Co.	16
14 Tue	Oneonta.....	N. Y	" "	94
15 Wed	Schenectady ..	"	" " [& G.	75
16 Thu	Gloversville...	"	N. Y, C and F., J	37
17 Fri	Troy......	"	F. J.&G; N.Y.C &H R.	59
18 Sat	Poughkeepsie.	"	N. Y. C. & H. R..	75
	SUNDAY.			
20 Mon	Albany........	N. Y.	N. Y. C. & H. R.	70
21 Tue	"	"		
22 Wed	Pittsfield	Mass	Boston & Albany	51
23 Thu	North Adams .	"	"	20
24 Fri	Greenfield....	"	Fitchburg	38
25 Sat	Holyoke.......	"	Boston & Maine	28
	SUNDAY.			
27 Mon	Springfield. ..	Mass	Boston & Maine	8
28 Tue	Waterbury....	Conn	N. Y. & N. Eng.	65
29 Wed	Danbury......	"	"	30
30 Thu	Bridgeport....	"	N. Y., N. H. & H.	59
31 Fri	New Haven ...	"	" "	18

JUNE.

DATE.	PLACE.	State.	RAILROAD.	Mls.
1 Sat	New Haven...	Conn		
	SUNDAY.			
3 Mon	Hartford......	Conn	N. Y., N. H. & H.	36
4 Tue	Norwich	"	N. Y. & N. Eng.	70
5 Wed	Woonsocket ..	R. I.	" "	61
6 Thu	Worcester	Mass	" "	54
7 Fri	"	"		
8 Sat	Fitchburg ...	"	Fitchburg.......	26
	SUNDAY.			
10 Mon	Boston	Mass	Old Colony......	73
11 Tue	"	"		
12 Wed	"	"		
13 Thu	"	"		
14 Fri	"	"		
15 Sat	"	"		
	SUNDAY.			

59

159

The Wild West's 1896 season, from April 18 through October 24, was yet another difficult series of mostly one-night stands; reproduced from pages 62–66 of the 1900 *Route-Book*.

For 1897, the show began in Brooklyn, New York, on April 12, and finished in Richmond on October 16; pages 66–69 detail every stop.

The 1898 season started in New York City on March 29 with a parade, then opened at Madison Square Garden the next day; pages 69–73 told the story.

The year 1899 began in New York again, from March 29; pages 73–76 covered all the stops.

The last page of the 1900 *Route-Book* summarized six challenging years.

160

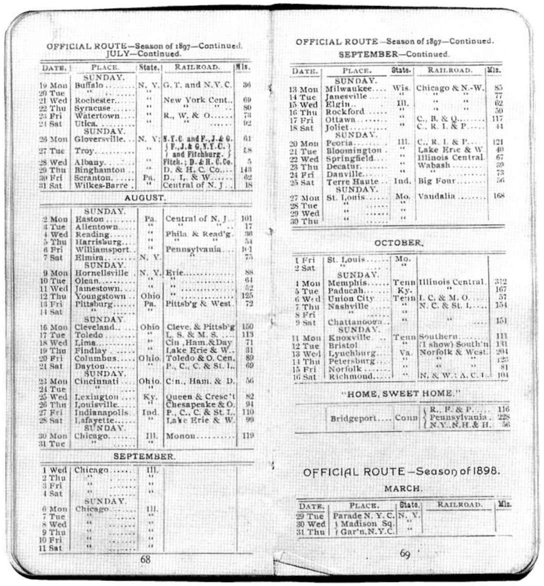

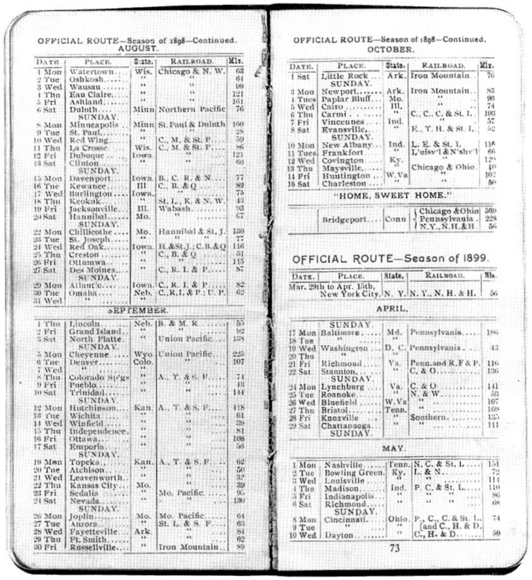

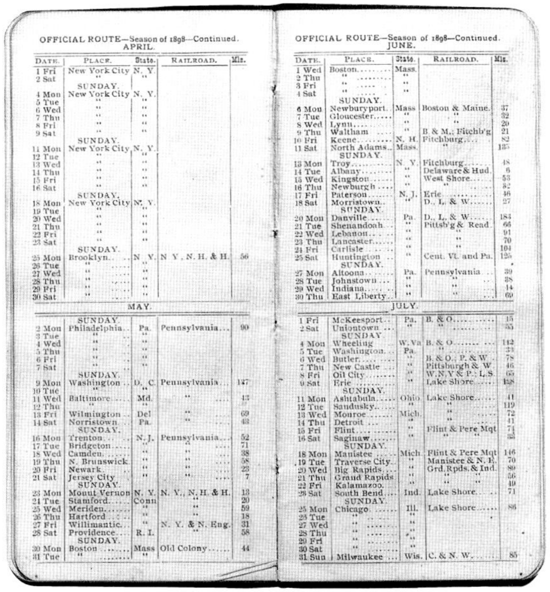

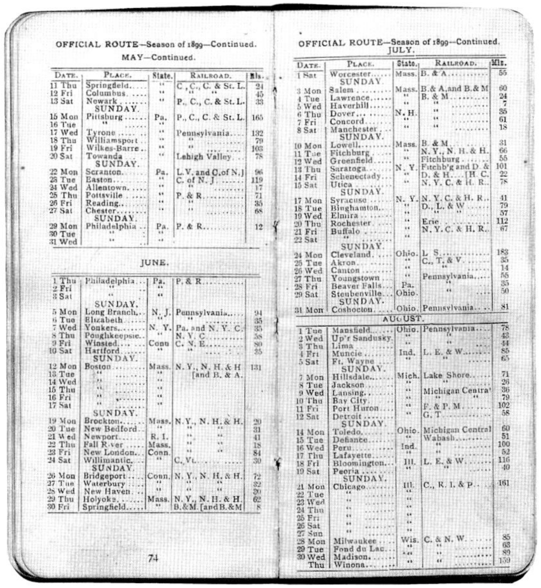

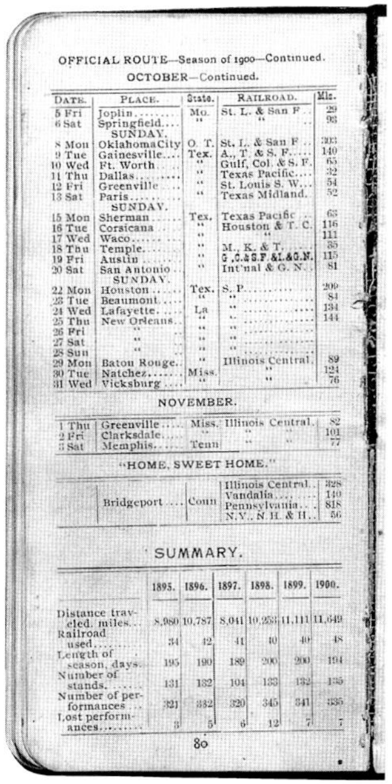

The Wild West a Main Attraction at the World's Fair

The World's Columbian Exposition (a.k.a. the Chicago World's Fair) was an event so grandiose that it remains to this day the standard by which all other fairs are judged. Over 27,500,000 people were in attendance.

The Wild West show was positioned at the entrance to the grounds, and some who came to see the fair attended the Wild West show and then left, more than satisfied. They thought the Wild West *was* the fair!

At times, the authenticity of the Wild West reached sensational proportions. As a stellar attraction for the fair, the show billed victorious Indian chiefs such as Rain-in-the-Face, the "slayer of Captain Tom Custer," drawing headline articles in the press. A masterful promotional stroke was achieved when Lt. Colonel George Armstrong Custer's chief scout, Curley, was introduced to Rain-in-the-Face and other Sioux, some of whom he had faced at the Battle of the Little Bighorn. From the Chicago *Globe*, April 29, 1893:

Buried the Hatchet
—
Sitting Bull's Slayer Meets the
Sioux Chief, Rain-in-
the-Face
COUNCIL OF THE BRAVES.
—
Curley, the Crow Indian, Is Over-
come with Emotion—
Other Events

Among the many features of the Wild West show was the reconciliation, yesterday afternoon, in the original cabin of the celebrated Mucapapa Sioux Chief, Sitting Bull, of the famous Crow Indian scout Curley and the present Sioux chief, Rain-in-the-Face.

Curley, it will be remembered, is held responsible by the Sioux Indians for the death of their great warrior during the late Indian outbreak at the Pine Ridge agency.[1]

Ever since the killing of Sitting Bull the Sioux Indians have sworn vengeance on the Crows and for nearly two years, until yesterday, Curley had not set eyes on a Sioux Indian, fearing that should he do so he would be killed on sight, which would certainly be his fate were he to return into their midst at Pine Ridge.

The starting gun from the "Wild Cowboy Race" and the prized Colt Single Action Army revolver, serial number 150681. Period photograph shows winner Gillespie at *left*, with Charles W. Smith. The quirt was another prize won by Gillespie, awarded by Dawes County, Nebraska. Items now on display at the Dawes County Historical Society.

Since Buffalo Bill has been in Chicago he has used every known method which his brain could conjure up to induce the scout to join his aggregation, but the "friendly" Indian refused to come on till the "pale face" dismissed the treacherous Sioux. Upon the promise of ample military protection, however, he finally agreed to join the aggregation.

When Curley arrived the meeting was again proposed, but the Crow strenuously refused till yesterday, when he was at last persuaded by Col. Cody and Maj. Burke to enter the dead chief's cabin.

Inside the cabin, squatted on buffalo robes, were the Sioux chiefs Red Cloud, Rocky Bear, Painted Horse, High Bear and Low Neck, presided over by Rain-in-the-Face. Just to the left of the great chief was the hatchet and pipe of peace. Outside the cabin were several squaws and a band of bucks.

The moment that Curley was announced a weird cry was emitted by the council of peace and the pipe was made ready. Arm in arm, Curley and Rain-in-the-Face left the hut and buried the hatchet. Returning to the hut the pipe of peace was passed around the circle and all went well till Curley's turn came. As the pipe was passed him by Rain-in-the-Face he broke down and commenced to cry like a baby; his eyes rolled from side to side and he watched every chief as a rat in a trap would a dog when some one was about to set it free. Notwithstanding the assurance of the Sioux chiefs that peace was at last restored he was not contented till he was taken from the hut and led to his own quarters. One Comanche and two Kiowa chiefs who are on their way to Washington on business with the government were also present at the meeting.

The Thousand-Mile Cowboy Race

As if the fair was not already grand enough, an event was conceived that, like the Congress of Rough Riders, caught the fancy of the riding and shooting public. In keeping with the flavor of Buffalo Bill's Wild West, the foremost entertainment attraction at the fair, the great cowboy race pitted ten contestants in a marathon from Chadron, Nebraska, to the Wild West show entrance in Chicago—a distance of one thousand miles.

The appealing array of prizes was listed in the Chicago *Times* of June 11, 1893, under the headline MAD RACE OF COWBOYS:

Aside from the laurel of glory which the riders will win there are other prizes, chief among which is $1,000 in gold, offered by the managers of the race; one of the finest Colt revolvers ever made, inlaid in silver, gold, and pearl; $500 divided into three prizes, offered by Col. Cody, and a fine cowboy saddle, given by an Omaha firm. Col. Cody will distribute the prizes on a designated time when the riders are all in.

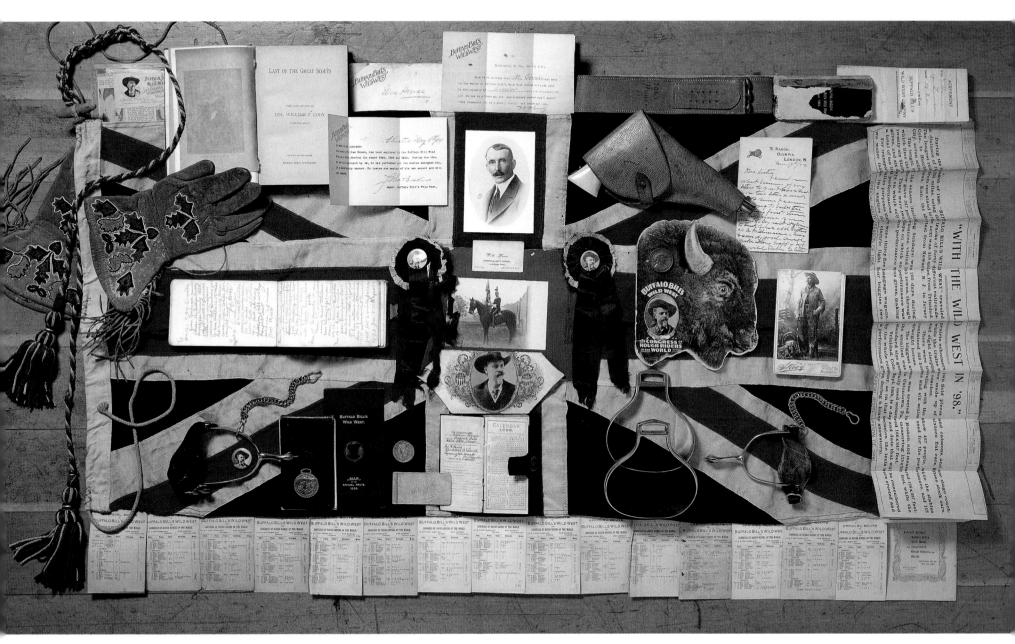

Memorabilia and ephemera of Lancer William House, who served with the Wild West in the 1898, 1899, and 1904 seasons and is pictured mounted at *center* and in portrait at *top center*. Listed in the 1899 *Route-Book* under "English Lancers," second only to Thomas Cook, Sergeant, as "W. House, Color Bearer." House's business card for the same season listed him as "Sword & Lance Expert, and Rough Rider" of "Buffalo Bill's Wild West." Includes rare contract for services for 1898 season, for which House signed up as a "Military Rider." On the back of the agreement, the "Rules and Regulations" included "Rule No. 27.—Penalty $1.00 to $5.00. For swearing, quarreling or loud, boisterous language about the establishment, cars, hotels or other places. Good behavior required at all times." Gauntlets a gift from Buffalo Bill.

Buffalo Bill committed to presenting a special prize of his own, the enticing sum of $500.

The race was scheduled to start on June 13, with Nebraska's Governor Crounse firing the starting gun, which itself was the most talked-about prize of all: a Colt Single Action Army revolver. Details in the Colt factory records identify the piece as .44-40 caliber, with 5½-inch barrel, engraved, with blued finished and gold-plated cylinder, carved ivory grips with ox-head motif, shipped to Harry Weir, Secretary, Cowboy Race, on May 6, 1893; there was only one gun in the shipment.

Reflecting its importance, the Colt Single Action was on view in Chadron at the start of the race. After the starting pistol shot, Harry Weir took the deluxe revolver personally and started after the cowboys by rail. He was conspicuous in wearing a huge white hat that almost hid him from view.

The press and public were captivated by this endurance trial, and the headlines in the Chadron *Citizen* of June 15 estimated the crowd watching the start at three thousand people. In order to ensure no undue hardship on the horses, humane-society officials were present. It is little known today, but endurance races are still run, usually of fifty or one hundred miles in a single day, and officials from humane groups are present as a standard procedure. Concerned about the humane question, newspaper reports clarified that Cody's $500 was to be given, according to the *World*, to the rider "who brings his horses in in the best condition. His prize is not therefore, an inducement to cruelty but the reverse."

Buffalo Bill's Wild West and Congress of Rough Riders of the World, pitting the White Eagle, guiding and guarding, against the Red Fox, waiting and watching. Matched pair of lithographs, the wagon train in distance behind Cody while the Indian encampment looms in the background behind Red Cloud. Made to sell as prints during the Chicago World's Fair. Each image measures 24⅜ × 19⅜ inches, ca. 1893.

164

THE WHITE EAGLE "COL. W. F. CODY = BUFFALO BILL" GUIDING AND GUARDING

THE RED FOX "RED CLOUD" WAITING AND WATCHING.

The press filed daily progress reports. After nearly two weeks in the saddle, the first rider reached Colonel Cody and the finish line. The Chicago *Evening Post* of June 27 told the story:

Cowboy Race Over.
John Berry the First of the Riders
to Reach This City.
Emmett Albright the Second.
Both Men Thoroughly Exhausted, but
Their Horses in Good Condition
—Prizes in Dispute

Colonel Cody was pleased with the race and results. He declared that there was a great deal more to the race then the mere first prize: "It will show the world what the native American horse is worth. European nations are watching the result of this race with interest. It is a test of the hardiness of the bronco and after the wonderful result of 150 miles in twenty-four hours, 1,040 miles in thirteen days and sixteen hours, there will be a rush for the American animal. European nations will want American-bred horses for their cavalry. Of course, on the entanglements of the riders and protests I am not in a position to decide, but I do say that the horses are in splendid condition. I was not surprised at that either, for it is just as I said in THE EVENING POST a few days ago—the cowboys know that the horse is their best friend and that its best endeavors can be brought out by kindness and care."

The dispute over the prizes was finally settled, as reported in the July 2 *Evening Post:*

Cowboy Prizes Divided.
The Contestants in the Famous Race Reach
an Amicable Settlement.

There was an amicable meeting yesterday held in Colonel Cody's dining tent at the Wild West camp of contestants and parties interested in the Chadron-Chicago cowboy race, when Mr. Hartzell, of the Chadron committee, was empowered by the committee and the cowboy racers present to refer the settlement of awards to Paul Fontaine, of the Humane Society. A general discussion of the circumstances connected with the race took place and all interested parties offered to abide, willingly and freely, in whatever award or decision Mr. Fontaine might make, the relative positions of the horses in the race not be[ing] considered by him.

The technical protest against Berry being in the race was upheld, but in consideration of the fact that he rode a fair, square race, and, as old Joe Gillespie expressed it, "Beat the race," the boys recognized him to the extent of agreeing to

Mr. Fontaine's decision by letting him have $175 out of the Buffalo Bill's Wild West purse of $500, together with the saddle given by Messrs. Montgomery, Ward & Co., of Chicago, for the first man in.

It was decided that Joe Gillespie was first in the race, as per the Chadron agreement, and he was awarded $50 of the Wild West purse, $200 of the Chadron purse and the revolver offered by Messrs. Colt.

Army Officers Endorse Buffalo Bill

With the guidance of Burke, Cody collected endorsements of his services as a scout for the army and published them profusely in programs. This artful public-relations and advertising technique served to verify the authenticity of Cody himself and also the reenactments presented in the Wild West. Beyond that, the statements rang true and were not contrived. The body of the quotations that follow appeared in the 1893 program, perfect timing for the Chicago World's Fair. Judging from the 1887 dates for several of the statements, they were likely collected in order to edify the British on the stature of Buffalo Bill, to coincide with the Wild West's first appearance in the United Kingdom. The endorsements have been rearranged in alphabetical order by officer name. Clearly, Cody had won the respect and admiration of the U.S. Army.

H. C. Bankhead, Brigadier General, Jersey City, 405 Bergen Avenue, February 7, 1887: *I fully and with pleasure indorse [sic] you as the veritable "Buffalo Bill," U.S. Scout, serving with the troops operating against hostile Indians in 1868, on the plains. I speak from personal knowledge, and from reports of officers and others, with whom you secured renown by your services as a scout and successful hunter. Your sojourn on the frontier at a time when it was a wild and sparsely settled section of the Continent, fully enables you to portray that in which I have personally participated—the Pioneer, Indian Fighter, and Frontiersman. Wishing you every success.*

Brevet Major General Eugene A. Carr, St. Louis, Missouri, May 7, 1885: *I take pleasure in saying that in*

an experience of about thirty years on the plains and in the mountains, I have seen a great many guides, scouts, trailers, and hunters, and Buffalo Bill (W. F. Cody) is King of them all. He has been with me in seven Indian fights, and his services have been invaluable.

George Crook, Brigadier General, Omaha, Nebraska, January 7, 1887: *I take great pleasure in testifying to the very efficient service rendered by you 'as a scout,' in the campaign against the Sioux Indians, during the year 1876. Also, that I have witnessed your Wild West Exhibition. I consider it the most realistic performance of the kind I have ever seen.*

S. W. Drum, Adjutant General, War Department, Washington, D.C., August 10, 1886: *Mr. William F. Cody was employed as Chief of Scouts under Generals Sheridan, Custer, Crook, Miles, Carr, and others, in their campaigns against hostile Indians on our frontier, and as such rendered very valuable and distinguished service.*

N. A. M. Dudley, Colonel, First Cavalry, Brevet Brigadier General, Fort Custer, Montana Territory [n.d.]: *I often recall your valuable services to the Government, as well as to myself, in years long gone by, specially during the Sioux difficulties, when you were attached to my command as Chief of Scouts. Your indomitable perseverance, incomprehensible instinct in discovering the trails of the Indians, particularly at night, no matter how dark or stormy, your physical powers of endurance in following the enemy until overtaken, and your unflinching courage, as exhibited on all occasions, won not only my own esteem and admiration, but that of the whole command. With my best wishes for your success, I remain your old friend.*

W. H. Emory, Major General, Washington, D.C., February 8, 1887: *Mr. Cody was chief guide and hunter to my command, when I commanded the District of North Platte, and he performed all his duties with marked excellence.*

James W. Forsyth, Colonel, Seventh Cavalry, Headquarters, Seventh Cavalry, Fort Mead, Dakota

Territory, February 14, 1887: *Your army career on the frontier, and your present enterprise of depicting scenes in the Far West, are so enthusiastically approved and commended by the American people and the most prominent men of the U.S. Army, that there is nothing left for me to say. I feel sure your new departure will be a success.*

James B. Fry, Assistant Adjutant-General, Brevet Major General, New York, December 28, 1886: *Recalling the many facts that came to me while I was Adjutant-General of the Division of the Missouri, under General Sheridan, bearing upon your efficiency, fidelity, and daring as a guide and scout over the country west of the Missouri River and east of the Rocky Mountains, I take pleasure in observing your success in depicting in the East the early life of the West.*

John H. King, Brevet Major General, Tallahassee, Florida, January 12, 1887: *I take great pleasure in recommending you to the public, as a man who has a high reputation in the army as a Scout. No one has ever shown more bravery on the Western plains than yourself. I wish you success in your proposed visit to Great Britain.*

Wesley Merritt, Brevet Major General, U.S. Military Academy, Late Major General Volunteers, West Point, New York, January 11, 1887: *I have known W. F. Cody (Buffalo Bill) for many years. He is a Western man of the best type, combining those qualities of enterprise, daring, good sense, and physical endurance which made him the superior of any scout I ever knew. He was cool and capable when surrounded by dangers, and his reports were always free from exaggeration. He is a gentleman in that better sense of the word which implies character, and he may be depended on under all circumstances. I wish him success.*

Brigadier General Nelson A. Miles, Los Angeles, California, January 7, 1878: *Having visited your great exhibition in St. Louis and New York City, I desire to congratulate you on the success of your enterprise. I was much interested in the various life-like representations*

Colonel Cody image lithographed on tin sign by Sentenne and Green, 227-29-31 Bleecker Street, New York, ca. 1895, 20 x 13½ inches. Imprinted with SINCERELY YOURS/W. F. CODY/"BUFFALO BILL." Some of Sharps pepperbox pistols carved with grip motif in cavalier image similar to that of Buffalo Bill. At *right,* Winchester Model 1873 rifles of marksmen George D. Snyder and Arizona Joe. Elaborate horsehair halter with rich original colors.

Cliff House, San Francisco, with a group of Indian performers; in *right* photo, enjoying the view of the Pacific Ocean from one of the most advantageous locations on the bay.

(*below*) Show troupe in front of Rodman Wanamaker's store, New York City, 1908.

Captain Jack Crawford:
The Poet Scout

A longtime friend and sometime rival of Buffalo Bill who shared his social conscience, John Wallace Crawford was known popularly as Captain Jack, the Poet Scout. Born in Carndonagh, County Donegal, northern Ireland, in 1847, Crawford emigrated to America in 1857. Adventure was in his blood. Ancestors had fought for Scotland's freedom, and his mother, Susie Wallace, was descended directly from Sir William Wallace, the legendary Scots chief. Crawford continued that family tradition. In his multifaceted life, he enjoyed friendships or acquaintances with a great many legends of the West. Among them were Ned Buntline, Texas Jack Omohundru, Wild Bill Hickok, Annie Oakley and Frank Butler, Sitting Bull, George Armstrong Custer, Billy the Kid, Pawnee Bill, and Theodore Roosevelt.

Despite the fact that the sum total of his formal schooling was approximately one month, Wallace gained national fame as a poet, traveling lecturer, and entertainer. Like Buffalo Bill, his reputation as an authentic American hero was on a solid foundation. Crawford was a veteran of frontline service during the Civil War, although several of his attempts to enlist for the Union war effort had been rebuffed due to his youth. Finally, as a volunteer with the Forty-eighth Pennsylvania, Crawford saw action, only to be severely wounded. While recuperating, Crawford was taught to read and write by a sister of charity. This education laid the foundation for his literary and theatrical career. After regaining his health, Crawford went West, where he was a scout for the army, while keeping a sharp eye out for gold and other precious metals. He served under General Crook in the Sitting Bull campaign of 1876. Later, he was appointed chief of scouts under General Wesley Merritt.

Crawford's writings and performances drew on his experiences as a soldier, as well as a scout, prospector and miner, hunter, rancher, and reformer. Following the Battle of Slim Buttes, Crawford heroically carried the press report for the New York

Presentations to the coterie of friends of Buffalo Bill. At *top*, officer's sword inscribed to Dr. D. Frank Powell, "White Beaver," by his battalion of the U.S. Volunteer Infantry. Etched detail from blade. Winchester Model 1895 carbine, part of a limited series of similarly got-up examples, given to friends such as M. R. "Gold Nugget Mike" Russell, serial number 38732, with silver stock plaques and names of recipients engraved on frame. Note deluxe checkered stocks. Another carbine in series, serial number 48751, was also given to Powell. The idea might have come from similar 1895s made for John R. Hegeman, serial numbers 20990 and 22417, the latter a present from Hegeman to General Nelson A. Miles. Still another of the genre, serial number 22590, was a gift to Cody from Captain Jack Crawford (and then from Cody to George T. Beck).

The tomahawk has an inscription marked on haft, as visible in detail.

A Broncho Philosopher
The Poet Scout

THE POET SCOUT

IS THE ONLY TRULY GENUINE
SCOUT-GUIDE AND INDIAN FIGHTER
NOW BEFORE THE AMERICAN PUBLIC

THE New York World said: "Jack Crawford is the only American Scout that has ever dignified literature." Permit us to present him to men and women, boys and girls of America with

An Introduction

When Senator Lamar of Mississippi was Secretary of the Interior, this is a copy of a letter of introduction from Senator Fair of Nevada and Generals Sheridan and Logan. This was twenty-one years ago:

WASHINGTON, D. C., June 8, 1886.

To the Honorable the Secretary of the Interior:

The bearer, Capt. Jack Crawford, "The Poet Scout," who seeks an interview with you with regard to his land interests in New Mexico, is a gentleman of intelligence and character. He served with credit as a soldier during the late war, and was recently chief of scouts with the army on the frontier, where he did good service in campaigns against the Indians. He is endorsed by Gen. Edward Hatch, Gen. E. A. Carr, Col. Wm. Laselle, Gen. Lew Wallace, Gen. Hancock and many other distinguished citizens and soldiers.

JAMES G. FAIR,
P. H. SHERIDAN,
JOHN A. LOGAN.

CAPT. JACK CRAWFORD

When a bit of sunshine hits ye'
After passin' of a cloud,
An' a fit of laughter gits ye'
An' yer spine is feelin' proud,
Don't forgit to up an' fling it
At a soul that's feelin' blue,
For the minit that ye sling it,
It's a boomerang to you.

BECAUSE "Capt Jack" has persistently refused to allow his name to be connected or in any way associated with the Yellow Dime Novel Literature that has created fake frontiersmen, they say he never was a scout. Read this from his Commanding General and note the date:

IN THE FIELD, NEAR EL PASO, TEXAS,
September 12, 1880.

To CAPT. JACK CRAWFORD, CHIEF OF SCOUTS:

My Dear Captain:—It is with sincere regret that I accept your resignation, and I am sure that I voice the sentiments of every officer in the command when I say that you will be much missed around the camp-fire and on the trail. There is no doubt but what your scout after Victorio into old Mexico, and the rapidity with which you located him in the Candaleria Mountains, and your fast ride to the nearest post, from whence you wired me at Fort Cummings, was the cause which led directly to his death by the Mexican troops; for through your energy, pluck and perseverance, our forces harassed and drove him until he was almost dismounted and without ammunition, an easy victim for the Mexican troops, whose commander ordered our forces out of Mexico as soon as they found Victorio was driven into their net. I trust that your mining venture will turn out as you anticipate, and I take pleasure in testifying to your courage, honesty and integrity.

Yours very respectfully,
GEO. P. RUEL,
Col. Commanding Column in the Field.

Boys, Boys, Boys! read this: From Gen. N. A.Miles, U. S. A.

LOS ANGELES, CAL., May 23, 1887.

* * * Your position with reference to that sensational kind of literature which for years past has, to say the least, done no good to the juvenile element of the country, is very commendable, and I think your labors in the field of legitimate literature will in time be even more fully recognized than perhaps you anticipate now.

Very truly yours,
NELSON A. MILES,
Brig. Gen'l U. S. A.

From the Gallant General, H. W. Lawton, when he was a captain in the United States Army:

FORT MARCY, NEW MEXICO, Jan. 20, 1883.

CAPT. JACK CRAWFORD,
FORT CRAIG, NEW MEXICO.

My Dear Crawford:—It seems as but adding a drop of water to an overflowing reservoir for me to add a testimonial to the many which you bear from distinguished officers of the army and from leading statesmen of the land, yet I desire to bear witness to your worth as a gentleman and an author, and your efficient services as a skilled and daring scout with the army on the frontier. During your service in the department with which I was connected, I always found you ready and eager for duty, and the first to respond to a call for volunteers when a dangerous mission was to be undertaken.

Many a camp-fire on the border has been enlivened by your inimitable powers of entertainment, with your own song and story, and many of my brother officers, with myself, have felt the hardships of an Indian campaign lessened by the enjoyment derived from that frisky tongue of yours when night had closed the weary march of the day. Wishing you every success in your new field, I am,

Very truly yours,
H. W. LAWTON,
Captain 4th United States Cavalry.

Back cover of large-format single-sheet brochure promoting Crawford, "The Only Truly Genuine Scout-Guide and Indian Fighter Now Before the American Public," a claim unwelcome in the Buffalo Bill camp. One side reprinted an article from *Farm and Fireside*, February 10, 1908, entitled "Whar the Hand o' God Is Seen"; the other side was a collection of endorsements and poetry.

Herald. This required evading the Indians and took four trying days, during which he covered four hundred miles. His final scouting assignments were in New Mexico against the Apaches. There, in the 1880s, his service again placed his life in jeopardy. Conditions were so threatening that settlement of the New Mexico territory had nearly ceased.

Crawford retired from army life in 1886, settling in Fort Craig, New Mexico. His career as a writer had already begun years before, mainly as a correspondent for daily newspapers, not a few of which were in New York City. His poems and articles appeared on a regular basis in magazines, adding to his growing popularity. His artfulness as a storyteller saw him performing before large crowds, holding them spellbound. To quote social activist and popular lecturer, philosopher, and author, Elbert Hubbard:

Jack Crawford is an orator, a poet, a man: and I'll go you a Stetson against a stogie that Harvard, Yale, Columbia and Princeton have not a man on their roster who can hold an audience of 2,000 people for two hours and not have a person leave or want to leave. Captain Jack can do it, and moreover can adapt himself to any kind of an audience, from Chicago newsboys to a parliament of religions. The man is a marvel of manly strength, fluid intelligence, flowing wit and oratorical grace.

Who taught Captain Jack to throw the lariat of his imagination over us and rope us hand and foot and put his brand upon us? Yes, that is what I mean—who educated him? God educated him.

Crawford's first book of poetry, *The Poet Scout: Verses and Songs,* appeared in 1879. This anthology expanded a reputation already substantial from appearances he made as a stage performer, a career which began in 1876 with a lead role in the Buffalo Bill Combination performance of *Life on the Border.* In the 1876–1877 season the show alternated with *The Red Right Hand; or, Buffalo Bill's First Scalp for Custer.* Like Cody, Crawford initially performed popular entertainments before the public beginning in the late fall, returning in the off-season to his life in the West. However, these shows were not limited to east of the Mississippi. In the spring of 1877, Cody and Crawford dazzled audiences for five weeks in San Francisco before traveling to Oakland and Sacramento and then to a six-week stint in Virginia City, Nevada.

The final night's engagement soiled their friendship: Crawford was wounded by a knife wielded by Cody during a reenactment of the fight with Yellow Hair. (Crawford portrayed the Indian chief.) The next day, Cody appeared in a matinee, but this time without Crawford. The two had also quarreled over financial matters; Crawford felt he was not paid his due.

(*clockwise from lower left*) Crawford with colorful jaguar-fringed coat, Civil War and other service-related medals, and a Colt Model 1878 Frontier Double Action revolver. Ca. late 1870s.

With his plated Winchester (the stocks checkered), Crawford reads a brochure or show program with his portrait emblazoned on front

The Winchester appears to be the Model 1876; held in Crawford's left hand is what looks like a rock, likely representing gold ore. Knife scabbard barely visible on his left hip; this time, he wears moccasins.

Crawford set up his own stage show, hitting the road as the Captain Jack Combination. His first appearances were in California, late in 1877, and they continued into early the following year. A reviewer in the Los Angeles *Herald* dubbed Crawford "the very beau ideal of a frontier hero. . . . [The play was rife with] exciting and romantic adventures."

Crawford then actively took up gold mining, heading in the spring of 1878 for the fields of the Cariboo region of British Columbia. Accompanying him were actors from his stage company. The troupe performed in Canada and prospected in its spare time. Soon abandoning show business, Crawford devoted seven months to seeking gold but with very little success. The long and lonely nights, however, inspired a torrent of poems. Luckless in mining, he returned to the stage.

In a financial crunch after sporadic performances (mainly in California), Crawford hired on as a scout with the military district of New Mexico, under command of Colonel Edward Hatch. Crawford's service as chief of scouts began by June 1880 at Fort Craig. The goal was to end depredations by the Apache chief Victorio.

While on this duty, Crawford kept a sharp eye out for mining opportunities. On one reconnaissance, he had a chance meeting with none other than the outlaw Billy the Kid—only about a year before

Capt. Jack Crawford
"THE POET SCOUT"

Headquarters: Knickerbocker Building
Fifth Ave. and Fourteenth St.   NEW YORK

Nashville Tenn Feb 25 — 1905 —

Theodore Green
Dear Sir

Here it is I want to
warn you however it is
N.Y. at the bottom
of a check

Capt Jack Crawford

With deluxe Remington rolling-block pistol, medals, and jaguar coat.

Letterhead showing Crawford's address in New York City, a place he frequently traveled to and where he was toast of the town. The bronze sculpture by August Zeller is a life-size bust. Elaborate base represented vignettes from the subject's peripatetic life.

SAY, PARD

When a bit of sunshine hits ye,
After passing of a cloud,
When a fit of laughter gits ye
An' yer spine is feelin' proud,
Don't fergit to up and fling it
At a soul that's feelin' blue,
For the minit that ye sling it
It's a boomerang to you.

"CAPT. JACK."

the Kid's death at the hands of Pat Garrett in Fort Sumner. Crawford, who thought dime novels had a bad influence on their readers, used the incident to preach against their influence.[2] He said the Kid blamed "Dime Novels, and a reckless love of adventure, [for driving] him from a good home and a loving mother, and frontier whiskey and bad associates did the rest."[3]

In mid-October, Crawford learned that troops had ended the Victorio menace by killing him and sixty Apache fighting men, along with several women and children. Crawford, credited with helping to track and locate Victorio, then resigned his position to resume his mining and acting careers. Thereafter, he set up residency in New Mexico for most of the rest of his life, although he later maintained a home in New York City. For the next five years, he concentrated on serving as a post trader at Fort Craig and in a general line of ranching and mining businesses.

Touring with fellow performer Will L. Visscher (who had formerly been with the Captain Jack Combination), Crawford resumed his show-business career in 1885. Performing first in New Mexico, they moved on to Kansas and then set up in St. Louis. At the same time, Doc Carver was in town with his newly formed Life on the Plains and the Great Wild West Combination. This full-blown Wild West show appealed to Crawford, who joined the troupe and remained with the show, ending up in New England.

His experiences with Carver's Wild West, the Cody Combination, and his own Combination made him realize that he could carve out a unique career by mixing lecturing, poetry readings, and the recitation of stories from his adventurous life. In 1886, this career began in earnest, with themes such as "The Campfire and the Trail." His preference was to have these appearances considered as "a frontier monologue and medley," not as lectures. Crawford also was known for a well-developed sense of humor, to the point that, as one observer expressed it, he could keep an "audience in one continuous uproar. . . . Humor flows from Capt. Jack like water from a sprinkling cart."[4] During this mix of activity, he continued acting on the stage, playing roles that reflected his authentic frontier reputation.

For the fall 1889 New Era Exposition in St. Joseph, Missouri—an event of a month's duration billed as the greatest show since the Centennial Exposition of 1876—Crawford was hired to organize the outdoor entertainment and set up displays of minerals. He created a village of over fifty authentic Apache Indians by hiring them off a reservation in New Mexico. Part of the show was a reenactment of Custer's Last Stand, with Crawford playing the role of Custer. Late in September, a disastrous fire wiped out the main exhibition building. Crawford, with another volunteer named Broncho John, bravely led a contingent of cowboys and Apaches into the conflagration to save the featured exhibit of the Marquis de Lafayette's coach.

Crawford's life on the lecture circuit consumed much of his time and energy for the next thirty years. From time to time, he interrupted his tours with positions or appointments, including four years as a U.S. Department of Justice special agent beginning late in 1889. Ferreting out illegal alcohol on Indian reservations was the focus of his job, a task he did with relish since he was an advocate of temperance. These years also added to his reputation as a genuine Western character and an expert on Indian life and culture. Further, the experience offered him the chance to speak before crowds and to meet an array of colorful personalities. Later, he received appointments as deputy U.S. marshal for Arizona and New Mexico. These assignments meant wide-ranging travel, more contacts, more exposure to the public, and an ever growing reputation.

In 1898, the poet scout set off for the Klondike, joining hordes of gold seekers but also continuing with an occasional speaking engagement or poetry reading before the rugged individualists of the north country. Ever the optimist, one of his poems was tailor-made for miners:

But joking all aside, good friends,
Success or failure all depends
On you. Each one must do his part,
Must work with hands and brain and heart,
For there is no such word as fail,
Except to those who will not sail
When winds are fair. So come what will,
Despite the rushing stream or hill,
Press on! and climb. Say "never die,"
And you will get there bye and bye.

In time, Crawford reluctantly decided that his partner in the mining project was a swindler and that the company in which he and others had invested was fraudulent. He returned to San Francisco in July 1899—disappointed, troubled, and in debt but richer in experience and ready to resume an active career on the lecture circuit. The Klondike proved to be the last of his great adventures—two years out of his life in which he returned with no gold but a wealth of stories to add to the bonanza of his lecture subjects.

Captain Jack versus Buffalo Bill

Buffalo Bill and Captain Jack had a long-standing friendship. However, it was strained from time to time with differences of opinion over money matters and an alleged lack of abstinence by Cody from demon alcohol. Crawford enjoyed a reputation as an advocate of clean living, free of spirituous beverages. Their differences are reflected in a popular commentary in Cody's autobiography: after Crawford delivered a gift of a bottle of whiskey—consigned by a friend for Cody—a distance of some three hundred miles through hazardous Indian country, Cody's comment was, "Jack Crawford is the only man I have ever known that could have brought that bottle of whiskey through without *accident* befalling it, for he is one of the very few teetotal scouts I ever met."[5]

During the summer of 1894, while Crawford was traveling in England, excerpts from a letter he sent to an old friend in Wichita were published by a local paper. These remarks stated it "seemed strange . . . that while the original and real Buffalo Bill [William Mathewson] was living in quiet modest retirement in Wichita, another claiming to be the original was setting the world on fire with stories of his wonderful deeds and hair breadth escapes."

In response, John M. Burke accused Crawford of being "a fraud and fake frontiersman." Angry letters crossed between Cody and Crawford, now both nationally famous. Previously, Captain Jack had been reluctant to attack Buffalo Bill publicly. But in this instance, their differences reached a wide audience.

Crawford had come to view Cody's Wild West performances as fictionalizing the saga of the real West. The genuine West was the dominant theme of Crawford's lectures and performances. He interpreted Cody's show as clearly a departure from realism—like a live-performance equivalent of the dime novels. Despite these distinctly antagonistic views, Crawford revealed his continued feeling of friendship for Cody by the presentation in 1899 of a Winchester inscribed COL. W. F. CODY, FROM CAPTAIN JACK.[6]

Crawford and His Poetry

Crawford published several volumes of poetry in his career, along with pieces in magazines and other publications and recitations on the stage. The published volumes ranged from *The Poet Scout: A Book of Song and Story* (1886) to the final *Whar' the Hand o' God Is Seen and Other Poems* (2d ed. 1913).

With literary and public fame, Crawford combined a prodigious output of articles, poems, and essays while crisscrossing the country with public speaking engagements and theatrical performances. It was generally unknown, however, that he relied on the assistance of editors for purifying his poetry and prose due to imperfections of spelling and punctuation. From around 1895 the editor was Marie Madison, whose qualifications included several plays in her own right, one of them with Captain Jack.

Samples of Crawford's poetry, innumerable endorsements, and biographical pronouncements appear in the illustrated booklet, *Souvenir of Song and Story*, published New Year's Day 1898. This thirty-page, 11¼ × 9¼-inch monograph also offered mining stock for the Captain Jack Crawford Alaska Prospecting and Mining Corporation—a venture capitalized at $250,000, with an office listed at 150 Nassau Street, New York City. Clearly, Captain Jack was multi-talented, though as a businessman he shared some of the same bad luck as Cody, particularly in his hopes of success as a miner.

Crawford's keen interest in firearms was reflected in his tribute to the Winchester rifle and a still longer poem, "The Olde Kentucky Rifle." Among lines from the latter tribute, ringing true for any collector or history buff:

> It was my lone companion when this
>   country was a wild,
> I loved it dear as father ever loved a
>   favored child.
> An' I've seed some skeery moments when
>   to me 'twas all in all,
> That ol' Kentucky rifle hangin' thar
>   ag'in the wall.

Crawford's ode to the Winchester was one of his less maudlin or banal efforts. By modern standards, however, he would hardly qualify as a major or even minor poet:

To My Winchester

> Thou are not sweet
> In disposition unto all, my dear;
> To some thou art most spiteful in thine
>   anger—
> Many have quailed in abject fright to hear
> Thy ringing tones in war's resounding
>   clangor.
> Although thy face may gleam with polished
>   smiles,

> Thou art a spitfire when the scene is
>   fitting,
> And gone are all thy sweet coquettish wiles
> When foes with mine their battle powers
>   are pitting
> In war's made heat.
> I love thee, dear,
> And love of loyal man was never placed
> Upon a more deserving, true companion,
> In western wanderings, when peril faced
> Our daily life, on plain, in gloomy
>   canyon.
> My trust in thee has never been betrayed,
> True as thy tempered steel I've always
>   found thee,
> In scenes of danger I was not afraid
> Though savage foemen lurked in rocks
>   around me,
> For thou wert near.
> Come, dear one, fling
> Thy moody silence off, and lift thy voice
> In song as in the days now gone
>   forever;
> For all the dangers past let us rejoice,
> I'll beat the time with thy quick-acting
>   lever.
> Sing in thy wildest tones, let not a note
> Be soft as note from tender woman,
> Sing as thou didst when from thy fiery
>   throat
> We hurled defiance at a foe inhuman.
> Sing, sweetheart, sing.
> Whoopa-la, my pet,
> Let war come if it must, and I will wed
> A thousand border men to girls like
>   you are,
> And with my wild Pegasus at their head
> We'll whip our weight in Spanish
>   Weyle cats sure.
> With truth and right, with liberty and love,
> With freedom's starry banner floating
>   o'er us,

> With faith and trust in Him who reigns
>   above
> All tyranny and wrong must melt be-
>   fore us
> For freedom yet.

In company with this poem, Crawford rendered a solid endorsement of the Winchester rifle: "The Winchester Rifle is by all odds the best small arm on earth, and always has been since first invented. More than 75 per cent. of the frontiersmen use the Winchester. For rapidity and accuracy it cannot be beaten."

Captain Jack and His Guns

The Winchester Model 1873 number 99609, richly engraved and presentation inscribed, is the only known example of that model with decoration by the factory composed of lines of poetry. The company's gift may well have been timed soon after Crawford's lengthy poetic tribute to that noble arm.

His Kentucky Rifle and Winchester poems are a reflection of Crawford's love of guns and shooting. His collection numbered several pieces, three of the best of which are pictured on these pages. Documentation of a selection of Crawford guns and memorabilia appeared in a receipt from the organizing committee for the centennial celebration of Fort Bliss, El Paso, Texas. The receipt, signed by Victor B. Gilbert, County Judge, lists the following, each identified with a serial number:

Items loaned for Anniversary by Mrs. Willis B. (Irene) Shontz [from the Captain Jack Crawford Collection]:

Portable desk of Captain Jack Crawford, famous Army Scout.

#13221—Colt gun taken as a trophy at Slim Buttes fight, 1876.

#11832—Spencer Repeating Rifle gun taken as trophy from Chief American Horse.

#5720—Manhattan gun given to Captain Jack by General Custer of the 7th. Cav.

The End of the Trail

Camp chair of General Custer and portable desk of Custer, given to Captain Jack

#12022—Silver Watch, a gift to Captain Jack from Army Scout "Texas Jack".

#367895—Silver Watch, a gift to Captain Jack from Attorney General Richard Olney.

#18313—Winchester gun, a gift to Captain Jack for "Buffalo Bill" Cody.

#1—Colt ball and cap gun, a gift to Captain Jack from "Buffalo Bill" Cody.

#32074—Winchester gun used by Captain Jack in New Mexico.

#15758—Winchester gun used by Captain Jack when he was Chief of Army Scouts.

#51687—Winchester gun used by Captain Jack in "West" Shows [a nickel-plated Saddle Ring Carbine].

#56595—Colt 38 gun, a gift to Captain Jack from Robert T. Lincoln.

#186213—Colt ball and cap gun, a gift to Captain Jack from "Wild Bill" Hickok.

#454794—Smith & Wesson gun, a gift to Captain Jack from W. A. Bell.

Clearly, Captain Jack was a collector and a pioneer enthusiast of the Wild West who happened also to have experienced the times himself. Gifts of guns from gunmakers are known to have come to him from the factories of Colt, Winchester, and Remington. During some appearances, he set up displays of arms from his growing collection.

In his lecture performances, Crawford often clutched a Winchester Model 1873 or Lightning Colt rifle in one hand while, as part of his Western costume, he wore a six-shooter in a holster. A climax to some of these appearances was a demonstration of how Wild Bill Hickok would deal with two desperadoes, coming at him front and back. Crawford would whip out his Colt revolver, fire a blank at each imagined foe, and then depart the stage to excited applause from his enraptured audience.

Crawford remained solidly engaged in a whirlwind of activities and tours. He was claimed by death on February 27, 1917—some six weeks after the death of his longtime friend and sometime unfriendly rival, Buffalo Bill. Both wanted the public to understand and appreciate what the West was about: freedom, self-reliance, hard work, bravery, courage, stamina, sacrifice, and opportunity. Cody's message came first from the stage and then largely from the show arena. Crawford's came mainly from the stage or lectern through his educational pronouncements and entertainments. Only briefly was Crawford a Wild West performer. Although his fame was less enduring, Crawford deserves to be recognized as successful in his own way as his legendary rival was in his.

Winchester Model 1873 presentation, serial number 499609, a .22 rimfire caliber; finished in gold, nickel, and silver plating, with blued half-octagonal barrel and case-hardened hammer and trigger. For other firearms of Crawford or ones he presented to friends, see R. L. Wilson, *The Peacemakers*.

Buffalo Bill and Pawnee Bill as partners, ca. 1908–1912. Gold-plated Colt Single Action Army revolvers inscribed on backstrap MAJOR GORDON W. LILLIE; Single Action at *right* a .44 smoothbore, specially ordered from factory by Lillie. Cabinet cards include adoring wife May, who became an expert shot and equestrian. U.S. Lithograph Company documents foreboding problems. Programs became thinner but were still colorful.

Chapter 8

Colonel Cody and Major Lillie

1908-1912

The triumphs of the European tours, the Chicago World's Fair, and numerous engagements in New York City were distant memories as Cody approached old age. In his early sixties, Cody was hounded by debt and, though older, he seemed none the wiser in business dealings. He remained fortunate in having loyal friends and the continued adulation of millions of members of the public. One of those acquaintances from the early days tried to help out the aging scout: Gordon W. "Pawnee Bill" Lillie, himself an accomplished showman and a "man with a record, a name."

The partnership that developed is all the more interesting because Pawnee Bill wrote about it in a detailed and intimate memoir. A copy of the twenty-eight-page, single-spaced saga was found by Greg Martin at an antique show, accompanied by memorabilia of both stars. Other copies of the manuscript are known, including the most vital, a complete set, provided directly from the family to Pawnee Bill's biographer, Glenn Shirley.*

Promotional display of approximately 19 inches in height to attract the public.

Lillie's extraordinary record began when he—as a nine-year-old boy—first saw Cody, with Wild Bill Hickok and Texas Jack Omohundro, in Bloomington, Illinois. The three were on tour during the *Scouts of the Prairie* days. Much of Lillie's story deals with the years in which the two Bills were partners in Buffalo Bill's Wild West and Pawnee Bill's Far East. During the show season, they lived together, traveling in the same private railroad car, touring the United States and Canada. Their road trips began in 1909 and continued until 1913. Published here for the first time, these recollections bring alive that long-lost era—vital times for both and for the future of Wild West entertainments. Pawnee Bill's abiding affection for his old partner, Buffalo Bill, is evident throughout.[1]

*The authors are grateful to Glenn Shirley, author, *Pawnee Bill: A Biography of Major Gordon W. Lillie,* and to Western Publications, for permission to quote from manuscript material, copyright for which is held by Mr. Shirley.

My earliest recollection of Col. W. F. Cody, Buffalo Bill, was as a small boy . . . hearing my dear mother read to me stories of him in the "Saturday Night", a publication similar to the Saturday Evening Post of today. [One day] mother sent me on an errand . . . after school which took me into the center of my home town, Bloomington, Ill. As I passed along Main street looking West, I saw in front of the St. Nicholas Hotel, which was then the best and most popular hotel in town, a large crowd. Thinking it was a fight, boy like, I hurried to the spot as fast as I could run but the thrill I got was not only greater than any I had ever received from a fight, but was the greatest I had ever received in my life.

There in the center of this immense crowd sat three frontier's men clad in big sombreros with long hair falling to their shoulders and buffalo robe coats. They were relating experiences of the plains to each other. These men were Buffalo Bill, Wild Bill Hickcock, and Texas Jack [Omohundro]. They were to appear at the Schroders Opera House that night in a play called "The Scouts of the Plains".

Many years after, my father moved his flouring mill thirty five miles [south] of Wichita, Kans., to a little town called Wellington. . . . The milling business did not appeal to me so I drifted into the Indian Territory and after a year or two among the Pawnee Indians learned their language [and] through the influence of Adler Steveson and Senator David Davis, succeeded in being appointed interpreter and teacher in the Government school at Pawnee Agency. There was a traders store, a community boarding house, a big Indian boarding school, and the U.S. Indian Agent's Office constituted the entire white settlement. . . .

As I entered the boarding house one evening I was asked by the manager if I would accept as a room-mate a young man who I had observed at dinner that day, to which I gave my ascent [sic]. I found him to be Mr. Chas Burgess who had been sent by Buffalo Bill to get a half-dozen Pawnee Indians to take part in their play the coming winter. Major Bowman had objected to him taking them without first getting permission from the

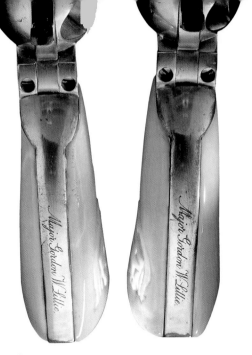

Pair of Pawnee Bill Colt Single Action Army revolvers, gold plated, with inscribed backstraps; .450 Boxer caliber, 5½-inch barrels; serial numbers 14844 and 14845; English proof markings; eagle and star motifs on bone grips.

Indian commissioner at Washington. This took the biggest part of a week . . . so in this way I became well acquainted with Mr. Burgess and found him most entertaining, as he had been with Col. Cody three years and . . . visited nearly every big city in the U.S. His stories of his travels fascinated me.

The Indian commissioner refused the permit [to] take the Indians. On his return he told Col. Cody that he had been refused to take the Indians but, he Said, "There is a young fellow down there in the service who talks Indian like a native, has long hair, and would be a good man for your Wild West Show" which was to be put on in 1883 as a new, thrilling line in the Show world. So I was engaged and took the Pawnees on to take part in the first and only Wild West performance ever given up to this time. It proved an ovation in every city, and its popularity was acclaimed at every point we visited.

I furnished the Indians for Col. Cody, and acted as his interpreter for the following two years, one season with the big Wild West show and one with the Prairie

Waif, or Buffalo Bill's Dutchman. Then I embarked in business for myself starting the second Wild West show, and operated with varied degrees of success, but the last three or four seasons prior to 1907 my shows had made a great deal of money.

[Buffalo Bill and Pawnee Bill Connect]

I was appearing in Wonderland Park Revere Beach, Mass. in 1907, when I received a message from W. W. Stewart, administrator of the Bailey estate, asking me to come to New York at once, as he had a great show proposition to make me that would make me rich. It was the combination of the Buffalo Bill and Pawnee Bill Shows. On the first visit, I left, feeling that there was no chance of the combination of the two shows. At the death of James A. Bailey, Mrs. Bailey wished to dispose of both the Barnum and Bailey, and the Buffalo Bill shows. They had picked on me for the Buffalo Bill Show, the Ringlings having picked the Barnum and Bailey shows the spring before.

The latter part of June I had another wire from Mr. Stewart asking me to meet the Buffalo Bill show at Keene, N.H. for a conference with Col. Cody. I arrived just as the show was over. I watched the crowd leave, which was very light, then went to Col. Cody's private tent. He greeted me cordially and asked if I had seen the show. "No," I said, "I arrived just as the people were leaving." We then had some further conversation about combining the two shows and I asked under what title the combined shows would operate. Col. replied, " 'Buffalo Bill's Wild West and Congress of Rough Riders of the World.' She has run for over thirty years under that title. There has never been an atom added to it nor taken from it," he replied. "Well, Col.", I said, "If I were in your place, I guess I would act just as you have about it but unless I could have the title of my show embodied in the title of the combined shows, I could in no way be interested." He invited me to take dinner with him but I had to refuse as I wanted to get back to my show, just as quickly as possible. As I took my leave the Colonel asked, "Can you tell me why our business is not better through New England?" "Yes, you are down here too late. I never could get any money in N.E. after the 20th day of June." I replied. "Why, I never heard of such a thing. I am quite sure I have played N.E. this late and even later in years gone by, and always made money," he said. "Well, maybe you can with your show, but I never could with mine. I always manage to be out by the 20th day of June." "We go into New York state next. What will we do there?" he asked. "A lot better, but you are in the edge of haying which will hurt you some." He then asked, "Well, from there we will go into Mich. What will we do there?" "Put all your extras in, every day. You will do all you can hold, as you will be in Mich. just right." I replied[.] "Well, Gordon," he said, "I am going to watch and see how your prophecies come out," he said, and bidding me good-bye, I hurried away to catch the train fully convinced and satisfied that the combination of the two shows was a closed incident for all times.

When the show reached New York State, I got a very friendly letter from the Col. saying they had made no money in N.E. but that the moment they had crossed the line into New York state, business had improved. When they reached Michigan he could not wait to write but wired me: "First town in Mich. Got all the extra seats in." The second or third day another wire stating: "All the extras in, and turned people away in a rain."

On a wire from Mr. Stewart, I went on again to New York. "What did you do to Col. Cody on your visit to Keene? He now thinks you are a sort of a wizard or superman. He is willing to any change in title you choose to make and is stronger for [you] than horse-radish." So after another conference with Col. Cody, we decided on the title "Buffalo Bill's Wild West and Pawnee Bill's Great Far East Combined" under which the shows operated for five years. After the deal was completed and the money was paid, I went on to the Buffalo Bill Show and met them at New Orleans. They had but three weeks yet to run, when they closed at Memphis about the middle of November, 1907. My reception was any thing but a glorious affair. Col. Cody

Pawnee Bill Single Action Army revolver, documented in the Colt factory records in rare .44 "smoothbore" with "slightly choked" 5½-inch barrel for shooting shot loads; blued finish; shipped to Lillie on April 30, 1891; serial number 140472. Shipment was of two revolvers of same description.

A few pairs of similar smoothbore revolvers were made on Lillie's order by the factory, of which this specimen is the only one known to the authors. Pawnee Bill was given a pair of pearl-gripped Single Actions by the factory in 1902; another set was given to him in 1906.

received me in a most cordial manner and I knew he meant it and was glad and delighted to have me there, for his faith in the handling of the show by the administrator was entirely gone, and several clashes between Col. Cody and the assistant manager . . . were most serious. In one of [these] the Col. struck the manager and knocked him down.

Orders came from headquarters in 28th St. New York City "Unless Cody apoligizes and begs your pardon close the show at once and ship it back to winter quarters, Bridgeport, Conn." The Col. held out till the last moment refusing to so humble himself but when he saw them making actual preparations to close the show, he asceeded [sic] and apoligized most humbly. This and a number of other less serious clashes had so wrought the Col. to a point where he realized since the death of Mr. Bailey there was no friendly sentiment left. It was just a cold dollar and cents proposition, so a change of management was welcomed by him. The relations between Cody and Bailey had always been most cordial and friendly. Mr. Bailey was a great admirer of Col. Cody, always staked him when he was short of money, and in fact was always ready and willing to assist and please him in every way possible, but when I sa[y] Col. Cody welcomed me that about ended it for the best I could say for the balance of the 619 (There were 620 people in the Company) members composing the Company that they received me in a respectful manner, a kind of an air of "I am against him, but he is now the big boss and I will have to be nice to him in order to hold my position".

I knew Col. Cody well from having worked for him as a boy, knew he was tempermental and made up my mind before I handed my money over to the administrator that I would get along with him. Nothing he could do would cause me to fall out with him, and now that I had met the balance of the troupe and saw they were against me, I was more determined in this resolve than ever. I had only been with the show two days when a business matter came up that compelled me to return to my Buffalo Ranch in Okla. so that I barely reached the show in Memphis the closing day and went in to Bridgeport, Conn. on the train.

[Pawnee Bill Takes the Reins]

All the performers, in fact every one around the show, including Col. Cody, left for their homes in the west. I with the treasurer, auditor, Johnie Baker, and the main bosses and enough working men to pack the show away went into winter quarters with the two big trains, and in the course of the next two weeks, had it packed away, in the buildings of the Barnum winter

Programs of Pawnee Bill's entertainments around the turn of the century. A buffalo-profile souvenir booklet of the Oklahoma ranch, dating after the Two Bills show.

quarters. When the Ringling Bros. had purchased the big Barnum show, the plant of the Buffalo Bill show went with it together with a contract allowing us to winter in the Barnum quarters, and also to rent from the Ringling Bros. the plant, for which we were to pay the sum of $25,000.00 per year as follows: $1,000.00 each week on the road for the first 25 weeks; then nothing more for the balance of the season. Our offices were in the Bailey building, 28th & Broadway, New York City.

My wife, known and extensively billed with the Pawnee Bill shows (as Miss May Lillie, Champion Lady Horse-back Shot of the World) was terribly against the combination of the two shows, arguing that as we had made plenty of money in the Pawnee Bill Show, [we] could continue to do so, as it was so well established and favorably known that it was so much easier for me to handle than the combined shows would be, but I was persistent and as the argument went on from day to day, and she had exhausted about all her most favorable points she declared, "If you go into this deal, I will never travel with it. I think this is the most crazy idea you have ever had. Worked 20 years (fifteen of them on a shoe-string) and now that you have your show on a good solid foundation, where you make more money than you need, you want to tear it all up. Tell me if you can any one good reason why you are even justified in considering such a deal. Have you got one? Just one?" "Yes," I declared, "I have one. One and no more. You know, May, we have worked almost night and day and as you say, have at last made a wonderful success, considered today one of the three best paying and most attractive show properties in the whole U.S. You also know that during that whole time, the Buffalo Bill show did all in their power to stop us, even to hiring our best performers, to stopping us for getting a permit from Washington to legally take the Indians off the reservation and I had to steal them, and take a chance of going to jail, or my show would have stopped; how they at every chance would go 30 to 50 miles out of their way to cover our paper with theirs, reading: 'Coming Soon;' when in many cases they had no intention of playing the town; and how the people have passed [us] up and waited for Buffalo Bill, who did not come. How our friends who saw it said, 'When the cable came from Antwerp, Belgium, the Pawnee Bill has failed' they all threw their hats in the air and 'Hurrahed' with delight and glee at our failure. Well here's my reason, the only one I have got, I want this combination of the two biggest Wild West shows in the World with myself as owner and general manager so that I may see these boys who threw their hats in the air and who worked so hard in many ways to down me, come to me and receive their pay check from my hand." "O bosh, all those things you are crying about are dead and buried long ago. Let them rest in peace. Why resurrect them at this late day? And you call yourself a business man, and the only reason you can advance why you should pull off this, the greatest financial and business event of your whole life is to get even with a lot of people who are not even in your class."

"Forget it? No never. I can never forget it. The wounds are healed, the scars will always remain. Had these things happened the last five years of the Pawnee Bill show I would have laughed at [them], considered it sport, but you know these hard knocks came when we were down and struggling to get up, when our purse was empty and when money was hard to get; when the price to get in was only 10c and 25c, that's why I will never forget." Mrs. Lillie kept her word. She never travelled with the combined show.

[The Two Bills Show Headquartered in New York]

Our offices on 28th St. were very nice. the General reception and office room, with a number of desks for the heads of the different departments, a room for Mr. Cook, the general Agent, and one for Mr. Baker, the Arena director, who was also the foster son of Col. Cody. Major Burke, general Press representative, had a desk in the reception room. Most of the early part of the winter I spent in Bridgeport, as I made a number of important changes in the equipment and general handling of the show. Buck Connor, now motion picture actor and director, was my private secretary, and by liberal use of the telephone with me, handled the office. On one of my weekend visits to New York, Buck confided in me that the talk around the office in my absence was that I was not big enough to handle the combined shows.

The night before, I had seen at the Opera House, a play called "Vie Wireless". It was the most wonderful scenic picture I had ever seen in my life, and on this account was the talk of New York, so the following morning, I called on the manager, complementing the wonderful production, and secured from him the address of the artist who had produced these wonderful scenic effects. They were the people who worked exclusively for the Shuberts. I asked them if they could make

Colt Single Action Army revolver, documented in the factory ledgers as 4¾-inch barrel, .45 Colt caliber, blued and case-hardened finish, serial number 292027, shipped April 18, 1907, to G. W. "Pawnee Bill" Lillie. This revolver was purchased just before the two Bills became closely allied professionally. The grips are of smooth patina, revealing age and wear from use in the show arena. Lack of shipping address in the factory records indicates the company might well have delivered the guns directly to Pawnee Bill while he was on tour. Delivery might have been made by a Colt factory employee. R. H. Wagner, Colt Historian Emeritus, has told the authors of delivering guns and parts to the 101 Ranch show on behalf of the Colt factory, with strict instructions to make sure he was paid on the spot for whatever was invoiced.

for me something for our show that would create a sensation equal to or greater than "Vie Wireless" for our
opening in Madison Square Garden which was to take
place in March. He said he thought so as he had so
much more room in the Garden in which to work effects. So in two weeks from that date I called on them
again and they had made for me a complete working
model of just what they could do for me in the Garden.
The model was great, everything suited me but the price
when [they] told me it would cost $75,000.00 I wilted.
That was a lot of money. This price was more than three
times what I had figured to put into it, but I felt sure it
would put our show over with a bang at least, even if it
did not create a sensation.

The day had arrived for our opening in the Garden. The putting up of this great scenic piece had taken
up two of our three days allotted for rehearsals. So early
of the third day, Mr. Baker was on the job. The scenery
had taken virtually all the space, back stage, leaving
merely a passageway barely big enough for three horses
to pass. Absolutely no room at all for props such as
stagecoaches, prairie-schooners, artillery pieces, horses,
camels, elephants, etc., etc. These all had to be kept in
the basement. The passageway on either side of the
stage was only 8 or 10 ft. wide and very steep. Mr. Baker,
Johnie, as he was always called, had worked all day and
far into the night trying to work the program, but at the
entrances and exits this enormous bunch of horsemen
and material would pile up in the passage-ways to the
basement, and to make matters worse the Far East had
been added to the program, with many new acts and
animals such as camels, elephants, water-buffalo, animals that had never before been carried with the show.
And while we had stabled our Far East animals in the
stable of the Wild West horses purposely to get them accustomed to them, and unafraid, and had had a good
effect but never before were the Wild West horses compelled to rub sides with the elephants, camels, Etc.
which made them frantic and in a number of instances
caused accidents to the riders.

Reports finally came to the front of the house where
I was very busy, arranging the smallest details incident

Agreement of October 30, 1911, between Buffalo Bill and Pawnee
Bill for continuing their partnership in the "Two Bills" show. The two
Bills seated together in full show regalia.

to the opening of the greatest show house in the World,
as it was billed in those days, that the show could not be
put on unless a large part of the scenery was removed.
This could not be done without ruining the whole scenic
effect. As I had always staged all of my performances, I
offered my services to assist John. He accepted them
with a weak heart, but I added my bit. First I engaged

12 big strong men with a hook rope they attached to the
backs of the vehicles without slacking the speed and
b[y] the 12 men hanging on to the rope let them down
into the basement without any delay. Then I stationed
men in the exits to keep them clear of all obstacles, and
to hurry the riders down the incline into the basement.
This alleviated a large part of our congestion but we yet
had considerable trouble to over-come. I saw Johnie did
not accept my services with a very good grace, so I took
him to one side and said to him "Johnie, I am the general manager of the show, and that is all I want to be. I
do not want to be the arena director, but I am positive I
can render you aid if you will allow me, and when we
get these first few shows over, and things are running
right, all the credit due I want you to have as you are
surely entitled to it. But you have put in so many hours
and the task has been so great that I can see where you
are losing your nerve." This had the proper effect. Johnie
put his shoulder to the wheel. We worked together all
that night and the following day up to noon.

The doors opened at one o'clock and what we
called the first dress rehearsal was given to a large
crowd, and the performance went off splendidly with
but few waits and mishaps. At night, the performance
which was advertised as the formal opening many important personages occupied the boxes, by invitation
from the management. Gen. Miles had come from
Washington with a party of prominent army officers
and their ladies, the Governor of the State of New
Yor[k], and New Jersey, the mayor of New York,
Richard Crocker, the leader of Tamany Hall and many
others, in fact the entire large circle of front row boxes
were occupied by important personages, well known in
those days. Every seat in the house was filled. The performances went off with a [bang], and wonderfully
smooth for the second performance. The United Press of
New York the following morning was loud in their
praise. Many of them mentioned the Far East as a welcome added attraction and giving us front-page stuff
with big head-lines.

The following day, Mr. Cook came to me and complimented me highly and also said Col. Cody was

pleased with the performance. "But," said he, "I sure had my troubles with the Colonel during rehearsals. I sat in a box with him and when the horses and people would pile up in the exits at the close of an act, he would go up in the air. Three different times during rehearsals he would take me to the Hoffman House and actually laid on the bed and cried, shedding real tears, and wail, saying, 'Pawnee Bill will ruin me. Never wanted this Far East thing. We have showed in the Garden many times before without all this big scenery, and the show was always good. What are we going to do, Cook? Cant you do something about it to straighten it out?' I tried to pacify him as best I could, under the circumstances but I myself, Major, was dubious that Johnie and you would ever be able to bring it out of the chaotic condition and make a real performance of it without removing a large part of the scenery and widening the exits. But you have, and you both deserve great credit for putting on what I think is the greatest Wild West and Far East performance ever appearing in the Garden."

I also stopped at the Hoffman House but I always got up at 6 o'clock and went over to the Garden. Col. never arose till about 9 and seldom came to the Garden until after lunch. I purposely avoided meeting him for several days, for after the dismal tale Cook had related to me I figured to give him plenty of time to quiet down, and then I knew with the excellent press we had received, that we would be sure to do a big business. The matinee of the second day was light. The night house was not what I had expected though the statement showed more money than the opening day, due to their being no invitation guests. The following day picked up, the afternoon being good, and the night house almost filled. The following Monday was big both afternoon and night. The night house being a complete sell-out with a slight turnaway. Tuesday during the Far East section of the performance, Col. Cody's valet brought me a note asking me to come back to his dressing room, as I entered, I noticed that he looked very happy. He extended his hand to me, saying, "Pard, put her there." As I grasped his hand I wondered what was coming next. With his other arm he pulled me up close to him saying,

"Major, we've got the world by the tail with a down hill pull. All my friends tell me we have got the greatest performance I have ever had." During our five years of partnership I dont think the Colonel ever said anything to me that pleased me quite so much. For I now knew that I had made good, which I knew from past experience when I worked for him as a boy, that that was absolutely essential in order to get along with him. When I had worked for him as a young man I looked upon him with awe, in fact I looked upon him as the greatest man I had ever met [or] seen. We only saw him during the performances or during our trips on the train, and I was not at all intimate with him or his disposition, but after the news went out of the combination of the two shows, I heard plenty.

[The Ringling Brothers and the Wild West Show]

One night as I was retiring at the . . . Hotel at Bridgeport, my phone rang and I found it was Mr. John Ringling. He said he and Otto, his brother, wanted to see me, so I quick, got dressed before they reached the room. They came up to talk over things in general, and the combination of the two shows in particular, the how's and whys that brought it about, etc. During our conversation, I mentioned to them that I was surprised that they did not buy the Buffalo Bill show and operate it as they already owned the Buffalo Bill [plant] and had to provide room for them to winter in their Barnum winter quarters, and that it was a show that they could handle easily, as it would draw money either ahead of or behind the Barnum show. "Well, I will tell

Letter from Pawnee Bill Lillie, dated July 18, 1927, to a Mr. Saunders on Pawnee Bill's Buffalo Ranch, Pawnee, Oklahoma. With signed sepia-tone portrait photograph of Pawnee Bill and envelope addressed to Whitelaw Saunders of Wawego, Kansas.

you why we didnt consider it, Major. You know Col. Cody is awful hard to get along with. No one can handle him without trouble. You know last season they nearly closed the show in the middle of the season on account of Col. Cody knocking the assistant manager down. They have that Wild West bunch lined up against all the Bailey end of the show, and the cowboys, Indians and Mexicans, with all them guns, tomahawks and war-clubs, keep the Bailey end of the show in dread and fear all of the time. Wait till you get opened and on [the] road. You'll have your trouble. They'll about scalp you."

"No, no, John, you are mistaken. You failed to take into consideration that I am and have always been one of that same tribe you have just mentioned, with their guns, tomahawks and war-clubs, and can weild [sic] them as good as they can. Furthermore, I am the boy that's going to do all the lining up of these people myself." "Well, Major, I will admit you probably are the best fitted person in the U.S. to handle him, but mark me, you wont get away with it without your trouble too. When fall comes you will know you have had a big job even if you get away with it." Here our conversation drifted to the purchase of the Barnum show by the Ringling Bros. John making the statement that they used very good judgment in the purchase, as the show the past season had cleared more than the purchase price of the entire property to which Mr. Otto ascented. . . .

The engagement at Madison Square Garden ended in a blaze of glory as our press agents would say. The last two weeks was a turn away every night with a number of turn aways at the matinee, something most unusual in the Garden. From N.Y. we went over to Brooklyn, this being our first opening under canvass. The canvass and seats had all been erected before we left the Garden, so that our first move was an easy task. The weather was damp, cold and cloudy the entire week, which materially hurt our business, and to add to our discomfort, a strike was pulled off among our hustlers [settled by Pawnee Bill by standing up to the strikers and backing his boss hustler]. . . .

[Major John Burke and Louis E. Cooke]

When we started to bill New York Mrs. Bailey's representative and the administrator came to my office to discuss matters pertaining to the operation of the show. Mr. Cook came in. He was in entire charge of the advertising, and the entire advance of the show. Mrs. Baileys representative suggested to Mr. Cook that too much money had been spent the previous year in advertising N.Y. and asked if he didnt think we could get along without the subway ads, as they were very expensive. "No, I dont," replied Mr. Cook, and asked me what I thought of it, to which I had to reply that I did not know, as I had never billed N.Y. this being my first appearance in N.Y. as a showman. They suggested to me that they cut out the subway advertising, to which I agreed, as it was the first disposition to reduce costs I had seen since my connection with the show, and for the further reason that it had been the first request they had made of me, and were the legal representatives of Mrs. Bailey I considered it bad policy to lock horns with them at the very first opportunity though Mr. Cook argued to the last moment that it was one of the best modes of advertising in N.Y. outside of the Press and I felt that he was right. This was months before we began our actual billing.

A number of times during the winter, Mr Cook had urged me to allow him to include the subways in our billing. I looked into the subway advertising considerably. I noticed the Hippodrome, the largest theatrical house in N.Y. used them, and a number of my best friends thought it one of the best forms of advertising in N.Y. so just before we started billing N.Y. I told Mr. Cook I would leave it entirely to his judgment. This I knew [was] equivalent to saying "Bill the subways." On the second or third day of our Brooklyn engagement, in stepped Mrs. Bailey's representative, (I do not mention names as one of them still lives in N.Y. the other went down on the Titanic), and entered a complaint about the N.Y. expense account for entertainment of the Press by Major Burke and also asked me what I was going to do about Mr. Cook's billing the subways, when we had all decided to eliminate it. "Well, don't you think it

Cody on horseback, late in career.

proved out the thing to do? Look at the enormous business we did in New York, more by far than the show has ever done before." "Yes I grant you this, but it was not the subways that did it. You deserve all the credit. It was that scenic backpiece and the addition of the Far East that made the business."

"Gentlemen, Mr. Cook had urged me many times after we had made our decision had been rendered to allow me to use the subway, and after a thorough investigation I decided that Cook was right, and told him to take them." "Well Major Lillie, we have also given this matter lots of thought and we have come over to request that you discharge both Louis E. Cook and Major John M. Burke, you have been doing lots of talk about economy and management and reducing costs, we believe that this would be two long strides in that direction, as these two are the most extravagant men in our employ and as these two positions carry with them the spending of over 70% of the daily expenses of the show you can never accomplish what you desire with these two men in these two important positions virtually the key to the situation." To say that I was thunder struck by this request is putting it mildly. I would not have been more surprised had they asked for my resignation. Louis E. Cook, called the Dean of general Agents, the highest priced general agent and justly so in the U.S. a man who had worked for Mr. Bailey in this same position, he was filling with us, for 12 or 15 years. Major John M. Burke, called the Dean of Press Agents, who had been with Col. Cody for over 30 years in class A with the highest salaried press agents in this country. He knew more managing editors and owners of big publications and called them by their first names than any press man who ever lived, was considered [an] authority on matters of early Western history, and his wonderful true western stories on Western heroes both of the red and the white race, were readily accepted by the press of the Country. These two men, and also, Johnie Baker, who had been with Col. Cody for over 30 years are the only three men left of the original Buffalo Bill Co. that Col. Cody ever made any special mention of to me, and he requested me more than once before the combination was completed, that I always keep these three men in their respective positions as long as they filled them properly and wanted to remain with us, and I had given him my promise that I would do this. Now I am requested to discharge two of these men, one of them for no cause for when I decided we should take the subways I assumed all responsibilities for him. The other one because his expense account entertaining the press men of N.Y. ran high.

"Gentlemen, where will you get capable men to take their places? All the big shows are open and all capable men are under contracts. There is no chance in the world for us to do this. We cannot get along without them. Then your request [is] not fair to them anyway. I am responsible for the billing of the subways. After investigation I found Cook was right, and consented for him to take them. As for Burke's excessive expense account I do not believe that we did half enough in entertaining the press, for I never in my life saw such liberal treatment of any show any place as was accorded us by the press of N.Y. City. And I feel that I will never live to pay off my obligation to them. Furthermore, we have yearly contracts with both of these gentlemen, and we

would have to pay them whether we used them or not during the season."

I knew Mrs. Bailey's representatives. Knew the great worth of these two men and that they knew as well as I did that there was no chance for us to get along without them. It gradually began to soak into me that this was a sort of challenge to me for a fight and what a day and what a time for one. The entire week to now had been cold and damp without a ray of sunshine. The business had gone from big business to nothing in one jump, with no prospect of improvement. I had also noticed that ever since the combination had been completed there was a disposition to find fault and to not approve anything that I did or suggested. They had not approved of the ordering of the expensive scenery, claiming that as this scenery could not be carried on the road, in meant an added expense of $2,500.00 per week for our three weeks in the garden.

"Well, Gentlemen, ["] I finally said, "I cannot grant this request. Before Col. Cody and I came to terms he mentioned these two men and also Johnie Baker and lauded their abilities and asked me if I did not think they were good men, and I told him that I thought they were as good, if not the best men, in their respective lines, and told him I would retain them as long as they successfully filled their positions. So you can see I cannot go back on that. Now if you want to see Col. Cody and talk the matter over with him, we can all get together and discuss the matter further. but i[n] view of the fact that Major Burke has been with him ever since the Wild West was first started, and that Mr. Cook has been with him 12 or more years, and he has a very high personal regard for him, outside of their ability in their respective lines, I do not believe there would be any use of it." "But, Major Lillie, you are the manager. Col. Cody does not enter into these business matters. He handles the back end of the show." "I know I am the manager thats why I object to granting this request, which I know is wrong and against the best interests of the show, and this particular thing you propose is of vital interest and concern to Col. Cody, and as long as I occupy my present position I will always consult him on

matters of importance, whether they be in connection with the front or the back of the show. (Everything connected with the business of the show is referred to as the front while everything connected with the performance is referred to as the back) Furthermore, he owns a third of the show and is equal owner with us."

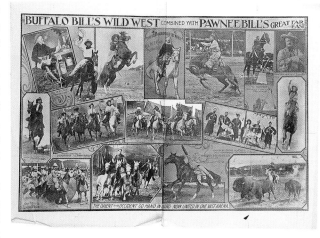

Vignettes from the Cody and Lillie entertainment.

[Buying out the Bailey Interests]

"Oh, no he isnt. He does not own one iota of the show. Not a penny in the show. We own outright his third of the show and hold a bill of sale signed by him, for it, including the titles "Buffalo Bill's Wild West, Buffalo Bill's Rough Riders of the World," and the right to use the picture of and the full title of Col. W. F. Cody, Buffalo Bill. Besides that, we hold his notes for over $70,000.00. This makes us the ⅔ owner against your ⅓ and I really think you do not give us due consideration in matters of vital importance concerning the show. Major, why dont you buy out our interests? We can see where your handling of the show does not coincide with our mode and idea of handling and that you are very headstrong and mean to handle it entirely in your way, not withstanding we are the majority owners. The only solution that we can see would be for you to buy us out then you can handle it to suit yourself, and when the

Show earns sufficient amount to pay off Col. Codys share you can deed back to him a third or a half of the show just as you and he agree. As matters are now going I can see a chance for it to lead to serious trouble, and I would regret to have to resort to legal means after our relations up to now have been so friendly. Well, Major, think it over, we will be over in a few days and talk it over further with you." With this they returned to N.Y. (Well, that's that). I thought they sold me a third interest together with giving me a lot of salve to the effect that they considered me the greatest Wild West manager in the country, etc. to get me tied in as an entering wedge to force me to buy the other ⅔ interest. I quite agreed with them on many of their statements, especially the one where they said they were afraid matters would get into serious complications, for I say plainly that this was their intentions, and with they owning the majority of the show, they could object to my mode of handling, have some restraining order issue, apply for a receiver and in that way take the management out of my hands. I talked it over with Col. Cody. He said he could do nothing to raise money, as owing to the last season in Europe they encountered Glanders with their horses and did not only lose their horses by the German authorities killing them but the authorities also burne[d] all their horse tents, canvass, harness, saddles, costumes, and everything came into contact with the horses. This caused the attendance of the show to fall off till it was pitiful to the extent that the show had lost over $300,000.00. This compell[ed] Col. to mortgage his ranches in North Platte, Neb, and Cody, Wyo. and his big modern hotel at Cody to help pay his share of the losses, and even this was not sufficient. He was also compelled to give them the bill of sale referred to by Mrs. Bailey's representatives, and some notes for the balance.

The entire week in Brooklyn was bad, being rainy, cold and windy so that the business showed a loss. Then we moved to Philadelphia, where the first two days were very bad, being bad weather. On Tuesday morning, the two representatives of Mrs. Bailey arrived, bent on making me buy the balance of the show. They made several pretty strong statements as to what they had decided to do, if things about the show were not changed. In fact they were in a manner—veiled threats. The business being bad I think, had a depressing influence on them. I am sure they left New York with the sole intention of putting some kind of a deal over with me if it was possible to do so. Finally, I asked them what kind of a deal they would make with me if I undertook to buy it. I explained to them that it meant a pretty big load for me as I had already paid out about $50,000.00 in cash for the other ⅓ interest and my share of the wintering of it. After some figuring they made me an offer of $66,666.66 for their two thirds interest and me to take up the notes and mortgages they held of Col Cody's or to endorse them as a guarantee of payment. There was one of the notes for about $12,000.00 which have been given by Col. Cody to James A. Bailey in London, Eng. at a time when the show was making plenty of money, that Col. Cody claimed that he had paid. Col. said that Mr. Bailey had taken it out of his share of the profits, had given him a receipt in full for the money, promising to send the note on to him the next time he visited their main office in New York City, where the note was filed. For some unexplainable reason this had never been done, and as Col. had lost or misplaced his receipt for the money, at the death of Mr. Bailey the estate held the note with nothing to show that it had ever been paid. I knew all about it for I had had the matter up with the administrator, trying to get it straightened out for the Col. but up to now had accomplished nothing as the Col. had been unable to produce any proof that he had paid it. "If I could raise the cash, could you not make some concession for it and what do you intend to do about the note that Col. Cody has already paid?" I asked. After some little argument between them, they finally agreed to throw out the $12,000.00 note and to throw off all the interest then due, which was quite an

Postcard of Buffalo Bill and friends at Wild Bill Hickok's grave, Deadwood, South Dakota, with two letters and envelope from Cody to his friend Mike Russell, with photograph of Cody taken in Leeds, England, signed "To M. R. Russell/from his friend/W. F. Cody." Russell's Model 1895 Winchester carbine, from the series presented by Buffalo Bill, pictured in Chapter 7.

amount. "Will you give until tomorrow noon to see what I can do about raising the money?" I asked. "All right, we will[.] Be here at noon tomorrow and if you can raise the money it will be a go." I knew I could raise it, for all I had to do was to draw a check on the Fidelity Trust Co. of Philadelphia where I had the amount, but it meant the depletion of nearly all my cash I wanted to have some time to think it over and to talk it over with Mr. Geist, the President of the Fidelity Trust Co. The last week's poor business had also dampened my ardor, while I knew the weather entirely responsible for it, still the fact that we were losing money daily had a bad effect, but after some talk with Mr. [?] I decided to go through with it. Wednesday morning when I arose, I saw the glorious sunlight flooding the earth, warming the chilly air, my nerve all came back. I could hardly wait to reach the Trust Co. to consumate the deal. All the bills of sale for properties[,] notes, and titles we transferred to me and a deed to the Bailey ⅔ interest. The note which had been paid was endorsed and returned to me without cost, this note being turned over to Col. W. F. Cody. My check for the full amount was passed to them, thus making me the sole owner of the Buffalo Bill's Wild West and Pawnee Bill's Great Far East combined show. I had a verbal understanding with the Col. that when the shows would clear the amount equal to the value of the show that with his one half he would pay me and I would deed back to him one half my equity in the shows. This was later done[.]

When I left the Trust Co. I felt like the man, I imagine feels, as he steps away from jail, for ever since I discovered the trick that was being worked on me, that I had been enticed and flattered into this deal in order to compel me to buy the balance of it, the thing had been a constant worry to me. I now know that this awful load was lifted from my shoulders and I was free again.

[The Two Bills Show Owned by the Two Bills]

It was about 6 o'clock when I reached the show lot. I found Col. Cody had gone down to the private car for dinner, so being anxious to bear the good news to the

One of the many cabinet cards with photograph taken by Stacy, from the Two Bills period.

Col. I joined him. He was just sitting down to dinner, and as I took my place at the table opposite him, I threw down the London note before him. "Have you ever seen that before?" I asked. "You bet. That's the Bailey $12,000.00 note. How did you get it?" "By buying them out, lock, stock and barrell. We are now sole and equal owners of the show. Your half interest to rest in my name until such time as the show makes enough that your half of the profits will pay it off, then I will deed back to you the half interest." "How about this $12,000.00 note?" the Col. asked. "I just made them throw that in, and also to knock off the interest on all the other notes. So you are now through paying interest, as I will [not] charge you on interest on these other notes. I dont believe in paying interest." "That's bully, Major. You have relieved my mind. I have a few little obligations in the way of small notes to some good per-

sonal friends of mine that I will have to take care of, then I will straighten up with you. The matinee today was great the best [we've] had since we left New York City, and the show went over big. Every one seemed to be pleased with it. I feel sure we were right at last."

The balance of the Philadelphia engagement was immense, the last three night houses being turn-aways and all the matinees were big, showing gross receipts of over 45,000.00 on the week. . . . The following Sunday in looking over the weekly statements, the Col. says, "Did you notice, the moment the Bailey interest got out, the business picked up? Derned if I dont think they were a couple of Jonnahs. We are lucky to have gotten rid of them."

The following week we played Wilmington, Baltimore, and Washington. At the latter stop, we were honored by the presence of our President, Wm. H. Taft, and also our good friend, Gen. Miles honored us again and a great many of the Ambassadors and Digni[t]aries of

Lithograph of similar period as Stacy cabinet card image.

Foreign Countries so that the boxes looked like the Far East had come to see the Far East, as the bright flashy costumes of the foreign legations such as China, Japan, India etc., almost outshone the colors and costumes of our Far East section. . . .

When we reached Indiana [Cody was pestered by a man who wanted to take him up in a balloon] . . . the Colonel lost his patience, rising from his chair he said, "Look here, young man, just tell Mr. X—with my compliments if I had 30 years to stay here and didn't have anything to do, I wouldn't go up in his derned baloon." As the young man made his escape with a broad smile, he looked at me and winked. The Col. then said to me, "What do you think of that? Baloon ascentions, what will they expect or want me to do next? No sir, I draw the line there. Why, when I built my big new barn on the North Platte ranch, I crawled up to the roof to get a view of the ranch. When I looked down over the side, it made my head go round like a top. The earth suits me pretty well."

When we reached the Dakotas on our way to the Coast we showed a small town giving only a matinee performance, as we had a long run to our next stopping place. The show was speedily loaded after the matinee, and by 7 o'clock, we had been on the road an hour, and were just entering what was known as the 'Bad Lands'. I had never seen them but had heard much about them from the Pawnee Indians. As it began to get dark the Col. suggested that we not put on the lights in our car, as it was a bright moonlight night, it would give us a better opportunity to see the freak formations. We sat up till nearly midnight enjoying the scenery and relating reminiscences of the early days.

[Colonel Cody and His Gold-Mining Interests]

The Col. finally ran onto gold mining and said that all his life he had wanted to own a gold mine. "I have a small mine right now at or near [Oracle], Ariz., which lays up in the Catalina Mts. 57 miles from Tuscon; Tuscon being the closest railroad point makes expensive operation, as everything has to be hauled this 57 miles by freight wagons, but according to my manager and part-ner, who is an expert mining engineer, we have an inexhaustible supply of rich ore some of it testing over $100.00 per ton. Major, wouldnt it be great if a fellow had a good gold mine, so that when he needed more money all he would have to do would be to sen[d] some miners down in the mines and bring it up. In that way would not be taking a thing away from any one else. You know in most businesses what you gain has to be taken away from some one else. In other words as you gain wealth, some one or some others get poorer, in the proportion that you become wealthy, but with a gold mine this does not happen. All you have to do is just go down in the ground and get it without taking a thing away from anyone." "Yes, Col." I said, "That would be great, but I think the Lord has always been pretty good to you. In fact you have had a gold mine ever since I

Signed lithograph, from watercolor painting. 34 × 21¼ inches.

knew you." "What do you mean?" asked the Col. "This old mine that we are now operating, the one we are riding on, right now, in my opinion. She is the biggest and best gold mine you or I will ever have[.] You know she has given you all your ranches, your hotels, and in fact every thing you have. And in my opinion she is and has always been the best gold mine you will ever own." "Yes," said the Col. "She has been a pretty good old mine,["] but as the years went by, I saw him send three, four, and as high as five, thousand every month or so to Tuscon[sic] for his mine. I remember, distinctly, the Col. coming to me more than once, putting out his hand, he would say, "Shake hands with your millionaire partner." As I shook his hand he would hand me a telegram saying, "Read that." The telegrams all read about alike I have read so many of them that I am sure that I can quote one verbatim viz—"Just stuck three foot vein of Tunkston. Fine quality, at 400 ft. level. Essays $300.00 per ton. Looks like inexhaustable supply" Then within the next two or three weeks, another telegram which would read, viz: August Bills due, better send $5,000.00 to the First Nat'l Bank of Tucson.

This same operation was pulled on him time after time, and it always worked. It got to be a joke with us at the front door, Charley Thompson, my assistant manager, would often say to me, when we [see] him get a telegram, "Well, they have either made another strike at the mine or the months bills are due." I relate the above to show you the trusting nature of the man. If he was for you at all, nothing ever excited his suspicions against you. Col. Cody, to me was more like a child in his business dealings, he apparently cared nothing for money, except when he wanted, or needed it to spend, then if he did not have it, or could not borrow it, it made him sick; he would go to bed. I have witnessed this myself. The finish of the gold mine came some 3 years later one spring when he arrived in N.Y. prepatory to our opening, he said to me, "What do you think I found my mining partner doing? We found that he was doubling the prices on everything he bought [and] taking the other half for himself, and on those ten mining claims that he

Buffalo Bill's Savage self-loading pistol, presented by the company in 1911. Mother-of-pearl grips, engraved frame and barrel; blued finish; .32 caliber; serial number 33177. Inscribed on backstrap COL. W. F. CODY accompanied by scroll flourishes. See program advertisement of ca. 1910, quoting Cody, Appendix H.

talked me into buying, saying the big vein of ore we had just struck on our property run directly under all 10 of them, and that he could buy them if taken at once at $3,000.00 per claim, later wiring me that he had succeeded in closing the deal for the 10 claims at $250.00 and to wire $5,000.00 to bind the bargain at once, which I did. We find he bought those 10 claims at $250.00 each. Can you beat that? But we have him under arrest. I dont know whether I will be able to recover anything or not, but if I dont he will very likely go up. . . ."

In the fall, I asked him what he had done about his mining partner, and he said, that on advice from his lawyer in Tucson, who wrote him that his case was going to be hard to make stick, he suggested withdrawing the suit, which I did. "That must have cost you considerable, Col." I suggested. "Yes, somewhere between $125,000.00 and $150,000.00, and no salvage. The taxes have not been paid for the last two years, and with this years' taxes it will about wipe out what the property is worth."

During the whole time this mining deal was going on, the Col. had often intimated that he would like to have me interested in it with him, that he wanted me to look the property over, but I had no intention of going into it, as I know nothing about mining, but I did say to him if we ever got near to it with the show I would run over and see it. So the year we went to the Pacific coast, on the day we showed Riverside, Calif. the Col. made all arrangements for me to visit his mines. Arriving on the lot in the morning he called me to him saying, "Your train leaves at 6 o'clock" "For where?" I asked. "Tucson" he replied. "I have both your railway and pullman reservations. I have also wired the hotel man to meet you at the train and take you out the 57 miles in the car and have wired my partner to have my log cabin fixed up for you, and I know you will enjoy it." I did not want to leave the show at this time as we had two very long runs before reaching Tuscon and I felt my presence was necessary. But my remonstrances were of no avail. I went. The next morning I was met by the car as I

stepped off the train, and by 9 o'clock was passing through the forest of giant uca [sic] cactus. A wonderful sight. We reached the mines about noon[.] My entire visit reminded me of plays I had seen wherein some mine away up in the mountains was the seat of action. There was the Chinese cook and assistant. All the miners were Mexicans, the foreman with the long-drooping mustache, the Col.'s partner, to me I pictured as the villan of the play; the spacious log cabin built especially for the Col. and occupied by him yearly for a month or so during the winter, with a spectacular big fire-place, Navajo rugs on the floor, mounted heads on the wall; with a few pictures of noted Indian chiefs and a Chinese servant nicely dressed in stiff starched white loose trousers and a jacket; who kept the cabin immaculate; the fire going in the fire-place, and who stood at attention constantly ready to do something to please you. The only [thing] missing was the little cute s[o]ubrette, who the villian preys on, but in this case I pictured the Col. filling this important part, thus, the cast was complete and perfect; the setting beautiful, with real atmosphere in this little tragedy that cost the Col. at least $150,000.00. But this was only one of many that kept the Col.'s bank account depleted but apparently never made him any wiser. He was no more than out of one until he was into another.

[Katherine Clemmons, British Actress, and Other Women]

The [Katherine Clemmons] episode, which had just preceded the mine disaster was fully as costly. This I only knew from things the Col. had told me. She had accompanied him during their European tours and had been presented to many of the nobility as his niece. On their return, she brought back with her, 20 big wardrobe trunks which cost a small fortune to fill with costly raiment, jewelry, etc. A close friend of the Col.'s who had often taken dinner with them told me when the waiter handed her a bill of fare, she invariably would ask for another one. Then, placing the one on top of the other, so that only the prices were exposed, she would study the prices only. When she found something marked 3-4-

5 or even more dollars she would say, "This ought to be good. Let's see what it is." And if to her liking, she would order.

The winter before the first opening in the Garden all the big papers all over the country were carrying stories on the [Howard] Gould-Clements divorce trial. In talking to me about it, the Col. said, "I was offered $60,000.00 if I would go on the witness stand and give certain testimony. It was I who introduced her to Gould. The season we played at Erastina Park, Statton Island, Mr. Gould who was a good friend of mine often ran down to see me. He loved horses, and would frequently take a ride on one of my saddle horses. One day Catharine said to me, "Col. who is that young man who calls on you so often, and sometimes rides your Ishan horse?" I told her it was Mr. Gould. "Is he of the Gould family who has so much money?" she asked. "Yes," I said "His daddy wa[s] Jay Gould who had more money than anybody and he and his brothers and sisters got it all. If you would like to meet him, I will introduce him to you the next time he comes down." No sooner was she introduced than she got busy right now. She not only set her cap for him, but she was determined to make him wear it. Shortly after the introduction Mr. Gould went to Europe. She followed him and after many sensational stories that went through the American papers of their courtship culminating with the announcement and describing their wedding in Paris[.] Then the more sensational and salacious episodes during their married life, their divorce trial, resulting in Mr. Gould obtaining his freedom, but costing him a fortune. The final settlement involved more than $100,000.00 according to the reports. This closed another of the Col.'s tragedies or comedies as the reader may class it.

I myself, knew Miss Lidia Devere well who was a daughter of Tony Devere, the humpty-dumpty clown, the best known clown of 50 years ago. She was considered one of the most handsome women of the stage, and played the opposite lead to him in his great play "The Prairie Waif" but when he took to the Wild West Show she dropped out of his life. Miss Isabel who as a girl of

18, a chum of the Col.'s daughter, Irma, and was introduced to him by the daughter, was a very beautiful girl. She and Irma had both attended a Seminary near Washington D.C. and were very dear and close friends. When the show played Washington, they attended the performance and at the close they went back to the Col.'s dressing tent. A strong attachment sprung up between them and it was reported that the Col. attempted to obtain a divorce that he might marry her, though there was a difference of about 40 years in their ages.

Miss Platt who was playing the beauty in "Every Woman" was the last close friend of Col. Cody that I knew of. She, with her mother, visited our show for a week once, when we played Chicago, and during our five years as partners he paid her attention periodically.

[On the Road Again]

The show encountered considerable bad weather the first season, then again owing to a contract existing prior to the combination in which a division of territory had been made with the Barnum show, we getting the short end of it, we did not have a big town that we did not get it after the Ringlings had played it with their Barnum show, therefore cutting off considerable from our gross receipts. This I had determined to change the coming year. At the close of the season Mr. Cook said to me, "Mr. John Ringling wants to see you about the division of territory for the coming season." "Do you consider that a good idea," I asked. "Oh, yes" he replied, "We have always done it. You see, that eliminated all opposition between the two biggest shows in the country. It is a great saving of paper, labor, time, etc." "Well Mr. Cook, show me where we had a single big town ahead of the Barnum show last season. Every big town we had this year, we got it after the Barnum show had played it." "Well, we made money in them, didnt we?" he asked. "Yes, but I am positive that we would have made considerable more had we been first in them, and had them fresh. Then again I dont like this thing of playing second fiddle. If they divide this year they will give me half, not take what they want and give us all that is left." The show was no more than landed in the winter quarters and we had gotten settled in our offices on 28th St. than Mr. Ringling called on me urging me to divide [words missing here] the same argument that I had to Mr. Cook as to why I did not want such an arrangement, and showing him where the past season we had second on all the big towns. John saw I was wise as to what had really happened but he says, "Well, Major, I have laid out the first two weeks of our route[.] Suppose we look them over." Which we did. Noting they had Easton, Scranton, Wilkes Barre, on their route, I said, "Why, John, you had these three towns last fall late. You dont want them again this spring. These three towns virtually belong to us." "O, yes, we do," he said, "These towns are always good for us, no matter when we take them, but I tell you what we can do, Major, suppose I give you these three towns. We will stay out of them and you give us Erie, Rochester, and Buffalo instead." Neither of us had played the last three mentioned towns the past season. He had intentionally put these three good fresh towns on my route and the three Penna. towns which he had played the fall before and did not want again on his route so that he would have something to trade that he did not want for something we both wanted, in other words; trading something for . . . something. I caught the idea. "No, John," I said, "I prefer for each of us to go ahead without any division. I am willing to sign any kind of an agreement not to fight in opposition where our routes conflict, but I want to try one season my way." John didn't like my attitude and so expressed himself. This in a way caused a breach between the Ringlings and me that lasted as long as I remained in the show business. The handling of the Madison Square Garden was entirely a political affair . . . [various interests expected to receive business, or problems might develop with city inspectors]. That evening the chief of the plain-clothes men of N.Y. City who was a very close friend of mine, brought his mother to see our show. As I passed them two coupons for their seats, "I have seen your show two or three times Major. If I would not be interfering with your business, I should like to come back after the crowds get in and talk with you." He said as we sat in the front door of the show, talking . . . I related to him our predicament [on getting a performance site in Mt. Vernon, New York], and lamenting that I did not see how we could overcome it, as it was the only lot available in or near Mt. Vernon. After some thought he said, "I can fix that for you." "You'll put me under ever-lasting obligations to you if you can. How can it be done?" I asked. "Just don't pay any license at all. Stay away from the city hall. Dont go near it." "Why, we wouldnt dare do it that way, would we? What would I say if the chief of police or the inspector of licenses comes around and wants to see our license?" "No one will come around to inspect or see your license. Leave that all to me. I tell you to do it this way because it's not only the easiest way out, but the only way I see to handle it, so you will not lose your afternoon performance." As I had no other plans and could figure out no plausible way to handle it, I accepted his offer[.] We stayed away from City Hall, played Mt. Vernon on the advertised date, and like the Arabs of old folded our tents and silently stole away. If a policeman, inspector or other city official set foot on our lot that day, I did not see him.

[Colonel Cody and His Notes]

During our Brooklyn engagement, Mr——, a very well known actor of that day, called on me and presented a note for $5,000.00 past due, given him by Col. Cody, and demanding instant payment. I took him back to the Col.'s tent. The Col. acknowledged the transaction and asked me to pay it and charge it to his personal account. "But Col. your account is somewhat over-drawn now, on account of your 3 week's bill at the Waldorf which was some $1400.00 and furthermore as I made large remittances to our printers here had just about depleted our cash account, I do not see how it can be possible for us to pay this note before the latter part of the Philadelphia engagement, which was the next week." With this I left Mr—— with the Col. and went back to the front of the show. It was fully an hour before Mr.—— made his appearance at the front of the show. He was excited and made it good and plain to me that

Stock certificate issued to Wm. F. Cody for 1,000 shares of the Cody-Dyer Arizona Mining and Milling Company, March 25, 1913. The Irma Hotel and the Historical Pictures Company were two of his other investments that were a drain on finances.

he came over to collect on this note, and that he was going to do it. I explained to him again that we could not pay at this time. "And why?"—but that if he would present it the latter part of the Philadelphia engagement I would guarantee payment on it. But this did not satisfy him. He said, "No sir. Nothing but the money." I explained to him that this was entirely a personal obligation of Col. Cody's, that the show company nor myself were in no way obligated, and that just at this time Col. Cody happens to be over-drawn, and has no money. "But we can take care of it next week. I am willing to guarantee it personally." But this did not satisfy him. He finally said, "I came over for this money. This note is considerably past due, and as I said before I am not going to leave until it's paid, and unless you consent to pay it at once, I am going to have an attachment issued against the property of the show." This began to sound serious to me. I had no idea he would go this strong, for I knew Col. Cody, and he were great friends, and had been for many years, but from his positive manner, I was convinced that he meant just what he said. So I went back to see Col. Cody. I had stopped at the treasurer's wagon and found we only had about $12,000.00 in the safe, where we should have $20,000.00, that being the amount we were supposed to always have and never paid any printers or out-side bills except from surplus running above this amount. I found the Col. in bed. He said he was sick. "Where are you sick?" I asked. "All over," he said, "its my nerves. They always go back on me when any one threatens to attach the show. Did you fix it up with him? What does he say?" "Well, Col. I have talked with him for half an hour and used every argument and even agreed to guarantee the note by my personal endorsement and also by the endorsement of the show Company, provided he would wait till the latter part of the Philadelphia engagement. But his reply was 'I came after this money. The note is past due, and if I dont get it, I am going to attach the show' " "Yes, that's just what he said to me. I cant understand him. He has loaned me money before and has always been lenient with me. Cant you do something to fix it up? Something must be done to get it off my mind, or I will not be able to go into the performance tonight.[" "]I stopped at the treasurers wagon on my way here and found your account about $400.00 over-drawn. [Y]ou know your bill from the Waldorf for the four weeks was $1422.40. We only have $12,000.00 in the treasury of the show, where we should have at least $20,000.00 paying $5,000.00 and the interest would bring us down to less then $7,000.00, which could easily be wiped out by two or three rainy days." "Now, Major, please pay this note. We will get along, I know even if it rains. I have lots of good friends in N.Y. that I can draw $5,000.00 from any time I want to, but we are sure to have some good weather. We have had bad weather now for over a week. I look for a change of weather tomorrow, and if we do, business will pick up right now." I saw the Col. was mentally in a bad way. I had never before seen him in such condition. I felt sorry for him and wanted to relieve his anxiety. I said, "All right, Col. We will pay it and charge to your account." This I did, and as soon as it was endorsed by the drawee I took the note back and turned it over to him. He was like a child in expressing his joy and gratitude. He grabbed me by the hand, and leaping from his bed, he kept saying, "I thank you! I thank you! I will never forget you for this. You have relieved my mind." etc. etc. This matter had put me to thinking and wondering if he might not have quite a number of these notes out among his friends. He had mentioned to me at one time, he owed Mr. McDonald, a banker at North Platte $20,000.00 and I knew that the season before, he had drawn very little money from the show, as his share had been used in liquidating his losses in Europe, to the Bailey estate.

In the fall of the year, R. M. Bickerstaff, the manager of the U.S. Lithograph Co. came on to the show to consult me about making our paper for the coming season. I related to him the whole story of what had occurred in Brooklyn in the spring of the year on the $5,000.00 note and how it had depleted our treasury at a most inopportune time. "What I am afraid of, Bick. Suppose a note would come up like this for $20,000 or even more from someone who would insist on immediate payment and we were in Arkansas, Kallamazoo, or Oshkosh, away off from our friends and you know the Col. draws his money just as fast as any surplus shows up, so that he never has any great amount of surplus and if a thing like this would come at a time when business was slack, or after a siege of rainy weather, and our treasury was low It might cause us a lot of trouble. You know what an attachment against us would mean. Big headlines in all the papers all over the country "Buffalo Bill and Pawnee Bill Broke—Show attached, etc." "I'll tell you what I would do if I were you, Major; incorporate the company. This is a protection that you have outside of your incorporated company." "This is a fine idea, Bick, I think I will take it up with the Col. and if he is agreeable at the close of the season we will come in to N.Y. and have it fixed up."

[Incorporating the Two Bills Show]

The show closed at Richmond, Va. in good weather, and a big crowd, something unusual this late in the season, it being about the 20th of Nov. The Penna. R[ailwa]y ran a special Pullman train from Richmond into N.Y. just to carry our people. . . . On our trip to N.Y. the Col. generously offered, and insisted on me taking the big double bed in the state-room but I refused and occupied the single berth at the side. Our train left Richmond about midnight[.] Early the next morning we stopped in Baltimore for a change of engines and crews. I was up, as I am an early riser, and succeeded in getting a cup of coffee and a ham sandwich. "Can you fix me up a cup of coffee, in something that I can take to the train?" I asked. The boy was trying to figure out a way when the engine of our train gave two shrill whistles and I knew I must go but I succeeded in getting two ham sandwiches and a piece of apple pie for the Col. and arrived at our train as it was moving out, it being about 6 A.M. I did not disturb the Col. till about 10 o'clock, when the porter advised me that the Col. was up. "How about it? Had any breakfast?" I asked as I entered the door. "No sir, just got up.

But I am as hungry as a wolfe in a snow-storm. Any chance to get something to eat?" "Not a chance. I was up at Baltimore about 5:30 this morning and got a cup of coffee and a sandwich and got 2 ham sandwiches and a piece of apple pie for you, and was getting some coffee when the whistle of our train gave the signal to leave, and I just barely made it as the train was pulling out." I said, handing him the sandwiches and pie. "Fine, fine. I have had many a worse breakfast than this," and he devoured the last crumb with a relish and washed it down with ice-water. Our train was moved on a very fast schedule, so that we reached N.Y. by noon. The Col. and I with Mr. Bickerstaff as legal advisor, went to Trenton, N.J. where the Buffalo Bill's Wild West and Pawnee Bill's Far East Company was incorporated; Col. W. F. Cody, President; G. W. Lillie, Vice-pres. and general manager; Chas Metius, treasurer, and Harry Stratton, Secretary and Attorney for the Company. We were incorporated under the laws of the State of New Jersey, with an office established at Bromley Inn in charge of Mr. Stratton, as the law provided. The Col. caught the first train west for his home at Cody, Wyo. in the Rocky Mts. He had a wonderful hunting lodge which he called "Pauhaska Tee-Pee" made of big pine logs with the bark on them[.] One big living room below with a very large fire-place made of freak rock formation and a number of sleeping rooms above. The Col. once said to me, "You know, Major, by the time our season closes I am just about all in. The constant noise and turmoil both days and nights just wears on a fellows nerves. By the time our seven months season is up, I can hardly wait till I reach my hunting lodge away up in the Rockies, almost at the eastern entrance to the Yellowstone Park. I take a bunch of congenial fellows with me, all good friends of mine, a good cook, and plenty of good stuff to eat and drink. We go up there and hunt, play cards, relax and rest for 3 or 4 weeks, and it always brings me back to my old self again." I caught our train as it went through Jersey City and went on into Bridgeport, our winter quarters with it. After storing every thing away, placing the mechanics and painters at work, rebuilding, repair-

Promissory note for $1,000, dated Sioux City, Iowa, September 7, 1912, to H. H. Cross. Debts like these were a looming financial nightmare for Cody; sometimes he had forgotten about them, but, somehow, he never flinched from honoring commitments.

ing and painting our two big train-loads of material including the two trains of 50 cars, I went to our offices on 28th St. N.Y. and reviewed, approved and ordered the many changes and improvements to be made in our equipment program, executive staff, and advance brigades; also took up with Mr. Cook our route for the following year.

[Pawnee Bill Buys the Wild West Plant]

So by about Dec. 10th I was preparing for my annual visit to my Buffalo Ranch in Oklahoma, and to visit my dear old father and mother who counted the days from the time I left one year until my return the following fall. My trunks were packed and my reservations had been secured when I received a wire from Mr. Otto Ringling, the manager of the Barnum & Bailey Shows, saying he wanted to see me before I left for Okla. So I caught the first train out for Bridgeport. Mr Ringling said, "You know, wintering the two shows here in the same quarters crowds us both too much, makes it unpleasant for both shows. I sent for you thinking I might be able to sell you the Buffalo Bill plant, then you could established your own winter quarters, and be more independent." "You know, Mr. Ringling, I was forced to buy out the interests of the Bailey estate in our show, which included Mr. Cody's interests. Cody and I are now equal partners, but at present I am carrying the whole load, as the Col. owed so many of his friends that he was unable to pay me any money on his half interest the past season, and it will be up to me to supply the money to winter, repair, and put the show out for next season. But if we have as good a season the next year as we had this past season, I might consider it next fall when we come in." "But, Major, I will name you a price that is so low it will be almost like paying rent. [Pawnee Bill made an offer to the Ringling Brothers, to buy out their interest in the show's plant, his friend Tom Smith sharing in the deal.] So at Christmas time I wired the Ringlings as follows: "Will give you $40,000.00 for the plant; 20 down and 20 before we leave in the spring[.]" I had my doubts about them accepting this offer. I rather expected a counter offer of

$45,000.00 but the reply came back the same day; "We accept your offer. Signed, Ringling Bros." So I wrote Tom my offer of $40,000.00 had been accepted and enclosed their wire to him. I also made him an offer to go in with me equally on buying the plant and after all costs of operation, we would divide the profits, he to be general manager and in possession of the plant at all times, and to receive and pay out all moneys. When I reached winter quarters, Tom was there waiting for me. At our first conference, he handed over the Ringling telegram together with a draft on the Carnegie Trust Co. of Pittsburg for $20,000.00 made out in his name but endorsed on the back "Pay to the Ringling Bros. Tom Smith." This was to pay Tom's half. When I delivered it to Mr. Otto Ringling, he says "How about the other $20,000.00?" I replied, "You know, Mr. Ringling, I wired you I would pay you that before we left winter quarters in the spring." "Yes, I know," he said, "But is it going to distress you or cause you any trouble to raise it?" "I may have to borrow it or part of it. I wont know till all our winter quarter bills and expenses are paid," I replied. "Well, Major, I tell you what to do. After you open next spring, you just mail me a check for $1,000.00 at the end of each week for the first 20 weeks, same as you did the rent money last year, and that will be satisfactory to me." "Why, that's more than satisfactory," I replied, "I consider that a great favor and will never forget it, and hope at some time I may be able to show you my appreciation in a more substantial manner." Otto was considere[d] the hub of the Ringling Bros. in financial matters. He was called "The King". He was a bachelor, about 45 years old, rather morose, and quiet, and had the reputation of being very close in business matters. This held true in small matters, but in big deals I found him the biggest man I had ever dealt with. I found him an agreeable honorable, high-class gentleman, and an incessant worker. This also held true with all the other brothers.

The following spring we opened in the Garden again, using our big scenic background of the year before with but few changes. But the action of the "spec" had been added too, and as a culminating feature, I had engaged an Arab [Ishmael] with a diving act, who had just reached America, and our opening was to be his first appearance before an Amer. audience. [The dismal failure of this highly touted and spectacular act, in a seventy-foot dive, caused potential public-relations problems. The performer lost his nerve after a few nights of dazzling and daring performances, and the act had to be canceled. It required Major Burke's] most seductive, persuasive powers to keep this story out of the papers. . . . We had to strike out all our dive-of-death [materials] from our advertising, even sent our lithographer over the whole city, to take down the dive of death papers. The papers gave the incident a lot of space heading it "The Man who Lost His Nerve." The failure of Ishmael to do the dip of death cost us a pretty penny.

[Competition with the Barnum Circus—
a Papering War]

There was little out of the regular show life this season, excepting two big circus fights with the Barnum Show. During our three weeks engagement in the Garden, the Barnum show played across the N.E. States and back again, so that we clashed in New York State at Albany, and in every town clear across the State to Buffalo. We had succeeded in getting into all the towns first with our advertising cars, and brigades. I felt very good about it, as this was my first chance to show the Barnum people why I did not want to divide the territory as they had wanted me to do. . . . [A papering battle developed between the Barnum interests and the Wild West and Far East in which both sides were covering over advertising on the road with aggressive advance teams. Suit was filed by the Wild West and Far East against the Barnums, and there was a flurry of court action. In the end, at a chance meeting at a restaurant in New York, Lillie and John Ringling agreed to drop the action:] . . . "We will just settle our lawyers bills and we will call the case off."

[Colonel Cody and Major Lillie]

During our entire five years association as partners there never was but once that Col. and I stood on the brink of 'falling out'. It occurred the day we played Tulsa, Okla. that fall 1909. It was as windy and dusty a day as I had ever seen in Oklahoma. The lot was fully two miles east of town, knowing the Col.'s abhorence to dust in the arena I had sent into to Tulsa, and engaged two sprinkling carts, which with our two made four. These we kept busy all day, hauling water and sprinkling it on the arena. But as the haul was two miles the arena had been plowed the spring before and the sun that day was about as hot as I had ever seen it, it was impossible to allay the dust. We would no more than put a load of water on than the hot sun and wind would take it up. So that during the afternoon matinee, which was crowded, the dust was something awful, after each of the big horse acts. The dust was so heavy you could not see across the arena. An old friend of mine, J. C. Wrightsman, a very wealthy oil man of Tulsa had invited me to take dinner with him at the Petroleum Club. He came after me in a big, new car about five o'clock in the evening. As I went out to meet him, the Col. walked into the marquet. Mr. Wrightsman spying him, asked me if that was not Buffalo Bill. "Havent you ever met him?" I asked. "No, I should like very much to know him." So I introduced him to the Col. and he invited the Col. to go to dinner with us. "Oh, I can't leave here. Someone has to stay around here to attend to business. The Major can go, I'll look after things till he gets back." I could see plainly that he was all unnerved and worried and I knew it was caused by the dust in the arena. I also knew I had taken every precaution and made every effort to prevent it. It was a physical impossibility. All the sprinkling carts in Okla. could not have done it. I knew too, that at this time between the afternoon and evening shows, from four to seven o'clock was the only lull during the show's day, and was perfectly safe to leave the ground. His remarks cut me to the quick, made me heartsick. As we drove towards Tulsa in silence Mr. Wrightsman said, "Major, I guess you know,

I am aware of who runs the show. That was funny of the Col. wasn't it?" I knew Mr. Wrightsman had noticed how this had hurt me and was anxious to relieve me if he could. We had a most wonderful dinner at the Petroleum Club, and I enjoyed it. The following morning at Bartlesville, Okla. Col. came in to the office wagon, looking over the statement of the day before, remarked that our night house had fallen off terribly. "Yes," I said[.] "That was entirely due to the dust at the afternoon performance.

["]Every one was covered with it and left the show with a feeling of disgust, that they never wanted to see another show." I explained to him too that I had hired extra sprinkling carts and done all in my power to keep the dust down, but it was a physical impossibility. "Do you know what I intend to do next season, Col.? You had Mr. Ernest Cook (no relation of Louis E. Cook, our general agent) here the last season before I took charge." The Col. sensed right away that I was going to say something, so he says, "Major, let's get out of the wagon, were we can talk privately." The ticket wagon being a very busy place in the morning, and there were three or four people in the wagon at that time. So we walked around to the end of the wagon and stopped in the shade. But the country people were beginning to arrive on the lot, and crowded around us so that we could not talk privately so we walked over to a new house that was about completed, just off of our lot and sat in the shade of the porch. So I said, "As I was saying in the wagon, you had Mr. Cook as manager before I came here[.] You think he is a good manager dont you?" "Yes," said the Col. "He was a very good manager." "Well," I continued, "I am going to employ him entirely at my expense next season. I am going to put the show in thorough shape during the winter and stay with it in the spring until the rainy season is over and the show is running smoothly, then I will turn the entire management over to Mr. Cook and am going out to my buffalo ranch and stay until fall, when I will come back and take charge again." "Why, what's the matter, Major, what's wrong?" asked the Col. "Simply this," I said,

"things dont suit me around here. I have been in the show business 25 years and this is the first time I did not feel at home around my own show and I am not contented and happy with it." The Col. looked me over a few moments, studied and then said, "If there is any body around the show that is the back end of it, that you dont like or that annoys you, let me know who it is, and I will fire them forthwith." But I refused to enter any complaint, though the Col. well knew there were certain of his old employees who had talked against me in a manner such as they should not have done, and continued to work for the show. But I told him 'no' I did not want him to discharge any one. Finally he said, "Well Major . . . if you are not here with the show next season I wont go either" and we walked back to the lot, he going back to his private tent.

For the next three or four weeks, things passed off quietly. The Col. came regularly to the ticket wagon, we passed remarks about the weather or the attendance the day before, but while our relations were entirely pleasant, they [s]eemed somewhat strained[.] About four weeks later, he sent his valet, around with a note, asking me to come back during the Far East Section of the show, as at this time, he had about 45 minutes that he had nothing to do.

As I entered his tent, he cordially placed an easy chair, handed me a cigar, and as I bit the end from it, struck a match, and held it for me to light, then taking another chair almost opposite from me, sat down, and asked "How would you like to make a million dollars?" "Fine," I said, "if I do not have to kill any one or rob a bank to do it." "No sir, you wont have to do either and it will be easy. You know for over 30 years I have been traveling over the length and breadth of this country and also Europe. There are people now who saw me, when they were youngsters that now have grandchildren. There are many old people who have not seen me since their youth. If they thought they only had one more chance to ever see me again, I believe [they] would flock to the show in great numbers. My idea is to advertise next year and the year following as the two

farewell seasons of Buffalo Bill in person. Make it good and strong that this will be their last chance to see me. You know it will take two seasons to cover the U.S. and Canada. Now you mark my word. They will come from far and near in such numbers that we are going to have to increase our big arena and our seating capacity also. It will make a million dollars each season. That's a half a million apiece for each of us each season or a million apiece for each of us for the two seasons. You know, Major, I do not expect to live more than a couple of hundred years, and if I am ever to get any rest, pleasure, and recreation, I must do it pretty soon. I will want you each day to ride in the arena with me and I will tell the people that at the end of the two farewell seasons I will retire to my T. E. Ranch, Cody, Wyo." "Col., I quite agree with you about the farewell tours. You may have got your sights a little high on the amounts we will each make, but I do believe it means a great increase in our business." Which it did, something over $800,000.00 on the two seasons.

[Colonel Cody and Money]

The Col. spent his [money] like a drunken sailor. In the fall of the first farewell tour, the Col. had me draw within about two weeks, three checks, two for $3,000.00 each, and one for $4,000.00 all in favor of the manager of his ranch in Wyo. When he drew the last one he said to me, "You know, we are haying out on the ranch and it takes a lot of money." "Is it alfalfa?" I asked. "No, it's wild prairie hay" "Wild hay, in our country, Col. sells for about $4.00 per ton. There are a number of big ranch contractors in our country who make a business of putting up hay for the big cattle ranchers at from $1.00 to $1.50 per ton and make money at it. I dont think there's a ranch in Okla. that spends $10,000.00 in haying." "That is a good deal, isnt it? I hadnt thought of it before." he said[.] The day we played North Platte, he gave his daughter a check for $3,000.00 and a large touring car costing probably $3,000.00 more. His hotel bills of a spring in New York for three or four weeks, at the Waldorf or H[o]ffman House would run from $1,200.00 to $1,800.00[.] He did not spend money by the 50's and 100's but always by the 1000's[.]

The first of the farewell tours, the one when we went to California was much the largest of the two, and on the closing day at Little Rock, the Col. borrowed $12,000.00 from me and when we got into winter quarters and had balanced the books for the season, we found that he was $5,500.00 over-drawn on his personal account, so I took this up for him, in order to balance our season's books. Here was $17,500.00 he borrowed at the close of the largest season we had during our association as partners.

When we played Cleveland, Ohio, that season he bought a big White Steamer for his hotels in Wyo. and shipped it and the chauffeur with it, as the White people recommended. I do not remember the cost of this car, but I know the price was more than I had ever heard mentioned for an automobile, something like $12,000.00[.] It was a car that carried about 20 people. Thus his money got away from him. Later, I talked the matter of the farewell tours over with Mr. Cook[.] As to making this two of the greatest gala seasons the show had ever had. We improved all the physical property, and also put on a very extravagant performance, all of the various troupes were increased in number; we carried over 70 of the finest big Sioux Indians I had ever seen together.

[A Private Railroad Car]

This was the year I bought our fine almost-new private car. The season before, some train master had told the Col. that if our section ever got into a serious wreck, we would both be killed, that our private car was the oldest one in the train, and that in a wreck, the oldest or weaker always succumbs to the stronger, so the Col. asked me to get a new private car. I succeeded in buying a most wonderful private car of the Penna. R[ailwa]y. one of two cars they had built at a cost of $30,000.00 each, to use for private parties of 12 persons or less, and as it was not an all steel car, they could not take it through the tunnel into N.Y. The parties occupying it had to go over to Jersey City to get into it. This

they objected to, and had in many cases lost business on account of it.

So I purchased one of them. I had it sent to the R.R. shops and entirely remodeled, cutting down the kitchen and putting in a bathroom, two wonderful staterooms, a large dining and observation room, with two duofolds that made up as settes during the day, thus reducing the capacity from 12 to 4 persons. I had put in a great deal of my time at the shops during the reconstruction of this car, and had picked out or approved all the changes and things that went into it, even to the tapestry covering the duofold. I was proud of the success in the transformation I had wrought, making it into the greatest private car for two people with accomodations for two extras, in case we had visitors, I had ever seen. The superintendent of constructions also expressed himself in the same manner so that when the Col. arrived in N.Y. in the spring for our opening I made a special trip with him over to Trenton, N.J., our new winter quarters. I pointed out to him, the many changes I had made, the wonderful strength of this car, it being an all steel framed car. The wonderful lighting and water system. As we entered the big observation room, the Col. standing about the center, turning around slowly and inspecting the walls, I thought he was admiring the beautiful wood work, when to my surprise he turned to me and says, "Major, I dont believe I have seen a mirror in this entire car." "Oh yes," I replied, "We have two nice, large beveled mirrors in each of our private washrooms." "I know, but dont you think we ought to have a nice big mirror across over that writing desk? You know in our old [P]atti car, there were mirrors every place, and I sure liked that."

The [P]atti car had been built for Adalaid [Adelina] Patti, the great opera star and was touted and advertised as the most beautiful car ever built and used by her during her tours of America. It was then bought by Mr. Bailey, for the Buffalo Bill Shows[.] The interior was exquisite. All the wood work being rosewood hand-carved. The brass work being very artistic, the same being gold plate. Every panel in the car being

bevelled plate mirror, so that sitting in any room, and almost in any position, you could look any direction, and see your reflection in a mirror. This was what so pleased the Colonel.

Many times have I seen him sitting in the center of our observation room, with large double windows on either side, especially on our Sunday runs, so that as we passed the various stations in the country towns the crowds who invariably came to the station to see our two trains pass through, could see him, and what pleasure he got out of it. If the train stopped for orders, or for any purpose, and there was a big crowd, he would invariabl[y] take from his inside pocket, his big comb, run it through his long, gray curly hair, put on his large sombrero, and nearly always would say to me, "I better get out and do a little advertising," strolled out to the observation end, and walked from side to side of the large platform, apparently taking in the town but his prime object to give the crowd a better chance to see him.

Colonel's two big fort[e]s in the show business was his personality and his ability to capitalize it from an advertising standpoint. He had no business or executive ability, could not even organize or handle his own show; never had any thought of tomorrow, or laying up for a rainy day. Money to him was only made to spend or to aid and make others happy, not for himself. Providence had always provided him and always would. He was born under a lucky star.

[Advertising the Two Bills]

When the combination was formed and completed the first thing I did was to engage the best artist in New York to make a composite picture of our two heads, making a perfect bust of Col. in the foreground, with a bust of myself in the background. The face and about a quarter of the bust just protruding in advance of his, making a most beautiful combination. This I proposed to use on every piece of printed matter as a kind of trade mark. Mr. X—, who made it, has never been surpassed to this day, on this kind of work. I had him bring it to the Hoffman House. He and I had placed it against the head of my bed in my sleeping room, arranged the lights as best we could to get the greatest effect, then I brought the Col. to the room to see it.

As he entered he walked straight to the foot of my bed, gazed at the picture, intently, for several moments, then stepping to the right, then to the left, observing it from the different angles, remarked, "This is a beautiful piece of work, as I have ever seen. Especially good of my head, just one little criticism I might make if you will allow me." "Certainly, certainly," said the artist, as he raised from his chair and approached the foot of the bed. "I have always been credited with having a very handsome ear, and you will notice you have it almost covered with that lock of hair. Couldnt that be fixed by cutting out that lock of hair so as to get a good view of the ear?" "I certainly can, and since you mention it, I think it will be an improvement. I will take it and make this change and return with it tomorrow about this time." This he did, and the following day the Colonel gave his universal approval. This was profusely used in all our printing till the close of the shows.

[Financial Pressure on the Two Bills Show]

At Denver in 1913. The second year of the farewell season was not so large as the first. The beginning of the season was big and gave as great promise as the first, so that up to the fourth day of July, we had cleared about $125,000.00, but immediately following the Fourth the business fell off so that by the time we closed in Richmond, Va. Nov. 20th, we had lost back about $40,000.00. Three weeks before our closing, I went to the Colonel, explaining that unless the business improved, we would each have to advance about $20,000.00 at Richmond Va. to pay off the hold-backs, etc., [.] This he said he would be unable to do, so it was necessary for me to advance the entire $40,000.00, in order to close the show and pay all bills. But before the Col. left for the West, I had a long talk with him about the money necessary to winter and put the show in order for the season of 1913, and explained to him that, as I had advanced all the money to pay off with I could not advance all the money with which to winter the

show, as it would take all of my spare money to do it and I did not want to open the show without some money in the treasury. He said he would have to have some money to go West on, as he was absolutely broke. "I'm square with you now, am I not?" "Yes," I said, "All but the little money you have drawn on your personal accounts which overdrew it, and the $20,000.00 I advanced you being your half to close the show with." "This bad business cant last always. You will find next season will be all right. I have had several slumps like this before. They all have them. Look at the price of cotton, 3¼c, [no] wonder we could get no money in the south, but she will be all right in the spring. Mark my word. I tell you Major what you do, find out what I owe in my personal account[."] ([O]n being advised it was $32,000) he said, "I will give you my note for $10,000.00 backed by a mortgage on my Irma hotel and contents at Cody, Wyo. There is one picture hanging in the barroom worth more than that, the picture of me on horseback, by Rosie Bonheur in Paris. I will need this 6800.00 to go home on and pay off some little indebtedness I will have. The home folks always expect me to pay up when I return home at the end of the season." "But, Col. I am not sure I can do this unless you are sure you can raise your half of the winter expense," I said. "Oh, there will be no trouble about that. I can raise it among my friends as soon as I reach home. The last three years have put me out of debt, the only money I will owe will be this $10,000.00 and the $20,000.00 you can take out of the first money we make next spring. The $20,000.00 for winter quarters I will send you as soon as I reach the west."

So I loaned him the $10,000.00. As he handed me his note and the mortgage on the Irma hotel property, he asked me as a favor not to [put] the mortgage on record at present, that he would guarantee me nothing would go on record ahead of my mortgage and that later he would advise me when to put in on record. A month after we got into winter quarters and the bills began to fall due, I wrote the Col. about his half of the winter-quarter's money, saying: "The bills are now

falling due["] and that I now needed it. To which he wrote me, "I am going Denver in a few days. I will have no trouble to raise it there, and will send it to you just as soon as I can make the necessary arrangements etc."

[The Pressure of Worsening Financial Woes]

The matter ran on another month and no money, so I wrote him again a stronger letter than the first one, explaining to him that I must have the money at once, that our bills for January were now past due and must be paid. A few days before this I had seen an Associated Dispatch in the New York papers "Buffalo Bill to head the Great Sells-Floto Show" being the headline and a short write-up, but the day following this publication I received the following wire; "Pay no attention to reports in Newspaper. I have done nothing that will interfere with our shows. Will have money in a few days and will send it to you immediately [after] I get it. W. F. Cody". So I paid [no] attention to the newspaper account. So several others appeared in the next three or four weeks, all of them connecting the Col.'s name with the Sells-Floto Circus. Also, I began to receive wires and letters from every one we did business with and from many of my friends, to all of which I replied there was nothing to it. It was just newspaper talk. I could not see at the time how there could be any thing to it for the Col. was now a full half as he had paid me up in full for the property and all he now owed me was just the amounts created, that past fall also I was well satisfied the amount of his debts on the outside among his friends had all been paid. So from my point of view, I could not and would not have attached any importance to these press reports, even if the Col. had not wired me to the contrary, for I now knew he had a $50,000.00 investment in the show, which was absolutely worthless to him without his presence, and that he could not afford to give this up.

About the middle of February, I got a wire from him that he was sending the money by mail. When it arrived there was but $15,000.00, writing me he would try to send the other $5,000.00 later, but also suggesting that I try to make this do until we got on the road. But when we got on the road, we were in reality worse off *than in winter quarters. We opened in bad weather which continued for three or four weeks, preventing us from making any money. During the winter when Mr. Cook and I were discussing the route he submitted one going south, taking in all the larger towns along the Atlantic Coast then going out of the South via Atlanta, Ga., and Memphis, Tenn., and across to Chicago, as we were on our way to the N.W. I objected to this route, arguing that while I had never made the South in the spring, I had always understood it was only good in the fall, after cotton picking time, but Mr. Cook argued that things had changed, that the spring was now good in the South as they raised all the early berries & vegetables both for the East and the West, and that their real and biggest harvest was in the spring. "Why," he said, "The Barnum show, on the biggest season they ever had made it over this very route that I have laid out for us to take, and furthermore, over this route we will be entirely free from opposition." So I consented to it which all the big showmen blamed our bad business to.*

I do not believe there was a chance for us to have gotten money any place, Philadelphia, N.Y. City, Baltimore where the show had never before in 30 years failed to get money, all fell down, in fact the business was off in every town that we showed. It looked to me like we were the power of some Jinx. Of course, I think also, the farewell tours being continued over into the third season, had considerable to do with our bad season. The fall before, the Col. asked me one day what I thought we could do with a third farewell season. "Nothing at all," I said, "As we have no place to go. We have used up all the country with the two past seasons, and would have to repeat in almost every town we make." "Mr. Cook says that will make not one whit difference, that Sarah Bernhart had made a dozen farewell tours, going over nearly the same routes each year, and that each time the business was better." "Well, I hope it will prove out so with us," I said, "But I have no faith in it." So the show was billed in a farewell tour the third time. I made out a statement after we had been out 100 days, showing we had suffered an average loss of $403.00 per day. During

that season from the opening to the close in November there were just three cities where the business approached our old standards. They were Norfork [Norfolk] Va., Davenport, Iowa, and Omaha, Neb. Even Chicago, one of the best W.W. towns in the U.S. showed a loss on the entire week.

When we had been out a couple of months, the Col. asked me if I believed in Jonahs. "No" I said, "Not much, though I am superstitious about Friday and 13 and you know, Col. this is 1913," I said. "Have you noticed the yellow cat Miss Burgess carries around with her every place? Clarence says he thinks that's the Jonah and derned if I dont believe it too. I wish you would issue an order that all pets must be sent away from the show. That you will find will settle the Jonah." We had a rule on our printed contracts which read: no pets of any nature will be carried with the show. But as Miss Burgess was a sister of Mrs. Johnie Baker, no remonstrance till now had ever been made, so I had overlooked it. "Suppose you mention this to Miss Burgess, or to Johnie and tell him as you have me that it annoys you, and I am sure they will be glad to send the cat away." So it was sent back home but apparently had no effect on the business which continued bad right on up to the close.

[Printing Bills Precipitate the End]

Our printing bills were in arrears and the printers were beginning to press us for money. They came on to Chicago to see what was best to do. I suggested they put Mr. Bickerstaff in charge of our finances, as a sort of a receiver. This they would not do. All were favorable except the U.S. Lithograph Co. who were our largest creditors, and who swayed the sentiment of the others "Let's wait till we reach Denver. If the business does not improve by that time, we will then decide what is best to do" they said. . . .

The U.S. had already decided what they [would] do in conjunction with H. H. Tammen of the Sells-Floto Show, they had decided when we reached Denver, they would attach this show for the printers bill, and for the $20,000.00 Tammen had loaned to Col. Cody. They

would then put the show up and sell it as a whole. Mr. Tammen would buy it in. The show would then continue on its route with every thing intact except myself.

During our engagement in Chicago, one of my best friends came to me and said, "If you allow this show to go into Denver, you will never leave there with it. You will lose your show. This man Tammen, means to take it away from you. He holds a bill of sale of all of Col.'s interests, and also a contract with Col. Cody to go with the Sells-Floto Show for the coming season. He finds you hold the whip hand with your contract with Col. Cody and is determined to take your interest in the show away from you and throw you out as the easiest solution. You know Col. Cody borrowed $20,000.00 from Tammen last winter." "I know he did," I said, "But I didnt borrow any thing from him, and if he holds a contract for Col. Cody's services, he is not going to do any thing that will injure the title of Buffalo Bill, and he cant do the things you say, and keep it out of the papers." "Yes, he can, he holds Denver in the palm of his hand. He owns the biggest newspaper there, The Post, and can do anything he wants to."

The day we showed Omaha I saw a Mr. Warner taking an inventory of the show property. I asked him what he meant by this. He said that he as an employee of Mr. Tammen's had been ordered by him to get a list of all the property of the show. On the morning we arrived in Denver I left the train early and on arrival at the show grounds was served with attachment papers in the name of the U.S. Lithograph Co. at N.Y. and Cincinnati. A deputy was put in charge of our ticket wagon, and several were placed around the show ground. There was nothing in the papers about it but during Monday and Tuesday, every one buying tickets, observed the law was in charge of our show. The report became general over town, and when Wednesday morning came, the show having filled its engagement, and was still standing on the lot, the news story was too big to keep out of the papers. It was broadcast the length and breadth of the country. The story was so great it had got away from them. An order was obtained from

the court ordering the sale of the property, small hand
bills about 5 × 6 in. were struck off and a few were
posted about the grounds. They didnt put up many as
they were not seeking buyers, as they already had the
buyer in the person of Mr. Tammen. Through my attorney I got out an injunction, and on the day of the sale
stopped it on the ground that Mr. Tom Smith, my partner in the plant owned one half of that property, thus
the first sale was stopped, but Tammen gave bonds, and
after about a week, the property was advertised to sell
again.

[Pawnee Bill Tries to Save the Show]

Leaving word at the desk of the Savoya Hotel that
if any one asked for me, give them my Buffalo Ranch
address at Pawnee, Okla. I took the night train for
Trenton, N.J. where our Company had been incorporated and early in the morning of the second sale day a
wire was received by [the] U.S. Marshall, at Denver,
who was in charge: "Stop all proceedings, ancilliary receiver has been appointed and is now on his way to take
charge." This was a knock out for Mr. Tammen. He now
saw his scheme of throwing me out and proceeding on
the route without me was stopped for good. So he ordered the advance cars back, discharged all people excepting a sufficient number to take care of the stock. In
the meantime Tammen also had placed an attachment
on the show property for $20,000.00, both companies
attaching also in addition to all the show property, my
ranch and home in Pawnee. The show property was
eventually sold in Denver. Tom Smith suing Tammen
for $50,000.00 damage and recovering $43,000.00.

As time went on the Tammen people and the U.S.
Lithograph Co. fell out, so that the U.S. people were
afraid to proceed with their case in Denver on account
of the influence Tammen had over the courts, had the
case transferred to the Pawnee County Court. When the
case came to trial, after it had proceeded for an hour or
two, the prosecution asked for a recess, at which time
they offered to call the case off, provided I would call
everything off against them. This I refused to do, asking
a bonus of $3,000.00 with which to pay my attornies.

This they refused, and the case proceeded until the middle of the afternoon, when they asked for another recess, at which time they consented to withdraw their suit and give me $3,000.00 provided I would withdraw a suit which I had entered against them for damages. This I consented to do, and proper settlement was made through contracts drawn by the attornies for both sides. Thus ended the show's and show life for me.

[The Last Meeting of Cody and Lillie]

Several years later I was in N.Y. City, and I with a number of friends dropped in to the new Astor House at Times Square for lunch. We were ushered to a table just a few feet from one occupied by Col. Cody and a party of friends. Col. came right over and greeted me most cordially[.] After we had finished our lunch, the Col. asked me to step over to the ladies entrance, saying he wanted to speak to me confidentially. This I did. He put his arm around me and said, "Major, the people do not want to see me under the circus tent [Cody suggested that he and Pawnee Bill rejoin forces, and start fresh with another Wild West and Far East show]. . . . They want to see me in the open arena. That's what the public wants." But I assured the Col. I was afraid this could not be done, as it would cost at least ½ million dollar[s] to do it. This was the last time, I ever saw the Col. . . . but he still lives in my memory as the ideal of my boyhood days [when I first] saw him, one of the biggest and best men I ever knew.

Pawnee Bill and May Manning, ca. 1886; photos taken a few years after young Lillie had first seen Buffalo Bill in Bloomington, Illinois. Lillie introduced Manning to the world of the Wild West, from a sophisticated Philadelphia and Ivy League background. She became an expert at riding and shooting, and the couple's story was brought to life in Pawnee Bill's own memoirs, as well as Glenn Shirley's *Pawnee Bill: A Biography of Major Gordon W. Lillie.* Denver Public Library, Western History Department.

Cody and his entertainments, 1913–1917. Winchester Model 1897 shotgun at *top*, made for Johnny Baker. Colt Lightning rifle *below*, in .22 caliber, presented to Dr. B. F. Longstreet by Kickapoo Medicine Encampment; bronze tomahawk also with Kickapoo associations. Dime novels, letterheads, programs, A. D. M. Cooper artwork, Cody with children, family death notice, and grave site represent hectic and failing final years.

Chapter 9

✦

Sells-Floto, the 101 Ranch, and the End of the Trail 1912–1917

Old age did not come gracefully for Buffalo Bill. In his final years, he was plagued by financial woes, though he remained sturdy in health until nearly the end. Indebted to Harry Tammen, Cody agreed to tour with the Sells-Floto Circus and Buffalo Bill's Wild West in 1913, 1914, and 1915. The tension between the two accelerated, and once when Tammen had to meet with Cody to iron out a difference over Cody's debts, the old scout was considering drastic measures: to a friend Cody announced he was prepared to kill Tammen! Meeting in Lawrence, Kansas, the wily businessman was afraid to enter Cody's tent until assured of his personal safety.

The grueling schedule of appearances proved the continuing mettle of Buffalo Bill: in 1915 alone, there were 366 performances over a 183-day period, and Cody did not miss a single show. When a rainstorm caused flooding at the show grounds in Fort Madison, Iowa, only Cody and five others of the four-hundred-person troupe and staff remained to save the women and children.

In scout pose; Winchester 1873 at hand. Signed and dated May 13, 1911, to R. J. Walker, with lengthy inscription attesting to Walker's service as a soldier and his experience on the plains.

For the 1916 season, the old scout toured with an outfit called Miller and Arlington Wild West Show Co., Inc., Presents "Buffalo Bill" (Himself) Combined with the 101 Ranch Shows. A scarce program provided the public with an overview of hyperbolic proportions:

One of the big surprises of the year has been the amalgamation of the famous Buffalo Bill and 101 Ranch shows. Both exhibitions have been known to the public for many years, because they typified all that was best in the line of frontier exhibitions. The fact that the combined shows are exhibiting in this city, and that Buffalo Bill is here in person, is creating very general interest.

The new military spectacle which the combined Buffalo Bill (himself) and 101 Ranch shows offer this season, is entitled "Preparedness," and to judge from comments elsewhere the title is a very fitting one. The purpose of the display is not only to afford the patrons of the show a big realistic military display, with all the color and thrills of so strenuous an entertainment but also to arouse public interest in the enlargement of the army and in "Preparedness" for defense in case of possible attack.

All the soldiers utilized in the new Buffalo Bill–101 Ranch military spectacle, "Preparedness," are "loaned" by

215

Dressed for the show arena, with Winchester Model 1873; rare in that it was signed and dated twice.

the United States War Department, which has granted the men furloughs in order to participate in the display and to give it genuineness. The display has already had a very marked effect in stimulating enlistments. Col. Wm. F. Cody (Buffalo Bill) actively participates in the military maneuvers as well as in the battle between United States cavalrymen and a band of Indians led by the famous Sioux, Chief Iron Tail, which is a stirring feature of the exhibition. . . . He is accompanied by over a hundred Sioux and other Indians, with their squaws and papooses. . . .

While the principal feature of the combined Buffalo Bill–101 Ranch shows is the big "Preparedness" spectacle, which is the amusement sensation of the season, the frontier

features always naturally associated with the name of Buffalo Bill, have not been neglected, and scores of Indians, cowboys, cowgirls and other characteristic people of the ranch and prairie present a vivid picture of life on the border. . . .

The time will come, no doubt, when Buffalo Bill, whose name is so closely associated with the history of the West and the Indian warfare of the Borderland, will be a tradition. Today he is an institution, linking the present with a part that will always stand out as an historic cameo in the story of "the making of the West." Buffalo Bill belongs to the history of the United States, and no story of the subjugation of the wild Indian tribes is complete without a record of his participation in it.

Marksmanship remained a highlight of the show, represented by Edith Tantlinger, "The Oklahoma Indian Girl." Midway through the same program, she is pictured holding a Winchester Model 1897 shotgun. The caption reads:

Edith Tantlinger . . . is the crack shot with the show. She is an expert with the rifle, revolver and shotgun and handles the lariat with dexterity.

[She is] a native of Oklahoma, where she received her first training in shooting quail, deer, bear, etc., in the Wichita Mountains, near Fort Sill, Oklahoma.

Vern Tantlinger, who was either Edith's husband or her brother, was chief of the cowboys. His picture,

An aging Buffalo Bill; buffalo-head stickpin on cravat.

With little girl in dress sitting on his knee; on show lot in an unidentified city. Personal Cody frame, a number of which were made up for Buffalo Bill and family, believed done in North Platte.

Louisa Frederici "Lulu" Cody, in a domestic pose she preferred.

next to hers, shows him holding a boomerang in each hand. He is identified further as "a native of this country who spent several years in the wilds of Australia and learned to handle 'The Australian Boomerang' very skillfully." The right half of a poster promoting Princess Wenona, pictured in Chapter 3, advertised Edith Tantlinger.

The introduction to the Buffalo Bill and 101 Ranch program closed with a flourish, which in retrospect was a last hurrah for Cody, for 1916 was his last tour under canvas.

Buffalo Bill was the first to realize the romance and picturesqueness of Indian and cowboy life from an exhibition standpoint, and he introduced the life of the mountains and prairies to the people of the East. He visualized the dangers of the Overland trail and savage incursions of the Indians upon the settlements of the white pioneers, the outlawry of the border, the stagecoach hold-up, the buffalo hunt, the round-up, the sports and pastimes of the cowboys and cowgirls and all the other incidental features of life in the Far West; and the picture he presented was a true one, for it was taken from his own life. In addition to thus perpetuating the "story of the West" in the form of a great exhibition, the life and exploits of Buffalo Bill have been preserved in many volumes of real stories of the Wildest West and even in motion pictures.

Buffalo Bill: Exhibition Shooter and Sportsman

Cody's reputation as a hunter and marksman remained one of the attractions that brought millions to see him. Riding in the showring with his trusty Winchester, reenacting the old days of buffalo hunting on the plains, and shooting aerial targets while on horseback were staple performances of the Wild West act almost to the end.

Shots on the stage had served to draw the public to his earlier performances in the Combination days. In a Combination show in Chicago in 1881, Cody put on "an exhibition of Fancy Rifle Shooting, in which he is pre-eminent and alone. *Note*—The audience will please take particular notice of the twenty different positions that Mr. Cody holds his rifle in making his fancy shots."

Programs and posters reminded the public that the entertainments had key elements of shooting and guns, horses and riding. An 1898 poster had as its theme "Marksmanship—Foot and Horseback." This sheet advertisement was printed in at least three variations and sizes by the Enquirer Job Printing Company. The illustration showed Cody on horseback,

An Indian with a basket of glass balls, assisting Buffalo Bill in showing the public his skills as a practical "all-round shot." From the 1899 program and pictured in several others as well.

From the 1899 program and used frequently in other editions, Cody running buffalo to camp. Scene likely an inspiration to engravers for embellishing firearms of the day.

firing his Winchester at glass balls, while Annie Oakley stood firing her shotgun, and Johnny Baker lay on his back firing his gun.

Cody had particular ideas about his own brand of marksmanship, as described in various programs. Quoting from page 13 of the 1902 publication, under the title "A Practical 'All-Round Shot' ":

In contradistinction of the many so-called "fancy shots" that have for years been before the public, "BUFFALO BILL" is what may be termed a "practical marksman," and where that expression's full meaning is understood, he is looked upon as a marvellous "all-round shot." That is, a man of deadly aim in any emergency, with any weapon—a small Derringer, a Colt's, a shot-gun, a carbine, a blunderbuss, or a rifle—at any foe, red or white; at any game—[prairie] chicken, jack-rabbit, antelope, deer, buffalo, bear, or elk; at the swiftest bird or soaring eagle; on foot, in any position; on horseback, at any speed. To be such a marksman is only the result of years of necessity for exercising the faculties of instantaneous measurement of distance, acuteness of vision—in fact, an eagle eye and iron nerves—to think quick, to resolve, to fire, to kill. As a hunter these gifts have rendered him famous and gained him plaudits from admiring officers, noblemen, sportsmen and competitors in the chase, and compelled the respect and fear of his implacable Indian foes. That he exists to-day is the result of the training that enables a man in the most startling exigency to command himself, and to meet the circumstances face to face, whatever they may be, and achieve by cool precision deserved victory in the field, and embellish history with deeds of heroism. MR CODY still gives an exhibition of his ability by shooting objects thrown in the air while galloping at full speed, executing difficulties that would receive commendation if accomplished on foot, and which can only be fully appreciated by those who have attempted the feat while experiencing a rapid pace when occupying "a seat in the saddle."

Exhibition shooters and gifted marksmen. At *center*, presentation J. M. Marlin falling-block rifle from Dr. John Ruth to Hon. E. H. Pardee, 1879; serial number 1199, .22 rimfire, 26-inch octagon barrel. *Top*, two rifles of Tom Pringle (a.k.a. T. H. Ford): Marlin Model 1892, .22 rimfire, serial number 123275; and Winchester Model 1892, serial number 262395, silver plated and in .32-20 smoothbore. *Bottom*, a Model 1873 presentation from Winchester to Arizona Joe, in .32-20 caliber, serial number 447861; Joe on horseback in cabinet-card photo. The silver-plated Model 1873 .22 short, inscribed on mortise cover GEO. D. SNYDER, believed to be from the Snyder Brothers Wild West, serial number 472556B. *Left to right*, beneath Arizona Joe rifle, coins shot by Oakley, Cody, and (on watch-fob chain) Baker.

Just how accomplished Cody was as a marksman was described in a laudatory article in the Hamilton (Ontario) *Daily Spectator* on August 27, 1885:

Wild Western Scenes

—

Buffalo Bill's Great Show in Hamilton

—

Cowboys and Indians Engage in Bloodless Combats—Sitting Bull and His Braves— Vivid Picture of Frontier Life

. . . Johnnie Baker "the Cowboy Kid," did some wonderful rifle shooting at short range, holding his rifle in a dozen difficult positions and never failing to hit the mark. Miss Annie Oakley also did some very clever marksmanship (or rather markswomanship) with both rifle and shot-gun. But the best shooting was done by Buffalo Bill himself. He shot at 24 clay pigeons sprung from a trap, hitting 21 and missing 3, in 1 minute and 18 seconds. He also did some splen[d]id shooting with his horse running at full speed. An Indian galloping alongside him flung about a dozen balls into the air in quick succession, and Mr. Cody broke [e]very one of them.

Cody's use of shot to hit the glass-ball targets was a point of some controversy in his day. Writing to his sister, Julia Goodman, in 1884, he stated proudly: "I am improving wonderfully in my shooting, don't take a back seat from Carver or [Bogardus]. . . . I broke 87 glass balls out of one hundred thrown from a trap 21 yards rise with a shotgun riding a horse at full speed. I have broken 76 out of a hundred with a rifle running full speed."

The loads he used in the shot cartridges were .44-40 caliber, having a thin projectile of paper, which was designed to drop out of the trajectory as the charge came out of the barrel—which reduced leading in the rifling. The approximate charge was twenty grains of black powder, considered a mid-range load, and a quarter ounce of no. 7½ chilled shot. Most of the impacts took place approximately twenty yards from the muzzle, and at that range the spread of the charge was estimated at about two to three inches. Using shot shells on horseback, often going full tilt, made the glass balls less difficult to shoot than with a single lead projectile. However, these hits

were still difficult. Safety was a crucial factor: the charge of shot would dissipate after about eighty to one hundred yards, whereas a bullet could go for a half mile or more with devastating effect. Once, while shooting in Baltimore, Cody had hit a child in the audience! The boy recovered, and thereafter Cody and he maintained a correspondence over a period of years. That accident made Cody all the more concerned about the use of proper cartridges; for him, shot was the only answer.

Hunters and Marksmen

From Colonel Cody's May 1889 Paris souvenir and invitation book are reminders of the hunt with the Grand Duke Alexis, a visit of a delegation from a team of American marksmen, and an invitation from the Marquis de Mores to see some rifles. An F. Machise sent a note to Cody in which he stated "no doubt you will remember my name as that of the Englishman to the Suite of the Grand Duke Alexis when you accompanied His Imperial Highness to the Buffalo Hunt in the Nebraska Plains. And [whom] you received [so] amiably in your tent at the American Exhibition in London." Machise wished to introduce to Cody "Count Stanislas Ozarorsky, who is desirous to make your acquaintance, and whom I am sure you will receive with your usual kindness." The count, of course, was a fellow sportsman and hunter.

Cody also received an undated flier from the Massachusetts Volunteer Militia Rifle Team, a distinguished group then competing in international matches. The team had prepared a handsome giveaway that pictured two trophies they had won, the Hilton and the Soldier of Marathon; the document listed all the members. The last on the list, W. M. Farrow, became a well-known writer on shooting and established a distinguished record as a crack competitive shot:

During the Paris engagement of 1889, Theodore Roosevelt's old nemesis, the Marquis de Mores, with whom T.R. nearly fought a duel (with Winchester rifles), invited Cody to lunch at the Restaurant de France au Trocadera. The postscript to the marquis's letter was a tantalizing invitation for any keen shot: "If you come at my house at 11.30 [July 6] I will show you my rifles and we will go together." Among the marquis's arsenal were some magnificent Winchester and Colt firearms; further, he was an experienced horseman, shooter, and hunter. The marquis died in 1896 in Algeria, fighting bandits on the desert in a Hollywood-style pitched battle.

Bowie knife of the Marquis de Mores, documented on the scabbard, shortly after the nobleman's death, with a finely lettered paper label in French. Translation: "Hunting Knife/of Marquis de Mores/Explorer/Sale Guerin in Brusselles/at the Fort Chabrol." Made by James Dixon and Sons, Sheffield, and so marked. Etched on the left side of the blade inside the fuller: EXPLORATEUR. Bright steel blade of 10½ inches; overall length, 16 inches. Checkered ebony handle and German-silver mounts.

The Marquis de Mores was a heroic and at the same time somewhat tragic figure in the second half of the nineteenth century. Organizer of a major cattle operation in the Dakota Territory and developer of a meat-packing facility, he was instrumental in building the town of Medora. A keen enthusiast of guns and hunting, he was a rival of Theodore Roosevelt. This knife was likely seen by Cody if he indeed visited the marquis's house in Paris in 1889, per the marquis's invitation.

Arizona John Burke on "Expert Shooting"

One of the Cody intimates, both as friend and master publicist, John Burke authored the laudatory *Buffalo Bill from Prairie to Palace,* published by Rand McNally in 1893. Tied in with the best year in the history of the Wild West, Burke flooded the book with promotional angles. Prefaced with a print showing Cody "Breaking Glass Balls at Full Speed," Chapter VI bears the title "Expert Shooting." The five-page text has relevance today. Burke's pronouncements fail to qualify as "politically correct" and the "fad" for shooting has subsided, yet to catch on with new generations from the ever increasing population of urban dwellers:

Every custom, vocation, or study that has for its object the protection of home, self, or one's just rights, the defense of the weak or the protection of the innocent, is justly denominated "manly," and commands universal respect and admiration. If such attributes or qualifications as a steady nerve, a

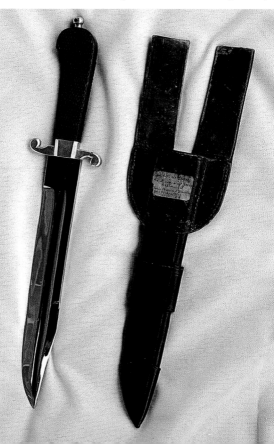

clear, penetrating gaze, and intensity and earnestness of purpose, are combined with quickness of action and courageous bearing, the admiration grows stronger and the respect deeper.

Years ago scarcely anybody save the professional duelist would ever have thought of making an accomplishment of rifle or pistol shooting, unless, like the enlisted soldier or the dweller on the prairies, a practical knowledge of fire-arms and their uses became an absolute necessity for self-protection or the performance of duty. Yet now so-called "fancy shooting" is considered rather a "fad," and its aptest exponents are objects of laudation and applause. The huntsman is no longer a slayer of game and wild beasts as a means of subsistence for himself and family, or for sale to neighbors or in the public market. The elephant is now rarely killed for his tusks, the tiger for his skin, or the buffalo (what few there are left of this species) for his flesh. Now the "chase" is a mere sport, like "hunting the covers" in Merrie England, and men boast of their prowess as hunters much as they do of their skill at billiards. Yet an expert with the rifle or the pistol is an object of applause and admiration, and even the more courageous of the fair sex love to try their skill at a target. For a time the old pastime of archery was revived, but, whether its difficulties or its present-day impracticability was the cause, it has been abandoned by the fashionable world, and shooting-galleries are now the "thing" rather than archery clubs.[1]

In the march of progress the club, the lance, the javelin, and the long-bow have been thrown aside, and modern invention has given us the cannon, the shotgun, the musket, the rifle, and the pistol. Some writers have even argued, and ably too, that the invention of gunpowder had a most powerful and active effect upon the civilization of the world.

However, the acts of aiming and discharging the projectile, and successfully striking the target, be it animate or inanimate, possess a rare fascination for the world at large. . . .

How different from [the target shooter, the hunter, and the soldier] is the daring scout, the intrepid cowboy, the faithful guide, [of] the unsettled West. To either of these danger is so constant, so frequent in its visitations, that it has become an expected presence. An ear quick to detect a rustle of the leaves, a footfall on the turf, the click of the hammer of a rifle; an eye to instantaneously penetrate into the thickness of the brush; to detect, locate, and photograph a shifting speck on the horizon; to measure distance at a glance, and to fix the threatening target's vulnerable point in an instant are absolute necessities. Added to these, as an absolute essential, must be nerves as tense as steel. A tremor of the arm, nay, the slightest quiver of a muscle, that sends the bullet a hair's-breadth from the point aimed at, may cost not only the death

S&W First Model Single Shot .22 pistol, richly decorated by either Oscar or Eugene Young, gold plated and with mother-of-pearl grips; serial number 18073; 10-inch barrel. Specially made in 1898 for factory exhibition use. Shipped April 25, 1916, to Whitney Sporting Goods, Denver, along with S&W Military and Police number 11632. A similar First Model Single Shot pistol was made for Annie Oakley, as noted in Chapters 5 and 7.

of the shooter, but the lives of those depending on him for safety. No fancy shooting this; for more than life—honor and reputation, the preservation of sacred trusts and cherished lives committed to his care, depend upon his coolness, his courage, and his accuracy. In a moment all will be over for good or ill, and upon his single personality all depends. The stake is fearful.

These indubitable facts considered, is it surprising that these danger-baptized heroes of the West stand to-day as the most marvelous marksmen of the world?

The amateur sportsman, the society expert rifle-shot, the ambitious youth, and even woman, to whom all real manly exploits and true heroism are admirable, all take sincere pleasure in witnessing the feats of marksmanship of the cowboy, scout, or guide expert, and wonder at his marvelous accuracy. It is because actual necessity was the foundation upon which their expertness was built that these surpass all others in the science. What appears wonderful to others is in them but the perfection of art.

Looking at expert shooting as a pastime, a science, or a means of protection or self-preservation, the awakening of the manhood of the country and the up-growing youth to its possibilities is surely to be commended and encouraged. No man is more to be credited with the accomplishment of this than Gen. W. F. Cody. His romantic and picturesque history and his wonderful accomplishments have attracted to him the attention of America and Europe, and no one man is more capable of exemplifying the science of shooting than he. A graduate, with high honors, of the school of expert shooting is taught by the best practice and actual experience, he is master of his art. The object-lessons he gives are of incalculable benefit to the ambitious student of marksmanship, and sources of delight to all. His trusty rifle is now a social friend, whose intimacy is founded on dangers averted, heroic deeds accomplished, and honors nobly won.

Buffalo Bill: Gun Collector

Just how many firearms Cody owned over the years is unknown today, but the number that has survived is limited. At one time, his collection was substantial—though unlike Annie Oakley, he did not have them grouped together in his tent or cluttering up an apartment in New York City! His favorite and most historic rifle, Lucretia Borgia, is the keystone to the Buffalo Bill arms collection. Considering how many times it was shot, and the use it was subjected to on the plains, it is remarkable the treasure survived at all.

As Cody's fame became more widespread, gunmakers honored him with special gifts. Winchester advertised consistently in his show programs, and his arsenal grew. In time, however, his generosity cut into the size of his collection, since he tended to present guns to friends in an overly generous fashion.

What the Buffalo Bill Historical Center has in its holdings represents the remains of his original collection: Lucretia Borgia comes first, then, in a loose chronological order:

pair of eighteenth-century flintlock pistols, crudely inscribed to Cody from W. E. Plummer, England, 1903

flintlock U.S. martial pistol by A. Waters of Milbury, Massachusetts

over and under mule-ear percussion rifle with patchbox and ramrod marked "W. E. Robbins"

Remington New Model Army revolver, believed taken from Yellow Hair when Cody shot him

Metropolitan Navy Model revolver (no. 6088)

Remington Rolling Block rifle from Colonel George Leroy Brown, who had received it from Cody (no. 1423)

Frank Wesson single-shot rifle associated with Cody and Luther North (no. 372)

Belgian flintlock trade rifle, painted red, probably used by an Arab in the Wild West show—given to Cody by Annie Oakley

Winchester Model 1873 rifle given to Will Richard by Cody (no. 6745; a .44-40 smoothbore)

pair of Colt Single Action Army revolvers, nickel plated and with bone handles (nos. 54057, 54070—from W. F. Schneider)

Winchester Model 1873 Carbine believed used by Cody (no. 229894B)

Cody's best Model 1873 rifle, gold plated and engraved (no. 494993)

Winchester Model 1873 rifle (no. 607678)

Winchester Model 1886 rifle (no. 53507)

E. Thomas Jr., Chicago, double-barrel shotgun (barrels only, with case)

Marlin Model 1894 rifle (from Zach Sutley, who had received it from Cody; no. 278024)

Winchester Model 1894 rifle (no. 463269)

Winchester Model 1895 Carbine (no. 22590), engraved on the receiver with Cody's name (the gift from Captain Jack, later presented to George T. Beck)

Winchester Model 1895 rifle (no. 42123)

Buffalo Bill's guns presently on loan to the historical center include a Colt Single Action Army revolver (number 129108) inscribed WILLIAM F. CODY. Some privately owned pieces are featured in this book, and a few of the period photographs show Cody with guns known today to be in private or museum collections.

Cody Queried about Guns and Featured in Advertisements

Besides his marksmanship on stages and in arenas and his repeated use of guns afield, Cody was sometimes asked questions by reporters and the public about firearms subjects. A fascinating letter in the 1887 tour diary shows that even women were captivated by the subject of Cody and his guns. Writing on June 10 from her fashionable address on Curzon Street in London's Mayfair district, Carolyn Creyke gushed with enthusiasm and requested that Cody come for a visit:

I should so much like to show you our house & my rifles, & several of my friends are most anxious to make your acquaintance[.] Can I persuade you & your daughter [Arta] to come & see me on Wednesday afternoon next—(the 15th) at any time after your performance. We should be so pleased. If at any time you thought of having an ivory sight the best gun maker in London lives close to me, & I could get it done for [you] if you liked. It would cost 2 guineas but the difference it makes in shooting on dark days or in the twilight is quite extraordinary, & I am sure if you have not already tried it, you would find it would answer at your evening performances— Hoping to see you on Wednesday. . . .

Caroline Creyke

The identity of the gunmaker remains unknown, but evidently Cody was experiencing some difficulty with his shooting during evening performances.

From the Colt factory alone Cody received such presents as a richly engraved and inlaid Burgess Model lever-action rifle on which the frame panel scene depicted a scout shooting a buffalo. The date of presentation, July 26, 1883, coincided with performances Cody was then making in Hartford.[2] A Single Action Army Target Model was made for him, deluxe engraved, with gold-inlaid inscription, and pearl grips; other specials were made up in the conventional Single Action Army, in double actions, and in semiautomatics. While not considered a devotee of automatic pistols, records show that one of the first Colt pistols of this type, a Model 1902 Military (number 14940) was gold inlaid COL. WM. F. CODY and presented to him by the factory.

A full-page advertisement from the Colt company in a program from around 1910 noted that "Colt Revolvers have been adopted by the United States Army and Navy, by the Police, Militia, and are used by Buffalo Bill's Wild West Show. THEY ARE THE BEST."

Cody was quoted endorsing the new Savage semiautomatic pistol, the advertisement stating:

A friend gave me a 10 shot Savage Automatic Pistol for Christmas. It is the first automatic I ever owned or fired. I had turned them down without trial, and stuck to an old army revolver. To-day I took the old revolver and the Savage Automatic out and fired each fifty times making, to my surprise, a much better score with the automatic than I could with my old pet gun.

Among other promotional statements, the advertisement noted that the "world's crack shots, like Col. Cody, 'Bat' Masterson and Dr. Carver, say it beats any revolver. . . . Write to-day for 'The Tenderfoot's Turn,' a fascinating book (free) about famous crack shots, by 'Bat' Masterson."

Handsomely styled Winchester advertisements appeared not infrequently in the programs. Judging from pictures of Cody spanning over thirty years, his favorite sporting and frontier rifle was the Model 1873. Rarely is he shown with any other make or model. The Winchester, he maintained, was "the boss."

Wild West arsenal wagon. Model 1895 Winchester rifle, at *left*, same as used by President Theodore Roosevelt on his African safari and by Colonel Cody on his hunting expeditions. Rifle, number 69193, in Buffalo Bill Museum, Golden, Colorado; a gift to Cody from Johnny Baker. Note numerous rifles and Single Action Colt revolvers, as well as several gun boxes, cartridge cases, and targets and a commercial Winchester sign. Ca. 1913.

Buffalo Bill Cody et al. on Film

Watching Cody and the Wild West on film brings alive their performances, despite the Keystone Kops–style quick movement of film footage from that time. The panorama of the preshow parade and the show itself are presented, as are action shots of Buffalo Bill firing blanks at buffalo charging around the arena.

The earliest film ever made of Cody was by Thomas Edison in West Orange, New Jersey. That footage, of Cody firing a Model 1873 Winchester—now believed lost—was made at the same time as Edison's film of Annie Oakley. More films were made by Edison in 1898 and by Biograph in 1902. Still later, Cody and Pawnee Bill organized a film company and copyrighted a production in 1912.

Finally, the Col. W. F. Cody (Buffalo Bill) Historical Pictures Company was formed in 1913. This production firm made at least eight single-reel silent films, including footage shot at the Pine Ridge Indian Reservation featuring Cody, such stalwart veterans of the Indian Wars as Nelson A. Miles, Indians including Short Bull, Flat Iron, and No Neck, and other members of the Wild West troupe. The Battle of Wounded Knee was staged anew. From mid-February to early March 1914, Cody went on a lecture tour, where selections of his movies were shown.

Wild West–show footage featuring gunfire or arms-related scenes ranged from Cody hunting buffalo on horseback—firing blanks in his Winchester 1873 at about eight of the beasts—to firing at glass balls, also from horseback. An Indian rides near Cody, throwing up the targets, as they gallop around the showring. Other footage shows buffalo running into the arena, quickly pursued by Cody, mounted on his white horse and riding like the master equestrian that he was. Winchester in hand, he shifts into a gallop and chases the buffalo across the field and out of the arena—continuously firing his rifle. Cody then returns to the arena and chases and fires at more buffalo. Sometimes, he fires his Winchester with only one hand, just like the old days on the prairie!

One of the more filmable Wild West vignettes was the old Deadwood stagecoach riding around the

Lithograph poster making clear that the star himself will appear in both parades and performances, Santa Cruz, May 7. Checking *Route-Books* establishes precise dates of performances up to and including final year. Poster dated 1914, in fine print. *Top* image only: 26½ × 18½ inches.

ring, pulled by a six-horse team and moving at a rapid pace. Passengers are shown on top and inside. Then come the Indians in hot pursuit. Shooting goes back and forth between pursuer and pursued. A fight breaks out on top of the stagecoach. Then the cowboys arrive and chase off the Indians amid dust from horse hooves and coach wheels and smoke from the black-powder blanks. At the end, the triumphant cowboys escort the coach, saved again from the redskins, out of the arena.

Other sequences show Indians and cowboys shooting at each other and chasing each other around the arena. Cleverly orchestrated, some horses fall over, and some riders play dead.

A sequence presenting a reenactment of the Battle of Summit Springs features gunfire when the camp comes alive, under siege by attacking mounted troops, led by Buffalo Bill. He fires his Winchester '73, billowing clouds of smoke.

A shooting demonstration by Johnny Baker is pure magic. Standing next to a table laden with several guns, he fires as fast as he can, keeping four assistants furiously busy. Three assistants load the traps,

Buffalo Bill Stetson with satin hat band. The brand was a Cody favorite, as advertised in some of the show programs. From a 1900 edition, picturing Cody wearing a hat similar to this one, the body of the half-page advertisement proudly stated:

"Years ago we made specially for Colonel Cody, the 'Buffalo Bill,' a soft hat of quite tremendous proportions. This style has been adopted and worn ever since by him and many of his Western companions.

"Out-door life is hard on hats, and the continued patronage of these men is a strong endorsement of the satisfaction and wonderful wear that go with every 'Stetson.'

"There are Stetson Hats for the fashionably-dressed men of the big cities, for the cowboy, the military man, the agriculturist, and everyone else. Vastly different in style, but highest quality always."

A half-page advertisement in a 1912 program pictured Cody wearing a Stetson. The photograph was inscribed with his signature and the notation " 'Buffalo Bill' wore a Stetson for 40 years." Cody has been credited as the originator of the ten-gallon hat.

the fourth helps Baker. He fires his side-by-side double-barrel shotguns and pump-action Model 1897 Winchesters with tremendous speed. The clay-pigeon traps are set up three abreast. With his back to these, he bends over and fires between his legs. He lies on a stool and fires backward; a handler holds his legs as he stands on his head, this time with a double-barrel shotgun! Springing back on his feet, he gingerly throws the gun to a handler when finished. Sometimes the gun barrels seem precariously aimed at his assistants!

In one series, a cannon-drill team with a caisson pulled by six horses charges around the arena. U.S. artillery and cavalry drill units are also shown. A six-horse artillery unit with caisson comes into the arena at speed, then yet another six-horse artillery unit arrives. One cannon is set up for the crowd and then dismantled to move again. The horses then proceed to tow off both cannon sets.

From Prince Albert to Chief Plenty Coups

Not filmed in the show arena yet still a fascinating bit of historical footage is the presentation of a Winchester Model 1895 rifle by Prince Albert of Monaco to Chief Plenty Coups of the Crow Nation. The presentation appears to be taking place on Main Street, Cody, Wyoming, near the Irma Hotel. Buffalo Bill acts as interpreter and master of ceremonies. With Prince Albert and Cody standing in the foreground, the five Indians, all in full dress, ride toward them, Plenty Coups dismounts and comes over to meet his highness, who is dressed in a dark suit and wearing a hat. Both gentlemen shake hands and enter into an animated conversation. Buffalo Bill holds the rifle in his left hand.

The footage is captioned, and at this point the subtitle reads: "I wish to present you with this rifle to kill game only, not to fire against the white man, and hope you will keep it as long as you live."

Sells-Floto Circus advertising postcard, with carved buffalo-motif bone-handled letter opener measuring 12⅜ inches; the silver ferrule is inscribed COL. W. F. CODY BUFFALO BILL "DUKE" MAY 27, 1902. The other side is inscribed FRANK MCGRANN TO J. H. WOLF. A similarly carved buffalo-motif umbrella or whip handle is on display at the Buffalo Bill Historical Center.

Prince Albert of Monaco, visiting Cody, Wyoming, and about to present Winchester Model 1895 rifle to a chief, believed to be Plenty Coups. The rifle held by Cody at *left*. The event was captured on motion-picture film, and the tribe still has the Winchester, which was inlaid with an engraved plaque on the right side of the stock. 1913.

Prince Albert presents the chief with the Winchester. The happy Plenty Coups clutches the rifle and shakes his royal highness's hand. The caption has Plenty Coups reply: "You are a ruler in a country across the Big Lake. I, too, am a ruler. My people once ruled this entire land. I thank you for your gift and ask you to accept this belt as a token of remembrance." His highness admires the handsome belt, which is adorned with beadwork.

The Winchester still belongs to the Crow Nation and is currently exhibited at the Chief Plenty Coups State Monument, Pryor, Montana. An engraved presentation plaque was inlaid on the stock. However, since the Crows had traditionally been friendly to the whites, the on-screen admonition against shooting them with the rifle was Hollywood inspired.

Prince Albert and Cody at Camp Monaco

A hunting film was shot on what was billed on-screen as the last hunt of Buffalo Bill. The site was near Cody, Wyoming, adjacent to Yellowstone Park and was called by the participants Camp Monaco. The three hunters were Prince Albert, Cody, and Cody friend A. A. Anderson, a wealthy enthusiast of the West and of Buffalo Bill. With their guide leading the way, the three ride out of camp on horseback and vanish from the picture frame. Cody is the fourth and last rider, and he waves a hearty good-bye.

In one of the sequences, a tree falls into campfire flames while Cody, chopping wood at the time, doesn't miss a beat, keeping up his swing! Meanwhile, men rush to prevent the fire from getting out of control.

An old tree was marked with a handsomely painted Camp Monaco sign. In later years, this landmark was damaged by fire. The stump was removed and brought to Cody, where the historic marker is now on display in the Philip R. Goodwin Camp Scene at the Cody Firearms Museum.

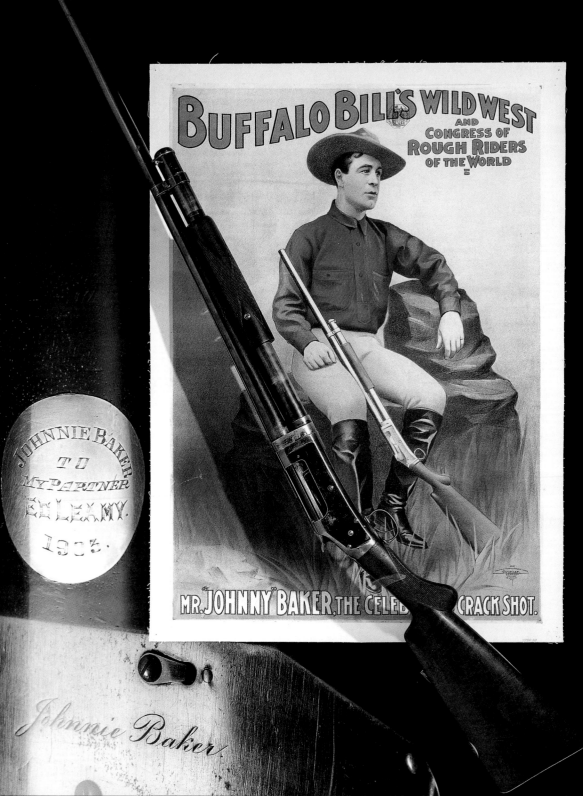

The Life of Buffalo Bill (Col. Cody)

In 1912, *The Life of Buffalo Bill (Col. Cody)* was produced and copyrighted by the Buffalo Bill and Pawnee Bill Film Company, 145 East Forty-fifth Street, New York City. This ambitious production, in three reels, told Cody's life story, beginning with a scene in which he rides through a river, looking for Indians or game. Cody rides up to the camera, with hat back, left hand up, as if sighting Indians or wildlife, his trusty Winchester '73 rifle clutched in his right hand.

The star dismounts, lays down his reins, and then his Winchester. Taking his lariat off the saddle horn, he ties it to the reins, dropping them on the ground. Next, he loosens the cinch of the custom-made saddle on his light-colored horse and removes the saddle and blanket, setting them on the ground.

Headings are presented to identify the film's sequences; clearly, several claim lineage from Wild West–show performances. Since there is a story line to the sequence, however, the film is much more advanced than the Wild West and is classified as one of the first Westerns. Cody was attempting to move the Wild West show from the arena into movie theaters. But in his sixties, he was a bit old to become a cinema star and capitalize on the new medium, try as he did. Plenty of action was sandwiched between each sequence:

(*left*) Specially built Winchester Model 1897 shotgun; note spellings of Baker's first name; serial number 190091. In 1903, Baker presented this gun to his friend Jed Leamy (manager of a circus troupe of trapeze artists). Winchester factory records note: 28-inch barrel, takedown, checkered stock, pistol grip, slide handle checkered, oil finish, engraved JOHNNIE BAKER, pull 13½ inches, drop at heel 2¾ inches, drop at comb 1¾ inches; received in warehouse December 3, 1902, and shipped same date. Ledger records one other shotgun with same specifications and on same order number, now in Buffalo Bill Historical Center collection, serial 190092. Baker also had specially built Model 1897 numbers E410405 and 410411, both in 12 gauge, and both inscribed with his name. Poster 27½ × 19½ inches.

One of the rarest of Wild West posters, seven feet high, shows the armed Baker and Annie Oakley standing in front of Oakley's tent, ca. 1898; printed by Enquirer Job Printing Company, Cincinnati, Ohio.

(*above*) Johnny Baker's custom-made and cased Colt Model 1889 .38 New Army and Navy revolver, serial number 15475. Reflecting keen interest of Baker and Cody in firearms, this revolver was shipped in 1895, accompanied by a deluxe .44 Bisley Single Action Target revolver, gold inlaid, inscribed COL. W. F. CODY/BUFFALO BILL. Baker also received a .44 New Service revolver, the 7½-inch barrel specially made as a smoothbore. Detail shows coin shot by Baker, inscribed and turned into a watch fob.

At the end, Cody stands up, holding reins in his hand, and gets ready to resaddle his horse. Putting his blanket on the horse's back, he then throws on his saddle and prepares to cinch it up. Cody takes a while to seat his saddle, then gathers together his lariat and puts that on the back of his saddle. Like at the end of so many Westerns to follow, our hero is ready to ride off into the sunset!

Johnny Baker: Trick Shot and Cody's Foster Son

No stranger to the cinema and Buffalo Bill's most loyal friend and partisan, Johnny Baker was still with Cody's show in 1916, some thirty-three years after first appearing as the Cowboy Kid. Baker's career paralleled the history of Buffalo Bill's Wild West. Nearing old age, Baker's life story was prepared by the old

performer himself. The biography began with his birthday, January 13, 1869, at North Platte, Nebraska:

When Buffalo Bill moved with his family back to the little western town of North Platte in 1876 . . . I got my first glimpse of this famous frontiersman[. He] became my idol and I soon was on friendly terms with him. He had just lost his own little son who was just my age, 7 years, so from then on I was a member of the Cody family. I attended school with his daughter [Orra] until 1883 when the Wild West show was organized. Buffalo Bill took me with the show, and for the next 35 years I was with the show continually. During that long period of time I missed only 9 performances. . . .

I was considered an expert marksman at the age of 14 years[, having] won the Boys championship at the age of 12.

1888 Defeated a Mr Vandergrift 3 straight matches at clay birds, making a score of 100 straight double rise, and 98 and 97 single rise.

1891 at Hamburg Germany broke 1000 flying objects out of 1016 shots fired.

Have appeared before the public in shooting exhibitions 12,600 times and have used in these exhibitions over a million rounds of ammunition.

In 1917 a horse fell with me during parade and I was forced to retire from active work. . . .

Have appeared before about all the crowned heads of Europe and have been presented to many of them, including Queen Victoria, King Edward VII, King George, Queen Alexandria, the Kings of Saxony, Denmark, Belgium, (not the present King Albert), Serbia, the [Shah] of Persia, Franz Joseph, The Czarina of Austria, The President of France, The King of Italy and Royal family, etc., etc. Also the present Prince of Wales and Prince George, his brother.

An adept organizer and one of the closest of the troupe to Cody himself, Baker became "arenic director," as revealed in the flamboyant text of several editions of the show programs. To quote from that of 1902:

"Petit Jean," as Johnny Baker was known in France, firing with two handguns at Le Fusil de Chasse, a Paris club for aficionados of guns and hunting, 1905. At *right*, his set of Model 1897 Winchester pump shotguns.

Through perserverance and his aptness for learning he has become a most valuable assistant to Colonel CODY, so much so that he is now Arenic Director, looking after all matters pertaining to the Exhibition, and has shown himself to be thoroughly familiar in the art of conducting the entire entertainment without an interruption. He is an admirable stage manager, and it is to him that the care of the large army of men is assigned.

The 1916 show program praised Baker's thrilling demonstration before a shooting club in France:

In the many years young Baker has been touring with his sponsor, "Buffalo Bill," in many countries, no marksman has been subjected to more trying tests than he. To dispel the incredulity with which the public is affected, probably with reasonable excuse on account of "trick shooting" chicanery, one of the many instances when the young American was asked to "face the music" under official inspection of the most stringent order, may be related. During the visit to Paris, 1905, the Premier Shooting Club of France, famed for its many Monte Carlo winners, "Les Tireurs de Chasse" Isle de Bellingcourt Seine, extended an invitation to him to join them in friendly competition and give a private exhibition to the gentlemen and ladies of the club. A number of the most accomplished members, in fact "top-notchers," were found at the traps and it was a trial the severity of which can only be expressed as he himself did in the phrase, "I most certainly felt I was up against it." It was "miss and out" and at the 38th bird, Baker was solitary and alone and had shot from the extreme mark. They presented him with a solid gold cup, although he protested that he was unaware that one was at stake, they said "we did and you earned it." At request, he gave an exhibition of every possible shot known to his repertoire, interspersed with many, including "The Tower Shot," entirely new to him and with a record of 198 out of 200 tries, he received the plaudits of enthusiastic blue-blooded auditors, connoiseurs of the game, who fully appreciated the task they had set him and the cleverness and style in which he had accomplished it.

This was further emphasized by their presentation to him of a special gold medal and a parchment, making him an honorary member of the club for life, a generous tribute to a representative American Marksman

Baker died in Denver at the age of sixty-two on April 22, 1931. He was loyal to Cody to the end, and a newspaper report says that an hour and a half before his death he whispered to his wife at bedside: "Keep alive the memory of Pahaska [the Indian name of Colonel Cody]."

Promotional lithograph poster of health potion Sagwa, touted as a cure-all. Printed by the J. Ottmann Litho. Company, Puck Bldg., New York City, copyright 1892. 28 ¥ 41½ inches. Inside back cover of Kickapoo booklet at *lower right*.

Guns of Johnny Baker

Like so many of his marksmen contemporaries, Baker had a taste for fine guns. He had a few that were custom-built and others that had been presented to him. One of the earliest of the latter was the Westley Richards 12-gauge side-by-side shotgun from Buffalo Bill. And one of the best in handguns was a Colt Model 1889 New Army and Navy, with gold inlaid sideplate monogram and ivory grips. Two of his special Winchester shotguns are known, both Model 1897s, one of them at the Buffalo Bill Historical Center and the other as pictured here. His name was engraved in script on each frame by the factory.

Yet to be identified was a revolver that young Baker ordered in a letter addressed to Hugh Harbison, for many years the secretary of the Colt company. As Cody's adopted son and a rapidly ascending star in his own right, Baker could open doors often closed to other professional shooters. His order was for a .32-caliber revolver and reflects Baker's practiced eye for fine guns. However, Colonel Cody should have insisted that the Cowboy Kid extend his schooling, considering the abysmal spelling and grammar:

July 12 1888   Staten Island
Mr Hugh Hobison [sic]
Dear Sir—The gun I would want would be a 32. As for the finish I dont care how that is just an ordinary finish would do, but couldn't you finish it with the nickle and gold as I would want use it on the stag[e] If I can afford to geet it will let you know what to do when I see your price I should think you would let me have it pretty low because I will keep it before the public all the time Awaiting your Reply I am Dear
Sir Yours Respty
Johnie Baker

A few of Baker's guns are known today, but, as has been the fate of so many arms of the celebrated exhibition shooters, most have disappeared.

Model 1895 Winchester carbine number 55455 was a gift to Cody from Baker, with elaborate inscribed silver plaque on right side of the buttstock:

TO MY GOVERNOR
Col. W. F. Cody
FROM
Johnny Baker
—1906—
"NOT TRANSFERABLE"

In order to make sure Buffalo Bill did not give the carbine away, Baker included the special notation in the final line.

The most recent discovery, the Winchester Model 1897 shotgun later presented by Baker to his friend Jed Leamy, was found in the mid-1990s in Australia.

Kickapoo Indian Medicine Company

Contemporary with the brilliant showmanship and unerring marksmanship of Buffalo Bill and Johnny Baker, two enterprising businessmen combined their skills and intuitions into a medicine show that in some respects rivaled the success of Buffalo Bill's Wild West. This ingenious business was known as the Kickapoo Indian Medicine Company, and the entrepreneurs were Texas Charlie Bigelow and John E. Healy.

Indians were considered by many whites to have special powers in matters of health, fitness, and sickness through a knowledge of herbs, roots, bark, and other natural substances. Catering to public gullibility, wily salesmen touted products for which they claimed Indian origins. The Kickapoo Indian Medicine Company operated first in Boston (1881–1884), then in New York (1884–1887), in New Haven for ten years, and finally removed to Clintonville, Connecticut. This august firm was able to boast an endorsement from none other than Buffalo Bill himself: "Kickapoo Indian Sagwa . . . is the only remedy the Indians ever use, and has been known to them for ages. An Indian would as soon be without his horse, gun or blanket as without Sagwa."

The company headquarters in New Haven were touted by Healy and Bigelow in language that would have done their hero, P. T. Barnum, proud:

Near by the river front on Grand Avenue, New Haven, Conn., stands a towering massive warehouse; into this you are invited to visit the uncultured sons of the plain and forest, who assist in carrying on one of the most original enterprises on the continent. In the upper portions of the building these sons of the far west find a home; in fact, it is their hunting grounds *(pro tem.)*, and if one will but shut one's eyes to the fact that a roof is between himself and heaven, there is little or nothing left for imagination. It is here the Indians are received prior to being consigned to their duties in the extensive factory or to encampments upon the road. Another portion of the building is occupied with tents erected and equipped exactly as though they formed a settlement on the plains. The clothing and food supplies of the band are scattered about with that unstudied elegance of disorder which, as the initiated are well aware, forms a great attraction to the free and easy red and pale faces, constituting the grandest charm of life away from the trammels of civilization.[3]

The building was termed the principal wigwam, and the owners boasted a private museum in the building, replete with displays of weaponry, curios, artifacts, and wild-animal trophies. Guests were allowed a guarded look at these authentic treasures. All this served to back up Kickapoo claims of the merit of their healing tonics.

Packages of Kickapoo Indian remedies had a caution stamp, looking much like a cigar band, imprinted with Indian motifs and the legend: CAUTION NONE GENUINE WITHOUT THIS OUR SEAL & SIGNATURE WHICH MUST BE ENTIRE AND UNBROKEN. In script was the signature "Healy & Bigelow."

A stream of publications was produced for the faithful, with enticing titles such as *The Indian Illustrated Magazine* and *The Kickapoo Indian Dream Book*. The reader was encouraged to be temperate and to follow such homilies as:

I am Chief of the Kickapoo Indian tribe
And am strong as a brave can be,
Not brandy, nor whiskey do I imbibe,

By George H. Walker and Company, lithographers, Boston, this poster includes portraits of the Kickapoo Medicine Company's partners. Rare image measures 20 x 24 inches. The rifle is the presentation Colt Lightning .22 given to Dr. Longstreet (detail of stock plaque page 233); inside front cover from rare Kickapoo catalogue at *lower right*. Motif on broadside at *lower left* based on George Catlin print.

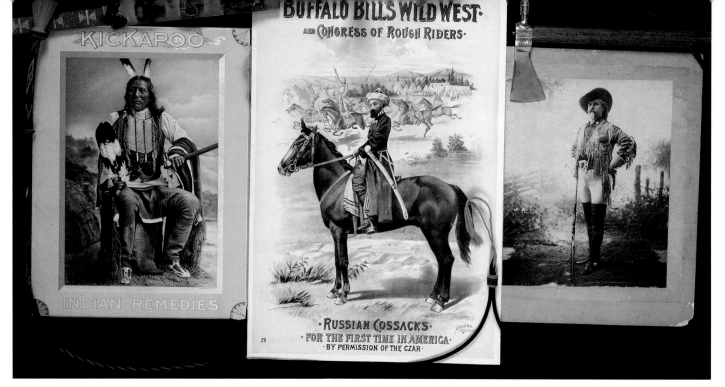

Nor the Chinaman's poisonous tea.
But Indian Sagwa I often do take,
For it's good for man at least.
It cures the body of many an ache,
And stomach for many a feast.

The publications combined advice on health and medical matters with entertainments, information, and promotions on the Kickapoo product line.

One such publication, *Kickapoo Indians: Life and Scenes Among the Indians,* ran feature articles, poetry, maps, and even biographies of Buffalo Bill and the vanquished George Armstrong Custer. Texas Charlie became a heroic figure in these articles and in dime novels. Brooks McNamara interprets the phenomenon:

In their magazines, Healy and Bigelow were turning themselves into frontier heroes. The old raw West was rapidly dying out, replaced by a picturesque literary and theatrical West created by popular authors, showmen, and publicists. Healy and Bigelow, like Buffalo Bill Cody, were products of the nostalgia that accompanied the closing of the frontier; and like Cody their reputation as heroic Western figures was

chiefly the result of a carefully conceived public relations campaign.[4]

The main difference between Healy and Bigelow and Buffalo Bill was that the latter was a bona fide frontier hero.

Healy and Bigelow developed their own medicine show with Indian performers whose job it was to help sell Kickapoo patent medicines. The Indians acted out scenes of terror, reflecting their reputation to city folk and the uninitiated, and at the same time performed domestic roles, the latter intended to help move the products. These encampments traveled about much like Cody's Wild West but were not on as grand a scale. Some whites also served the company, which claimed over eight hundred employees by the late 1880s. Alas, the actual Indians were never Kickapoos but primarily Eastern tribes like the Iroquois and tribes from the West like the Sioux, Blackfoot, and Cherokee. A few were hired from reservations, as was done by Cody, and some were enticed away from Buffalo Bill's Wild West.

From *left*, Kickapoo promotion by J. Ottmann Litho. Company, Puck Bldg., New York City; Chief Red Spear; 23⅛ × 17⅛ inches. Cossack riders by A. Hoen and Company; 30¼ × 20⅞ inches. Unusually large Cody photograph by Stacy, Brooklyn, New York. Redstone and carved-wood effigy pipe. Reins of a horsehair bridle, late nineteenth century. The tomahawk was a presentation to White Beaver.

Flier promoting the Kickapoo encampments; note reference to "Sharp Shooting" at bottom. For other side, see image on page 231. 28⅜ × 5⅞ inches.

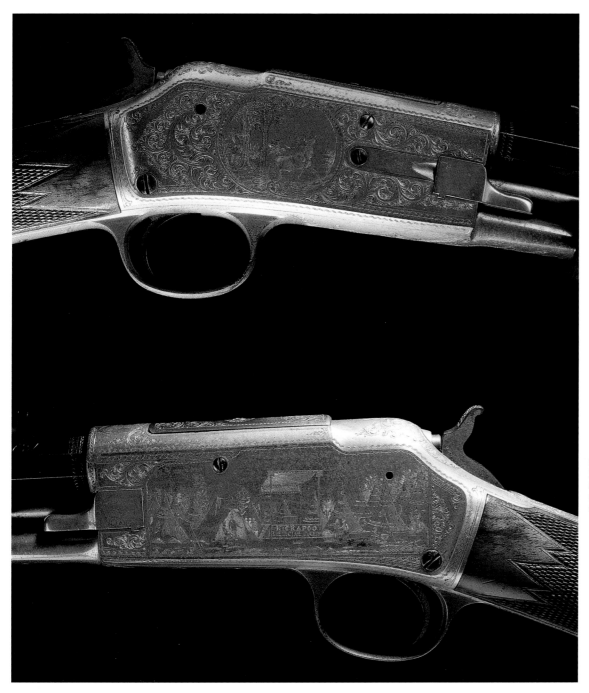

Serial 10570 Colt Lightning .22 rifle; left side with finely detailed inscription KICKAPOO/MEDICINE CAMP, at entrance. Right side panel scene as more often associated with deluxe Winchester lever action rifles of the day. Inscription one of the longest and finest of any observed on a presentation Colt.

Kickapoo encampments traveled about the country, set up to ply their trade, and encouraged public visits. Tents and teepees offered places for consulting with the public, and there were accommodations for stage demonstrations or performances— some of these pure vaudeville. The smallest encampment might be a handful of participants, supervised by the official company agent. The biggest was organized in Chicago, composed of approximately 135 plus two bands of musicians! Posters advertised "Free To All! Indian Medicine Camps. . . . A Novel and Interesting Performance by the Kickapoo, Warm Spring & Pawnee Tribes of Wild Western Indians. . . . Full War Costumes. . . . Representing All Points of Interest in the Indian Country."

An 1883 playbill from an encampment in Albany advertised a program featuring "Fancy Rifle Shooting, Holding the Rifle in twenty different positions by the noted Scout and Indian Fighter, TEXAS CHARLIE. The Rifle used is from the celebrated Wesson Rifle Co., of Worcester, Mass." Texas Charlie, one of several known to have laid claim to the title "champion rifle shot of the world," was also advertised in the 1883 billing as lecturing on Indian "ways, customs and habits." Still another show, also in Albany, presented the fancy rifle shooting of Mr. and Mrs. Charles Fox.

So popular were the Kickapoo encampments that for several years perhaps as many as one hundred units of various sizes were out and about in the United States and Canada, with some in the West Indies as well. Badgered by competition from cheap imitators of the original and, like the Wild West shows, confronted with motion pictures as competition for the public's time and interest, the Kickapoo Indian Medicine Company ceased doing encampments and traveling shows prior to World War I. Healy had sold out to Bigelow in the 1890s and moved to Australia. In 1912, Bigelow moved to England. The last sales of Kickapoo products were through drug and general stores; the company went out of business in the 1920s. A substantial collection of Kickapoo memorabilia and records, including sev-

eral Winchester lever-action rifles, is in the Peabody Museum of Natural History at Yale University.

By far the finest Kickapoo rifle ever made—and the premier slide action built by the Colt company— is a .22 caliber that is associated directly with the Kickapoo encampments. Factory records identify the rifle, serial number 10570, as engraved and inscribed, finished in half nickel and gold plating, with an octagon barrel, special sights, special pistol grip and checkered stocks, and the monogram BFL. The elegant presentation stock plaque has a eleven-line-long inscription! The Worcester *Telegram* told of the presentation in its August 29, 1890, issue:

Dr. Longstreet of the Indian camp on Pleasant St. was treated to an agreeable surprise, last evening, by the presentation of a handsome rifle to him by his fellow campers. The presentation was a complete surprise to the Doctor, but he showed his appreciation of the gift in a neat speech in which he promised to entertain his donors with an exhibition of his skills as a marksman. . . . [The rifle] will be placed on exhibition today in the window of E. S. Knowle's gun store.

The magnificent rifle was equal to any known to have been presented to Buffalo Bill, Annie Oakley, or any of the other exhibition shooters.

A. D. M. Cooper, Frontier Artist

A showman of a different mettle was Astley David Montague Cooper, an artist who numbered Buffalo Bill among his broad range of clients and friends. Cooper was born in St. Louis, Missouri, in 1858, one of a handful of artists native to the pre–Civil War West. His fascination with the West had been influenced by his grandfather, Major Benjamin O'Fallon, who served as an Indian agent prior to 1832 on the Upper Missouri and Yellowstone rivers. O'Fallon is reputed to have owned several Indian paintings by George Catlin, an artist whose work influenced Cooper. As a young student, he reportedly attended art classes in Paris.

After attending Washington University in St. Louis, Cooper traveled throughout the West sketching and painting the Plains Indians. With the fortune

A. D. M. Cooper, frontier artist.

of good timing, *Frank Leslie's Weekly* assigned him to cover the Custer campaign against the Sioux in the spring of 1876. Luckily, Cooper was elsewhere during the Battle of the Little Bighorn.

In 1882, Cooper opened a studio in San Francisco, where he continued to work for Leslie's magazine. An assignment for several studies of General Grant, visiting the Bay Area, gained Cooper widespread recognition. In 1909, the artist moved to San Jose, where he built an exotic studio in the form of an Egyptian temple. Like Frederic Remington, Cooper was a collector of Western memorabilia, which were important props for his pictures. Among his admirable group of Indian artifacts was an eagle-feather war bonnet that had belonged to Chief Red Cloud.

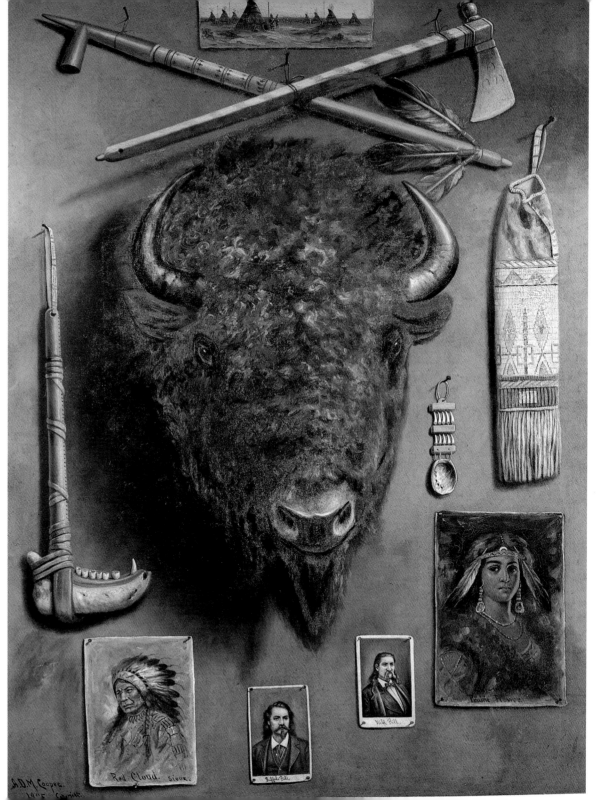

Cooper became known nationally and internationally for his Western paintings. He and Cody had much in common: both were thoroughly acquainted with Western life and each in his own way became an allegorical chronicler of a vanishing phase of American history. Cooper's paintings captured the vastness of the Western landscape and the Indians who lived in harmony with nature. His studies became symbols of a way of life that had disappeared long before he had stopped painting them.

Cody purchased several paintings from Cooper, among them one noted in *After the Hunt*, by Alfred Frankenstin:

His best work, . . . however is the undated life of buffalo head, Indian weapons and photographs of Buffalo Bill and other Western notables which hangs at the head of staircase, in the Hotel Irma at Cody, Wyoming. All the paintings of the Irma came from Buffalo Bill's collection and this one was doubtlessly executed expressly for the famous man.

A. D. M. Cooper died in San Jose in 1924. Much of what remained of his collection and studio was bought by Greg Martin in the 1970s; that material is largely intact to this day.

The Last Days of the Great Scout

Old, tired and still broke, Buffalo Bill finished the 1916 show season, despite the need to be helped onto his horse and to take a few breaths in steeling himself to ride around the arena. There were times when he circled the showring in a carriage. One poster shows Cody seated in a carriage and is headlined: "Buffalo Bill 'Still Holds the Reins' Personally Directs Every Performance and Gives Daily Receptions." The final performance for the 1916 season was in Portsmouth,

Trompe l'oeil artist's palette portrait tribute (1905) to American Indians, accompanied by one of Cooper's favored themes: trompe l'oeil of buffalo, with vignettes of Indian artifacts, and *carte de visite* views of Buffalo Bill and Wild Bill Hickok. The Indian portrait on *left* identified as Red Cloud Sioux, the other as Indian princess Prairie Flower. 70 × 52 inches.

Souvenir show banner, felt.

Reverse-glass Cody portrait, from the Julia Cody Goodman Collection. 26½ × 20¼ inches, including Cody family frame. Ca. 1915.

Holding open book. Taken in 1907 by a Cody photographer, F. J. Hiscock.

by a cold and then a nervous collapse, was life threatening. Once again in Denver, it was clear that Cody was nearing the end of the trail.

The news went out that Buffalo Bill, seventy-one years of age, was near death. Not long before he died, Cody was quoted as stating to Louisa that she should not worry, "I've still got my boots on. I'll be alright."[5] But his condition faltered, and on the tenth of January 1917, he died. Despite his will, which directed burial in Wyoming, Buffalo Bill was laid to rest on Lookout Mountain. Not long before his demise, Cody supposedly remarked to Louisa: "I want to be buried on top of Mount Lookout. It's right over Denver. You can look down into four states there. It's pretty up there. I want to be buried up there—instead of Wyoming."[6] What impact an alleged $10,000 payment to Louisa by Harry Tammen had on the burial site remains a matter of conjecture.

The news of Cody's death brought front-page headlines across the country and tributes from far and wide. The funeral was one of grand proportions, yet to be equaled in the annals of the state of Colorado. Tributes from Annie Oakley, General Nelson Miles, and Theodore Roosevelt captured Cody's multifaceted career and his impact on his times:

> [He] was the kindest hearted, broadest minded, simplest, most loyal man I ever knew. . . . He was courtesy itself, and more like a patron than an employer. . . . His relations with everyone he came in contact with were the most cordial and trusting of any man I ever saw.
>
> Annie Oakley

> Colonel Cody was a high-minded gentleman, and a great scout. He performed a great work in the West for the pioneers and for the generations coming after them and his exploits will live forever in history.
>
> General Nelson A. Miles

> An American of Americans. . . . He embodied those traits of courage, strength and self-reliant hardihood which are vital to the well-being of the nation.
>
> Theodore Roosevelt

Virginia, on November 11. Undaunted, the old scout was already making plans for the 1917 season.

Ready for a rest, he headed for Denver for a relaxing visit with his sister May before returning to Cody. In Wyoming, he planned to relax for the winter and devote his time to a series of memoirs for William Randolph Hearst. On reaching Denver, Cody looked so weakened that May called together his only surviving child, Irma, his sister Julia, and Louisa. Their presence helped to revive him. Resuming his travels, Cody rested for a few weeks at the TE Ranch, returned to Denver, and enjoyed the healthy surroundings of Glenwood Springs early in January. But it was soon evident that his condition, aggravated

Plans for an elaborate grave site on Lookout Mountain never materialized. The site today is relatively simple, accompanied by the Buffalo Bill Memorial Museum, a pet project of Johnny Baker, and by souvenir shops and restaurants.

Johnny Baker Carries On

Teaming up with champion boxer Jess Willard and showman Edward Arlington, Johnny Baker organized a new show for the 1917 season. "Let My Show Go On!" was the headline on the last of the Buffalo Bill programs. Now billed as "The Buffalo Bill Wild West Show & Circus," the presentation combined the old Wild West elements of the stagecoach holdup, the Pony Express, and the wagon train, with entertainments on the order of the Congress of Rough Riders, along with such circus acts as Hajaiaji, a Hindu nail walker, the lady midget Princess Suzanne, the clever

monkey Prince Charles, and an oriental mystic and fortune-teller.

Baker was billed as the arena director and the brief program carried a one-page biography, nearly the same as that from the 101 Ranch and Buffalo Bill (Himself) program of the previous year. Only two references in the program indicated that Baker was continuing his shooting act: first, in the biography, "His continued association with the show as its arenic director and champion rifle shot ensures the survival of the real Buffalo Bill spirit and inspiration"; second, the back cover was a full-page advertisement from Winchester, the bottom of which read: "WINCHESTER ARMS and AMMUNITION used exclusively by JOHNNY BAKER and THE BUFFALO BILL WILD WEST SHOWS."

The 1917 tour continued through November. However, due to World War I, Baker's riding accident

(*left*) Show programs, *top row, left to right,* 1887, 1884, 1886, 1885, showing program fare, 1893, and 1890 (in German, printed in Vienna). *Middle* row, 1893, 1894 (open to show New York panorama on back), 1895 (open to show travel map on back), 1898*, 1899, 1900 (painting of Cody by his friend Frederic Remington, adapted from one of several done for Helen Cody Wetmore's *Last of the Great Scouts*), and 1901. *Bottom,* 1902 (open to show colorful advertisement on back), 1902 (England; back shown for unusual advertisement), 1903 (back cover; also England), 1907, 1907*, 1910, and 1910.

*Advance couriers, often mistaken for programs.

(*right*) Show programs, *left to right, at top,* 1910 and ca. 1910; *middle,* ca. 1915 and 1914; *bottom,* 1914–1915 and the last, following Cody's death, 1917.

that year, and other complications, the final curtain then fell on the last season of the Wild West.

"Buffalo Bill 'Still Holds the Reins,'" though on a buckboard. As of 1914, Cody no longer executed his shooting demonstration or was an active figure in any of the performances, which he introduced instead. Sometimes he was more comfortable appearing at the show opening in a carriage and no longer riding about on horseback. Copyright 1913 by the U.S. Lithograph Company, Cincinnati and New York, Russell Morgan print number 15325, 26 × 39 inches.

January 14, 1917, front page of the *San Antonio Express*. Fittingly, the Winchester Model 1873 rifle was discontinued not long after Cody's death. His passing was mourned by all shooters and sportsmen: Buffalo Bill, like Theodore Roosevelt, had promoted the vigorous outdoor life—the life they, too, loved.

Period postcard of grave site on Lookout Mountain. Although plans called for a grand monument to Cody, a large gravestone and protected, landscaped surroundings were the best that was achieved at the time.

Buffalo Bill and 101 Ranch Wild West Shows, combined, 1916 season. Despite the aging star, the show still presented an impressive front.

The PASSING—
of the LAST
GREAT SCOUT

"Buffalo Bill" Greatest Plainsman the West Ever Knew, a Unique Figure in Development of Country—A Picturesque Pioneer Who Has Given Young America Many Thrills—Honor His Memory Today.

Bordered with authentic Indian, wildlife, and shooting artifacts, this broad array of Buffalo Bill collectibles (most predating his death) demonstrates his mastery of merchandising—though not all of these were under control of Cody and his associates. Many of these items also reveal high manufacturing quality and intriguing style; products from later periods tended to become gimmicky and less refined.

Chapter 10

✠◉✠

Enjoying the Wild West

Museums and Historic Sites

Collector, historian, reenactor, museum and historic-site devotee, armchair traveler, bibliophile, film and television fan, and die-hard tourist—Buffalo Bill's Wild West offers something for everyone. There is a seemingly endless variety of collectibles, a reasonable number of museums and historic sites, a fair number of events, a growing library of publications, and a gradually mushrooming collection of films and television programming related to the Wild West. There is even a place to see a modern interpretation of Buffalo Bill's Wild West—at EuroDisney outside of Paris, where it is the most popular live entertainment, playing to sell-out audiences since its opening in 1992.

Buffalo Bill and the Wild West have a universal following and their own international language. The book *The Peacemakers,* which featured Buffalo Bill as much as any other Western character, has appeared in several printings and has been translated into four languages. This book itself promises to be published in at least five languages. Since the death of Cody, Buffalo Bill and his Wild West have never had a more popular following than *right now.*

Appearing in Appendix I is a list of museums and historic sites with strong tie-ins to the Wild West. These range from the foremost institution of them all—the Buffalo Bill Historical Center—to a litany of museums and places whose cooperation helped to make this book a reality. Nearly all have brochures listing hours and general descriptions of their holdings and programs. In some cases, the hordes of visitors restrict the available time of staff for handling inquiries. But it always helps with any institution to become a paying member, and that kind of support is crucial for their continuing activity and programs.

Considering the difficult weather in the locales where museums such as the Buffalo Bill Historical Center and the Buffalo Bill Ranch are situated, sometimes a site will be shut down or have shorter hours for the winter months. Summer visits are so crowded at the historical center that from June through September the doors are open from 7 A.M. to 8 P.M.! Weather problems do not hamper the Autry Museum of Western Heritage in Los Angeles, which is open every day except most Mondays, Christmas, and Thanksgiving.

Visiting in Cody, Wyoming, has the added attraction of being located only about an hour's drive from the eastern entrance to Yellowstone Park. The historical-center complex began as the Buffalo Bill Museum, founded soon after Cody died. Not a few of his descendants have remained active in the organization since the institution's beginnings.

The center is the museum equivalent of Mecca for any Buffalo Bill and Wild West enthusiast. One can even walk into a true shrine: Buffalo Bill's boyhood home from Le Claire. You can also see "Lucretia Borgia" and much, much more! The thousands of square feet of historic and artistic treasures are unmatched anywhere in the world. Besides the Buffalo Bill Museum, the center offers the Cody Firearms Museum, the Plains Indian Museum, the Whitney Gallery of Western Art, the McCracken Research Library, and the Kriendler Gallery of Contemporary Western Art. An annual fund-raising event in September is a highlight of the center's year.

Though a relatively young institution, the Autry Museum of Western Heritage is a powerhouse in its

Collector Michael Del Castello with richly detailed carved bass-wood figure of Buffalo Bill by Jim Smock, Santa Barbara, California. The scout holds a Winchester Model 1873 rifle and favorite Stetson. Cody stands six feet, two inches; the overall height of the sculpture (counting base) is six feet, six inches.

Material from Del Castello Collection on loan for special exhibition at the Royal Armouries Museum, Leeds, England, summer 1999, as well as on show at other institutions. Collection began with interest in advertising artifacts and American folk art, at which the Wild West had ingenious skills and capabilities. Much of the material was assembled by working with friend and fellow collector Greg Martin.

own right. In an imposing Spanish Mission–style structure, the Autry's exhibits celebrate the West from its historic roots up through the largely romantic interpretations of the electronic entertainment media and the printed word. The art and artifacts (not the least of which is a breathtaking arms collection), the Wells Fargo Theater, and a serious research library are conveniently located at Los Angeles's Griffith Park. The annual fund-raising gala, usually held in September, is the social highlight of the Autry year; that of 1997 celebrated Gene Autry's ninetieth birthday, and the auction reached a $900,000 gross, with the featured deluxe Colt revolver (by Al White and Andrew Bourbon) fetching a record $42,500.

Wild Bill Hickok's Deadwood is undergoing a revival of sorts, thanks to casino gambling. However, don't expect to find the actual No. 10 Saloon, since the original burned down, and the site of the new No. 10 is a distance away. Expert Joe Rosa believes the original is now a parking lot near the Eagle Brewery! Deadwood is still worth a visit, and the Wild Bill grave site should not be missed.

For Cody's Kansas roots, the Kansas State Historical Society, in Topeka, is a leading source and its library one of the best. The society is located in the Kansas History Center complex, featuring a splendid museum that is well worth visiting.

In Nebraska, the Nebraska State Historical Society in Lincoln has its own wealth of material, largely from Mrs. Julia Cody Goodman and including important information on the subject of Chief Yellow Hair. The Buffalo Bill Ranch is maintained as a historic site by the Nebraska Game and Parks Commission and offers sixteen acres of the original North Platte Scout's Rest ranch, the barn, and the comfortable ranch house begun on the colonel's orders in 1886.

In Colorado, Lookout Mountain's Buffalo Bill Memorial Museum and the burial site are veritable Cody shrines. The museum was founded in 1921, launched by Johnny Baker as a memorial and a site to exhibit collections of his own and memorabilia of Buffalo Bill. Baker's poster collection is considered of the first rank. The view, which was a favorite of Cody himself, takes in the Rocky Mountains and the Great Plains. In Denver, the Western History Department of the Denver Public Library has an extraordinary array of images, as well as Nate Salsbury scrapbooks, Cody correspondence, and other important holdings.

The Circus World Museum in Baraboo, Wisconsin, has the finest known poster of Annie Oakley, the Buffalo Bill's Wild West ticket wagon (handsomely restored), and enough other material to make it another worthy visit. Additionally, the close association of the Wild West's history with circus personalities such as James A. Bailey contributes to the museum's appeal.

For the World's Fair cowboy race, the Dawes County Historical Society Museum in Chadron, Nebraska, is the place to visit. The original Colt revolver prize is one of the icons of the American West.

The Woolaroc Museum in Bartlesville, Oklahoma, displays a rich collection of the 101 Ranch. The late Philip R. Phillips had a wealth of stories about the Miller Brothers, some of whom he had met. Phillips saw the show as a boy, and the experience was instrumental in his devotion to arms collecting. The Pawnee Bill Museum in Pawnee, Oklahoma, offers G. W. Lillie's ranch and ranch house and exhibits that honor this stalwart of the Wild West–show circuit and his wife.

The National Cowboy Hall of Fame in Oklahoma City ranks as one of the sites to see for anyone keen on the great American West and particularly on understanding the role of the cowboy. The rodeo, so closely tied to Wild West shows, is represented at the museum by several exhibits and by the hall of fame of cowboy champions.

For Annie Oakley devotees, Greenville and Vandalia, Ohio, and Nutley, New Jersey, are crucial sites in addition to the Buffalo Bill Historical Center and the Autry Museum. The Garst Museum of the Darke County Historical Society in Greenville is tantamount to an Annie Oakley and Frank Butler shrine, and the Oakley and Butler grave site is not far away. Grandniece Bess Edwards has been working toward her goal of establishing an Oakley memorial site through the Annie Oakley Foundation, a project well worth public support. The Nutley Museum in Nutley, New Jersey, offers some of Oakley's firearms and other exhibits; it is located not more than forty-five minutes from New York City.

Vandalia houses the Trapshooting Hall of Fame and Museum at the site of the Grand American, the Amateur Trapshooting Association's annual championships. Located adjacent to the Dayton Airport, the hall of fame and museum celebrate the history and the giants of this sport, back to Bogardus, Carver, Oakley, and Butler. A research library is part of the complex.

Washington, D.C., boasts the Smithsonian Institution's National Museum of American History, a must for anyone trying to appreciate our culture. Though the complex has suffered in recent years from controversy over questions of interpretation, the collections are extraordinary, more general in their dealing with the American West rather than specific to the Wild West of Cody et al. Some of the challenging and often obscure papers for researchers are housed at the National Archives in Washington and were crucial to the monumental work of scholar Don Russell.

Nearby Fairfax, Virginia, houses the much more focused National Firearms Museum. A nonprofit institution established with the support of the National Rifle Association, the museum has over three thou-

Promotional Wild West lithographs of cowboys rounding up and lassoing wild horses with similarly styled theme of three cowboys on bucking broncos. Cowboys on broncos, 29 × 42 inches; the roundup scene smaller in height and larger in width. Both signed by the Forbes Company, of Boston and New York.

sand firearms and many thousands of artifacts, shooting trophies, medals, documents, and memorabilia. The beautifully presented exhibits specifically chronicle the role of firearms in America, concentrating on art and craftsmanship, history, mechanics, and romance.

Buffalo Bill Collectibles

The craze for collectibles and souvenirs of B-movie Western heroes, Disney characters, and even rock-

Brochures of museums, research facilities, and historic sites with Wild West connections, along with collectibles ranging from the antique to the contemporary. The shoulder-patch collection by Willabee and Ward, Norwalk, Connecticut, honoring fifty of the greatest U.S. firearms, includes references to Buffalo Bill and Annie Oakley. Wild West accountant Harry Piel's scrapbook at *right*, open to page with Iron Tail profile, and note that the chief was the inspiration for the buffalo nickel. Box for Buffalo Bill gun horse bits in frontispiece to this chapter made by North and Judd, New Britain, Connecticut; German silver used for the Single Action–type revolver. The Wild West Game copyright McLoughlin Brothers, New York, 1896. Sheet music at *left* dedicated to the memory of Colonel Cody, 1924; it represents outpouring of grief on the scout's passing and a myriad of efforts to honor his memory.

Scarce "Buffalo Bill"–model pocket revolver with advertisement by the Western Gun Works of Chicago. It is unlikely that Cody authorized manufacture of this type of gun under his name. The advertising skirts any specific reference to Cody himself. In any event, this marketing ploy underscores the widespread fame of Buffalo Bill. Ca. 1880–1890.

At *bottom*, presentation engagement or wedding gift of a serving knife and fork, engraved, with inscription. NS monogram on fork. Handle of knife in fluted and chased silver. Not pictured, the casing of leather, silk, and velvet. Other serving knives and fork appear to be commemorative in nature.

Front and back of a promotional calendar for the Wild West performance at Earl's Court, London, summer 1892, and an example of the astute promotional acumen of Cody's "Department of Publicity." The 1899 *Route-Book* listed no less than eleven men and one woman in that department, with advertising cars nos. 1 and 2 (each staffed in their own right), a staff for "Bill Posters" (eleven men), three lithographers, and a staff for "Excursion Bill Posters" (eleven more men), an "Opposition Brigade" (five men: including a lithographer, a boss bill poster, and two bill posters); finally, two more staff were listed as "Layers-Out"!

and-roll bands was pioneered by the master marketers and merchandisers of Buffalo Bill and the Wild West. Long before Gene Autry cap guns or Mickey Mouse watches or Pink Floyd T-shirts, there were the Wild West programs, cabinet-card photographs, posters, dime novels, buttons, toys, ad infinitum. Arizona John M. Burke and his creative staff knew how to do it.

For the collector, a book of dreams is James W. Wojtowicz's *The W. F. Cody Buffalo Bill Collector's Guide with Values.* (Price estimates are subjective figures, and some items will be worth more to certain collectors than to others.) The scope and variety of Cody collectibles almost defies the imagination, but Wojtowicz's book goes a long way toward showing them. This handsome volume presents for the first time illustrations of every Wild West program for every season. Rare route sheets are also published, as is virtually the complete array of Buffalo Bill collectibles. For the Wild West and Colonel Cody collector, Wojtowicz has been able to systematize this vast field and bring an orderliness to the subject that will be instrumental in spurring collecting in a substantial way.

Buffalo Bill collectibles did not stop with the death of Cody himself. Many boys and girls since have had some Buffalo Bill item thrust into a Christmas stocking or given as a birthday treat. Those phenomena continue at a solid pace.

The Dime Novels

Counting dime novels alone, the bibliography on Cody and inspired by Wild West characters is enormous. Don Russell estimated the number at 557 originals—the majority in the series "Buffalo Bill Stories"—and some 1,143 reprints. Russell summed this up most emphatically:

Nothing that William F. Cody did in life, nor all the traveling of Buffalo Bill's Wild West nor all the efforts of Major Burke and his corps of press agents, did as much to impress the name of Buffalo Bill upon several generations not only of young Americans but also of boys and men throughout the world as the dime novels. Of twenty-five million words, only two have survived— Buffalo Bill—but that survival in itself has contributed enormously to the legend. The glamour attached to Buffalo Bill and the West he personified has been reflected in billions more of words than have been strung together in the never ending stream of Westerns— books, melodrama, musical comedy, motion pictures, radio, television, even ballet, and grand opera.[1]

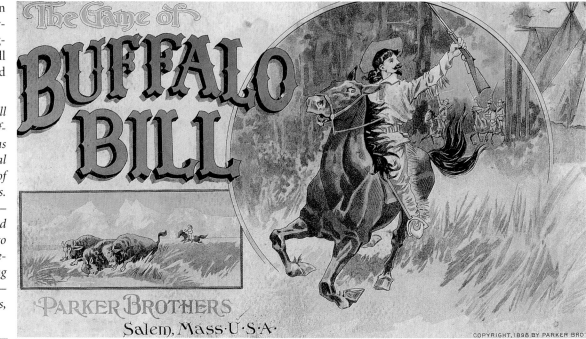

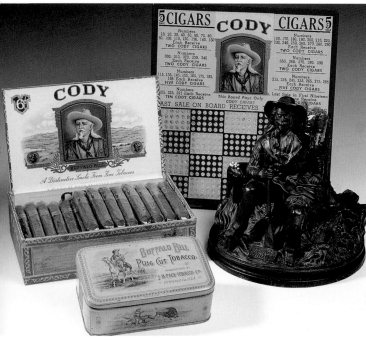

In collecting dime novels, one needs to be aware that the paper used was pulp with a high, self-destructive acid content. Therefore, these publications are extremely fragile. Eventually, they will turn to dust. Means of deacidification, however, can deal with that not inexpensive problem. Contact a paper conservator for advice on how to proceed. A library in your area will be able to offer advice, since any book collection with holdings postdating the dawn of the industrial age is confronted with the same problem.

"The Game of Buffalo Bill," Parker Brothers, Salem, Massachusetts, copyright 1898. Colored lithograph cover to game box. Board game with routes, much like trails followed by a wagon train.

Box of Buffalo Bill–brand cigars, tin of Buffalo Bill plug tobacco, game board that lists choices of Buffalo Bill cigars, and pot-metal casting of seated Buffalo Bill cigar and match holder. Note hunting scenes on tobacco tin. Casting and tobacco tin believed to be from the late nineteenth century; remaining items from the early twentieth.

Ledgers of the Gun Factories

The records of Winchester, Colt, Marlin, and Smith & Wesson all carry occasional historical information on Buffalo Bill firearms, but they are not considered complete. Sometimes, shipment was made to dealers without the factory annotating the records to specify the ultimate recipient. Other extenuating circumstances might also preclude a proper ledger-entry identification.

Guns shipped to some Wild West cast members, such as Pawnee Bill Lillie, are documented in the Colt records. But most of the firearms that had associations with troupe members will not have factory identifications. Either the records were lost or the purchases were not made directly from the factories. Old-time dealers, such as the William Read store in Boston, suppliers of a special Colt Single Action for Johnny Baker, have long since gone out of business, their records likely lost forever.

Factory-ledger entries are the purest form of documentation. Several examples of such evidence appear here. Collectors need to be extremely sophisticated in assessing the evidence that accompanies so-called historical firearms. The authors have even seen instances where factory letters describing historical firearms have been associated with guns that were created at much later dates!

Collecting and Dealing

Auction houses that sell in the Wild West arena range from the "big guns"—Sotheby's, Christie's, and Butterfield and Butterfield—to the smaller but more specialized operations such as the Old West Auction

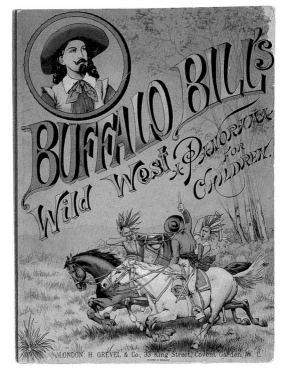

"Buffalo Bill's Wild West Panorama for Children," colored lithograph cover. Panorama opened all the way reveals scenes of Buffalo Bill, the Wild West show, Indians, and wildlife (see page 244). Note appearance of Cody in vignette on front cover, more like a cavalier than a figure of the Wild West.

of the Dick and Terry Engel Auction Company and the Brian Lebel Old West Show and Auction. The Engel and Lebel sales are annual events in Cody, Wyoming, and in the summer of 1997 were timed to coincide with the annual meeting of the Winchester Club of America. Witherell's Americana Auctions was the source of a rare matched pair of Doc Carver and Buffalo Bill posters, which caused a sensation and set record poster prices. Swann's auction galleries in New York have been known to come up with some tantalizing items. Another New York gallery is that of collector and dealer Martin Lane, launched under the tried-and-true name of Bannerman's. Of course, local auction houses might well have material, considering the widespread travels of the Wild West Show over so many years.

It is not generally understood that arms collectors tend to dabble in any number of antiquarian fields because guns relate to a myriad of other subjects. As a result, not a few arms collectors become very competent general historians. In the firearms line, Wild West items could turn up at any one of several galleries or at gun shows where such memorabilia is as likely to be found as anywhere. For listings of dealers and auction houses, the reader is referred to the wealth of magazines and other periodicals on firearms and the West. Further, the author's annual book, *The Official Price Guide to Gun Collecting*, presents names and addresses and listings of publications as they deal with firearms subjects. The guide also contains a listing of dealers in arms books, many of whom can be helpful with Wild West themes.

Magazines and Newspapers

For listings of estate sales and a myriad of other sources of memorabilia and collectibles, the aficionado needs to peruse publications such as *Arts and Antiques Weekly, Maine Antiques Digest,* and the more urbane *Art and Auction.* These publications contain so many possible sources that in some instances the collector virtually becomes a dealer as ef-

Silk scarf with portraits of Cody and one of Nate Salsbury, along with seven Indians from the Wild West show, among them Sitting Bull and Red Shirt. Ca. late 1880s.

Buffalo choker for scarf, carved in ivory by Fred Glasier and presented to Cody ca. 1904. On composition mounting.

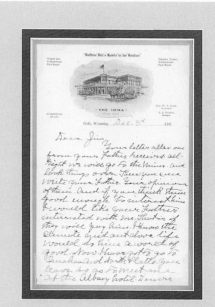

Buffalo Bill in chauffeur-driven car in front of the Irma Hotel. Note to friend Jim Morris on the hotel letterhead, dated December 3, referring to meeting with Jim's father and Jim about mining interests and to a later meeting in Denver at the Albany Hotel. Meantime, Cody was to visit North Platte and Omaha.

Locks of hair from the head of Buffalo Bill. An intimate item once in the Julia Cody Goodman Collection.

forts escalate in the exciting chase for material. Some collectors rely heavily on dealers to help in the search or to act on their behalf. More specific to firearms are journals such as *Gun List, Man at Arms, The Gun Report,* and *The Shotgun News.*

Among other magazines that fan the flames of Wild West collecting are *Cowboys and Indians, American Cowboy, Cowboy Magazine, True West,* and, of course, publications by several of the museums noted above. Wild West antique arms subjects are only occasionally dealt with by the large circulation publications: *American Rifleman, Guns and Ammo, Guns, Shooting Times, Gun World,* and the publication of the Single Action Shooting Society.

Books, New and Out-of-Print

For titles currently in print, Barnes and Noble, Borders, et al. have adopted modern merchandising magic and high-tech search engines to locate hard-to-find titles. Of course, nearly every bookstore in America has volumes related to the Wild West. And there are several levels of collecting titles in the genre.

Museum stores can be helpful, such as at the Buffalo Bill Historical Center, where the experts employed by the museum played a role in the selection of titles. The same is true at the Autry Museum and some of the other institutions listed above.

For antiquarian booksellers who specialize in titles on the West and are likely to handle material that is from the pantheon of Buffalo Bill's Wild West, the reader should consult with the Antiquarian Booksellers' Association of America at 50 Rockefeller Plaza, New York, N.Y. 10020-1680. These are considered the foremost dealers in books and manuscripts, and a visit to the book fairs of this group is an experience not to be missed.

Among specialized mail-order firearms-related (and often sometimes Wild West–related) book operations to consult are Jim and Theresa Earle's Early West Books, College Station, Texas; the Rutgers Book Center, Highland Park, New Jersey; Dixie Gunworks, Union City, Tennessee; Tom Rowe's R and R Books, Livonia, New York; Bert Garber, Covington, Louisiana; and Ray Riling Arms Books, Philadelphia, Pennsylvania. Some of these companies also appear at trade shows (mainly gun-collector events), and most also carry out-of-print titles.

E-Mail and the Internet

The fastest growing category of information dissemination on the broad subject of the West—of which Buffalo Bill's Wild West is a central theme—is the World Wide Web. If needed, have someone who is cognizant of computer technology assist you in a search.

The Wild West in the Movies and on Television

The movies play a role in keeping the memory of Buffalo Bill and the Wild West alive, but for authenticity such productions are consistently wanting. For example, Richard Frost, former curator of the Buffalo

White chinaware shaving mug and table-setting pieces from the Irma Hotel. Marked made by GREENWOOD CHINA, TRENTON, NEW JERSEY, for use by "The Irma." The plated silverware marked on the handles THE IRMA, and with maker stamping ONEIDA COMMUNITY. Hotel pictures taken at the time of the grand opening, ca. 1902. Hotel still in operation, billed as "Buffalo Bill's Hotel in the Rockies." In cold weather, radiators make historic pings and rattles, adding to charm. Remarkable bar in dining room traditionally (though erroneously) credited as gift from Queen Victoria! Suites named after celebrities and friends of Buffalo Bill.

Bill Museum, leveled scathing criticism against Robert Altman's *Buffalo Bill and the Indians:* too much emphasis on show-business sham and not enough on the real Buffalo Bill. Also, for many, the West is too serious a subject to be the target of ridicule. On the other hand, the original Wild West characters often had finely attuned senses of humor and were the first to poke fun at themselves and at each other—Buffalo Bill among them.

Films inspired by Buffalo Bill are many and varied and could be the subject of a book of their own, though they are dime novels in cinema form. One of the best known is *Buffalo Bill,* starring Joel McCrea and released in 1944. Any Western buff will find *The BFI Companion to the Western* a sourcebook filled with fascinating detail.

The archive of film and stage productions on Annie Oakley captured the public's fancy more so than did attempts at Buffalo Bill programming and is more distinguished. The first feature film, entitled *Annie Oakley* (1935), starring Barbara Stanwyck, is usually considered the most authentic depiction of her life to date. George Stevens was the director and Melvyn Douglas portrayed Buffalo Bill. Many who saw the film could remember having seen the original Oakley.

Greatly romanticized and presenting Annie too much as a country girl, the Rodgers and Hammerstein production of *Annie Get Your Gun* hit Broadway in May 1946. Irving Berlin wrote fifteen songs for that heavy-duty production, which had Joshua Logan as director and a book by Herbert and Dorothy Fields. Against a backdrop of spectacular sets designed by the legendary Jo Mielziner, Ethel Merman played the lead role. The show opened to a packed house and rave reviews in New York's Imperial Theater. The run on Broadway lasted for some three years—an astounding 1,159 performances. For the hundredth performance, a Model 1892 Winchester that had been one of Oakley's own was lent by Mrs. Spencer T. Olin.

A touring company production of *Annie Get Your Gun* began in 1947, with Mary Martin in the lead role. After playing in no less than forty-nine cities, the tour closed. Later revivals included one at New York's Lincoln Center in 1966.

On Thanksgiving eve in 1957, Mary Martin appeared on television in *Annie Get Your Gun,* which she proudly said had been practiced and rehearsed to the point that it was as perfect as they could make it. Summer-stock productions of this classic occur from time to time, and about every generation should expect to see *Annie Get Your Gun* back on Broadway. There is no telling how many times the show has

been performed by local casts and in high-school and college productions.

Annie Get Your Gun on film starred Betty Hutton, with Howard Keel as Frank Butler. That 1950 Metro-Goldwyn-Mayer production was originally slated to star Judy Garland, but the petite performer was ill and could not appear.

Theaters around the country hold Western film festivals, where old-time stars are sometimes present for autograph sessions. Among the collector newspapers in this specialized field are *Big Reel*, *Classic Images*, and *Westerns and Serials*.

For television production, besides an occasional rerun of old film and television fare and the programming of the Western Channel, the viewer should follow particularly the A&E and Discovery networks on cable and satellite. The former broadcasts reruns of the award-winning *The Real West*, hosted by Kenny Rogers, which includes features on both Buffalo Bill and the Wild West and on Annie

Oakley. The hour-long segment "The Guns That Tamed the West" remains the best presentation yet done by national television on the role of firearms in the Western saga.

Annie Oakley Legacy: Greenville, Ohio

In the last week of July, beginning on a Tuesday and ending with a one-and-a-half-mile-long parade on Sunday, the city of Greenville mushrooms from a population of 12,000 to more than 75,000. In celebration of Annie Oakley, beginning with a pilgrimage to her grave site, the festival event has grown to attract visitors from around the United States and from abroad. Once held on the grounds of the Darke County Historical Society, the Annie Oakley Festival

Cole Younger's Smith & Wesson Model 3 Russian First Model Single Action revolver, used by the outlaw in the James and Younger Gang's Northfield, Minnesota, bank raid of September 7, 1876. Surrendered September 21 by Younger on his capture by the posse of Sheriff James Glispin near Madelia, Minnesota. Revolver, accompanied by memorabilia, remained for many years in the possession of the sheriff and then his heirs. Serial number 28009; nickel plated, with ivory grips; .44 Russian caliber; 8-inch barrel. The letterhead and envelope testify to the later collaboration of Younger and Frank James in their own Wild West show, ca. 1903 and 1908.

Foldout Wild West postcard, accompanying presentation Winchester rifles from Cody to his friends Leonard and Hattie Horr. Buffalo Bill was a friend of their stepfather, David McFall, a founder of the town of Cody, whose Hart Mountain Inn had been named at Bill's suggestion. McFall married Aurilla Horr, taking in Hattie and Leonard, her children from a first marriage. Both children looked upon Buffalo Bill as a father figure. Model 1873 Winchester, in .38-40 caliber, with shotgun steel buttplate; German-silver plaque on butt, documenting presentation; serial number 470446B. Model 1890 Winchester, in .22 short, with inscription engraved on barrel breech; serial number 39485.

Dr. Paul Fees has commented on Cody's generosity with gifts of guns: "The Horr children, like the children of several other pioneer families [in Cody], were favorites of Buffalo Bill. . . . He is known to have made several such gifts after 1895, all Winchesters. After 1895 he is known to have purchased and presented several Model 1895 Winchesters in .30 government or .405 calibers to adult friends. The firearms gifts to children were made for lighter cartridges. . . . The engraving on both is consistent with the engraving which Cody had done for him locally for presentation to area families. In fact, the barrel engraving 'HATTIE HORR FROM COL. W. F. CODY' is identical to the barrel engraving on a Model 1885 Winchester in .22 short which Buffalo Bill presented to another Cody-area child after 1895. The engravings were done by the same hand, probably at the same time. Since Buffalo Bill's visits to Cody always occurred in the late fall and winter, it may be possible to find newspaper accounts of these firearms as Christmas gifts."

Souvenirs made after Cody's death and marketed by the Lookout Mountain memorial complex. The spurs of brass and German silver; relief-cast German-silver buffalo-head motifs. The W. F. CODY is a facsimile of Cody's signature. Spurs with an anchor stamping and other markings. Souvenir spoon engraved OMAHA and with Buffalo Bill on horseback pursuing buffalo in bowl with ruby eye set on handle.

Reenactments, Associations, and Commemorative Guns

In commemoration of the 150th anniversary of Cody's birth in the summer of 1996, the Cody rodeo grounds hosted a reenactment of Buffalo Bill's Wild West. The performances were based as closely as possible on the original entertainments, with local talent portraying Cody, Annie Oakley, Sitting Bull, and other stars. Even the music of the Wild West Cowboy Band was re-created. An annual celebrity shoot sponsored by the Cody Firearms Museum each summer carries on the tradition of marksmanship, an appropriate tie-in with the sharpshooter after whom the museum is named.

A compact disc and audiotape re-creation of the Wild West Cowboy Band by the Americus Brass Band brings alive the splendid music of the Wild West. As standard fare in the original show's performances, the music entertainments open with "The Star-Spangled Banner," followed by Handel's "See, the Conquering Hero Comes." Third in the eighteen-part recording is the Biograph recording of Buffalo Bill introducing the Congress of Rough Riders of the World. Listening to Cody's melodious voice is a particularly memorable and stirring experience.

The compact-disc liner notes would surprise most listeners with the fact that Buffalo Bill and the band were instrumental in adoption of "The Star-Spangled Banner" as the national anthem of the United States. The compact disc and tape even pay homage to the crackle of gunfire, the Indian war and ceremonial music, and the whooping and hollering that spectators heard in actual performances.

The new sport of cowboy action shooting is yet another mode of reenacting past Wild West realities. Members of the Single Action Shooting Society assume colorful nicknames, often based on real-life characters, dress up in period costumes, and are usually armed to the teeth. The matches—which involve firing live rounds at challenging targets—have been written up in *The Wall Street Journal* and have become a consequential factor in the firearms and am-

(a.k.a. Anniefest) has grown so grand that in the summer of 1997 many of the festivities moved to the Darke County Fairgrounds. Among the dignitaries present at the 1997 event was Sonna Warvell, the lead Annie Oakley from the EuroDisney Buffalo Bill's Wild West Show. Bess Moses Edwards, Annie Oakley Foundation president (and Oakley relative), counts such patrons on her board as Gene Autry, Jamie Lee Curtis, Monte Hale, Lowell Thomas Jr., and Holly-

wood film producer William Self. Among others involved with the foundation are Oakley authors Glenda Riley and Shirl Kasper.

Bess Edwards is the most active promoter of her celebrated ancestor. Her enthusiasm and dedication are the driving force behind the foundation's quarterly publication *Taking Aim*, and her energies extend from dealing with media queries to promoting postage stamps (only one done so far, part of the faulted Western Legends series) to tabulating virtually anything that helps to celebrate the memory of Darke County's favorite daughter.

Topperwein memorabilia, along with Ad Topperwein's specially built Colt Model 1877 Lightning revolver of .38 caliber; serial number 163470; low front sight and no hammer spur. Coins and cartridge case shot in special exhibitions, advertised free by Winchester.

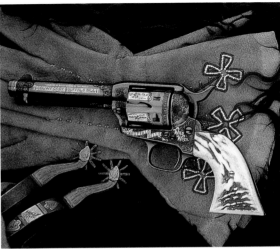

Shooting champion Rudy Etchen (*left*) on a pigeon shoot with Gary Cooper, Sun Valley, Idaho, 1958. Etchen, often termed the greatest shotgunner of all time, is one of the shooting world's all-stars, continuing in the spirit and marksmanship of the champions of old. Etchen's parents were extraordinary shots, and he learned many pointers of exhibition shooting from Ad and Plinky Topperwein. Practically all of Etchen's shotgun competition has been done with an 870 Remington pump; one of the first ten made was presented to him by the factory in 1950. Forty-seven years later, he was given serial number 6,000,001! Cooper and Etchen sometimes traded guns for the day's shooting; thus, the actor has the shooter's old faithful Model 870, while the marksman holds Cooper's Browning Grade II over-and-under.

A salute to the 150th anniversary of William F. Cody's birth, issued by America Remembers, 1996. Issue limited to 500, .45 Long Colt caliber, 4¾-inch barrel, stag grips. On the right side: gold highlights of buffalo and of Cody as scout guiding the Fifth Cavalry through Cheyenne country. The America Remembers Sesquicentennial Model 94 .30-30 Winchester had relief laser-carved walnut stocks, etched and 24-karat gold- and nickel-plated frame and cocking lever, and blued barrel and magazine tube; production was limited to 300.

munition business. A whole new market has opened up for Winchester, Colt, Navy Arms, Uberti, and Ruger (the Vaquero is advertised as "the gun that would have won the West") and for black-powder cartridge makers, holster, spur, and saddle makers, clothiers, ad infinitum. Two of the leading participants in these festivities, Phil and Linda Spangenberger, even have their own Wild West show, and the company has performed in the Far East and England as well as in the United States.

For fans of the 101 Ranch, Jerry and Ruth Murphey organized the 101 Ranch Collectors Association in 1986. An affiliated group, the 101 Ranch Old Timers, had been founded in 1966 by Robert Long and Mike Sokoll and was made up of the select group of surviving 101 Ranch employees and performers. Members of the latter association are honorary members of the former. On the hundredth anniver-

sary of the ranch in 1993, a gala celebration was held at the Marland Mansion in Ponca City, Oklahoma, and the Murpheys published a seventy-eight-page centennial book. The address of the association is published in Appendix I, along with lists of museums and historic sites.

Appendix I also lists the address of the Texas Jack Association, from whom a detailed brochure is available. The organization holds occasional meetings and has several members who are part of the Omohundro family. Among honorary members are descendants of the Earl of Dunraven and of Buffalo Bill. The brochure even pictures Texas Jack's grave site, a handsome marker donated by Buffalo Bill, John M. Burke, and Johnny Baker.

Ever since the spectacular success of the Buffalo Bill Winchester commemorative Model 94 rifle and carbine—with sales exceeding 112,000—special series

of guns have been issued honoring Buffalo Bill, Annie Oakley, and the Wild West. Winchester built six thousand Model 9422 Annie Oakleys in 1982, Colt made three thousand Buntline .45 New Frontier Single Actions in 1979, and 250 hand-engraved Buffalo Bill Single Action Army deluxe revolvers in 1981. Additionally, the U.S. Society of Arms and Armour (formerly the U.S. Historical Society) issued a Single Action Army revolver and a Model 94 Winchester,

(*above*) Buffalo Bill's Wild West Show at EuroDisney. From *left*, Tim Reevis (Sitting Bull), Jean-Philippe Delavault (artistic director), Teri Matter (Annie Oakley), Royal Armouries' Museum Director Guy Wilson, and John Waller, the museum's director of live demonstrations. This visit to the theme park was to organize details for the exhibition of the Michael Del Castello Collection at the Royal Armouries in summer 1999.

Performers portraying Annie Oakley, Buffalo Bill, and Sitting Bull, at center arena. Oakley, played by Sonna Warvell, is about to fire double-action revolver.

each with tie-ins to Buffalo Bill's 150th birthday, in 1996. The American Historical Foundation issued a firing reproduction of Wild Bill Hickok's Model 1851 Navy Colts. From the Franklin Mint came a nonfiring replica of a Buffalo Bill Model 1849 Pocket revolver and the finest of his 1873 Winchesters (based on original specimens at the Buffalo Bill Historical Center).

In 1998, Marlin issued the Model 1897 Annie Oakley, a lever-action .22, with 18½-inch tapered octagonal barrel, adjustable Marble semibuckhorn rear sight, and Marble front sight with brass bead. The blued frame was roll engraved, and Oakley's signature appeared in gold on the bolt. In keeping with the styling of rifles preferred by the subject herself, the pistol-grip stock was of select walnut, checkered.

Special-issue firearms are also planned as tie-ins with this book and its accompanying traveling museum exhibition.

Long Wolf and Rose Ghost Dog Return from London

In a human-interest story that grabbed media attention around the world, the remains of fifty-nine-year-old Sioux chief Long Wolf and seven-year-old Rose Ghost Dog (a.k.a. White Star) were finally exhumed from their 105-year-old grave site in an obscure London cemetery and returned to tribal lands at Wounded Knee, South Dakota. Both had died while on tour with Buffalo Bill's Wild West, according to press reports in 1892.

Their grave in West London had been forgotten for decades until a British woman ran across a reference to it and was instrumental in launching a campaign to return the bodies to their native lands. Not all the descendants of the two were in favor of disturbing the bodies, believing that to do so meant that someone else must die to occupy the emptied grave site.

A week after the remains were exhumed, the reburial took place, preceded by a ceremony in a Wounded Knee park. A procession then moved to the burial ground, four horsemen riding solemnly behind the hearse. Descendants and onlookers accompanied the procession on foot, some attired in traditional Sioux costumes.

Entire troupe against one of several handsomely painted backdrops, with stagecoach. Cheering audience raising arms as part of supercharged festivities.

A great-granddaughter of Long Wolf, Jessie Black Feather, eighty-six years old, said she felt "much better bringing my grandpa back to rest." Her grandmother had been with the chief in London, and the couple had been with the Wild West for approximately six years.

In the procession's trek to the burial site, four stops were made to honor the four directions recognized as holy in traditional Sioux belief. For days before and during the sacred interment ceremony at Wounded Knee, howling thirty- and forty-mile-per-hour winds were interpreted by tribal elders as a "sacred sign of greeting" according to a Reuters wire-service report. These winds were "paying respect to the dead." Following interment, the party returned to the village of Wolf Creek for a traditional Sioux feast and exchange of gifts among those who took part in the ceremony. A descendant of Rose Ghost Dog, Chris Eagle Hawk, said the feelings of his family were of "pain and abandonment. . . . I told my children you can go on. You don't have to carry this sorrow on to another generation."[2]

EuroDisney: The Wild West Returns

Leave it to Disney, however, to take the Wild West back to its roots and to create a revival based on the traditions firmly established over a century before. Buffalo Bill's Wild West Show at EuroDisney, opened in 1992, is history repeating itself. The most popular performing attraction at the world-famous theme park, by the fall of 1997 the extravaganza had drawn over three million spectators in almost four thousand performances. The new Wild West has outdone the first one in Paris in 1889 by far.

Two shows a day, both complete with barbecue dinners, run the cast of thirty, supported by a behind-the-scenes crew of over twenty-five, through many of the same maneuvers as the original troupe of Cody's Wild West. Against dramatic and strikingly lit backgrounds and announced by a "barker" or by performers portraying Cody and Oakley, the show

retains its original charm and sparkle. The attendance numbers 1,058 for each sold-out performance.

Buffalo Bill makes his grand entry, cowboys and Indians charge about the arena with athletic skill and enthusiastic fervor, Annie Oakley fires away with her legendary marksmanship, cowboys round up longhorn steers and perform Western music, Indians stalk the wily buffalo, the stagecoach is chased and held up, rodeo events abound, and Sitting Bull makes a majestic appearance. The public's excitement remains at a fever pitch throughout. The cast, including rodeo clowns and even waiters, rousts the audience into participation, with contests between members selected from the audience and cheering matches between sections of the gallery. For much of the ninety-minute performance, a musical score sets the tone for each segment of the show.

Oakley's marksmanship is cleverly done using blanks, fired speedily and frequently from her pair of double-action revolvers and from her lever-action Winchester-style carbines. The blanks are specially loaded for the troupe in the United States. Cody also carries a revolver (a double-action one), and fires a few shots himself. Oakley shoots out the flames on a large chandelier, fires at a huge bull's-eye target bedecked with flags, and often shoots from horseback as she circles the arena at daring speeds—just like the Oakley of old.

Blowups of original Wild West posters, period photographs, artifacts (some of them antique), a huge Western-style bar, dance-hall girls and bartenders in period costumes, and cowboy hats for every visitor are part of the ambience. To quote from the brochure:

Hoop 'n Holler in the wild, wild west!

Free cowboy hat with admission

Imagine a herd of stampeding buffalo, longhorn steers and as many Cowboys and Indians whooping and hollering right before your very eyes!

Add to that a runaway stage coach, a shoot-em up showdown, Annie Oakley's sharpshooting, rough riding showmanship, a delicious all-you-can-eat Texas-style barbecue, and you'll have yourself a night you'll never forget!

Nearly all cast members are from the United States and are genuine cowboys and experienced riders. A few of the Indians are descended from original performers in the Wild West of Cody's day, and several are descended from warriors from the mountains, plains, and the Southwest. Clearly, the troupe knows how to ride, though injury from their bold and daring performances is a risk that even Annie Oakley takes in each performance.

William F. Cody: A Heroic Figure

This book owes a debt to the consummate scholars of Cody, experts such as Paul Fees, Joseph G. Rosa, and the late Don Russell. This work is not intended to be the last word on Cody's life but rather is a celebration of the incredible world in which he excelled and will always remain unequaled, as well as of the extraordinary universe of the West that Cody, more than anyone else, influenced and personified.[3]

Not only is American culture the richer and more fascinating because of his unique legacy, but so is the rest of the world's. Imagine the millions internationally since the 1870s who have vicariously lived the dream of the Old West through Cody's autobiography, his stage and arena career, the movies, television shows, and books about his life and times, and even the dime novels, the comic books, cap guns, endless souvenirs, and collectors' items.

And then there is the hard evidence, spiraling in value as more people learn of the genre (many collectors would prefer that the field not get too big, which would thereby dry up the availability of collectibles): photographs, prints, paintings, costumes, watches and stickpins, cuff links, Stetson hats, boots, saddles, and probably the most treasured of all icons, his guns, such as the priceless Lucretia Borgia. Many of the best of these prized objects will never belong to a private party; they are either already in museums or will be soon.

That Cody had a vivid imagination and was a tall-story teller is part of his charm and just one more

March 20th 94
Cody Wyo

To my good Friend
Larry
from
Fred Garlow
Grandson of
"Buffalo Bill"

Colonel William F. Cody's grandson, Frederick H. Garlow, with the Winchester Model 94 "Buffalo Bill" Commemorative.

reason why he was one of America's most beloved characters—and always will be. Further, more than anyone, Buffalo Bill contributed to making the West the captivating subject that it has been for well over a century. The West will reign long after the junk entertainment—the sitcoms, the rot-your-mind rubbish that is standard television fare—has been forgotten. There will always be the West. When one thinks of this genre, first and foremost one thinks of Buffalo Bill: the brilliant scout and frontier hero who became larger than life—a legend in his own lifetime.

To repeat those memorable lines at the end of the film *Buffalo Bill*, when our hero, portrayed by Joel McCrea, recites an emotional arena farewell to his public: "Now the time has come to say . . . good-bye. . . . And so my little comrades up in the gallery and you grown-ups who used to sit there . . . good-bye. God bless you."

In response, a young fan's high-pitched voice shouts from the peanut gallery: "And God bless *you*, too, Buffalo Bill!"

Promotional image of Fred Garlow, a grandson of Buffalo Bill, taken at the time he traveled extensively in endorsing the Buffalo Bill Commemorative Winchester Model 94 rifle series for the Winchester factory. Royalties from Winchester for the sale of these arms raised over $600,000 for the Buffalo Bill Historical Center's firearms collection, then known as the Winchester Gun Museum. Garlow had sat on his grandfather's knee as a child; his parents died when he was a child. With a striking resemblance to Buffalo Bill, Garlow had been a professional hunting guide and became a dedicated supporter of the Cody museum complex. A photograph with his brother, Bill, and nephew Bill at the Camp Monaco site appeared in "Buffalo Bill and the Enduring West," *National Geographic*, July 1981.

Portrait of Buffalo Bill in old age. Farewell to the Last of the Great Scouts.

❧ Appendix A ❧

Buffalo Bill Guides the Sheridan Hunting Expedition

Cody's description of the grand hunt with General Sheridan and party took up much of Chapter XXIV in his autobiography:

Early in the month of September, 1871, information was received at Fort McPherson that General Sheridan and a party of invited friends were coming out to the post to have a grand hunt in the vicinity, and to explore the country from McPherson to Fort Hays, in Kansas. On the morning of September 22d they arrived in a special car at North Platte, a station on the Union Pacific, distant eighteen miles from Fort McPherson.

The party consisted of General Sheridan, Lawrence R. Jerome, James Gordon Bennett, of the New York Herald; *Leonard W. Jerome, Carroll Livingston, Major J. G. Hecksher, General Fitzhugh, General H. E. Davies, Captain M. Edward Rogers, Colonel J. Schuyler Crosby, Samuel Johnson, General Anson Stager, of the Western Union Telegraph Company; Charles Wilson, editor of the* Chicago Evening Journal; *General Rucker, Quartermaster-General, and Dr. Asch—the two last-named being of General Sheridan's staff. They were met at the station by General Emory and Major Brown, with a cavalry company as escort and a sufficient number of vehicles to carry the distinguished visitors and their baggage. . . .*

Lieutenant Hayes, the quartermaster of the expedition, arranged everything for the comfort of the party. One hundred cavalry under command of Major Brown were detailed as an escort. A train of sixteen wagons was provided to carry the baggage, supplies, and forage for the trip; and, besides these, there were three four-horse ambulances in which the guns were carried, and in which members of the party who became weary of the saddle might ride and rest. At General Sheridan's re-quest I was to accompany the expedition; he introduced me to all his friends, and gave me a good send-off. . . .

At five o'clock [the] next morning a cavalry bugle sounded the reville, and soon all were astir in the camp, preparatory to pulling out for the first day's march. I rose fresh and eager for the trip, and as it was a nobby and high-toned outfit which I was to accompany, I determined to put on a little style myself. So I dressed in a new suit of light buckskin, trimmed along the seams with fringes of the same material; and I put on a crimson shirt handsomely ornamented on the bosom, while on my head I wore a broad sombrero. Then mounting a snowy white horse—a gallant stepper—I rode down from the fort to the camp, rifle in hand. I felt first-rate that morning, and looked well.

The expedition was soon under way. . . . First in the line rode General Sheridan, followed by his guests, and then the orderlies. Then came the ambulances, in one of which were carried five greyhounds, brought along to course the antelope and rabbit. With the ambulances marched a pair of Indian ponies belonging to Lieutenant Hayes—captured during some Indian fight—and harnessed to a light wagon, which General Sheridan occasionally used. These little horses, but thirteen hands high, showed more vigor and endurance than any other of the animals we had with us. Following the ambulances came the main body of the escort and the supply wagons.

We marched seventeen miles the first day, and went into camp on Fox Creek, a tributary of the Republican. No hunting had as yet been done; but I informed the gentlemen of the party that we would strike the buffalo country the next day. A hundred or more questions were then asked me by this one and that one, and the whole evening was spent principally in buffalo talk. . . .

At three o'clock [the] next morning the bugle called us to an early start. We had breakfast at half-past four, and at six were in the saddle. All were eager to see and shoot the buffaloes, which I assured them we would certainly meet during the day. After marching five miles, the advance guard, of which I had the command, discovered six buffaloes grazing at a distance of about two miles from us. We returned to the hunters with this information, and they at once consulted with me as to the best way to attack the "enemy."

Acting upon my suggestions, Fitzhugh, Crosby, Lawrence Jerome, Livingston, Hecksher and Rogers, accompanied by myself as guide, rode through a convenient can[y]on to a point beyond the buffaloes, so that we were to the windward of the animals. The rest of the party made a detour of nearly five miles, keeping behind the crest of a hill. We charged down upon the buffaloes, at full gallop, and just then the other party emerged from their concealment and witnessed the exciting chase. The buffaloes started off in a line, single file. Fitzhugh, after a lively gallop, led us all and soon came alongside the rear buffalo, at which he fired. The animal faltered, and then with another shot Fitzhugh brought him to the ground. Crosby dashed by him and leveled another of the herd, while Livingston dropped a third. Those who were not directly engaged in the hunt now came up and congratulated the men upon their success, and Fitzhugh was at once hailed as the winner of the buffalo cup; while all sympathized with Hecksher, whose chance had been the best at the start, but who lost by reason of his horse falling and rolling over him.

The hunt being over, the column moved forward on its march. . . .

Upon reaching Pleasant Valley, on Medicine Creek, our party divided into two detachments—one hunting along the bank of the stream for elk or deer, and the other remaining with the main body of the escort. The elk hunters met with no success whatever, but the others ran across plenty of buffaloes, and nearly everybody killed one or more before the day was over. Lawrence Jerome made an excellent shot; while riding in an ambulance he killed a buffalo which attempted to cross the line of march. . . .

On the next morning, the 25th, we moved out of camp at eight o'clock. The party was very successful through the day in securing game, Hecksher, Fitzhugh, Livingston and Lieutenant Hayes; and in fact all did good shooting.

Lawrence Jerome persuaded me to let him ride Buckskin Joe, the best buffalo horse in the whole outfit, and on his back he did wonders among the buffaloes. Leonard Jerome, Bennett and Rogers also were very successful in buffalo hunting. . . .

Upon crossing the Republican river on the morning of the 26th, we came upon an immense number of buffaloes scattered over the country in every direction, as far as the eye could reach and all had an opportunity to do as much hunting as they wished. The wagons and troops moved slowly along in the direction of the next camp, while the hunters went off separately, or by twos and threes, in different directions, and all were rewarded with abundant success. Lawrence Jerome, however, had his career suddenly checked. He had dismounted to make a steady and careful shot, and thoughtlessly let go of the bridle. The buffalo failing to take a tumble, as he ought to have done, started off at a lively gait, followed by Buckskin Joe—the horse being determined to do some hunting on his own account—the last seen of him, he was a little ahead of the buffalo, and gaining slightly, leaving his late rider to his own reflections and the prospect of a tramp; his desolate condition was soon discovered and another horse warranted not to run under any provocation, was sent to him. It may be stated here that three days afterwards, as I subsequently learned, Buckskin Joe, all saddled and bridled, turned up at Fort McPherson.

260

We pitched our tents for the night in a charming spot on the bank of Beaver Creek. The game was so abundant that we remained there one day. This stopping place was called Camp Cody, in honor of the reader's humble servant.

The next day was spent in hunting jack-rabbits, coyotes, elks, antelopes and wild turkeys. We had a splendid dinner as will be seen from the following

BILL OF FARE

Soup.
Buffalo Tail.
Fish.
Cisco broiled, fried Dace.
Entrees.
Salmi of Prairie Dog, Stewed Rabbit, Fillet of Buffalo, Aux Champignons.
Roast.
Elk, Antelope, Black-tailed Deer, Wild Turkey.
Broiled.
Teal, Mallard, Antelope Chops, Buffalo-Calf Steaks, Young Wild Turkey.
Vegetables.
Sweet Potatoes, Mashed Potatoes, Green Peas.
Dessert.
Tapioca Pudding.
Wines.
Champagne Frappe, Champagne au Naturel, Claret, Whiskey, Brandy, Bass' Ale.
Coffee.

This I considered a pretty square meal for a party of hunters, and everybody did ample justice to it.

In the evening a court-martial was held, at which I presided as chief justice. We tried one of the gentlemen for aiding and abetting in the loss of a government horse, and for having something to do with the mysterious disappearance of a Colt's pistol. He was charged also with snoring in a manner that was regarded as fiendish, and with committing a variety of other less offenses too numerous to mention. [At the evening's horseplay, Cody proved an able and amusing entertainer—more experience to prepare him for a life before much larger audiences] . . .

[For the next three days, the party carried on the hunt, taking game along the way: on the twenty-eighth "buffaloes and turkeys," on the twenty-ninth in a march of twenty-four miles, "three buffaloes, two antelopes, two racoons, and three teal ducks," and on the thirtieth, traveling twenty-five miles, "nine turkeys, two rabbits, and three or four buffaloes."] We went into camp on the bank of the South Fork of the Solomon River, and called the place Camp Sam Johnson. We were now but forty-five miles from Fort Hays, the point at which General Sheridan and his guests expected to strike the Kansas Pacific Railway, and thence return home. That evening I volunteered to ride to Fort Hays and meet the party next day, bringing with me all the letters that might be at the post. Taking the best horse in the command I started out, expecting to make the trip in about four hours.

The next morning the command got an early start and traveled thirty miles to Saline River, where they made their last camp on the plains. As some of the party were attacking a herd of buffaloes, I rode in from Fort Hays and got into the middle of the herd, and killed a buffalo or two before the hunters observed me. I brought a large number of letters, which proved welcome reading matter.

In the evening we gathered around the camp-fire for the last time. . . . we all united in making that night the pleasantest of all that we had spent together. We had eloquent speeches, songs, and interesting anecdotes. I was called upon, and entertained the gentlemen with some lively Indian stories.

The excursionists reached Fort Hays, distant fifteen miles, on the morning of October 2d, where we pitched our tents for the last time. . . . That same afternoon General Sheridan and his guests took the train for the East, after bidding Major Brown, Lieutenant Hayes and myself a hearty good-bye, and expressing themselves as greatly pleased with their hunt, and the manner in which they had been escorted and guided.

Buffalo Bill's Wild West Ledgers, 1886–1887

At Swann's auction galleries in New York City in the early 1990s, Western Americana collector Martin J. Lane was able to purchase for Greg Martin three extremely rare business ledgers kept by Buffalo Bill's Wild West. Dated "May 9/86 to Sept 25/86," "Nov/86–Feb/87," and "Nov 24/86 to Mch 31/87," the books measure approximately 8 × 12¾ inches, and number 356, 333, and 361 pages respectively. Their contents provide a clear picture of the financials of such a complex enterprise, then fast becoming America's national entertainment. The books had come from an old New York law firm, where they had been placed due to a pending litigation in U.S. Circuit Court, District of New Jersey: *Frank C. Maeder v. Buffalo Bill's Wild West Co., et. al.*[1] By some miracle, the ledgers survived and appear to be the only such records in existence today.

The earliest two ledgers are indexed at the front, with numerous performers listed, along with subject headings including Animals, Books, Butcher, Bill Posting, Ammunition, Ads, Bar Acct, Cash, Country Teams, Feed, Express, Freight, Horses, Groceries, Hauling, Hotel, Incidentals, Job Print, Indian Goods, Indian Photos, Labor, Livery, License, Medicines, Meals, Newspapers, Profit & Loss, Pawnees, Police, Sioux, Rent, Sundries, R.R. [railroad], Saddles, Restaurant Receipts, Restaurant Acct, and Telegrams.

Among the accounts covered in all three volumes are the show's stars and top executives: Frank Butler and Annie Oakley, Johnny Baker, Broncho Bill, J. M. Burke, W. F. Cody, Tony and D. F. Escobel, Jim Kidd, John Y. Nelson, Nate Salsbury, William Sweeney, Frank Richmond, Lillian Smith, and Buck Taylor. Among others are A. Hoen (lithographs), Healy and Bigelow (of the Kickapoo Indian Medicine Company, also regarding lithographs), and the Great Western Company (lithographs).

The May 9, 1886, to September 25, 1886, Ledger

The body of material in the "May 9/86 to Sept 25/86" ledger begins with "W. F. Cody" and reveals that his average per month take was approximately $5,600 (for a total of $28,512.76). During the same five-month period, his expenses totaled some $10,602.26. The second page has the notation: "July 24. By Private arrangement with Mr Salsbury all accounts between Mr Cody & Mr Salsbury were Squared— and Each partner took ½ of Cash in Safe amounting to $12663.41 in all." A similar notation appears in the Salsbury section.

Some of Cody's expenses were $3,732 for "61 Horses," $1,025.10 for "R.R.," $70 to "Coyotte Bill," $35 for Hats, $101.75 to Lillian Smith, $71.10 for Ammunition, $130 to Jim Kidd, and $46.13 for "Indian Goods." Among Salsbury's expenses were $127.60 and $36.30 for "Legal acct," $35 for Parade Band, and $86.35 for a saddle for Cody. Salsbury's expenses totaled only $3,132.72.

Sums paid to performers are indicative of their rank and worth to the show: bandleader William Sweeney averaged $15 a week, a sum later increased to $30 (for a total of $365 for five months), while in the same period the Pawnee Indians received $3,664.92 and the Sioux $4,106.50. The Sioux account details sums paid to specific Indians, including American Horse, Antoine, and Antoine's squaw. Orator Frank Richmond received $1,007 in the five-month period, for an average of about $50 per week (the extra $7 covered a hotel expense). Tony Escobel averaged $50 per month, later increased to $60, and D. F. Escobel averaged $30 per month, raised to $40.

Butler and Oakley were paid $1,000 from May 12 through September 26, with their average weekly income at $50, the same sum as paid to Lillian Smith. These three (and Richmond) were the highest paid of the performers, and the highest outside of Cody, Salsbury, and Burke. Burke received $6,432.81 for the five-month period, of which $5,112.47 was expenses; his weekly salary was $75, with occasional deductions paid to Cody, Salsbury, and others. Stage manager Lew Parker received $25 per week, later raised to $50.

Gabriel Dumont, the chieftain in exile of Riel's rebellions in Canada, received $75 a month, while Sergeant Bates, Johnny Baker, and Jim Kidd received $50 per month (Kidd's was raised to $60, the same sum as paid to Broncho Bill). "Cowboy Sheriff" Con Groner received $175 per month, as did Buck Taylor (the latter raised to $185). Tom Duffy was paid $100 per month, soon raised to $110. Veteran stagecoach driver Fred Matthews received $50, then $60, per month. Miss Farrell was paid $50 per month, and John Y. Nelson Sr. received $80 per month.

A. Hoen was paid a total of $1,120 for lithographs, including $35 carried over from March 31. The Great Western Company received $529 in one payment. Job printing ran a total of about $3,355. One of the larger expense items was approximately $5,670 paid out for groceries. Rents paid for sites of perfor-

Ira Paine, who, acting as Carver's coach, gave his best services, and by word and action kept Dr. Carver fully informed as to how he should best manage when he was struggling against fearful odds. In the second thousand ball series the eye trouble commenced, which continued during the whole of the match. As eyes have no second wind it can be readily understood how difficult it was to accomplish the feat. The first hundred broken, taking only 5 minutes and 5 seconds, with but six misses, there were quite a number of 100 where as many as 20 and 30 were missed, with the time of 10, 12 and even 14 minutes, was called upon for his best efforts, and nerving himself he went to his task with a will and, shortening the time, made up the gap. There was a great feeling of relief when the last shot was fired, and the Doctor's friends took him in charge. Like Captain Bogardus, Dr. Carver is disinclined to make another match of this character. After all, *cui bono.* Such performances are certainly not amusing; they are even dreadfully monotonous. Public taste decries the exhibition of an overdriven horse. The glow of an achievement which shows endurance may be sought for; but, when life or limb are endangered, such reputation as may be acquired is out of proportion with the risk. One of Dr. Carver's handsome eyes is certainly worth more to him than five millions of broken glass balls, shot in any incalculable short space of time. We trust such time matches, prolonged without reason, will no longer be in vogue. In a certain sense only such trials may be useful in proving the efficiency of the arm, rather than that of the human machine; but then we can get at the excellence of a weapon by a purely mechanical plan. From the great merit of Dr. Carver's performance or that achieved by Captain Bogardus, we do not intend in the least to decry. As a representative, however, of public opinion, we must think that little is to be gained by exhibitions such as we have described.

Immediately after the match, Dr. Carver, quite exhausted after having shot his long fusillade, was put to bed and was carefully attended to. His eyes were terribly inflamed and painful, and the services of an occulist were called for.

Monday a representation of the FOREST AND STREAM AND ROD AND GUN, having called on Dr. Carver, found him in good spirits, and only suffering from his eyes. One of the eyes was closed and the other quite inflamed. A few days will possibly bring the Doctor quite round. The arms and chest of the rifleman show no signs of the terrible hard work he has gone through. Of course the head is a little dizzy, some old wounds about the skull Carver had received in his Indian fights paining him somewhat. The very abstemious life the Doctor has led will bring him to, we trust, in time.

[The official score was presented, with every shot listed, following each one hundred a tabulation of the total shots, total missed, and the time each hundred required. Those figures were then tabulated with a final total of seven hours, thirty-eight minutes, thirty seconds, with 712 misses; total hits 5,500.]

⊰ Appendix E ⊱

Annie Oakley on Ladies and Shooting

One of the most intriguing and revealing of Annie Oakley's published observations appeared in 1893. The piece, which also appeared in other papers, was entitled "Why Ladies Should Shoot."[1]

There are quite a number of reasons, in my opinion, why every lady who has the time, the means, and the opportunity, should learn the use of fire-arms.

Until recent years woman has been debarred to a great extent from participating in many sports, pastimes, and recreations which have hitherto been looked upon as fit only for the opposite sex.

Now, however, that her right to enjoy some of these healthy diversions, especially those of an out-of-door nature, are fully recognised, I am a believer in such diversions being taken advantage of to the fullest extent.

I do not wish to be understood to mean by this that woman should sacrifice home and family duties entirely merely for outside pleasure but that, feeling how true it is that health goes a great way towards making home life happy, no opportunity should be lost by my sex of indulging in outdoor sports, pastimes, and recreations, which are at once healthy in their tone and results and womanly in their character.

Under this category the use of fire-arms must come, for does not its practice as a rule bring one out into the open, where not only the fresh air may be breathed, but oftentimes the beauties of nature taken in at the same time.

If only as one means of benefiting the health, the use of firearms by woman is, therefore, well worth learning.

Then again, shooting is not only a healthy recreation, but a pleasurable one, and one in which both body and mind are brought into activity—the body in wielding or handling the weapon, and the mind in exercising judgment when aiming and firing at an object.

When learning the use of firearms, a woman learns at the same time confidence and self possession, for these qualities, together with good eyesight, nerve and judgment are *necessary in the handling of a gun or a revolver with anything like precision or accuracy.*

And are not these qualities of use also in daily life, and therefore all the more worthy of cultivation?

Further, every lady who has the chance should learn the use of firearms, so that she may be able to protect herself in times of danger.

It is a common remark that woman's only weapon is her tongue, but though this might have been true half a century ago it is not as true now, for are not many ladies now-a-days accomplished shots and fencers, etc., and proficient in exercises a knowledge of which is likely to come in useful in time of need for self-protection?

Still, the vast majority of my sex are greatly handicapped when danger comes, and, in my opinion, at least one great means whereby she can do something to equalise matters is by learning to handle a gun or revolver—the latter, of course, being the easiest to carry, and the most likely to prove useful in the greatest number of instances.

And now, having given one or two reasons why a lady should learn the use of firearms, I will proceed to give a few hints as to the best method which, in my opinion, she should pursue in acquiring a knowledge of the same.

There is no royal road to shooting, just as there is no royal road to knowledge. Some people follow one system and some another, but all have the same object in view—namely, the acquiring of a certain amount of proficiency in handling and using the weapon, be it rifle, revolver, or shotgun.

It is not in the capacity of all to become first-class shots, but by dint of hard work and perseverance any lady should be able to learn how to use firearms with some degree of skill.

It is best to commence, I should say, by using a light 22-calibre single-shot rifle, unloaded, and practising by pointing or aiming at a mark with it a few hundred times, care being always taken to keep the muzzle from pointing towards yourself or anyone else.

Having learned how to handle the rifle with ease, you should commence to shoot at a good-sized mark, having some friend who is acquainted with the use of firearms always by your side to give proper instructions. *It is best to learn in this way, as you can learn much quicker than by yourself, and at the same time you will not fall into many errors that you would be apt otherwise to do.*

Extra care is required in handling the revolver, as it is more complicated than the rifle, and, its being short, you are more apt to get the muzzle in a dangerous position. More time will also be necessary in learning how to use it.

The revolver will always be handy when travelling to those who care to carry it, as it will give you a feeling of security against danger and attack that will repay the trouble of taking it about with you, especially when journeying alone.

Having become proficient in the use of the rifle and revolver your next step should be to learn how to handle the shot-gun. For beginners I would recommend a light 20-bore, say about five pounds, loaded light at first, or until you get familiar with the recoil. Besides, a 20-bore gun will be found large enough for all practical purposes. In fact, some of my best scores in the field and at the trap have been made with a Lancaster 20-bore.

You should insist on accompanying your father or brother or intimate friends on their shooting excursions, and thus join with them in one of their healthy recreations, for if shooting is a healthy recreation for men, why not also for women?

As to how to dress when out on these excursions, I cannot very well tell you, except that the dress should vary with the climate and the time of year.

Personally, I have shot and fished in eleven different countries in various parts of the world, and have always made it a rule to dress warm in cold weather and cool in warm, being careful to keep my feet dry, and to have a light water-proof cape by me to use in case of rain.

My time is so fully occupied, or I might enter more fully into the subject; but I think the above will give the reader some idea of the reasons why a lady should learn the use of firearms, and how to proceed to do so.

⧹ Appendix F ⧸

"America: A Nation of Marksmen"

The "nation of marksmen" portrayed by Annie Oakley in the piece that follows remains a viable commentary.[1] There are far more Americans interested in the shooting sports than one would imagine from membership in the National Rifle Association (approximately 3.5 million in 1998) or even from the total number of hunting licenses issued annually (about 20 million as of 1998). And had the military draft not been eliminated, America's reputation as a nation of marksmen would stand significantly loftier than at present.

This on-the-mark piece by Oakley is in one respect more timely today than it was in 1907: numerically, there is by far a greater number of girls and women shooters at present than when this was written, led in spirit by the seventeen-year-old shooting marvel Kim Rhode, winner of the women's Olympic double trapshooting gold medal in the 1996 Atlanta Games. Despite the enormity of her achievement—which included defeating the best and most experienced female shots from around the world—Rhode was neither seen nor heard on a single major talk show and received scant press in mainstream publications or on radio or television.

America a Nation of Marksmen.
by Annie Oakley
The World's Greatest Woman Shot

After traveling through fourteen countries, meeting and competing with the best marksmen of each country, I can safely say America leads the world in shooting. I know that some who have visited the vaudevilles and seen the imported so-called colonels and captains giving their marvelous shooting exhibitions will not agree with me in this, but could they get back of the scenes and see how it was done, then would they say no truer words were ever spoken than those of the late P. T. Barnum when he said, "The American people like to be humbugged."

The laws of every big city prohibit dangerous shooting, such as shooting objects from the head, etc., but you can see it done right along, without any interference from the police, for the very simple reason that the shooter is deceiving the public. It is a well-known fact that one of these so-called champions, who was supposed to play a tune by hitting the keys on a piano, had his rifle jam so it wouldn't shoot, yet the piano never missed a note during the short time it took to get the rifle in working order again. Against Americans they invariably lose.

Not only does America produce the best shots, but it produces more of them. I think it would be a rare thing to find a family of any size where one of them at least did not own some kind of a firearm. Visit any suburban town after school hours and you will find young America out in force, either practising with the rifle or shooting at a mark or watching a chance to get a shot at some rabbit or bird. It is on record that one state alone issued more than 50,000 game licenses. Of course the Americans have many advantages over all other nations to become expert marksmen. In nearly every other country only the very wealthy can afford to own a gun or use one, as nearly all the shooting there is in protected game preserves, and it requires a license to even own a gun. We have very few such preserves in this country, and there always will be vast forests and marshes where the sportsman can find game.

Next to America I consider England produces the best marksmen, and let me say right here there is no better nor fairer sportsman than the Englishman. When I say this I know it to be true, as during my stay in that country I shot with many of the nobility and royalty, including the present king, then Prince of Wales, whom I first met at the London Gun Club and where he presented me with a handsome gold medal. Nearly one year after I met him at Wimbledon Rifle Range, during the big meet, where there were ten thousand people on the ground. I supposed he had forgotten me until he pushed his way through the crowd and, after shaking hands, insisted on he and myself having a few shots at the running deer, so-called because it is an iron deer 100 yds. distant, fixed on iron wheels to run down a steep incline. The shooter is supposed to place two shots in a small mark on the shoulder, and as it crosses very quickly it requires some skill and nerve, especially when ten thousand people are looking on, many of them crack shots themselves. Luckily we both made a very respectable score. Later I had the honor of giving several exhibitions before him and the present queen, and once while in Paris he [took] away a ten-cent piece which I had hit in the air with a . . . bullet.

I have been amused more than once when reading about how [some] Englishmen slaughter game on the reserves. These stories are very much exaggerated. The owner of an English game preserve will kill a lot of game sometimes, but if you are ever lucky enough to be his guest you will find his first thought is for you, as you will have the best stand, the best gun, and his best servant to wait upon you, and at the end of the day, if you bring in the most game, he will be more than pleased that you have done so. Any game that is left, after his friends have been taken care of, is sent to charitable hospitals or distributed among the deserving poor of the neighborhood, although it would bring a big price if sent to market.

One of the best sportsmen I ever met was an Englishman, Captain A. W. Money, for the past several years a resident of this country. As an all-round shot he had few equals, while his way of handling a gun was perfect, and although now nearing the allotted span of life he can more than hold his own with many of the younger marksmen.

Next to England, Italy produces the best shots and sportsmen. The grand prize at Monte Carlo, the greatest shooting event in the world, has been won more times by Italians than by any other nation, but in justice to America I will say that the restrictions imposed by the shooting committee there bar nearly all Americans. I found that out to my cost, as I made the trip, but was not allowed to compete. However, America has one win to her credit, as Mr. Pierre Lorillard did win the grand prize one year.

As to guns and clothes: hunting quail in the South I use

a light gun, say about six pounds, and load to correspond. As to dress, I wear a blouse waist, the skirt and gaiters made of light canvas and with light hunting shoes. Shooting ducks or geese in colder weather I use the same, only instead of canvas my suit is then made of Scotch tweed lined with flannel. As it is impossible to do much walking in long skirts when hunting[,] all mine are made to come about six or eight inches below the knee. When in the open fields, I use a hat with a wide brim, but in the woods a cap is best.

The color of the dress should correspond as near as possible with the surroundings. This rule does not apply to deer shooting. In this I always wear a red handkerchief as a protection against the new hunter, many of whom make it a rule to shoot at anything that moves, and although the fool killer has been written up time and again, the number seems to increase each year.[2] Nearly all ladies in starting in to hunt game shoot too quickly or before they have the proper aim. This can only be overcome by experience, but once overcome the amount of pleasure one can get from hunting over a pair of well broken dogs will more than repay the pains taken in learning to use a gun, and while you may return from the day's hunt tired and footsore you will find little use for doctor or medicine.

Although many of the rulers of Europe are ardent sportsmen, who love to hunt game, I think our President, Theodore Roosevelt, is a greater sportsman than all of them. He loves the sport not for the amount of game he gets alone, but for the exercise and out-door life. No distance seems too great for him when he starts for a hunt. There are no baited duck grounds or game preserves for him; all his hunting is done where game is wildest, and in the hardest kind of country. Although I have never had the pleasure of seeing him on one of his hunts, I have heard those who have been with him say that they have known him to hunt all day without having a chance to fire a shot at any kind of game. Yet when he returned to camp, although often wet and tired, his temper was not ruffled in the least, and the next morning he was up and ready to start out again. That is the kind of a President who inspires good marksmen and good soldiers. That he may live to be one hundred is the devout wish of every good American.

Some time since I read in an English paper that William Waldorf Astor had presented two hundred and fifty thousand dollars to the National Rifle Association of Great Britain, and I have been wondering why some of our millionaires have not done the same in this country. I am sure it would be money well spent.

The Italian Government takes great interest in the marksmanship of its soldiers, and gives them every opportunity to practice. When I first went to that country I could not understand why so many white targets with black bull's-eyes were painted on fences, ends of houses and walls; these were to be found at irregular distances and in all manner of places. It was several weeks before I found out what they were used for. One day a company of mountain soldiers came along on a trot, for the soldiers of Italy, instead of marching as the soldiers of many other nations do, always go on a dog-trot. When they came in sight of one of these targets they came to a full stop. The first line stopped, cocked their empty rifles, aimed at the bull's-eye and pulled the trigger, then dropped on their knees, so the next could do the same; and so on, until the entire company had done likewise.

Were we to believe all we read and hear, the cowboy and the "bad man" of the West were the greatest revolver shots in America. This, however, is far from being true. I can find more and better revolver shots right in New York than any place I know of. The cowboy and bad man have had their day, but when they were plenty they were very much over-rated, and depended more on the quickness of pulling the gun than on real marksmanship. There were two exceptions to this, however, one of whom was Ben Thompson, a Texan who had killed nineteen men before he was himself killed. He was an exceptionally fine shot, and so quick was he with the revolver that his opponent had little if any chance. He was a small man, mild mannered, very gentlemanly in appearance, and the last man one would pick out for a fighter. It was his boast that he never killed a man who did not try to kill him first. As most of his killing was done while he was marshal of one of the Texas towns, he was never troubled with the law. He was finally decoyed into a variety theatre in Dallas, Texas, and killed, but he killed two and crippled one before he went under. . . .

Here are a few don'ts that if adhered to may save an accident.

Don't shoot at a noise.

Don't shoot at a moving bush.

Don't shoot at small game, such as rabbits, grouse or squirrel with big ammunition.

Don't under any circumstances allow your gun muzzle to point for one moment at any living thing you do not mean to kill.

The Oakley Collection of Arms, Medals, and Trophies

Based on original press and others sources, we have compiled the following account of Oakley's medals. These descriptions were published in a variety of newspapers and journals, saved by the Butlers in their several scrapbooks. Some clippings were undated. Though the list is incomplete, it reveals the variety and quality of what was an amazing collection. Oakley herself spoke of these treasures, in the August 13, 1887, *Camp Sketches:*

Here is a case containing some of the medals I have won. There are twenty-three here in all. This magnificent gold one was presented to me by the members of the London Gun Club, when I gave an exhibition for them on June 11th. Do you know I think more of this than all the others put together, for it is the only medal this club, which is 'The Gun Club of the World,' have ever given away. . . . Here is the lady championship medal of America. . . . It was offered by a club in Eyrie, which was particularly keen about its being won by a stranger. . . . Now, look at the companion to the lady-championship one. . . . I was the only lady in this competition, but the only lady managed to break twenty-three balls out of twenty-five, and bear off the prize. . . . I have another medal here, which was given me upon the last day I was at the Madison-square Gardens, New York. The inscription upon it is, 'Presented by her New York lady friends, in commemoration of her fine and daring riding['].'' . . . presented to me for picking up my hat from the ground out of a side-saddle when riding at full speed.

From the *Kennel and Gun,* following a shooting demonstration in Pine Brook, New Jersey, on February 7, 1887, Oakley received a boxed gold medal, about one-and-a-half inches in circumference, inscribed: TO MISS OAKLEY, BY HER MANY FRIENDS AND ADMIRERS, FOR HER PERFORMANCE FEB. 7TH, 1887, AT FRANK CLASS' CLUB HOUSE GROUNDS, PINE BROOK, N.J. The obverse depicted a raised pigeon in full flight and was inscribed with the words AS A TOKEN OF SKILL.

From the *American Field,* April 13, 1889, at a match held at Pine Brook resort in New Jersey, where Oakley's medals were on display, came a gift of the Middlesex Gun Club, of "solid gold, the medal proper being held in the beak of a flying eagle, the bird being exquisitely fashioned."

The Springfield (Massachusetts) *Union* on October 26, 1887, referred to Oakley's popularity in England. She received a medal from Lord Mandeville after she had "divided a sweepstake with 10 entries with her host who presented her with a jubilee sovereign with his monogram and crest engraved upon it. [Another match was] at the grounds of Charles Lancaster. . . . She won by killing 41 out of 50 [blue-rock pigeons], in fine style. Mr. Lancaster presented her with a very handsome gold badge suitably engraved."

The Paris *Herald* ran the following, likely from November or December 1889:

A pigeon-shooting match was got up by the Club des Sports of [Lyons] in which Miss Annie Oakley was invited to take part. 'Little Sure Shot' was matched against the best local shooters: MM. Gazagne, de Saint-Trivier, Dufier, Bietrix, Coignet, Gauthier, Fraisse, all of whom were in turn vanquished. At the end of the match Miss Oakley was presented by the club with a medal as a souvenir of the occasion.—*Express de Lyon.*

A newspaper article without date or attribution (ca. 1887–1891), covering the same match, indicated that

after a very close and exciting contest, Miss Oakley won, beating all the crack wing-shots of Lyons, for which she was presented with a very handsome gold badge, valued at $200, and for an exhibition she gave with the rifle and revolver the club voted her an honorary membership and the club's gold medal. This is the first time a lady has ever had the honor conferred upon her.

An article based on a Frank Butler letter from Milan, Italy, in which the proud husband revealed that Oakley did quite well yet again in a pigeon tournament at Monte Carlo:

In the pigeon tournament . . . April 6 and 9 [1890], twenty-eight metres rise, twenty-five yards boundary, the first prize, 300 francs and gold medal, on April 6, was won by Dr. Bauer on eight straight kills; second prize, 200 francs and gold medal, was won by Annie Oakley on seven straight. April 9, same conditions, twenty one entries, Annie Oakley won first prize, 300 francs and gold medal, on eight straight.

From the *Belgian News,* June 5, 1891:

Miss O. *fetched* us her magnificent collection of medals and jewelry, presents from Royal and noble donors. . . . Various handsome gold and enamelled medals from different U.S. gun clubs, and a large medal in silver (oxidized) from the "Societe Nautique" of Lyons, the extraordinarily beautiful design and artistic finish of which stamped it as a French production. . . . a lovely shawl broach, representing a bat in moonstone with outstretched wings in gold, a valuable broach (saphire, garnets and pearls set in gold), from the Princess Gisella, daughter of the Empress of Austria. A bracelet, gold and diamonds from Prince Luitpold, Regent of Bavaria. "Bonnie Bessie" was wearing an elegant broach (diamonds and gold), presented to her by Baronesses Rothschild and Oppenheimer of Vienna.

The *American Field,* by William Bruce Leffingwell (ca. 1893–1895), revealed even more about the Oakley collection:

Besides the many beautiful gifts of laces, handkerchiefs and pottery which were given Miss Oakley when abroad, she has forty-five valuable medals, brooches, etc. . . . One of the prettiest of these valuable mementos is an oval pin presented by the Baroness de Horn, of Heidelburg. This has the photograph of the donor on the reverse side and shows the face [of] one of the most beautiful women in Europe. . . . A magnificent trophy is the medal won at Milan, Italy, where Miss Oakley defeated the prominent shots of Italy. She won $200 with this medal. The medal shows the old arena which has existed for 1,300 years and seats 30,000 people. . . . I wondered which she prized most, and when I inquired, her eyes moistened and she said "this!" and unpinned from her dress a medal which was to her as was the widow's mite, for it was all the giver possessed. . . . [presented to her by an orphan boy she had befriended; the medal was a gift bought with] the first money he ever earned [and] sent . . . to her with a suitable inscription. . . . It is Miss Oakley's mascot and she always wears it when shooting a match.

An unidentified press clipping (ca. 1912–1923) described Oakley receiving still another gold medal, this one from the Actors' Fund, after an August 19 (year unknown) benefit performance at the Polo Grounds

at which 14,000 people were present. Over $15,000 was realized for this worthy cause. . . . To-day she received the following letter. . . . we thank you for your fine exhibition . . . and we ask you to accept the accompanying gold medal as a souvenir of the occasion. . . . It was more than kind of you to volunteer, and your work aided greatly in making the afternoon the most successful of the kind in the history of New York amusements. . . . COHAN & HARRIS, New Amsterdam Theater."

And from the *Billboard*, an undated press clipping reads, "Miss Oakley showed us many valuable gold and silver trophies that had been presented to her by athletic clubs throughout the country, one from the N.Y. Press Club Athletic Club being a wonderful work of the jeweler's art."

Finally, the fate of all the medals except one was revealed in the Philadelphia *Public Ledger*, October 28, 1923:

For her hospital friends . . . and to their comfort went the proceeds from the assayed gold of her hundreds of championship medals—some from crowned heads of Europe whose thrones have gone down beneath the bloody hand of war. The beautiful medal awarded her for the "Championship of France" [from the Marseilles live-pigeon competition] is the only medal 'Little Sure Shot' saved.

❈Appendix H❈

Advertising in the Wild West Programs

Beginning in 1895, the use of advertising added a fresh commercial element to Buffalo Bill's Wild West programs. Several of the firms seen on those pages remain in business today. Poring over selected programs from 1895 through 1918 reveals the astute marketing of the Wild West machine and its successors. But as the shows declined, so did the advertising. Another casualty was the quality, size, and merit of the publications.

The style and appearance of these advertisements varied from year to year, with some ads repeated and some companies running variants of earlier ads. The selection illustrated here encompasses all the firearms and ammunition manufacturers and many of the companies that remain in business to this day or were in business into modern times. The nonfirearms advertisements were so numerous that space does not permit comprehensively listing or picturing every item. Due to the programs' rarity, not every year could be studied, though the total number of programs examined was approximately two dozen.

Shoot Blue Rocks.

USED EXCLUSIVELY BY
THIS SHOW..BEST AND
MOST RELIABLE..FOR
SALE BY ALL JOBBERS.

The Cleveland Target Co.
CLEVELAND, O.

Firearms, Ammunition, and Clay-Pigeon Makers:

Cleveland Target, clay pigeons (1897)

Colt's Patent Fire Arms, Hartford, Connecticut (1895)

Du Pont, E. I., de Nemours Powder, Wilmington, Delaware (ca. 1909)

Equitable Powder, St. Louis, Missouri (1902)

Harrington and Richardson Arms, Worcester, Massachusetts (1900, 1902, 1907, ca. 1909)

Hoxie Ammunition, Chicago, Illinois (1907)

Iver Johnson's Arms and Cycle Works, Fitchburg, Massachusetts (1902, 1907, ca. 1909, ca. 1910, 1910)

Marlin Firearms, New Haven, Connecticut, rifles (1907)

Parker Brothers, Meriden, Connecticut, shotguns (1902)

Remington Arms, Ilion, New York (1907)

Remington Arms Union Metallic Cartridge, New York (1916)

Savage Arms, Utica, New York, .32 automatic pistol, (ca. 1909, ca. 1910, 1910)

Stevens, J., Arms and Tool, Chicopee Falls, Massachusetts (1902, 1907, ca. 1909)

Union Metallic Cartridge, Bridgeport, Connecticut (1907)

United States Cartridge, Lowell, Massachusetts (ca. 1910)

White Flyer Targets and Traps, East Alton, Illinois (1902)

Winchester Repeating Arms, New Haven, Connecticut, rifles and ammunition (1897, 1899, 1900, 1902, 1907, ca. 1909, 1917)

Though not one of the more active advertisers, one clay-pigeon manufacturer, White Flyer, promoted their product in the pages of the Wild West program of 1902. The ad indicated: "In all our Exhibitions we recommend and use White Flyer Targets and Traps BECAUSE THEY ARE THE BEST." The manufacturer was the Western Trap and Target Company of East Alton, Illinois, which was affiliated with the Western Cartridge Company, controlled by the Olin family. Some twenty-nine years later, the Olin interests purchased the Winchester Repeating Arms Company, forming Winchester-Western.

viii

COLT'S

Lightning Magazine Rifles

REVOLVERS

and........

HAMMERLESS
SHOT GUNS.......

COLT'S
NEW POCKET
32 CALIBRE.

Colt Revolvers have been adopted by
the United States Army and Navy, by
the Police, Militia, and are used by

———— Buffalo Bill's Wild West Show.

THEY ARE THE BEST.

Colt's Patent Fire=Arms Mfg. Co.,

HARTFORD, CONN.

276

STEVENS

A MODERATE priced gun—that shoots well, looks well, wears well, handles well—is a STEVENS SINGLE or DOUBLE BARREL MODEL. Made in all standard lengths and gauges in Hammer and Hammerless styles.

For sale by all Merchants. If you cannot obtain, we ship direct, express prepaid, upon receipt of Catalog Price.

Send for 160-page Illustrated Catalog describing entire output. Has attractive cover in colors Mailed for 5 cents in stamps to pay postage.

J. STEVENS ARMS & TOOL CO.

P. O. BOX 77,

CHICOPEE FALLS, MASS.

STEVENS' RIFLES ARE USED BY PERFORMERS IN THE WILD WEST SHOW.

278

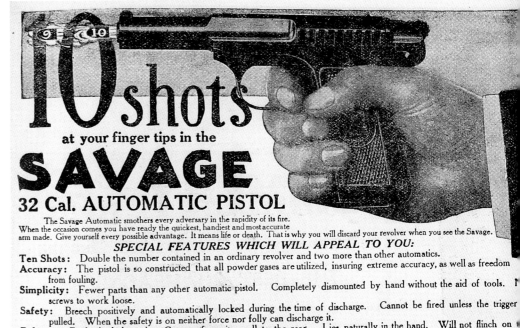

279

RIFLES AND CARTRIDGES

There are many makes of hunting rifles and cartridges, but Winchester—the **W** brand—have first call among sportsmen of experience. It is not sentiment, but quality and dependability that give them preference over all other makes. Not only are Winchester rifles and cartridges dependable, but they are made in calibers and types suitable for hunting all kinds of game. The high quality and entire dependability of Winchester guns and cartridges are maintained by the exercise of great care and experience in the selection of materials used in making them, and by thoroughly modern methods of manufacture. If you, like thousands of sportsmen, use Winchester rifles and cartridges, you are familiar with their superiority. If you haven't used them, a trial will convince you that you should.

THE GRAND PRIX—the highest possible honor—was awarded to Winchester Guns and Ammunition at the Panama-Pacific International Exposition.

EVERY GOOD GUN STORE IS A HEADQUARTERS
FOR WINCHESTER GUNS AND CARTRIDGES

**WINCHESTER ARMS and AMMUNITION used exclusively
by JOHNNY BAKER and THE BUFFALO BILL
WILD WEST SHOWS.**

Miscellaneous Manufacturers

Abbot-Downing, Concord, New Hampshire, Concord coach, wagons, wheels, axles, transportation, delivery wagons (1899)

Capewell Horse Shoe Nail, Hartford, Connecticut (ca. 1909)

Columbia Bicycles, Pope Manufacturing, Hartford, Connecticut, bicycles (1897)

Goodrich, B. F., tires, Akron, Ohio (1907)

Hamilton, Brown Shoe, Boston, Massachusetts, and St. Louis, Missouri (1910)

International Harvester Company of America, Galesburg, Illinois (ca. 1910)

Maxwell-Briscoe Motor, Tarrytown, New York (1910)

Meriden Britannia (International Silver), Meriden, Connecticut (1902)

National Cash Register, Dayton, Ohio (ca. 1910, 1910)

Parker Pen, Janesville, Wisconsin (1907)

Pierce-Arrow Motor Car, Buffalo, New York (ca. 1909)

Rogers Brothers (Meriden Britannia; International Silver), Meriden, Connecticut (1902)

Rogers, William, Hartford, Connecticut, silver-plated ware (1897)

Sherwin-Williams, Cleveland, Ohio, paints (1907, 1910)

Singer Manufacturing, sewing machines (1900)

Standard Oil, grease (ca. 1909)

Stetson, John B., Philadelphia, Pennsylvania, hats (1900, 1902, 1907, ca. 1909, ca. 1910, 1910)

Studebaker Brothers, South Bend, Indiana, automobiles (ca. 1910)

Underwood Typewriters (1900)

U.S. Playing Card Company, Cincinnati, Ohio, Congress playing cards (1897, 1899, 1900, 1902)

Veeder Manufacturing, Hartford, Connecticut, cyclometer for bicycles (1897)

White Sewing Machine, Cleveland, Ohio, bicycles (1897)

Willys-Overland, Toledo, Ohio, automobiles (ca. 1910)

282

The iron muscles for this daring deed

UNDERWOOD TYPEWRITERS
━ WIN ━

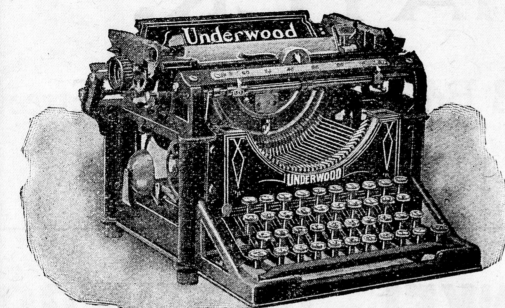

GOVERNMENT AWARDS CONTRACT FOR 250 MACHINES.

The Largest Order for Typewriters Ever Given.

Secretary Long, Navy Department, Washington, decided Saturday to accept the report of the special board appointed to investigate the merits of typewriters as to advantages, speed, durability, etc.

Decision was in favor of the bid made by the Wagner Typewriter Company for

250 UNDERWOOD TYPEWRITERS

and the Navy Department decided to accept their bid against the Remington, Densmore, Brooks, Rem-Sho, Jewett, Oliver, Hammond, and other typewriters in competition.

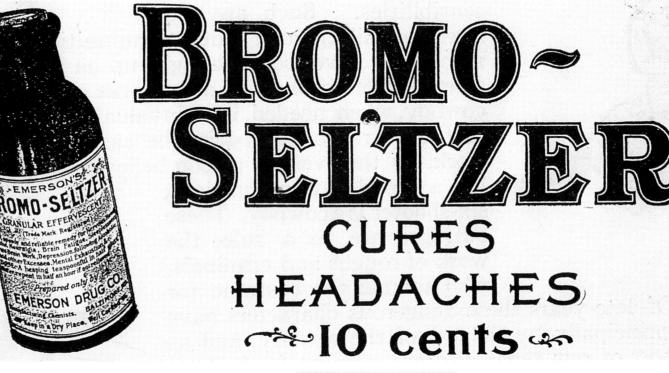

BROMO-SELTZER

CURES
HEADACHES
10 cents

Chew

BEEMAN'S
PEPSIN

(The Original Pepsin Gum.)

*Cures Indigestion
and Seasickness.*

WE HAVE IT.

FOR SALE BY ALL DRUGGISTS AND CONFECTIONERS.

LUDEN'S

5C. MENTHOL 5C.
COUGH
DROPS

GIVE INSTANT RELIEF

SOOTHE AND COOL THE
THROAT

SINGERS AND SPEAKERS
RECOMMEND THEM

"THE YELLOW PACKAGE"

W. H. LUDEN, READING, PA.

SOLD BY THIS SHOW.

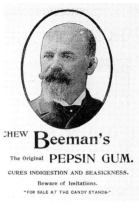

Chew **Beeman's**

The Original **PEPSIN GUM.**

CURES INDIGESTION AND SEASICKNESS.

Beware of Imitations.

"FOR SALE AT THE CANDY STANDS."

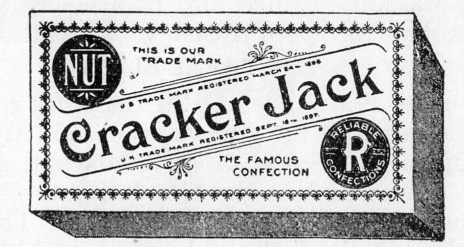

287

Railroads and Shipping Lines

Burlington (Chicago, Burlington and Quincy Railroad), Chicago, Illinois (1914)

Denver and Rio Grande Railroad (1914)

Missouri Pacific Railroad (1914)

Pacific Mail Steamship, San Francisco, California (1914)

Rock Island Railroad (1914)

Santa Fe Railroad, Chicago, Illinois (1914)

Union Pacific Railroad (1914)

Western Pacific Railroad (1914)

Beer, Gum, and Other Food or Drink or Household Suppliers, as Well as Stores and Wholesalers

Abraham and Straus, Brooklyn, New York, clothing, dry goods, theater booth, etc. (ca. 1909)

American Cereal, Quaker Oats (1900)

Anheuser Busch, St. Louis, Missouri, Budweiser beer (1907)

Baker, Walter, and Company, Dorchester, Massachusetts, cocoas and chocolates (1895)

Beeman's, Pepsin Chewing Gum (1895, 1897, 1899, 1907)

Borden's Condensed Milk, New York (1899, 1900)

"Bull" Durham Smoking Tobacco (ca. 1910, 1910)

Butcher Polish, Boston, Massachusetts (ca. 1910)

Cracker Jack (1907, ca. 1909, ca. 1910, 1910)

Emerson Drug, Baltimore, Maryland, Bromo-Seltzer (1907)

Heublein, G. F., and Brother, Hartford, Connecticut, A1 sauce, club punch, and cocktails, (1897, ca. 1910)

Kirk, H. B., and Company, New York, Old Crow Rye (1902)

Life Savers (1917)

Lord and Taylor, New York, wholesale distributors, onyx hose (ca. 1909)

Luden, W. H., Reading, Pennsylvania, Luden's cough drops (1907)

Mennen's Borated Talcum Toilet Powder (1897, 1899, 1900, 1902, 1907, ca. 1909, ca. 1910, 1910)

Narragansett Brewing, Providence, Rhode Island (1916)

Pabst Brewing, Milwaukee, Wisconsin, Pabst Blue Ribbon beer (1907, ca. 1909, ca. 1910, 1910)

Pond's Extract (1902)

Sears, Roebuck and Company, Chicago, Illinois, clothing, supplies (1895)

Slauson, A., and Company, New York, Scotch Mints, (ca. 1910, 1910)

Sloan, Dr. Earl S., Boston, Massachusetts, Sloan's liniment (1902)

Smith Brothers', Poughkeepsie, New York, cough drops (1895, 1899, 1900, 1902, 1907, ca. 1909)

Washburn, Crosby, Minneapolis, Minnesota, Gold Medal Flour (1899)

Wrigley, William, and Company, Chicago, Illinois, Wrigley's spearmint pepsin gum (1910)

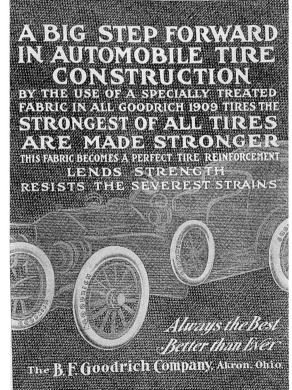

The
Pierce Arrow

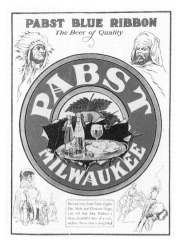

⊰ Appendix I ⊱

Museums and Historic Sites

W. F. "Buffalo Bill" Cody and the Wild West

Buffalo Bill Historical Center
Buffalo Bill Museum, Cody Firearms Museum,
Plains Indian Museum, Whitney Gallery of Western
Art, McCracken Research Library
Sheridan Avenue
Cody, Wyoming 82414

Autry Museum of Western Heritage
4700 Western Heritage Way
Los Angeles, California 90027

Circus World Museum
426 Water Street
Baraboo, Wisconsin 53913

Lookout Mountain
Buffalo Bill Memorial Museum and Grave
987½ Lookout Mountain Road
Golden, Colorado 80401

**Denver Public Library/Western History
Department**
10 West Fourteenth Avenue Parkway
Denver, Colorado 80204

Buffalo Bill Ranch
Rural Route 1, Box 229
North Platte, Nebraska 69101

Nebraska State Historical Society
1500 R Street
Lincoln, Nebraska 68501

**Kansas History Center, Kansas State Historical
Society**
6425 Southwest Sixth Avenue
Topeka, Kansas 66615

Annie Oakley

The Annie Oakley Foundation
Post Office Box 127
Greenville, Ohio 45331

**The Darke County Historical Society
The Garst Museum**
205 North Broadway
Greenville, Ohio 45331-2222

Nutley Museum
65 Church Street
Nutley, New Jersey 07110

Texas Jack Omohundro

The Texas Jack Association
Post Office Box 7000-185
Redondo Beach, California 90277

G. W. "Pawnee Bill" Lillie

Pawnee Bill Ranch Site, Museum, and Mansion
Post Office Box 493
Pawnee, Oklahoma 74058

Cowboys and Rodeos

National Cowboy Hall of Fame
1700 Northeast Sixty-third Street
Oklahoma City, Oklahoma 73111

Exhibition and Competition Shooters

Trapshooting Hall of Fame and Museum
601 W. National Road
Vandalia, Ohio 45377

National Firearms Museum
11250 Waples Mill Road
Fairfax, Virginia 22030

101 Ranch

Woolaroc Museum
State Highway 123
Bartlesville, Oklahoma 74003

101 Ranch Collectors Association
Ruth and Jerry Murphey
10701 Timbergrove Lane
Corpus Christi, Texas 78410

Thousand-Mile Cowboy Race, 1893

Dawes County Historical Society
Chadron, Nebraska 69337

National Museum of American History
Smithsonian Institution
Fourteenth Street and Constitution Avenue NW
Washington, D.C. 20560

The following museums are not noted in the text since their collections do not focus on Buffalo Bill's Wild West; an asterisk indicates membership in Museums West, a national association of Western museums of North America that also includes the Autry Museum of Western Heritage, the Buffalo Bill Historical Center, and the National Cowboy Hall of Fame. The reader can also consult the American Association of Museums, The Official Museum Directory, a mammoth publication issued annually by R. R. Bowker. For hotel accommodations, ask your travel agent to consider those belonging to the Association of Historic Hotels of the Rocky Mountain West, 1002 Walnut Street, Suite 201A, Boulder, Colorado 80302.

Amon Carter Museum of Western Art*
3501 Camp Bowie Boulevard
Fort Worth, Texas 76107

Eiteljorg Museum of American Indian and Western Art*
500 West Washington
Indianapolis, Indiana 46204

Thomas Gilcrease Institute of American History and Art*
1400 Gilcrease Museum Road
Tulsa, Oklahoma 74127

Glenbow Museum*
Calgary, Alberta, Canada

The Heard Museum*
22 East Monte Vista Road
Phoenix, Arizona 85004

Museum of the Mountain Man
Pinedale, Wyoming 82941

The National Museum of Wildlife Art*
10 North Center Street
Jackson, Wyoming 83001

Rockwell Museum*
111 Cedar Street
Corning, New York 14830

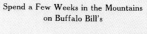

Buffalo Bill's Wild West silk scarf, by Hunting World, Inc.

Chapter 1

1. *The Life of Hon. William F. Cody, Known as Buffalo Bill the Famous Hunter, Scout, and Guide: An Autobiography* (Hartford: Frank E. Bliss, 1879; reprint, with a foreword by Don Russell, Lincoln: University of Nebraska Press, 1978). Cody qualified for the use of the title "Honorable" due to his (disputed) election to the Nebraska legislature in 1872. He never showed up to serve; the post was given to the opposing candidate, D. P. Ashburn. For further details on Cody's methods of writing and his use of other sources, see Russell's foreword to the 1978 edition.

2. John Willis to William F. Cody, October 4, 1897, Michael Del Castello Collection.

3. The Lou Simpson association has been the subject of some debate.

4. Cody, *Autobiography,* p. 154.

5. Ibid., pp. 154–56.

6. Ibid., p. 157.

7. Ibid., pp. 113–14.

8. Ibid., pp. 161–62.

9. The site is believed to be confirmed by the presence of such archaeological evidence as handblown beer and champagne bottles, as noted in Don Russell, *The Lives and Legends of Buffalo Bill* (Norman: University of Oklahoma Press, 1960), p. 93. Some historians have suggested that this hunting contest never took place and was made up by Cody for publicity purposes. As it is yet disproven, we present the story here partly due to its wealth of detail on Cody's hunting technique.

10. Cody, *Autobiography,* pp. 171–74.

11. Ibid., pp. 174–75.

12. Some discrepancies have been noted in Sheridan's calculations of distance; nevertheless, the ride was a feat of no little achievement.

13. Philip H. Sheridan, *Personal Memoirs* (New York, 1888), vol. 1, pp. 300–301.

14. Russell, *Lives and Legends,* p. 134.

15. Ibid., p. 134.

16. Ibid., pp. 134–35.

17. A driving gale concealed the sounds of the cavalry's hooves.

18. Cody, *Autobiography,* pp. 255–62.

19. Pond, Frederic E., *Life and Adventures of Ned Buntline,* Cadmus Book Shop, 1919, p. 6.

20. Cody, *Autobiography,* pp. 263–64.

21. Ibid., pp. 295–305.

22. Russell, *Lives and Legends,* p. 187.

23. Cody, *Autobiography,* pp. 313–15.

24. Russell, *Lives and Legends,* p. 187.

25. Cody, *Autobiography,* pp. 310–11.

26. Ibid., p. 320.

27. Pond, op. cit.

28. *Ellis County Star,* Hays City, Kansas, June 29, 1876, p. 4, as cited in Russell, op. cit., p. 220.

29. Russell, *Lives and Legends,* pp. 221–22.

30. Ibid., p. 226.

31. Ibid., p. 230.

32. Cody, *Autobiography,* pp. 355–56.

33. Ibid., p. 360.

34. O. H. Bentley, *History of Wichita and Sedgwick County Kansas,* Chicago: Cooper, 1910, vol. 1., pp. 291–92.

35. Russell, *Lives and Legends,* p. 91.

Chapter 2

1. The Earl of Dunraven, *Canadian Nights,* pp. 55–56, as cited by Russell, op. cit.

2. Cody, *Autobiography,* p. 316.

3. Ibid., p. 329.

4. "Famous Gunfighters of the Western Frontier," *Human Life,* January 1907, vol. 4, no. 4, pp. 7–9.

5. Don Russell, *The Wild West: A History of the Wild West Shows* (Fort Worth: Amon Carter Museum of Western Art, 1970). "First Episode" presents an enlightening early history of Wild West entertainments.

Chapter 3

1. Don Russell, *The Lives and Legends of Buffalo Bill* (Norman: University of Oklahoma Press, 1960), p. 291.

2. "The Letters of Doc Carver" (ed. by Raymond W. Thorp), *Outdoor Life-Outdoor Recreation,* vol. LXV, no. 4 (April 1930), p. 89, Russell, op. cit., p. 293.

3. Nate Salsbury, "The Origin of the Wild West Show," *Colorado Magazine* 32.3 (July 1955): pp. 205–8.

4. Louis Pfaller, " 'Enemies in '76, Friends in '85'—Sitting Bull and Buffalo Bill," *Prologue: The Journal of the National Archives* 1.2 (Fall 1969): pp. 7–31. This article presents a much more detailed study of Cody and Sitting Bull than we do and is based on records in the National Archives.

5. Ibid.

6. Ibid.

7. Ibid.

8. Ibid.

9. Ibid.

10. R. L. Wilson, *Winchester Engraving* (Palm Springs, Calif.: Beinfeld, 1991), p. 153.

Chapter 4

1. The title of colonel was bestowed on Cody by Governor John M. Thayer of Nebraska on March 8, 1887, when he appointed him "aide-de-camp of my staff with the rank of Colonel." On November 23, 1889, Colonel Cody received another appointment from Thayer, this time as aide-de-camp-in-chief "on the Staff of the Commander in Chief with the rank of Brigadier General." The latter document appeared in several Wild West programs, beginning soon after the appointment. Still later, Cody was commissioned a colonel as aide-de-camp on the staff of Silas A. Holcomb, when Holcomb was himself governor of Nebraska. Cody seemed more at ease with the rank of colonel than that of general.

2. For a well-worn example of the 1899 *Route-Book,* see the collage on Lancer William House in Chapter 7.

3. Nate Salsbury, "The Origin of the Wild West Show," *Colorado Magazine* 32.3 (July 1955): pp. 211–14.

4. Salsbury neglected to mention the name of the pope: it was Leo XIII, who served from 1878 to 1903.

5. Salsbury, "Origin of the Wild West Show," pp. 208–11.

6. Quoted in J. W. Buel, *Heroes of the Plains* (St. Louis, Missouri Historical Publishing Co.).

7. Albert H. Sanford, H. J. Hirshheimer, assisted by Robert F. Fries, *A History of La Crosse, Wisconsin, 1840–1900* (LaCrosse: LaCrosse County Historical Society, 1951), p. 216.

8. See R. L. Wilson, *The Peacemakers: Arms and Adventure in the American West* (New York: Random House, 1992), p. 299.

Chapter 6

1. Oakley remembered: "At first Colonel Cody entertained a grave doubt as to whether I should be able to withstand the recoil from a shot-gun. . . . I think I have pretty successfully demonstrated . . . that I have been able to bear up against it." However, in the first shooting demonstration in her three-day trial period, it was Nate Salsbury, the show's business manager, who watched her. To quote Oakley: "I afterwards heard that he told Colonel Cody that I was a real 'daisy' and completely laid the captain 'away in the shade.' " Annie Oakley, "The Story of My Life," unpublished ms., 1926, Garst Museum, Darke County Historical Society.

2. Ibid., p. 22.

3. "Miss Annie Oakley the Most Famous Girl-Shot in the World," *The Courier of London,* n.d., Annie Oakley and Frank Butler Scrapbook, 1887–1891, Buffalo Bill Historical Center, Cody, Wyo. In the scrapbook, the article is on a page facing other articles that are dated May 1, May 21, June 3, and June 11, 1887.

4. Oakley, "The Story of My Life," pp. 35–36.

5. "An Interview with Miss Annie Oakley," *The Dramatic Review,* June 10, 1887, Oakley and Butler Scrapbook, 1887–1891.

6. Annie Oakley, "Notes on the Rod and Gun," *Gameland* (March 1893), Oakley and Butler Scrapbook, 1893–1895, Buffalo Bill Historical Center, Cody, Wyo.

7. Undated and unidentified newspaper interview, from Annie Oakley/Frank Butler scrapbooks, Buffalo Bill Historical Center, McCracken Research Library.

8. Shirl Kasper, *Annie Oakley* (Norman: University of Oklahoma Press, 1992), p. 156.

9. Kasper, op. cit., p. 159.

10. Among the papers were the Bridgeport *Telegram-Union,* the Brooklyn *Citizen,* the Charleston *News and Courier,* the Chicago *Examiner* and *American,* the Hoboken *Observer,* the Jacksonville *Metropolis,* the New Orleans *Times-Democrat,* the Scranton *Truth,* and the St. Louis *Star.*

11. Theodore Roosevelt, with whom Oakley discussed the regiment, was strongly opposed to the concept.

12. Allentown *Democrat,* May 23, 1918.

13. Kasper, op. cit., pp. 226–27.

Chapter 7

1. Curley was not the slayer of Sitting Bull; this is poetic license on the part of the *Globe* reporter.

2. Despite his objections to these tomes, Crawford was the subject of at least three of them: two by Ned Buntline, the third by Prentiss Ingraham.

3. Darlis A. Miller, *Captain Jack Crawford, Buckskin Poet, Scout, and Showman* (Albuquerque: University of New Mexico Press, 1993), pp. 86–87.

4. Ibid, p. 173, citing the *Daily Optic,* Las Vegas, New Mexico, n.d.

5. *The Life of Hon. William F. Cody, Known as Buffalo Bill the Famous Hunter, Scout, and Guide: An Autobiography* (Hartford: Frank E. Bliss, 1879; reprint, with a foreword by Don Russell, Lincoln: University of Nebraska Press, 1978), p. 349.

6. Darlis A. Miller, *Captain Jack Crawford, Buckskin Poet, Scout, and Showman* (Albuquerque: University of New Mexico Press, 1993), p. 189.

Chapter 8

1. Pawnee Bill rarely indented; in order to make the manuscript easier to read, occasional indentations and subject headings have been inserted.

Chapter 9

1. Despite an initial false start, archery in modern times is a rapidly growing sport, with special hunting seasons in every American state and hunting practiced worldwide, even in Africa.

2. See R. L. Wilson, *The Peacemakers: Arms and Adventure in the American West* (New York: Random House, 1992), p. 292.

3. John E. Healy and Charlie Bigelow, *First Time of Everything.*

4. Brooks McNamara, *Step Right Up: An Illustrated History of the Medicine Show* (Garden City, N.Y.: Doubleday, 1976), p. 89.

5. Joseph G. Rosa and Robin May, *Buffalo Bill and His Wild West: A Pictorial Biography,* p. 217.

6. Ibid., pp. 217, 220.

Chapter 10

1. Don Russell, *The Lives and Legends of Buffalo Bill* (Norman: University of Oklahoma Press, 1960), p. 414.

2. *San Francisco Chronicle,* September 29, 1997, p. A8.

3. It's true that certain of Cody's entertainments made it appear that white settlers, cowboys, and frontiersmen were fighting back against red-man aggression—while in actual fact, circumstances, tragically, were quite the opposite. But his respect and admiration for the Indians, and their complementary feelings toward Cody, were clearly evident.

Appendix B

1. This is marked on the inside front cover of the "Nov 24/86 to Mch 31/87" ledger, which also includes the notation: "Defts' Ex. No. 48, H.D.O., Exc. May 20, 1909."

Appendix E

1. Annie Oakley, "Why Ladies Should Shoot," *The Shooting Times and British Sportsman,* August 26, 1893. Annie Oakley and Frank Butler Scrapbook, 1893–1895, Buffalo Bill Historical Center, Cody, Wyo.

Appendix F

1. Annie Oakley, "America: A Nation of Marksmen," *The Illustrated Outdoor News* 25.10 (April 1907).

2. In modern times, accident numbers actually decline.

Selected Bibliography

Research materials included original newspapers and periodicals; show programs; city, state, and regional directories; unpublished memoirs and correspondence; photographic sources; miscellaneous museums, historical-society and library archival materials; dealer and jobber advertising and correspondence; factory shipping ledgers; order books; and correspondence and interviews with numerous collectors, dealers, auction-house specialists, curators, historians, and students, as well as with descendants of original owners and users of arms and accoutrements and of Wild West–show members.

General Titles

Athearn, Robert G. The Mythic West in Twentieth-Century America. *Lawrence: University of Kansas Press, 1986.*

Barnum, P. T. Struggles and Triumphs or, Sixty Years' Recollections of P. T. Barnum, Including His Golden Rules for Money-Making. *Buffalo: The Courier Company, 1889.*

Billington, Ray Allen. Land of Savagery, Land of Promise: The European Image of the American Frontier in the Nineteenth Century. *Norman: University of Oklahoma Press, 1981.*

Bogardus, Adam H. Field, Cover, and Trap Shooting. *Prescott, Ariz.: Wolfe, 1988.*

Bold, Christine. Selling the Wild West: Popular Western Fiction, 1860 to 1960. *Bloomington: Indiana University Press, 1968.*

Burke, John M. Buffalo Bill from Prairie to Palace. *Chicago: Rand McNally, 1893.*

Buscombe, Edward. The BFI Companion to the Western. *New York: Atheneum, 1988.*

Carnes, Mark C., and Clyde Griffen. Meanings for Manhood: Constructions of Masculinity in Victorian America. *Chicago: University of Chicago Press, 1990.*

Cawelti, John. The Six-Gun Mystique. *2d ed. Bowling Green, Ohio: Bowling Green State University Popular Press, 1984.*

Cody, Louisa, in collaboration with Courtney Ryley Cooper. Memories of Buffalo Bill. *New York and London, 1920.*

Cody, William F. The Life of the Hon. William F. Cody, Known as Buffalo Bill, The Famous Hunter, Scout and Guide: An Autobiography. *Reprint. Lincoln: University of Nebraska Press, 1978. Original published in Hartford, Conn., 1879.*

———. Story of the Wild West and Camp-Fire Chats. *Philadelphia, 1888.*

Crawford, John W. The Broncho Book, Being Buck-Jumps in Verse. *East Aurora, N.Y.: The Roycrofters, 1908.*

———. Camp Fire Sparks. *Chicago: Charles H. Kerr, 1893.*

———. From Darkness into Light and Other Poems. *Chicago: R. R. McCabe, 1886.*

———. Lariattes: A Book of Poems and Favorite Recitations. *Sigourney, Iowa: William A. Bell, 1904.*

———. The Poet Scout: A Book of Song and Story. *New York: Funk and Wagnalls, 1886.*

———. The Poet Scout: Verses and Songs. *San Francisco: H. Keller, 1879.*

———. Whar' the Hand o' God Is Seen and Other Poems. *New York: New York Lyceum Publishing Co., 1910 (2d ed., 1913).*

Custer, General George A. My Life on the Plains. *New York, 1876.*

Danker, Donald F. Man of the Plains: Recollections of Luther North, 1856–1882. *Lincoln, Nebr., 1961.*

Dary, David. Cowboy Culture: A Saga of Five Centuries. *New York: Knopf, 1981.*

———. Entrepreneurs of the Old West. *New York: Knopf, 1986.*

Davies, Henry E. Ten Days on the Plains. *New York, 1871.*

Dippie, Brian W. Custer's Last Stand: The Anatomy of an American Myth. *Missoula: University of Montana, 1976.*

Disher, M. Willson. Greatest Show on Earth. *London, 1937.*

Dodge, Colonel Richard Irving. Our Wild Indians: Thirty-three Years' Personal Experience among the Red Men of the Great West. *Hartford, Conn.: A. D. Worthington, 1882.*

Dunraven, *the Earl of.* Canadian Nights. *New York, 1914.*

Durso, *Joseph.* Madison Square Garden: 100 Years of History. *New York: Simon and Schuster, 1979.*

Erskine, *Gladys Shaw.* Broncho Charlie, A Saga of the Saddle: The Autobiography of Broncho Charlie Miller. *London, 1935.*

Fees, *Paul, and Sarah E. Boehme.* Frontier America: Art and Treasures of the Old West from the Buffalo Bill Historical Center. *Cody, Wyo.: Buffalo Bill Historical Center, 1988.*

Fellows, *Dexter W., and Andrew A. Freeman.* This Way to the Big Show. *New York, 1936.*

Fenin, *George N., and William I. Iverson.* The Western from Silents to the Seventies. *New York: Grossman, 1973.*

Finerty, *John F.* War-Path and Bivouac, or the Conquest of the Sioux. *Norman: University of Oklahoma Press, 1961.*

Foote, *Stella Adelyne.* Letters from "Buffalo Bill." *Billings, 1954.*

Foreman, *Carolyn Thomas.* Indians Abroad. *Norman: University of Oklahoma Press, 1943.*

Fowler, *Gene.* Timberline: A Story of Bonfils and Tammen. *New York, 1933.*

Fox, *Charles P., and Tom Parkinson.* Billers, Banners, and Bombast: The Story of Circus Advertising. *Boulder, Colo., 1985.*

Fredriksson, *Kristine.* American Rodeo: From Buffalo Bill to Big Business. *College Station: Texas A&M University Press, 1985.*

Friedman, *Michael.* Cowboy Culture: The Last Frontier of American Antiques. *West Chester, Pa.: Schiffer, 1992.*

Frost, *Richard I., Leo A. Platteter, and Don Hedgpeth.* The West of Buffalo Bill. *New York: Abrams, 1970.*

Furnas, *J. C.* The Americans: A Social History of the United States, 1587–1914. *London, 1969.*

Gard, *Wayne.* The Great Buffalo Hunt. *New York: Knopf, 1959.*

Gibson, *Arrell Morgan.* The American Indian, Prehistory to the Present. *Lexington, Mass.: D. C. Heath, 1980.*

Gilbert, *Douglas.* American Vaudeville: Its Life and Times. *New York: Whittlesey House, 1940.*

Griffin, *Charles Eldridge.* Four Years in Europe with Buffalo Bill. *Albia, Iowa: Stage, 1908.*

Grossman, *James R., ed.* The Frontier in American Culture. *Berkeley: University of California Press, 1994.*

Havighurst, *Walter.* Annie Oakley of the Wild West. *New York: Macmillan, 1954.*

Hedren, *Paul L.* First Scalp for Custer: The Skirmish at Warbonnet Creek, Nebraska. *Glendale, Calif.: Arthur H. Clark, 1980.*

Hoxie, *Frederick E.* A Final Promise, The Campaign to Assimilate the Indians, 1880–1920. *Cambridge: Cambridge University Press, 1989.*

Hughes, *Richard B.* Pioneer Years in the Black Hills. *Ed. Agnes Wright Spring. Glendale, Calif.: Arthur H. Clark, 1957.*

Hutton, *Paul Andrew.* Phil Sheridan and His Army. *Lincoln: University of Nebraska Press, 1985.*

Inman, *Colonel Henry.* Buffalo Jones's Forty Years of Adventure. *Topeka: Crane, 1899.*

Johannsen, *Albert.* The House of Beadle and Adams and Its Dime and Nickel Novels: The Story of a Vanished Literature. *2 vols. Norman: University of Oklahoma Press, 1950.*

Jones, *Daryl.* The Dime Novel Western. *Bowling Green, Ohio: Bowling Green State University Popular Press, 1978.*

Jordan, *Teresa.* Cowgirls: Women of the American West. *Lincoln: University of Nebraska Press, 1991.*

Kasper, *Shirl.* Annie Oakley. *Norman: University of Oklahoma Press, 1992.*

Katzive, *David, ed.* Buffalo Bill and the Wild West. *Brooklyn: Brooklyn Museum, 1981.*

Knight, *Oliver.* Following the Indian Wars: The Story of the Newspaper Correspondents among the Indian Campaigners. *Norman: University of Oklahoma Press, 1960.*

Lamar, *Howard R., ed.* The Reader's Encyclopedia of the American West. *New York: Thomas Y. Crowell, 1977.*

LeCompte, *Mary Lou.* Cowgirls of the Rodeo: Pioneer Professional Athletes. *Urbana: University of Illinois Press, 1992.*

Leonard, *Elizabeth Jane, and Julia Cody Goodman.* Buffalo Bill: King of the Old West. *New York: Library Publishers, 1955.*

Logan, *Herschel C.* Buckskin and Satin. *Harrisburg, Pa.: Stackpole, 1954.*

Luther Standing Bear. My People the Sioux. *Lincoln: University of Nebraska Press, 1975.*

McCoy, *Colonel Tim, and Ronald McCoy.* Tim McCoy Remembers the Wild West. *Garden City, New York: Doubleday, 1977.*

McHugh, *Tom.* The Time of the Buffalo. *New York: Knopf, 1972.*

McLaughlin, *James.* My Friend the Indian. *Boston, 1926.*

McNamara, *Brooks.* Step Right Up: An Illustrated History of the American Medicine Show. *Garden City, N.Y.: Doubleday, 1976.*

Majors, Alexander. Seventy Years on the Frontier. *Chicago, 1893.*

Mead, James R. Hunting and Trading on the Great Plains, 1859–1875. *Norman: University of Oklahoma Press, 1986.*

Miles, Nelson A. Personal Recollections and Observations of General Nelson A. Miles. *Chicago: Werner, 1896.*

———. Serving the Republic. *Chicago, 1896.*

Miller, Darlis A. Captain Jack Crawford: Buckskin Poet, Scout, and Showman. *Albuquerque: University of New Mexico Press, 1993.*

Monaghan, Jay. The Great Rascal: The Life and Adventures of Ned Buntline. *New York: Crown, 1951.*

Moses, L. G. Wild West Shows and the Images of American Indians, 1883–1933. *Albuquerque: University of New Mexico Press, 1996.*

Mott, Frank Luther. A History of American Magazines, 1885–1905. *Cambridge, Mass.: Harvard University Press, 1957.*

Mumey, Nolie. Calamity Jane, 1852–1903: A History of Her Life and Adventure in the West. *Denver: Range Press, 1950.*

Nash, Gerald D. Creating the West: Historical Interpretations, 1890–1990. *Albuquerque: University of New Mexico Press, 1991.*

Neihardt, John G. (as told to). Black Elk Speaks. *Lincoln: University of Nebraska Press, 1932.*

Nelson, John Young. Fifty Years on the Trail: The Adventures of John Young Nelson, as Described to Harrington O'Reilly. *Norman: University of Oklahoma Press, 1963.*

Nolan, Paul T. John Wallace Crawford. *Boston: Twayne, 1981.*

———. Three Plays by J. W. (Capt. Jack) Crawford, An Experiment in Myth-Making. *The Hague: Mouton, 1966.*

Pearson, Edmund. Dime Novels; or, Following an Old Trail in Popular Literature. *Reprint. Port Washington, N.Y.: Kennikat Press, 1968.*

Prucha, Francis Paul. The Great Father: The United States Government and the American Indians. *2 vols. Lincoln: University of Nebraska Press, 1984.*

Regli, Adolph. The Real Book about Buffalo Bill. *Garden City, N.Y.: Franklin Watts, 1952.*

Rennert, Jack. One Hundred Posters of Buffalo Bill's Wild West Show. *New York: Darien House, 1976.*

Roach, Joyce Gibson. The Cowgirls. *Denton: University of North Texas Press, 1990.*

Rosa, Joseph G. They Called Him Wild Bill. *Norman: University of Oklahoma Press, 1982.*

———. The West of Wild Bill Hickok. *Norman: University of Oklahoma Press, 1982.*

———. Wild Bill Hickok: The Man and His Myth. *Lawrence: University Press of Kansas, 1996.*

Rosa, Joseph G., and Robin May. Buffalo Bill and His Wild West. *Lawrence: University of Kansas Press, 1989.*

———. Cowboy: The Man and the Myth. *London: New English Library, 1980.*

Russell, Don. The Lives and Legends of Buffalo Bill. *Norman: University of Oklahoma Press, 1960.*

———. Campaigning with King: Charles King, Chronicler of the Old Army. *Ed. Paul L. Hedren. Lincoln: University of Nebraska Press, 1991.*

———. The Wild West: A History of the Wild West Shows. *Fort Worth: Amon Carter Museum of Western Art, 1970.*

Rydell, Robert W. All the World's a Fair: Visions of Empire at American International Expositions, 1876–1916. *Chicago: University of Chicago Press, 1984.*

Sandoz, Mari. The Buffalo Hunters: The Story of the Hide Men. *New York: Hastings House, 1954.*

———. Hostiles and Friendlies. *Lincoln: University of Nebraska Press, 1959.*

Sanger, "Lord" George. Seventy Years a Showman. *London, 1927.*

Sarf, Wayne M. God Bless You, Buffalo Bill: A Layman's Guide to History and the Western Film. *Rutherford, N.J.: Fairleigh Dickinson University Press, 1983.*

Savage, William W., Jr. Cowboy Life: Reconstructing an American Myth. *Norman: University of Oklahoma Press, 1975.*

Sayers, Isabelle S. Annie Oakley and Buffalo Bill's Wild West. *New York: Dover, 1981.*

———. The Rifle Queen: Annie Oakley. *Ostrander, Ohio: n.p., 1973.*

Schubert, Charles, and Clara Mae LaVene. O. C. Marsh, Pioneer in Paleontology. *New Haven: Yale University Press, 1940.*

Sell, Henry Blackman, and Victor Weybright. Buffalo Bill and the Wild West. *New York: Oxford University Press, 1955.*

Sheridan, General Philip H. Personal Memoirs. *2 vols. New York, 1888.*

Shirley, Glenn. Pawnee Bill: A Biography of Major Gordon W. Lillie. *Albuquerque: University of New Mexico Press, 1958.*

Slotkin, Richard. The Fatal Environment: The Myth of the Frontier in the Age of Industrialization, 1800–1890. *New York: Atheneum, 1985.*

———. Gunfighter Nation: The Myth of the Frontier in Twentieth-Century America. *New York: Atheneum, 1992.*

Smith, Henry Nash. Virgin Land: The American West as Symbol and Myth. *New York: Random House, 1950.*

Smith, Sherry L. The View from Officers' Row: Army Perceptions of Western Indians. *Tucson: University of Arizona Press, 1990.*

Sprague, Marshall. A Gallery of Dudes. *Lincoln: University of Nebraska Press, 1967.*

Spring, Agnes Wright. The Cheyenne and Black Hills Stage and Express Routes. *Glendale, Calif.: Arthur H. Clark, 1949.*

Steckmesser, Kent Ladd. The Western Hero in History and Legend. *Norman: University of Oklahoma Press, 1965.*

Streeter, Floyd Benjamin. Ben Thompson: Man with a Gun. *New York: Frederick Fell, 1957.*

Swartwout, Annie Fern. Missie: An Historical Biography of Annie Oakley. *Blanchester, Ohio: Brown, 1947.*

Taylor, Lonn, and Ingrid Maar. The American Cowboy. *New York: Harper and Row, 1983.*

Thorp, Raymond W. "Wild West" Doc Carver: Spirit Gun of the West. *London: W. Foulsham, 1957.*

Thrapp, Dan L. Victorio and the Membres Apaches. *Norman: University of Oklahoma Press, 1974.*

Toll, Robert C. On with the Show: The First Century of Show Business in America. *New York: Oxford University Press, 1976.*

Utley, Robert M. Cavalier in Buckskin: George Armstrong Custer and the Western Military Frontier. *Norman: University of Oklahoma Press, 1988.*

———. Frontier Regulars: The United States Army and the Indian, 1866–1891. *New York: Macmillan, 1973.*

———. The Indian Frontier of the American West, 1846–1890. *Albuquerque: University of New Mexico Press, 1984.*

Van Steenwyck, Elizabeth. Women in Sports: Rodeo. *New York: Harvey House, 1978.*

Vestal, Stanley. Sitting Bull: Champion of the Sioux. *Norman: University of Oklahoma Press, 1957.*

Walker, Henry Pickering. The Wagonmasters. *Norman: University of Oklahoma Press, 1966.*

Wallace, Irving. The Fabulous Showman. *New York: Knopf, 1960.*

Walsh, Richard J., with Milton S. Salsbury. The Making of Buffalo Bill. *Indianapolis: Bobbs-Merrill, 1928.*

Webb, William E. Buffalo Land. *Cincinnati: E. Hannaford, 1872.*

Wecter, Dixon. The Hero in America: A Chronicle of Hero Worship. *Reprint. Ann Arbor: University of Michigan Press, 1963.*

Wetmore, Helen Cody. The Last of the Great Scouts: The Life of Col. W. F. Cody "Buffalo Bill." *London, 1901.*

White, G. Edward. The Eastern Establishment and the Western Experience. *New Haven: Yale University Press, 1968. Rpt. Austin: University of Texas Press, 1989.*

Wilder, Mitchell A., et al. The Wild West. *Fort Worth: Amon Carter Museum of Western Art, 1970.*

Wilson, Garff B. Three Hundred Years of American Drama and Theatre. *Englewood Cliffs, N.J.: Prentice-Hall, 1973.*

Wilson, R. L. The Book of Colt Firearms. *Minneapolis: Blue Book Publications, 1993.*

———. Colt: An American Legend. *New York: Abbeville Press, 1985.*

———. The Colt Engraving Book. *Forthcoming.*

———. The Book of Colt Engraving. *Los Angeles: Wallace Beinfeld Publications, 1974.*

———. Colt Engraving. *West Hollywood, California: Beinfeld Publishing Co., 1982.*

———. The Peacemakers: Arms and Adventure in the American West. *New York: Random House, 1992.*

———. Steel Canvas: The Art of American Arms. *New York: Random House, 1994.*

———. Winchester: An American Legend. *New York: Random House, 1991.*

———. Winchester Engraving. *Palm Springs, Calif.: Beinfeld, 1991.*

———. Winchester: The Golden Age of American Gunmaking and the Winchester 1 of 1000. *Cody, Wyo.: Buffalo Bill Historical Center, 1983.*

Winch, Frank. Thrilling Lives of Buffalo Bill and Pawnee Bill. *New York, 1911.*

Wojtowicz, James W. The W. F. Cody Buffalo Bill Collector's Guide with Values. *Paducah, Ky.: Collector Books, 1997.*

Wood-Clark, Sarah. Beautiful Daring Western Girls: Women of the Wild West Shows. *Cody, Wyo.: Buffalo Bill Historical Center, 1991.*

Woods, Lawrence M. British Gentlemen in the Wild West. *New York: Free Press, 1989.*

Yost, Nellie Snyder. Buffalo Bill: His Family, Friends, Fame, Failures, and Fortunes. *Chicago: Swallow Press, 1979.*

Monographs, Programs, and Miscellaneous

Buffalo Bill Dr. Carver The Wild West Rocky Mountain and Prairie Exhibition. *Program. Ca. 1883.*

Buffalo Bill (Himself) and 101 Ranch Wild West Combined. *Program. 1916.*

Buffalo Bill's Wild West. *Programs. Various years between 1884 and 1892.*

Buffalo Bill's Wild West and Congress of Rough Riders of the World. *Programs. Various years between 1893 and 1908.*

Buffalo Bill's Wild West and Pawnee Bill's Far East. *Programs. Ca. 1908–1913.*

Cahill, Luke. "An Indian Campaign and Buffalo Hunting with 'Buffalo Bill.' " Colorado Magazine 4.4 *(August 1927).*

Chauncey Yellow Robe. "The Menace of the Wild West Show." Quarterly Journal of the Society of American Indians 2 *(July/September 1914).*

Coleman, William S. E. "Buffalo Bill on Stage." Players. *N.d.*

Cooper, Tex. "I Knew Buffalo Bill." Frontier Times 33 *(Spring 1969).*

Crawford, Jack [John W.]. "The Government Scout." Outing 29 *(November 1893).*

———. *"In Memoriam, The Hero's Departed." New York: J. T. Altemus, 1885.*

———. *"Pursuit of Victorio."* Socorro County Historical Society *Publications in History 1 (February 1965).*

Davis, Tracy. "Annie Oakley and Her Ideal Husband of No Importance." In Janelle G. Reinelt and Joseph R. Roach, eds., Critical Theory and Performance. *(Ann Arbor: University of Michigan Press, 1992).*

Deahl, William E., Jr. "Buffalo Bill's Wild West Show, 1885." Annals of Wyoming 47.3 *(Fall 1975). See also Ph.D. diss., Southern Illinois University, 1974.*

Gray, John S. "Fact versus Fiction in the Kansas Boyhood of Buffalo Bill." Kansas History 8.1 *(Spring 1985).*

Higman, John. "The Reorientation of American Culture in the 1890's." In The Origins of Modern Consciousness. *Ed. John Weiss. Detroit: Wayne State University Press, 1965.*

Hornaday, William T. "The Extermination of the American Bison." Annual Report of the Smithsonian Institution, June 30, 1887, *vol. 2, pp. 367–548.*

Hutton, Paul A. "From Little Bighorn to Little Big Man: The Changing Image of a Western Hero in Popular Culture." The Western Historical Quarterly, *January 1976.*

Jones, Daryl D. "Blood 'n Thunder: Virgins, Villains, and Violence in the Dime Novel Western." Journal of Popular Culture 4 *(Fall 1970).*

Maguder, Theodore. "The Wild West, Bill, and Hartford." The Connecticut Historical Society Bulletin 48.2 *(Spring 1983).*

Marovitz, Sanford E. "Bridging the Continent with Romantic Western Realism." Journal of the West 19 *(January 1980).*

Miller, Ernest I. "Ned Buntline." Bulletin of the Historical and Philosophical Society of Ohio 10.1 *(January 1952).*

Moses, L. G. "Indians on the Midway: Wild West Shows and the Indian Bureau at World's Fairs, 1893–1904." South Dakota History 21 *(Fall 1991).*

———. *"Wild West Shows, Reformers and the Image of the American Indian, 1887–1914."* South Dakota History 4.3 *(Fall 1984).*

Nordin, Charles R. "Dr. W. F. Carver, 'Evil Spirit of the Plains.' " Nebraska History Magazine 10.4 *(October–December 1927).*

Oakley, Annie. Powders I Have Used. Wilmington: Du Pont Powder Company, 1914.

———. *"The Story of My Life." Unpublished manuscript, 1926.*

Pfaller, Louis. " 'Enemies in '76, Friends in '85': Sitting Bull and Buffalo Bill." Prologue: The Journal of the National Archives 1.2 *(Fall 1969).*

"Rare Recording by Buffalo Bill Is Given to the Library of Congress." Library of Congress Information Bulletin 41.11 *(March 12, 1982).*

Remington, Frederic. "Buffalo Bill in London." Harper's Weekly, *September 3, 1892.*

Russell, Don. "Cody, Kings, and Coronets: A Sprightly Account of Buffalo Bill's Wild West Show at Home and Abroad." American West 7 *(1970).*

———. *"Julia Goodman's Memoirs of Buffalo Bill."* Kansas Historical Quarterly 28.4 *(Winter 1962).*

Salsbury, Nate. "The Origin of the Wild West Show." Colorado Magazine 32.3 *(July 1955).*

Saum, Lewis O. " 'Astonishing the Natives,' Bringing the Wild West to Los Angeles." Montana: The Magazine of Western History 38 *(Summer 1988).*

Schwartz, Joseph. "The Wild West Show: 'Everything Genuine.' " Journal of Popular Culture 3 *(Spring 1970).*

Scorer, John G. "A Unique Character in American Literature, Captain Jack Crawford, 'The Poet Scout.' " Central Magazine 1 *(April 1895).*

Sells-Floto Buffalo Bill (Himself) Shows. *Programs. 1914–1915.*

Senelick, Lawrence, ed. "Shotgun Wedlock: Annie Oakley's Power Politics in the Wild West." Gender in Performance: The Presentation of Difference in the

Performing Arts, *pp. 141–57. Hanover: University Press of New England, 1992.*

Trennert, Robert A., Jr. "Selling Indian Education at World's Fairs and Expositions, 1893–1904." American Indian Quarterly *11 (Summer 1987).*

Correspondence, Manuscripts, and Official Records

*Johnny Baker Collection, Buffalo Bill Historical Center, Cody, Wyoming.**

*Seldon Bacon Papers, Buffalo Bill Historical Center, Cody, Wyoming.**

*Buffalo Bill Collection relevant to Great Britain, Germany, France/Belgium, Spain, Scandinavia/The Netherlands, Italy, Slavic countries, and Miscellaneous, Buffalo Bill Historical Center, Cody, Wyoming.**

Buffalo Bill's Wild West Cowboy Band, Buffalo Bill Historical Center, Cody, Wyoming.

*W. F. "Doc" Carver Scrapbooks, Buffalo Bill Historical Center, Cody, Wyoming.**

*William F. Cody Scrapbooks, Buffalo Bill Historical Center, Cody, Wyoming.**

*Peter H. Davidson Collection, Buffalo Bill Historical Center, Cody, Wyoming.**

Michael Del Castello Collection, miscellanous scrapbooks (including that of William F. Cody, 1889, Paris), correspondence, and Wild West–show programs, several items of which were in the Julia Cody Goodman Collection.

*Dime Novels and Related Literature, Buffalo Bill Historical Center, Cody, Wyoming.**

*H. H. Gunning Scrapbooks, Buffalo Bill Historical Center, Cody, Wyoming.**

*Itinerary of the Wild West (1883–1913). Buffalo Bill Historical Center, Cody, Wyoming. Tabulation of routes of Buffalo Bill's Wild West.**

Greg Martin Collection of Western Americana, San Francisco, California.

*Vincent Mercaldo, Buffalo Bill and Buffalo Bill's Wild West materials, Buffalo Bill Historical Center, Cody, Wyoming.**

*Annie Oakley and Frank Butler Scrapbooks, Buffalo Bill Historical Center, Cody, Wyoming.**

*Don Russell Collection, Buffalo Bill's Wild West, Buffalo Bill Historical Center, Cody, Wyoming.**

H.M. Queen Victoria's Journal (1887 and 1892), the Royal Archives, Windsor Castle, London.

*Wild West Show Correspondence, Buffalo Bill Historical Center, Cody, Wyoming.**

Wild West Show Ephemera, Buffalo Bill Historical Center, Cody, Wyoming.

*Available through the McCracken Research Library.

Acknowledgments, Photographic Notes, and Owner Credits

Acknowledgments

The Buffalo Bill's Wild West project began with an exhibition held at the University of California at Berkeley Museum in Danville, California. The site is an adjunct to Blackhawk, a luxury community founded by Ken Behring and Ken Hofmann. There, for public enjoyment, was the featured, summerlong display "Buffalo Bill's Wild West Show, Selections from the Greg Martin Collection." This comprehensive presentation, opening May 1 and running through September 6, 1993, sparked the collecting instincts of Michael Del Castello and inspired the creation of this book. We are grateful to Messrs. Behring and Hofmann and to their Educational Institute for enthusiastic support of the genesis of what became *Buffalo Bill's Wild West: An American Legend.*

We are also grateful to the following people and institutions:

Michael Del Castello, for his dedication and commitment, for the opportunity to study and research his extraordinary collection, and for his involvement in the loan exhibition at the Royal Armouries Museum, Leeds. This book would not have been possible or even conceivable without his assistance and insight and his unrelenting pursuit of making his Wild West collection the best in private hands;

Joseph F. Brownell, Chief Executive Officer, MDC Vacuum Products; Jayne Williams; and William H. Bentham, D.V.M., for their own special roles in seeing that the show and the project went on;

Petra Martin, for her stalwart involvement and brainstorming inspirations, appreciated as always;

The Buffalo Bill Historical Center, Byron Price, Director; Paul Fees, Ph.D., Senior Curator; Christine Houze, Assistant to Dr. Fees; Nathan E. Bender, Housel Curator of the McCracken Research Library; Frances B. Clymer, Librarian; Elizabeth Holmes, Associate Registrar; and Howard Madaus, Curator, Cody Firearms Museum, for seemingly endless assistance and insights on subjects they know so well and present uniquely to millions. Devendra Shrikhande, Staff Photographer, was responsible for the majority of images from the center, presented in Chapter 5. With particular thanks to Paul Fees and Frances Clymer, founts of information, who responded to every request with knowledge and enthusiasm; we are also grateful to Dr. Fees for his comments and suggestions on reading the entire manuscript;

The Autry Museum of Western Heritage, Mrs. Joanne D. Hale, Executive Director and CEO; and James Nottage, Chief Curator, for their generous and copious assistance on "one more book." Susan Einstein was responsible for photographing all the images from the museum, presented in Chapter 5; the materials were coordinated by James Nottage and Mary Ellen Hennessey Nottage, Collections Manager, and by Michael Fox, Curatorial Assistant. The authors are particularly pleased with the presentation of the treasures from the Autry and Buffalo Bill museums;

Guy Wilson, Director, Royal Armouries Museum, Leeds, for his dedication and innovation in the complexities of displaying the Michael Del Castello Collection in Leeds, scheduled for summer 1999. Also, John Waller, the museum's director of reenactments and live demonstrations, for his suggestions on the presentation of the Wild West material; and Graeme Rimer, Keeper of Weapons, for his insights;

Bill Garlow, Trustee of the Buffalo Bill Historical Center and a member of the Cody family, for his interest, insights, support, hospitality, and encouragement;

Ruth and Jerry Murphey, founders, the 101 Ranch Collectors Association, for unraveling the mystery of Lillian Smith and Princess Wenona and for arranging the photography of two striking color pages on the talented shootist;

Dennis J. and Julie A. Greene, for the guided tour of their unique Texas Jack Collection and for insights and information on their distinguished and colorful ancestor and on the Texas Jack Association;

Carolyn R. Vogel, for her intuitive grasp of the Wild West mystique and for the benefit of her several, often amusing, perceptions;

Doug Wicklund, Curator, National Firearms Museum, for color images and background details on Annie Oakley's deluxe Remington-Beals rifle;

Val J. Forgett, President and CEO, Navy Arms Company, for loan of the exquisite marksmanship medals, which added life to several color photographs;

Richard Rattenbury, Curator of History, National Cowboy Hall of Fame, for his own ideas, data, and suggestions;

James A. Hanson, Editor, *Museum of the Fur Trade Quarterly,* and to Mrs. Marguerite Radcliffe, Dawes County Historical Society, for arranging the photography and supplying background information on the Thousand-Mile Cowboy Race and the society's prized Colt Single Action Army revolver;

Tom Morrison, Superintendent, Buffalo Bill Ranch, North Platte, Nebraska, for clues on the

Thousand-Mile Cowboy Race and the facts on the ranch site;

Steve Friesen, Buffalo Bill Memorial Museum and Grave Site, Golden, Colorado, for aiding in finding a rare photograph of Johnny Baker and for guidance on that historic complex;

Keri Olson, Public Relations Director, Circus World Museum, for the packet of material and for answering questions on that unique and colorful fifty-acre establishment owned by the State Historical Society of Wisconsin;

Robert Landsdown, Woolaroc Museum, for brochures and assistance on that institution;

Kathleen Brown of the Museum of the Mountain Man, Pinedale, Wyoming, and Yasmin Braban of Rock Rabbit Productions, for their interest and efforts, even though we were unable to use the Pawnee Bill material from that institution's collections;

Randy Ledford and Wanda Green of the Pawnee Bill Ranch Site, for forwarding material on the ranch's collections;

Wallace Finley Dailey, Curator, Theodore Roosevelt Collection, The Houghton Library, Harvard University, for advice on associations between T.R. and Buffalo Bill;

Bess Edwards, President, the Annie Oakley Foundation, for sharing information and photographs, for her critical reading of Chapter 6, and for spreading the word about this book and loan-exhibition project;

David Tiene, President, Nutley Museum, for advising about Annie Oakley's New Jersey associations, and assisting with photography at the museum;

Judy Logan, Director, the Garst Museum, for providing pictures and information on the Oakley loving cup, the live-pigeon shooting medal, and other artifacts;

William Self, for making his selection of Annie Oakley material available for photography;

Eleanor Gehres, Manager, Western History Collection, Denver Public Library, for insights and help on the study of their impressive holdings;

George Miles, Curator, Western History Collection, Beinecke Rare Book and Manuscript Library, Yale University, for assistance with Nate Salsbury materials;

Milly Link, Amateur Trapshooting Hall of Fame and Museum, Vandalia, Ohio, for enlightenment on the world of clay-pigeon champions;

Officials of various other museums and historic sites listed in the appendixes, for assistance;

Riva Freifeld, for her research and efforts toward developing a television documentary on Buffalo Bill and Annie Oakley;

Glenda Riley, for assistance and counsel on the complex subject of Annie Oakley, in which her book on Oakley was invaluable;

Jean-Philippe Delavault, for the guided tour, front and back, of Buffalo Bill's Wild West Show at EuroDisney and for assistance with facts and photographs;

Bernard J. Osher and John Gallo, Butterfield and Butterfield, for their cooperation in accessing various materials, including the collection of Lancer William House;

Herb Glass, for supplying black-and-white photographs of the matched set of John Y. Nelson Colt Single Action Army revolvers;

Brad Witherell of Witherell's Americana Auctions, for his assistance in obtaining color transparencies of the rare Doc Carver poster;

Kathleen Hoyt, Historian, Colt's Manufacturing Company, for research documentation on rare firearms;

Norm Flayderman, for his customary aid in pictures and knowledge;

Thomas A. Conroy, for the fruits of his in-depth research on Buffalo Bill and the Combination in Rochester, New York;

Peter and Sandy Riva, for handling the complexities of contracts and arranging for the Peter Beard photography session;

H. Wayne Sheets, Executive Director, NRA Foundation, for his customary support and suggestions;

Paul J. Warden, President, America Remembers, and Robert A. Buerlein, President, American Historical Foundation, for assistance on special-issue projects relevant to Cody and his partners;

Dennis Adler, for his sharp eye in scouting for pictorial possibilities and for his valued still photography at Buffalo Bill's Wild West Show at EuroDisney;

Cynthia Bourbeau, for locating the obscure reference to Paul Gauguin's love of Buffalo Bill's Wild West, and his frequent attendance while the troupe was performing in Paris in 1889;

Rudy Etchen, for assembling an archive on his extraordinary life in the shooting world;

Joseph G. Rosa, for his aid in obtaining rare photographs;

Peter Buxtun, for his erudite assistance;

Richard Alan Dow, for his talents and assistance in editing a complicated manuscript;

John O. C. McCrillis, for assistance on Nate Salsbury and Texas Jack items;

Barbara Cromeenes, for keeping the wheels turning in Hadlyme, with the able aid of Judi Glover;

And Robert Loomis and colleagues at Random House, for their gentle encouragement on the fourth book in the American Arms series.

Photographic Notes

The authors are grateful to Peter Beard and Douglas Sandberg for their imaginative and inspired creativity. On location, Sandberg's equipment included a Toyo 4" × 5" view camera for layout shots and a Mamiya RZ67 medium-format camera for copy work. Lighting was usually daylight flash comprised of six thousand watts of Dynalight equipment.

The sessions with Beard were photographed with a Toyo view camera and Schnieder 210 and 135 mm lenses. An Italian FOBA upright camera stand was used to allow for unobstructed downward views. A large Lowell four-thousand-watt tungsten softbox was bounced onto white foamcore panels for even illumination with soft shadow.

The film was both tungsten and daylight Kodak Ektachrome, processed at Chromeworks in San Francisco.

The authors are also grateful to:

Kristine Sandberg, for her patience while we moved into her husband's studio, cluttering up family quarters with a myriad of subjects and even forcing the pet cat to fend for itself outside;

Michael Edwards, Sandberg's assistant on location when photographing at the Del Castello Collection;

Lucille Warters, formerly of the Buffalo Bill Historical Center;

The National Firearms Museum, National Rifle Association photography studio;

And photographers Dennis Adler, G. Allan Brown, Dennis Crowley, Sammy Gold, Jim Oliver, Rick Oltmans, Gary Putnam, and David Wesbrook, for sharing their skills through carefully rendered images.

Owner Credits

Except as credited otherwise, material in the book is from the collection of Michael Del Castello.

The authors are grateful to the following, for their generosity and full cooperation at providing assistance with images, and sometimes for providing the actual color transparencies or black-and-white prints: anonymous private collections, 15 (deringer set), 26–27, 44 (rifle), 47 and 48 (rifle), 221; Autry Museum of Western Heritage, 40, 42, 55 (E. E. Stubbs Whitney-Kennedy rifle), 109–19; Beinecke Library of Yale University, 33 (shotgun), 155 (revolver); James U. Blanchard, III, 13, 193; Buffalo Bill Historical Center, Buffalo Bill Museum, iii, 7, 19 (rifle), 23 (Yellow Hand artifacts), 51, 61, 77 (right), 90 (revolvers and holsters), 92, 99–108, 131 (letter), 132 (right), 139, 173 (at Penitentiary), 175 (Paris showgrounds and Cody birthday in London), 176, 178, 216 (top right), 225 (right); Buffalo Bill Memorial Museum and Grave Site, 228; Butterfield & Butterfield, Inc., 2 (miscellaneous items), 163; The Connecticut Historical Society, 184; Dawes County Historical Society, 262; Denver Public Library, Western History Department, 16, 33 (photo at right), 75, 142, 143, 145 (right); Disneyland/Paris, 254–55; Bess Edwards/Annie Oakley Foundation, 137 (bottom right); Rudy Etchen, 253; Norm Flayderman, 19 (revolver), 249 (right); Valmore Forgett, frontispiece (shooting medals), 40, 42, 70, 120, 137, 218; Garst Museum/The Darke County Historical Society, Inc., 140; Herb Glass, 77, (Nelson set from private collection, photographs courtesy Herb Glass); Howell H. Howard, 94; Martin J. Lane, 127, 172 (watch); Kansas State Historical Society, 25; Robert McNellis, 34 (right); Marlin Firearms Company, 134 (on loan to the Cody Firearms Museum); Greg and Petra Martin, (miscellaneous items in frontispiece and pages 2, 28, 31, 35, 40, 42, 54, 70, 120, 154, 167, 179, 180, 188, 204, 214, 218, 229, 231, 237, 239 (left), 240, 244, Cooper paintings on pages 30, 32, and 235, plus 17, 38 (left), 39 (right), 43, 190, 252; Ed Muderlak, 131 (center), Ruth and Jerry Murphey, 64–65; National Firearms Museum, 123 (rifle); Nutley Museum, 147, 149; Herb Peck, Jr., 9; Hans W. Schemke, 220; William Self, 130; Buck Stevens, 11; Paul Warden—America Remembers, 253 (right); R. L. Wilson, 15 (map), 257; Brad Witherell, 45; and James W. Wojtowicz, 4–6, illustrations from 1879 W. F. Cody autobiography.

About the Authors

R. L. Wilson has written some 30 books and over 250 articles on firearms and engraving. He is a historical consultant to private collectors and museums; music, art, and Italy's Mille Miglia are other interests. Greg Martin is the foremost antiquarian in the field of collectors' firearms, and is director of the Arms and Armor Department at Butterfield & Butterfield, San Francisco. Among other passions are shooting, art, food, wine, the California Gold Rush and its jewelry, and his estate vineyard, Puerta Dorada, in the Napa Valley.

Index

Note: Page numbers in *italics* refer to illustrations.

307